[redacted]

ROSARIO+VAMPIRE

3

TROLLS

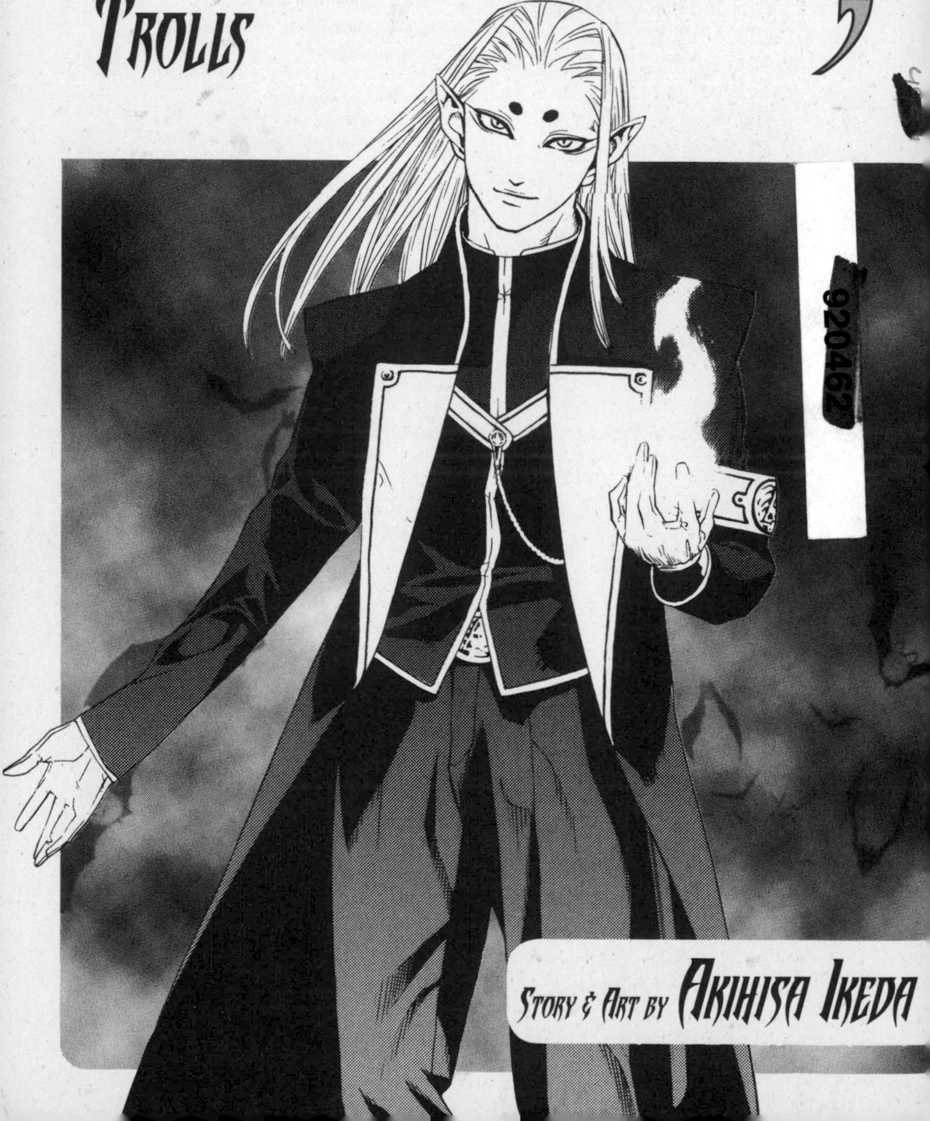

STORY & ART BY AKIHISA IKEDA

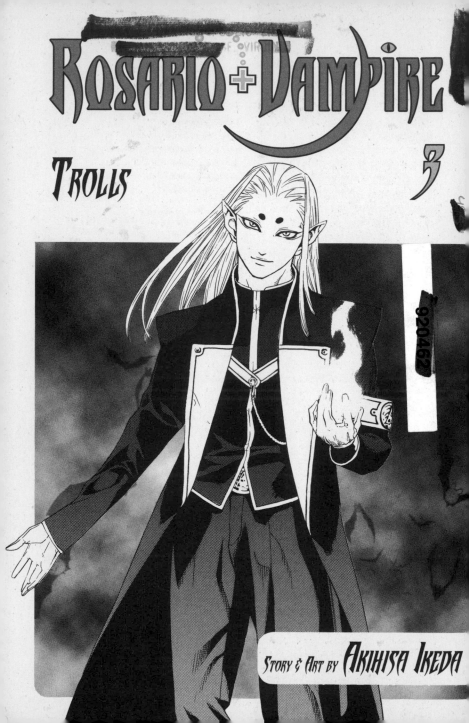

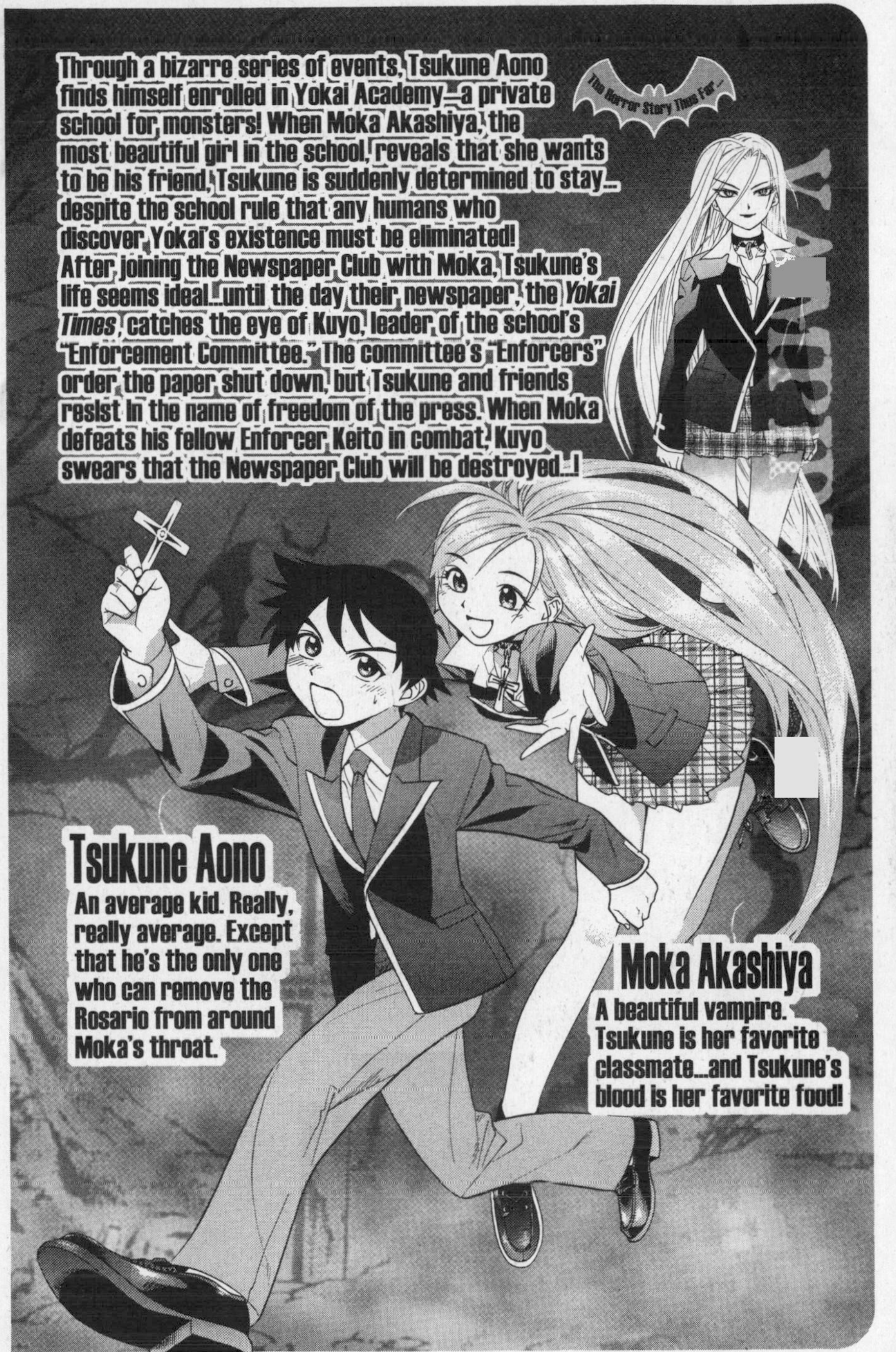
The Horror Story Thus Far...
Through a bizarre series of events, Tsukune Aono finds himself enrolled in Yokai Academy—a private school for monsters! When Moka Akashiya, the most beautiful girl in the school, reveals that she wants to be his friend, Tsukune is suddenly determined to stay... despite the school rule that any humans who discover Yokai's existence must be eliminated!
After joining the Newspaper Club with Moka, Tsukune's life seems ideal...until the day their newspaper, the *Yokai Times*, catches the eye of Kuyo, leader of the school's "Enforcement Committee." The committee's "Enforcers" order the paper shut down, but Tsukune and friends resist in the name of freedom of the press. When Moka defeats his fellow Enforcer Keito in combat, Kuyo swears that the Newspaper Club will be destroyed...!
Tsukune Aono
An average kid. Really, really average. Except that he's the only one who can remove the Rosario from around Moka's throat.
Moka Akashiya
A beautiful vampire. Tsukune is her favorite classmate...and Tsukune's blood is her favorite food!

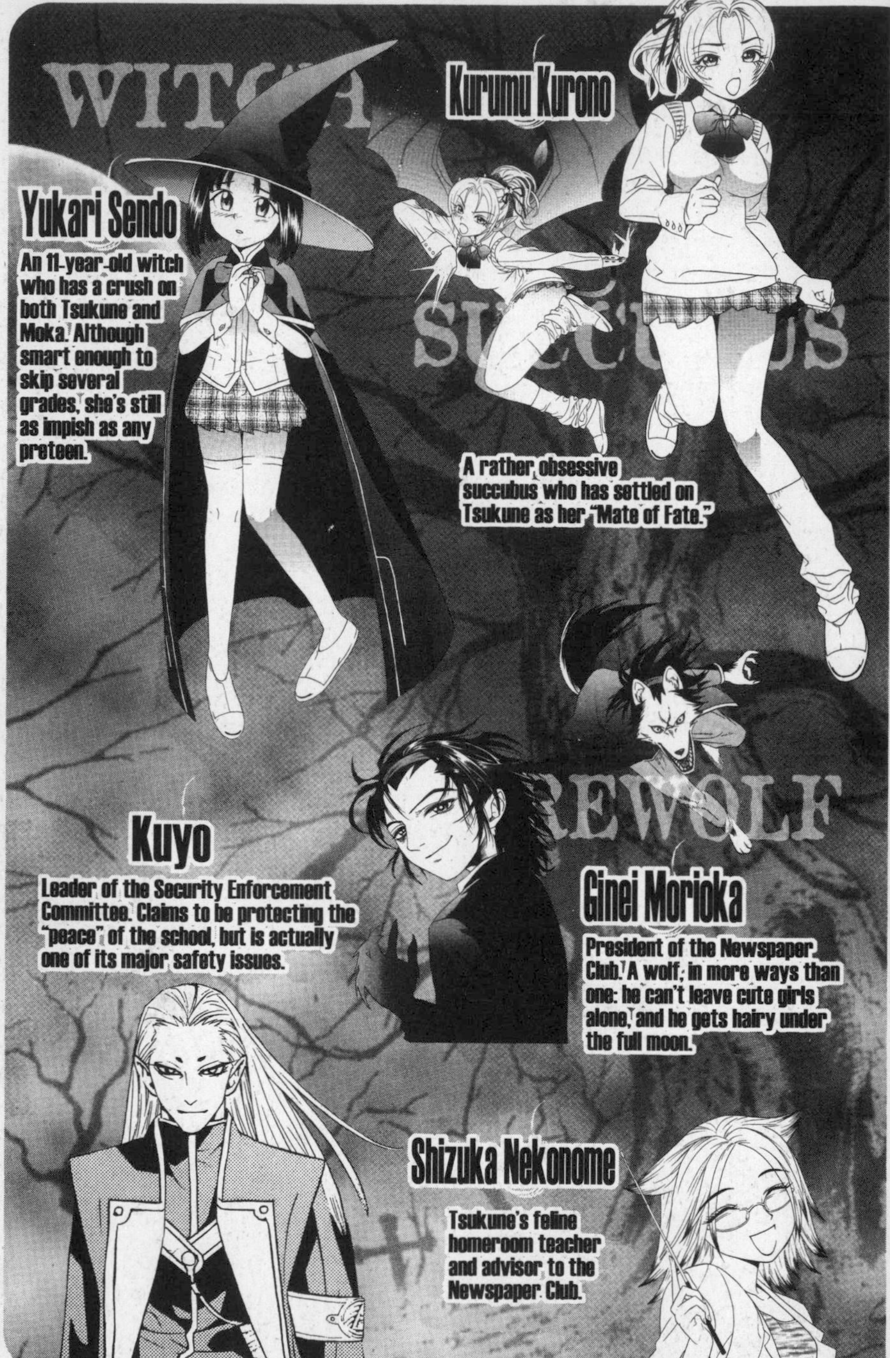
Kurumu Kurono
A rather obsessive succubus who has settled on Tsukune as her "Mate of Fate."
Yukari Sendo
An 11-year-old witch who has a crush on both Tsukune and Moka. Although smart enough to skip several grades, she's still as impish as any preteen.
Ginei Morioka
President of the Newspaper Club. A wolf, in more ways than one: he can't leave cute girls alone, and he gets hairy under the full moon.
Kuyo
Leader of the Security Enforcement Committee. Claims to be protecting the "peace" of the school, but is actually one of its major safety issues.
Shizuka Nekonome
Tsukune's feline homeroom teacher and advisor to the Newspaper Club.

CONTENTS

Volume 3: Trolls

9: The Secret

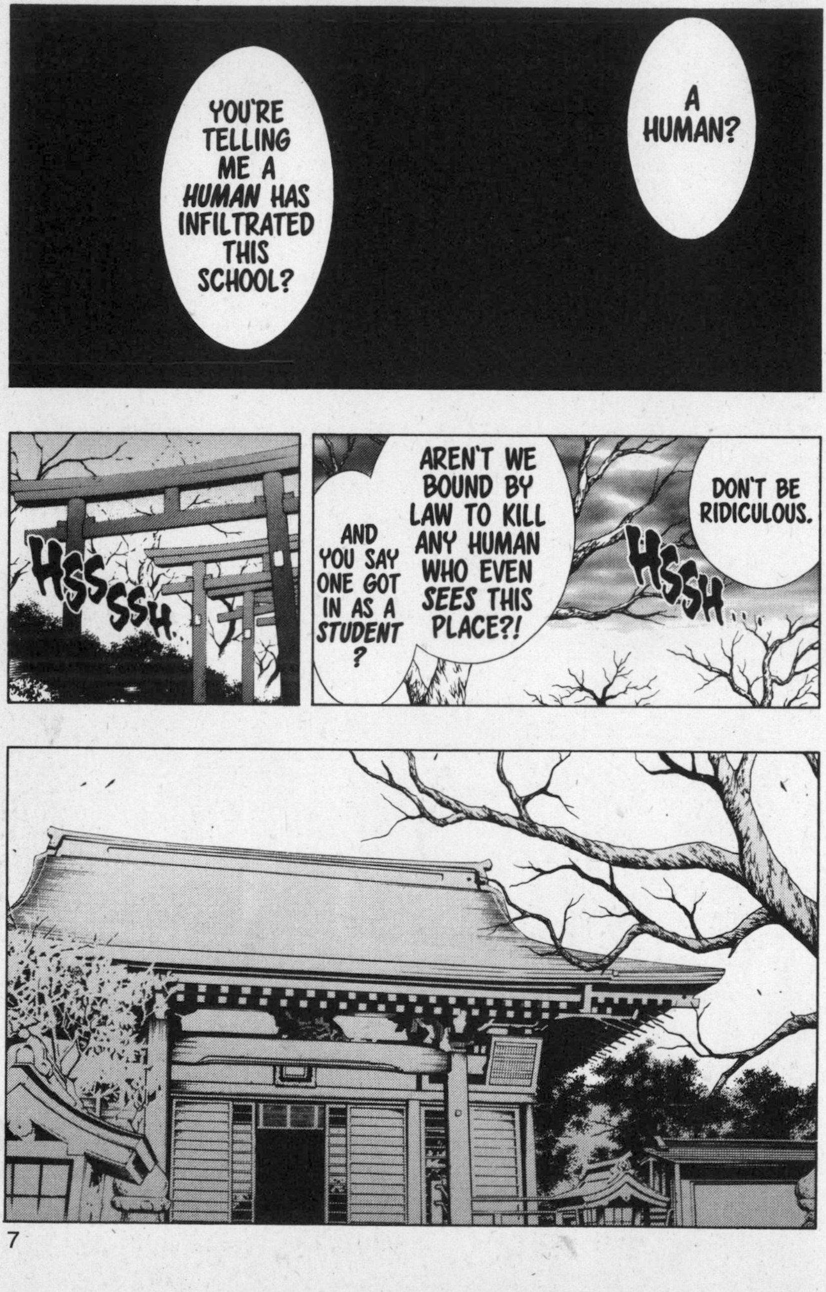
A HUMAN?
YOU'RE TELLING ME A *HUMAN* HAS INFILTRATED THIS SCHOOL?
DON'T BE RIDICULOUS.
HSSH...
AREN'T WE BOUND BY LAW TO KILL ANY HUMAN WHO EVEN *SEES* THIS PLACE?!
AND YOU SAY ONE GOT IN AS A *STUDENT*?
HSSSSH..

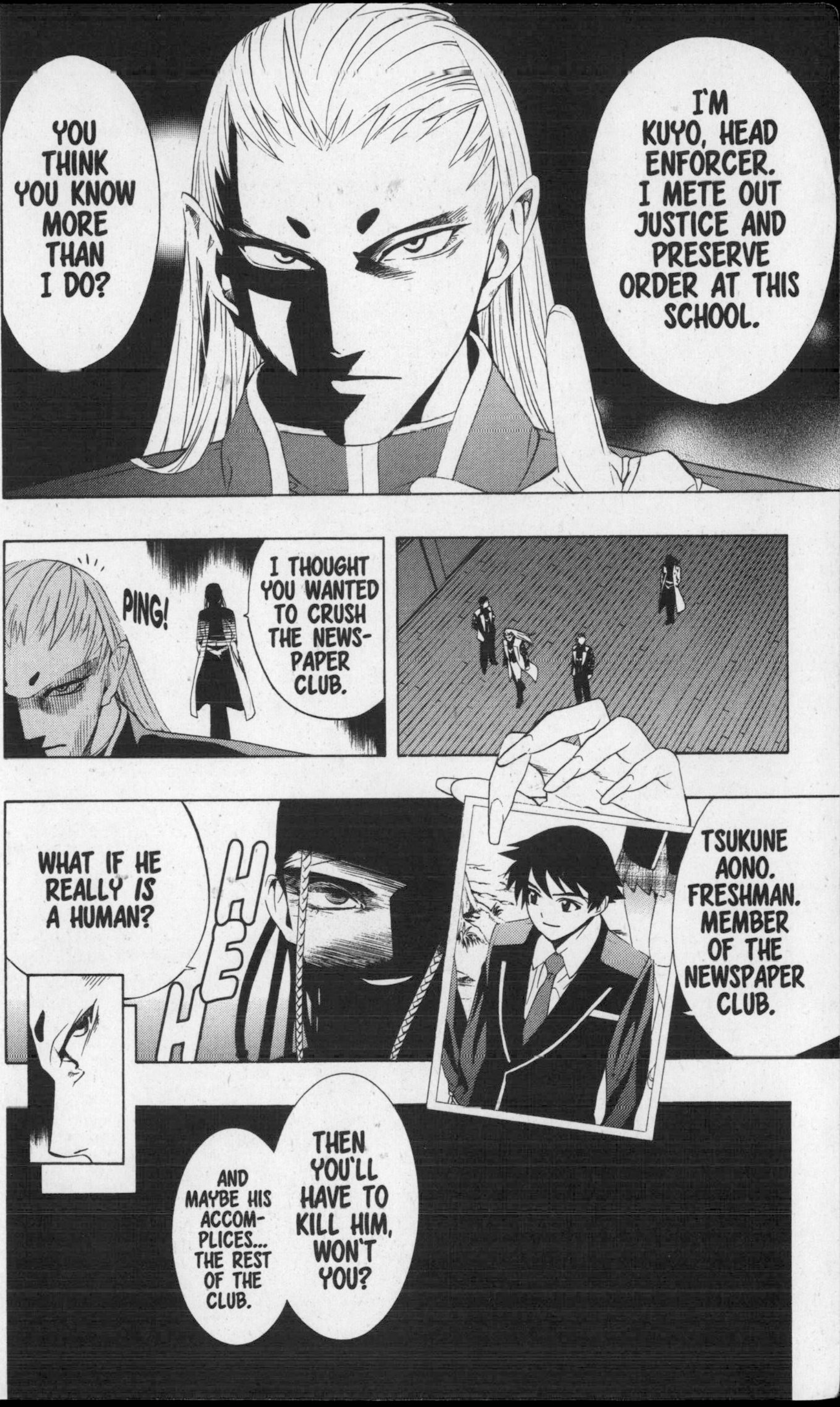
I'M KUYO, HEAD ENFORCER. I METE OUT JUSTICE AND PRESERVE ORDER AT THIS SCHOOL.
YOU THINK YOU KNOW MORE THAN I DO?
I THOUGHT YOU WANTED TO CRUSH THE NEWS-PAPER CLUB.
PING!
TSUKUNE AONO. FRESHMAN. MEMBER OF THE NEWSPAPER CLUB.
HEH
WHAT IF HE REALLY IS A HUMAN?
THEN YOU'LL HAVE TO KILL HIM, WON'T YOU?
AND MAYBE HIS ACCOMPLICES... THE REST OF THE CLUB.

9: The Secret

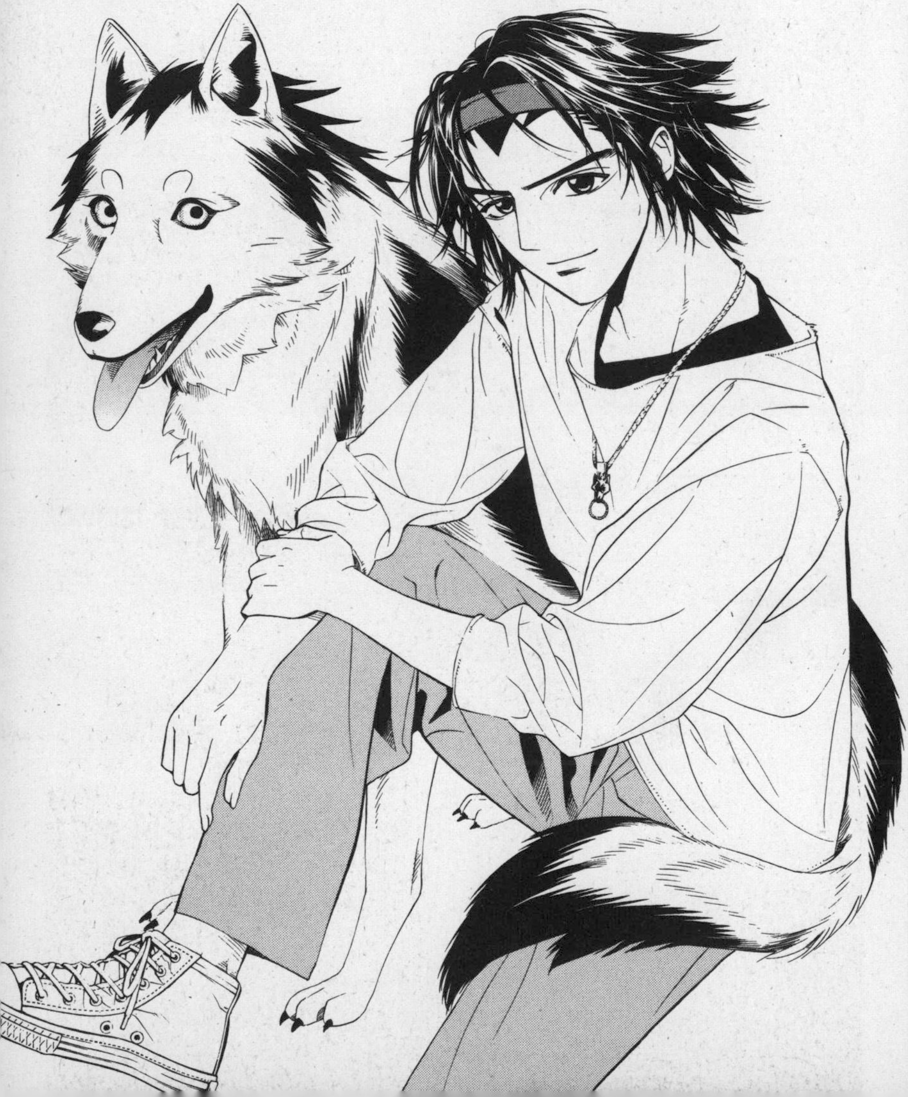

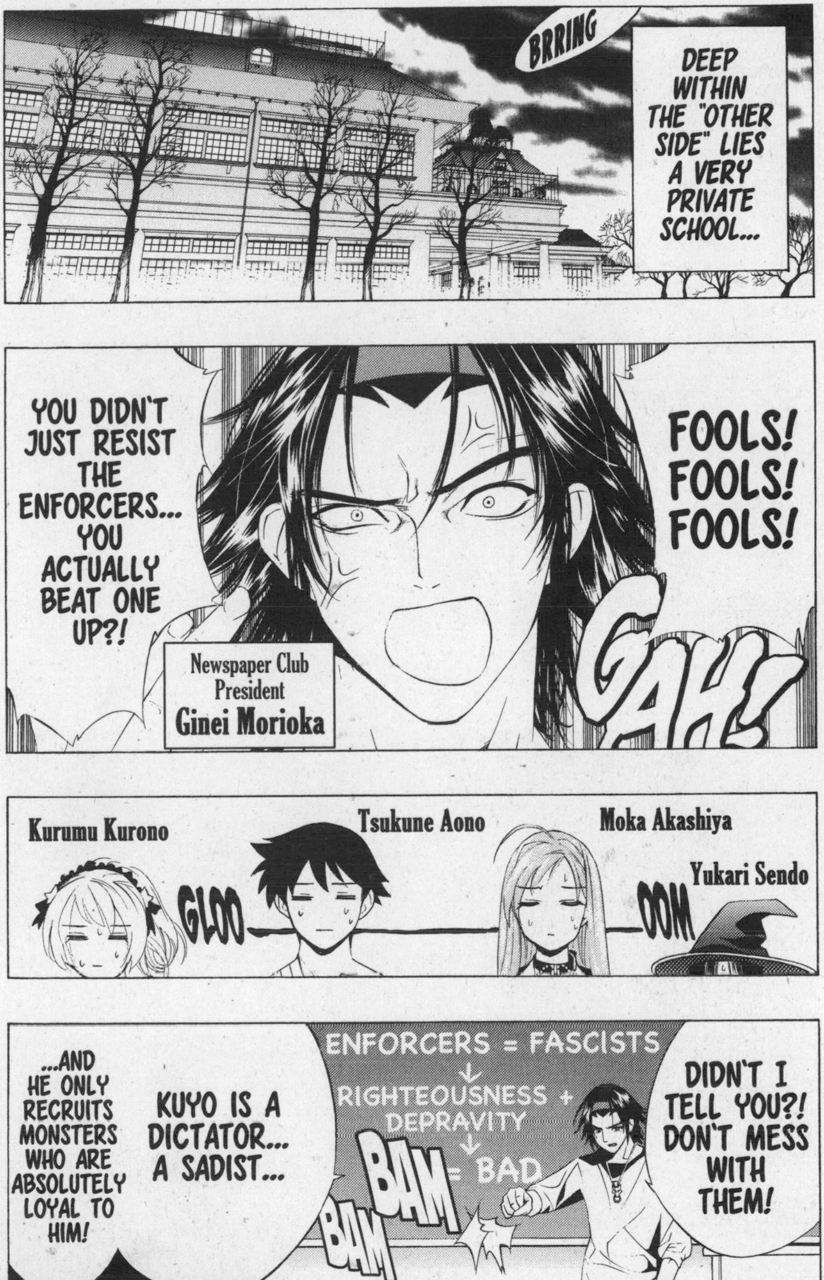
DEEP WITHIN THE "OTHER SIDE" LIES A VERY PRIVATE SCHOOL...
BRRING
FOOLS! FOOLS! FOOLS!
GAH!
YOU DIDN'T JUST RESIST THE ENFORCERS... YOU ACTUALLY BEAT ONE UP?!
Newspaper Club President Ginei Morioka
Yukari Sendo
Moka Akashiya
Tsukune Aono
Kurumu Kurono
GLOO—OOM
DIDN'T I TELL YOU?! DON'T MESS WITH THEM!
ENFORCERS = FASCISTS
↓
RIGHTEOUSNESS + DEPRAVITY
↓
= BAD
BAM BAM BAM
KUYO IS A DICTATOR... A SADIST...
...AND HE ONLY RECRUITS MONSTERS WHO ARE ABSOLUTELY LOYAL TO HIM!

READ THIS WAY

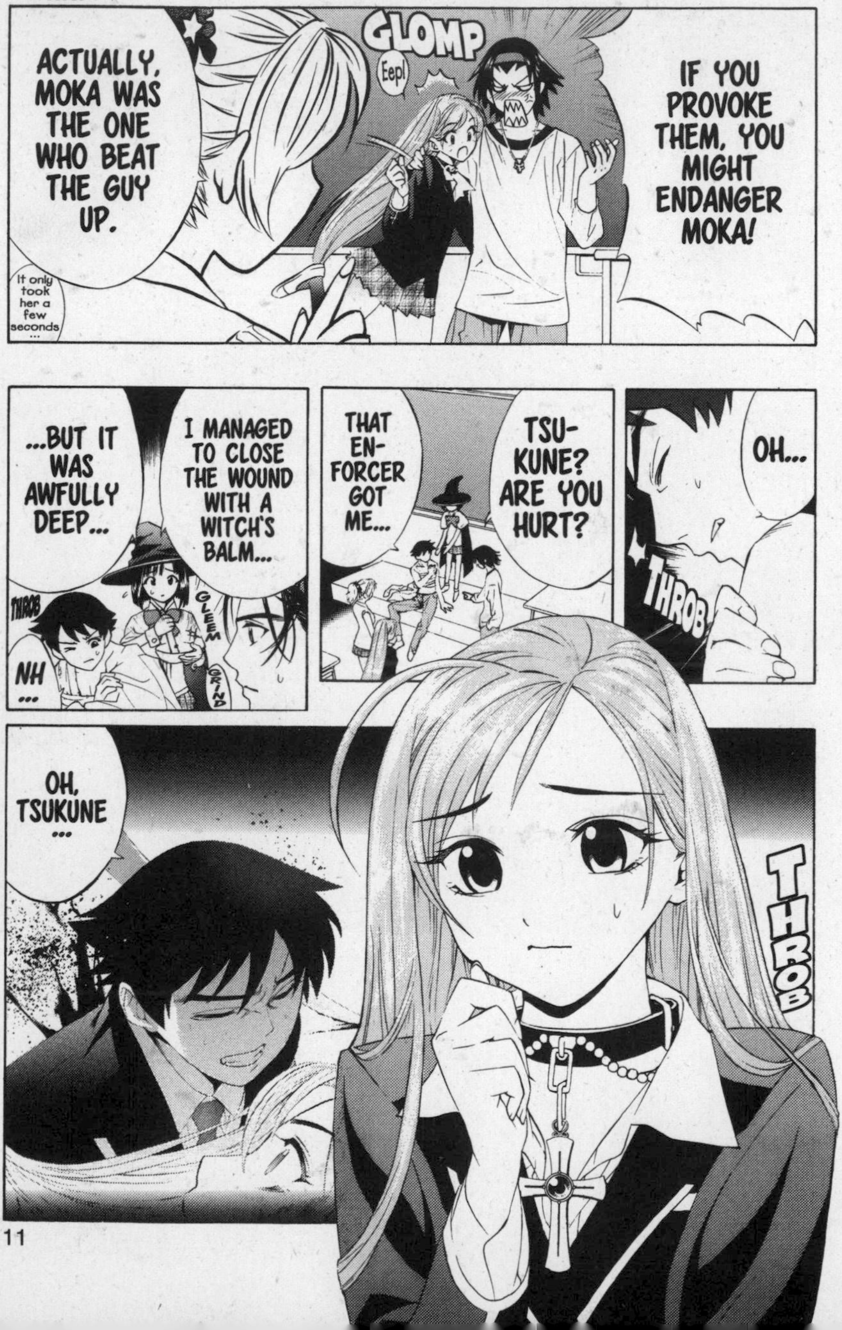
IF YOU PROVOKE THEM, YOU MIGHT ENDANGER MOKA!
GLOMP
Eep!
ACTUALLY, MOKA WAS THE ONE WHO BEAT THE GUY UP.
It only took her a few seconds...
OH...
THROB
TSU-KUNE? ARE YOU HURT?
THAT EN-FORCER GOT ME...
I MANAGED TO CLOSE THE WOUND WITH A WITCH'S BALM...
...BUT IT WAS AWFULLY DEEP...
GLEEM
GRIND
THROB
NH...
THROB
OH, TSUKUNE...

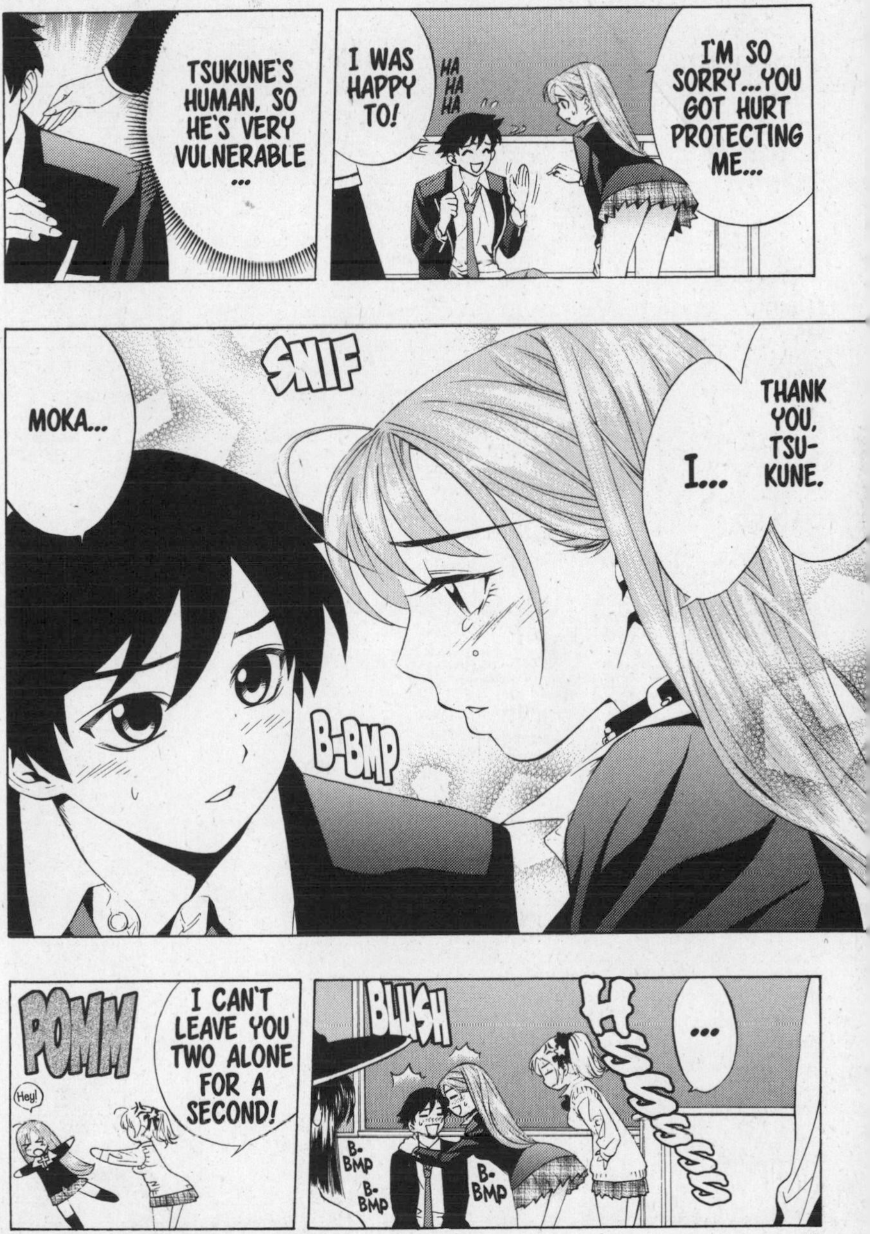
I'M SO SORRY...YOU GOT HURT PROTECTING ME...
HA HA HA
I WAS HAPPY TO!
TSUKUNE'S HUMAN, SO HE'S VERY VULNERABLE ...
THANK YOU, TSUKUNE.
I...
SNIF
MOKA...
B-BMP
...
HSSSSSS
BLUSH
B-BMP
B-BMP
B-BMP
I CAN'T LEAVE YOU TWO ALONE FOR A SECOND!
POMM
Hey!

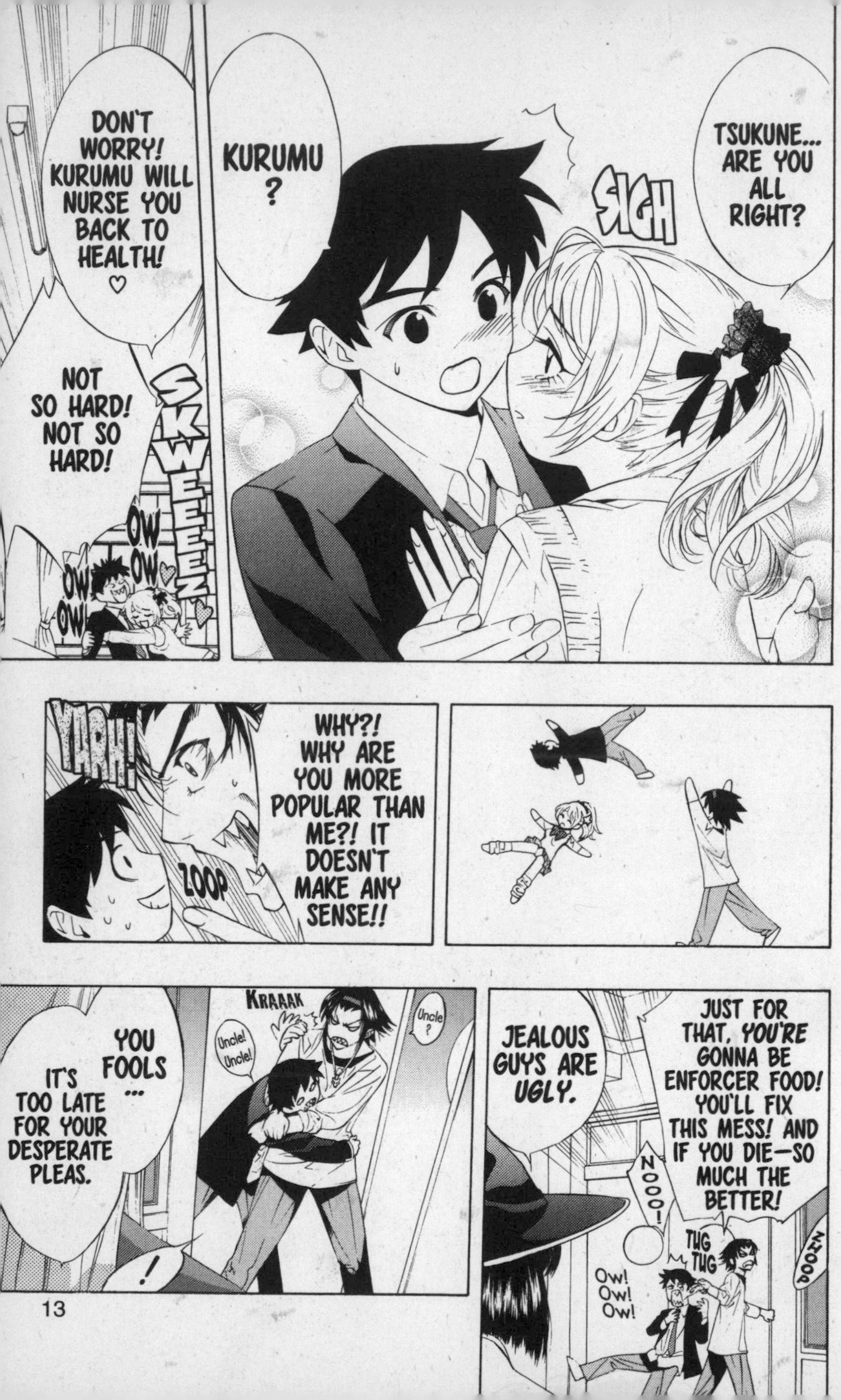
TSUKUNE... ARE YOU ALL RIGHT?
SIGH
KURUMU?
DON'T WORRY! KURUMU WILL NURSE YOU BACK TO HEALTH! ♡
NOT SO HARD! NOT SO HARD!
SKWEEEZ
OW OW
OW OW
YARH!
WHY?! WHY ARE YOU MORE POPULAR THAN ME?! IT DOESN'T MAKE ANY SENSE!!
ZOOP
JUST FOR THAT, YOU'RE GONNA BE ENFORCER FOOD! YOU'LL FIX THIS MESS! AND IF YOU DIE—SO MUCH THE BETTER!
JEALOUS GUYS ARE UGLY.
NOOOO!
ZWOOP
TUG TUG
Ow! Ow! Ow!
Uncle?
KRAAAK
Uncle! Uncle!
YOU FOOLS ...
IT'S TOO LATE FOR YOUR DESPERATE PLEAS.
!

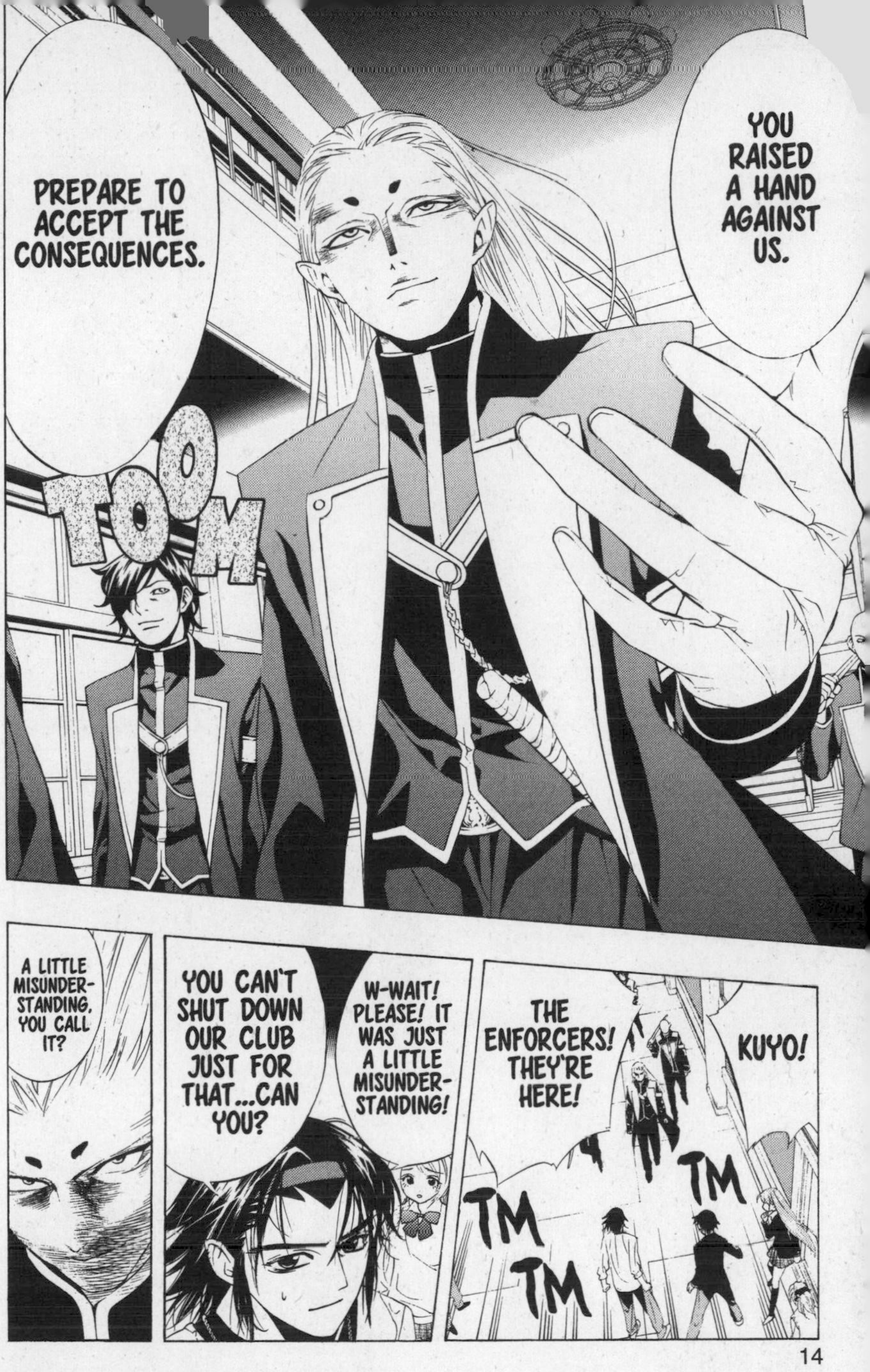
YOU RAISED A HAND AGAINST US.
PREPARE TO ACCEPT THE CONSEQUENCES.
TOOM
KUYO!
THE ENFORCERS! THEY'RE HERE!
TM
TM
TM
TM
W-WAIT! PLEASE! IT WAS JUST A LITTLE MISUNDER-STANDING!
YOU CAN'T SHUT DOWN OUR CLUB JUST FOR THAT...CAN YOU?
A LITTLE MISUNDER-STANDING, YOU CALL IT?

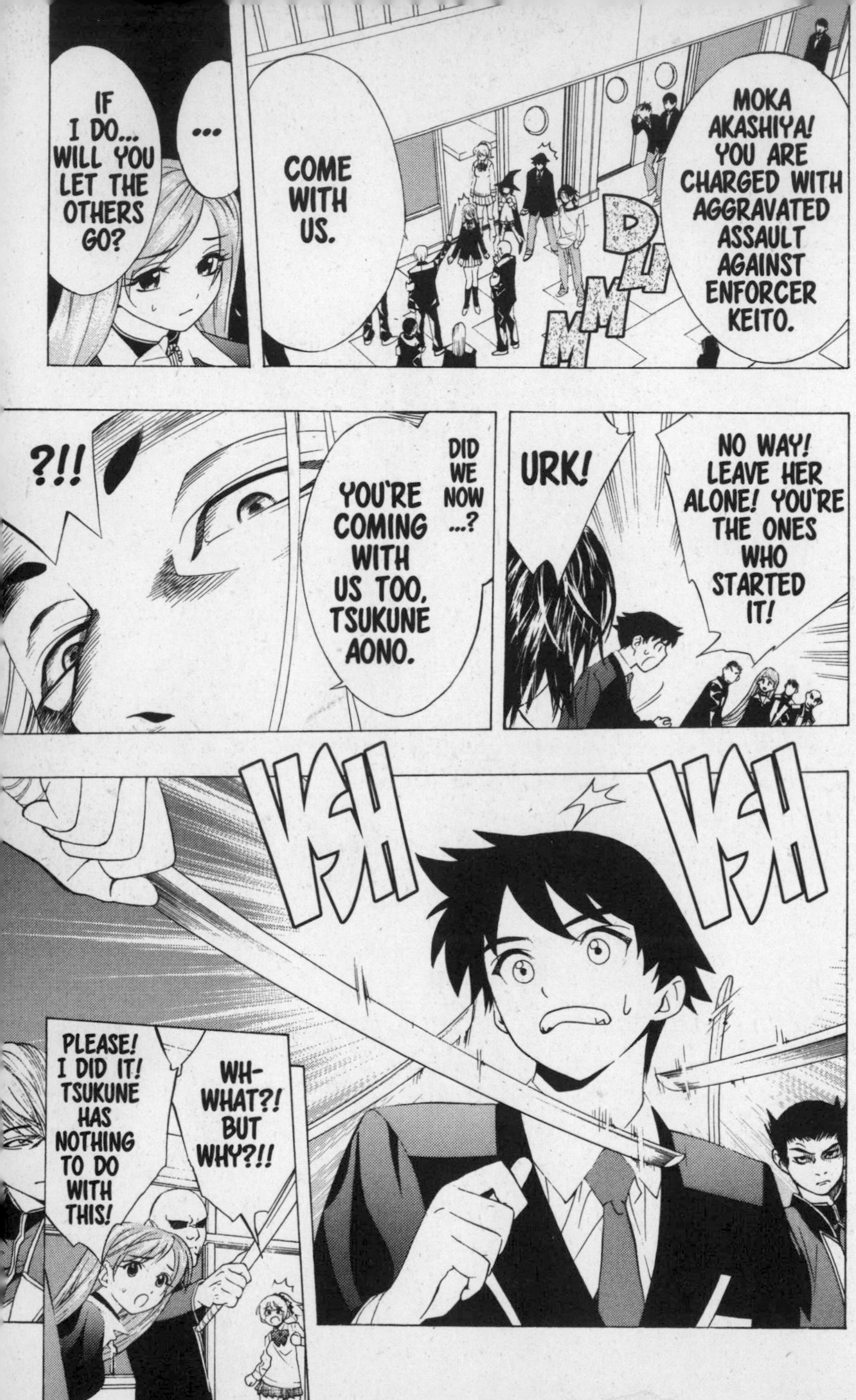
MOKA AKASHIYA! YOU ARE CHARGED WITH AGGRAVATED ASSAULT AGAINST ENFORCER KEITO.
DUMMM
COME WITH US.
...
IF I DO... WILL YOU LET THE OTHERS GO?
NO WAY! LEAVE HER ALONE! YOU'RE THE ONES WHO STARTED IT!
URK!
DID WE NOW ...?
YOU'RE COMING WITH US TOO, TSUKUNE AONO.
?!!
VSH
VSH
WH-WHAT?! BUT WHY?!!
PLEASE! I DID IT! TSUKUNE HAS NOTHING TO DO WITH THIS!

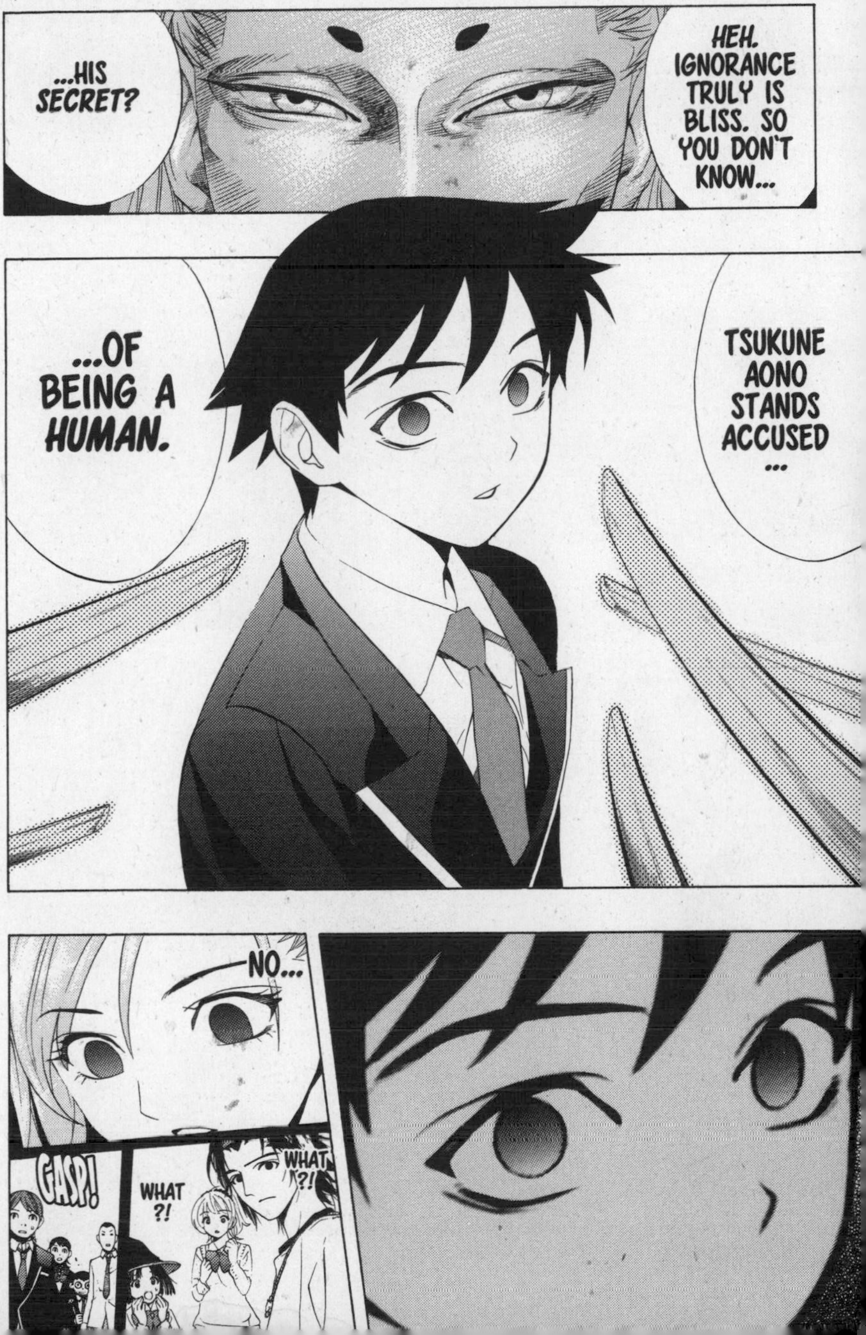
HEH. IGNORANCE TRULY IS BLISS. SO YOU DON'T KNOW...
...HIS SECRET?
TSUKUNE AONO STANDS ACCUSED ...
...OF BEING A HUMAN.
NO...
WHAT ?!
WHAT ?!
GASP!

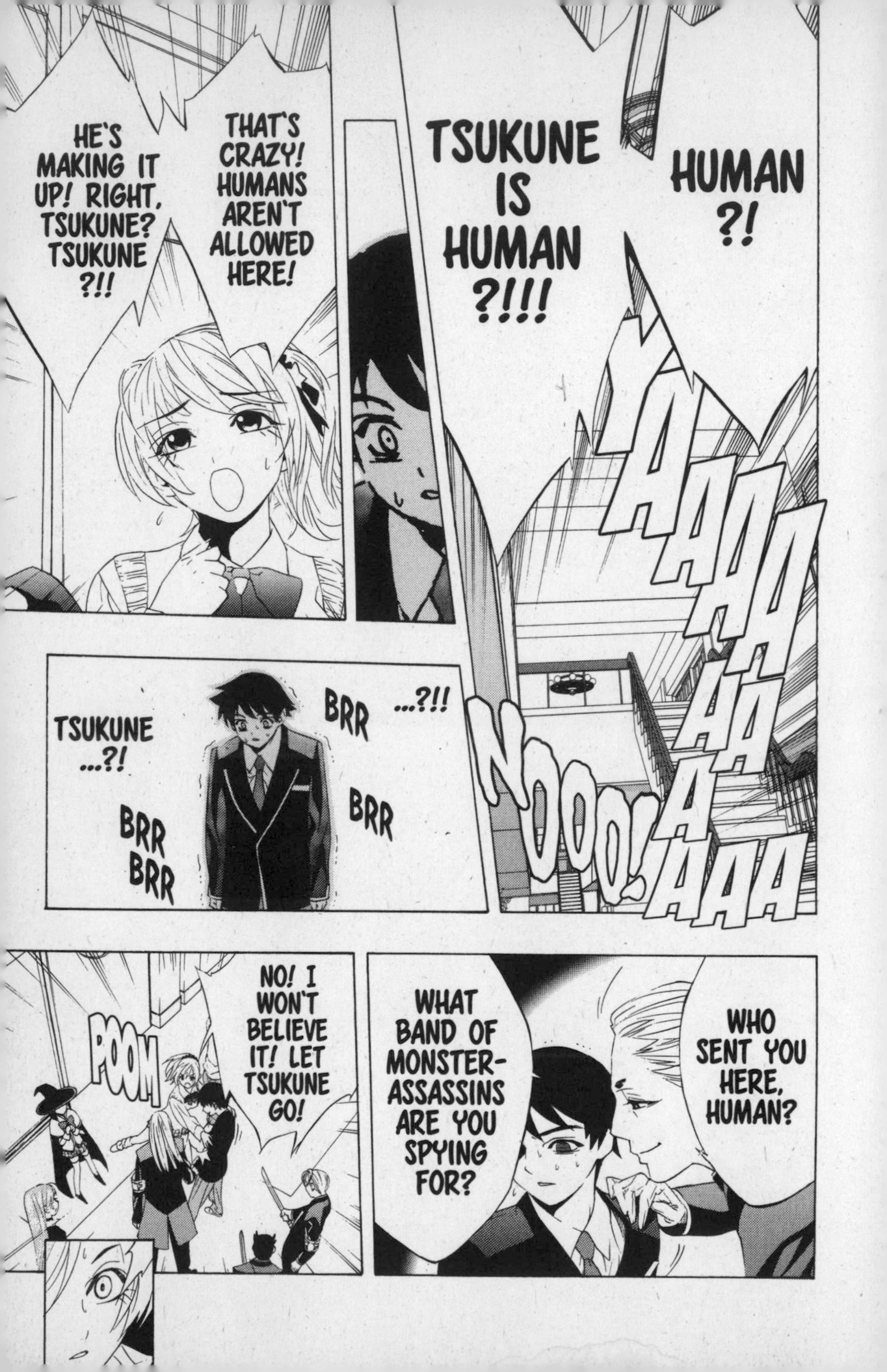
HUMAN ?!
TSUKUNE IS HUMAN ?!!!
AAAAAAAAAAAA
NOOOO!
THAT'S CRAZY! HUMANS AREN'T ALLOWED HERE!
HE'S MAKING IT UP! RIGHT, TSUKUNE? TSUKUNE ?!!
BRR
...?!!
TSUKUNE ...?!
BRR
BRR BRR
WHO SENT YOU HERE, HUMAN?
WHAT BAND OF MONSTER-ASSASSINS ARE YOU SPYING FOR?
NO! I WON'T BELIEVE IT! LET TSUKUNE GO!
POOM

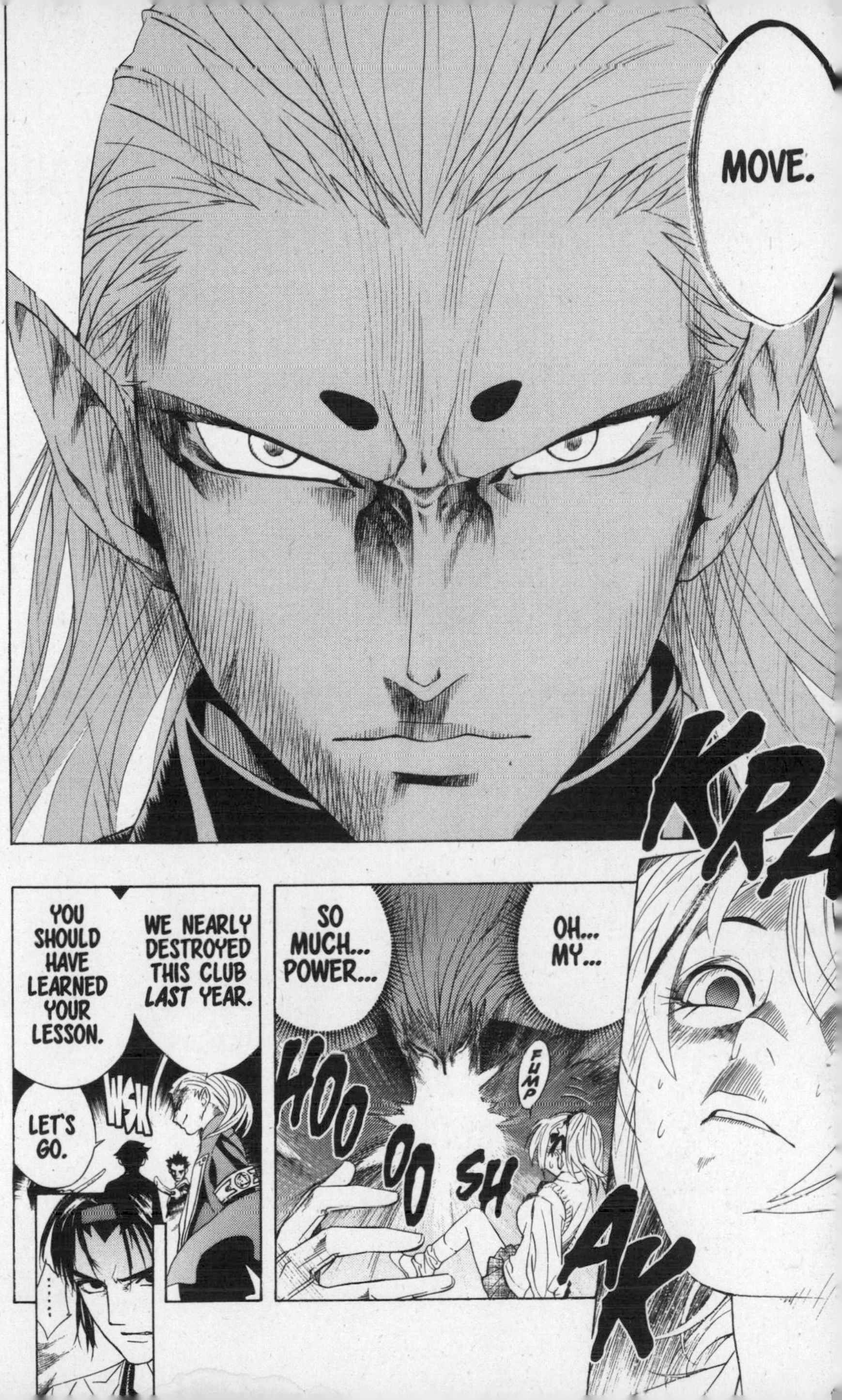
MOVE.
KRA
AK
OH... MY...
SO MUCH... POWER...
HOOOOSH
FUMP
WE NEARLY DESTROYED THIS CLUB LAST YEAR.
YOU SHOULD HAVE LEARNED YOUR LESSON.
WSK
LET'S GO.
......

READ THIS WAY

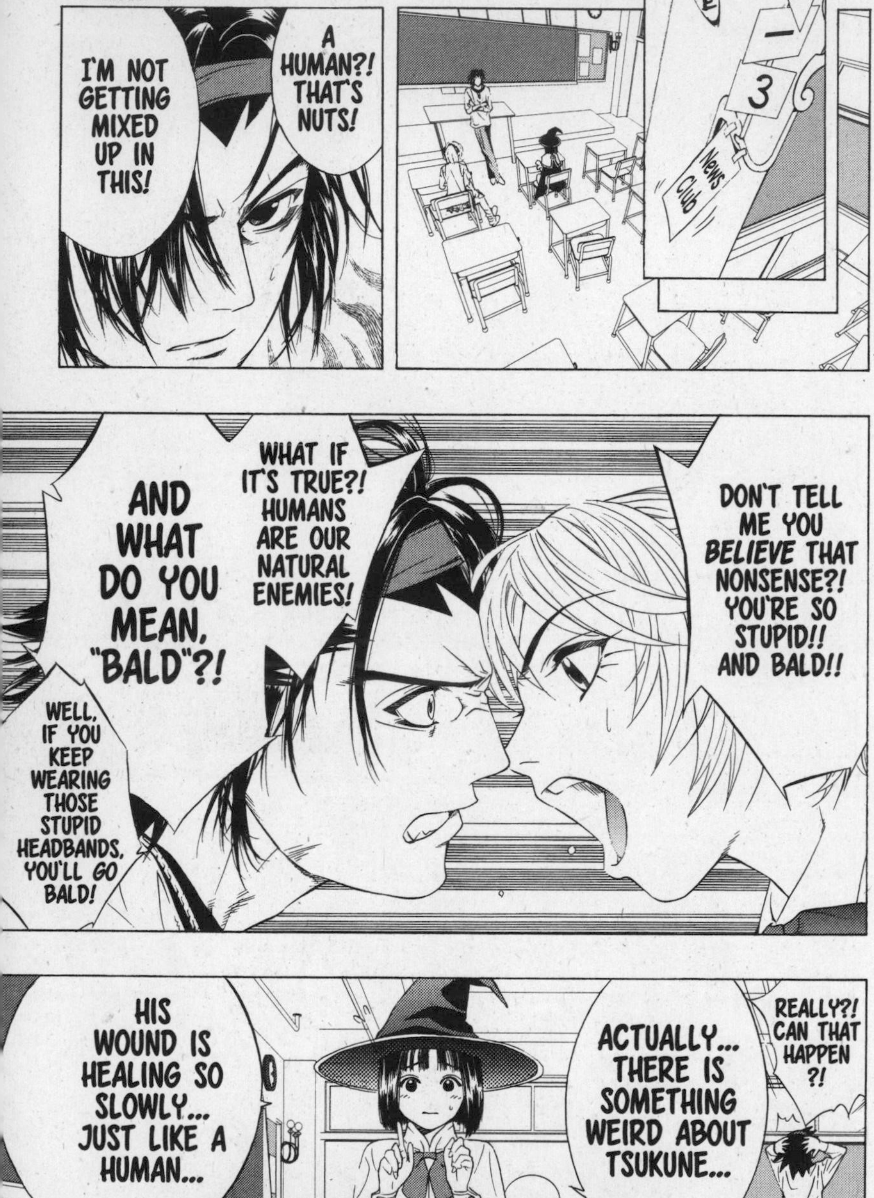
KREE
1-3
News Club
A HUMAN?! THAT'S NUTS!
I'M NOT GETTING MIXED UP IN THIS!
DON'T TELL ME YOU *BELIEVE* THAT NONSENSE?! YOU'RE SO STUPID!! AND BALD!!
WHAT IF IT'S TRUE?! HUMANS ARE OUR NATURAL ENEMIES!
AND WHAT DO YOU MEAN, "BALD"?!
WELL, IF YOU KEEP WEARING THOSE STUPID HEADBANDS, YOU'LL GO BALD!
REALLY?! CAN THAT HAPPEN?!
ACTUALLY... THERE IS SOMETHING WEIRD ABOUT TSUKUNE...
HIS WOUND IS HEALING SO SLOWLY... JUST LIKE A HUMAN...

[redacted]

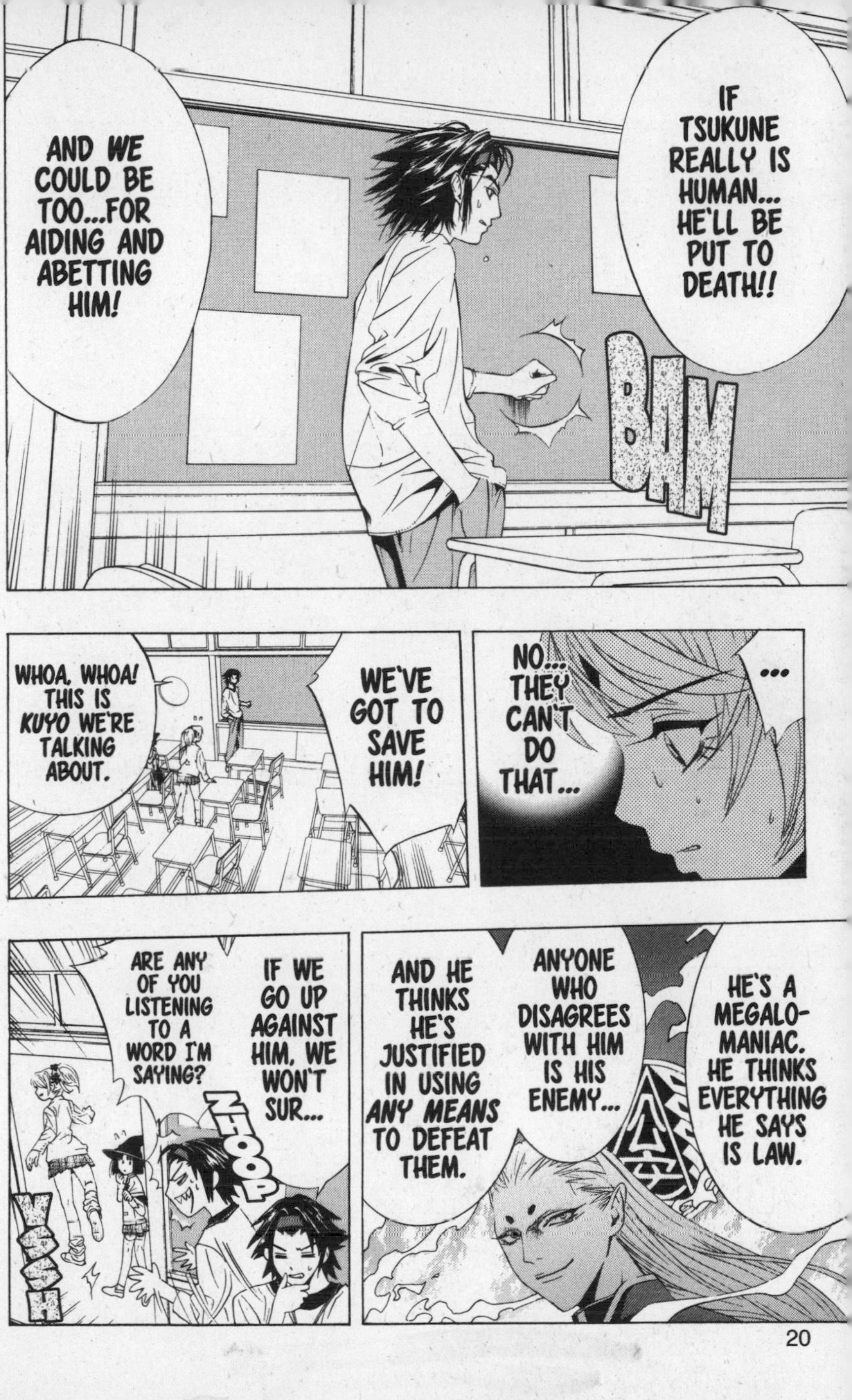
IF TSUKUNE REALLY IS HUMAN... HE'LL BE PUT TO DEATH!!
BAM
AND WE COULD BE TOO...FOR AIDING AND ABETTING HIM!
...
NO... THEY CAN'T DO THAT...
WE'VE GOT TO SAVE HIM!
WHOA, WHOA! THIS IS *KUYO* WE'RE TALKING ABOUT.
HE'S A MEGALO-MANIAC. HE THINKS EVERYTHING HE SAYS IS LAW.
ANYONE WHO DISAGREES WITH HIM IS HIS ENEMY...
AND HE THINKS HE'S JUSTIFIED IN USING *ANY MEANS* TO DEFEAT THEM.
IF WE GO UP AGAINST HIM, WE WON'T SUR...
ZHOOP
ARE ANY OF YOU LISTENING TO A WORD I'M SAYING?

READ THIS WAY

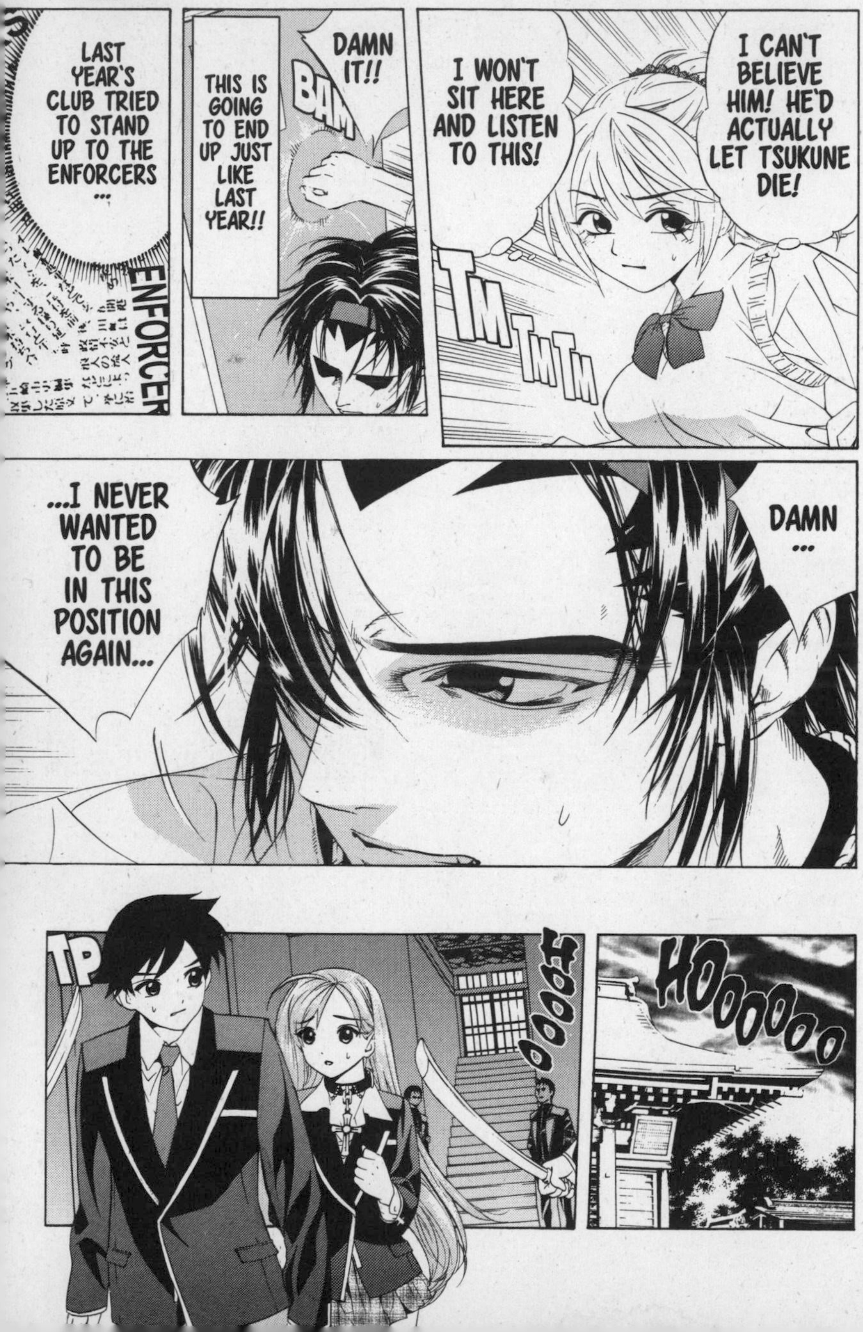

I CAN'T BELIEVE HIM! HE'D ACTUALLY LET TSUKUNE DIE!
I WON'T SIT HERE AND LISTEN TO THIS!
TMTMTM
DAMN IT!!
BAM
THIS IS GOING TO END UP JUST LIKE LAST YEAR!!
LAST YEAR'S CLUB TRIED TO STAND UP TO THE ENFORCERS ...
ENFORCER
DAMN ...
...I NEVER WANTED TO BE IN THIS POSITION AGAIN...
HOOOOOOO
HOOOOO
TP

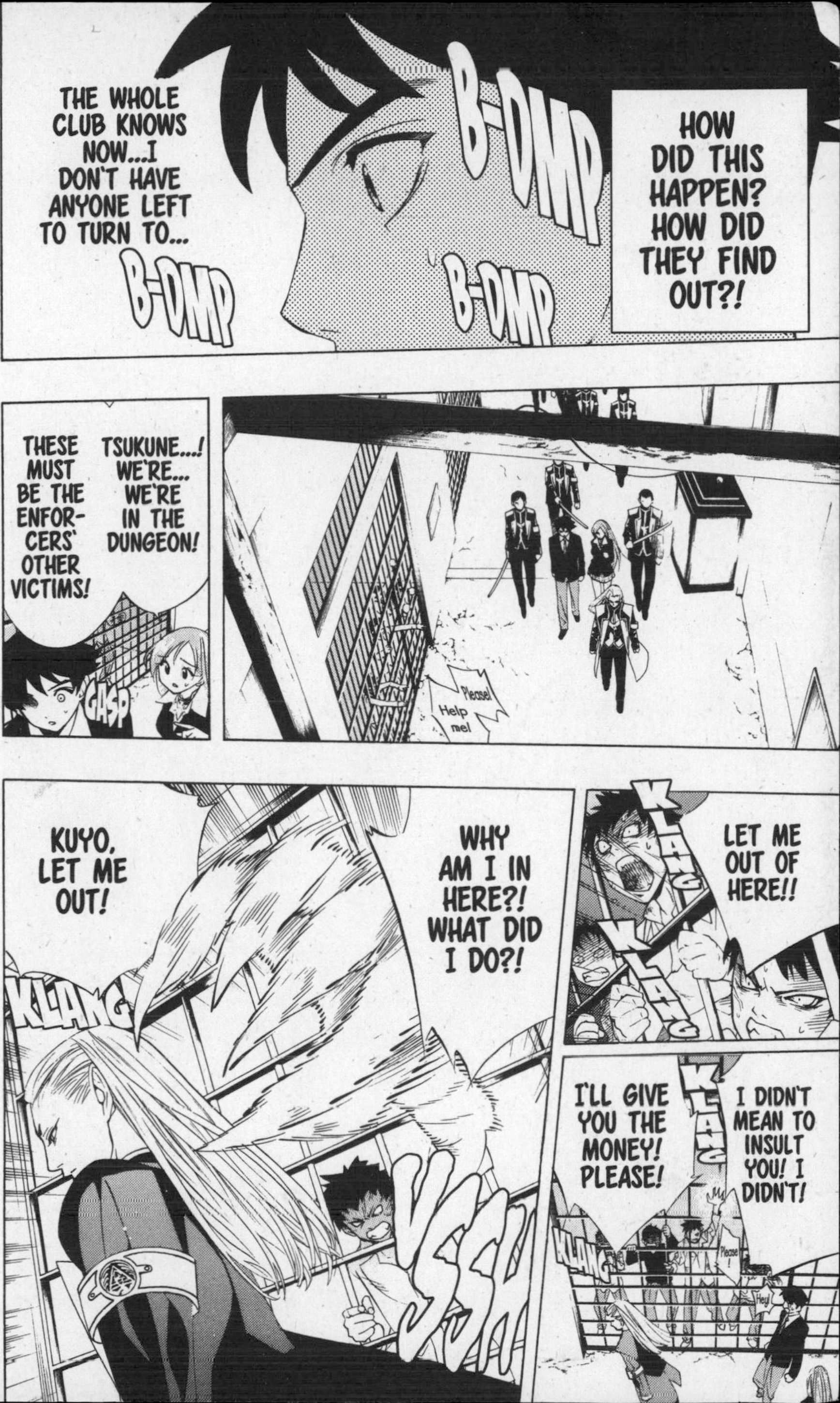
B-DMP
HOW DID THIS HAPPEN? HOW DID THEY FIND OUT?!
THE WHOLE CLUB KNOWS NOW...I DON'T HAVE ANYONE LEFT TO TURN TO...
B-DMP
B-DMP
Please! Help me!
TSUKUNE...! WE'RE... WE'RE IN THE DUNGEON!
THESE MUST BE THE ENFORCERS' OTHER VICTIMS!
GASP
KLANG
LET ME OUT OF HERE!!
KLANG
KLANG
I DIDN'T MEAN TO INSULT YOU! I DIDN'T!
KLANG
I'LL GIVE YOU THE MONEY! PLEASE!
Please!
KLANG
Hey!
WHY AM I IN HERE?! WHAT DID I DO?!
KUYO, LET ME OUT!
KLANG

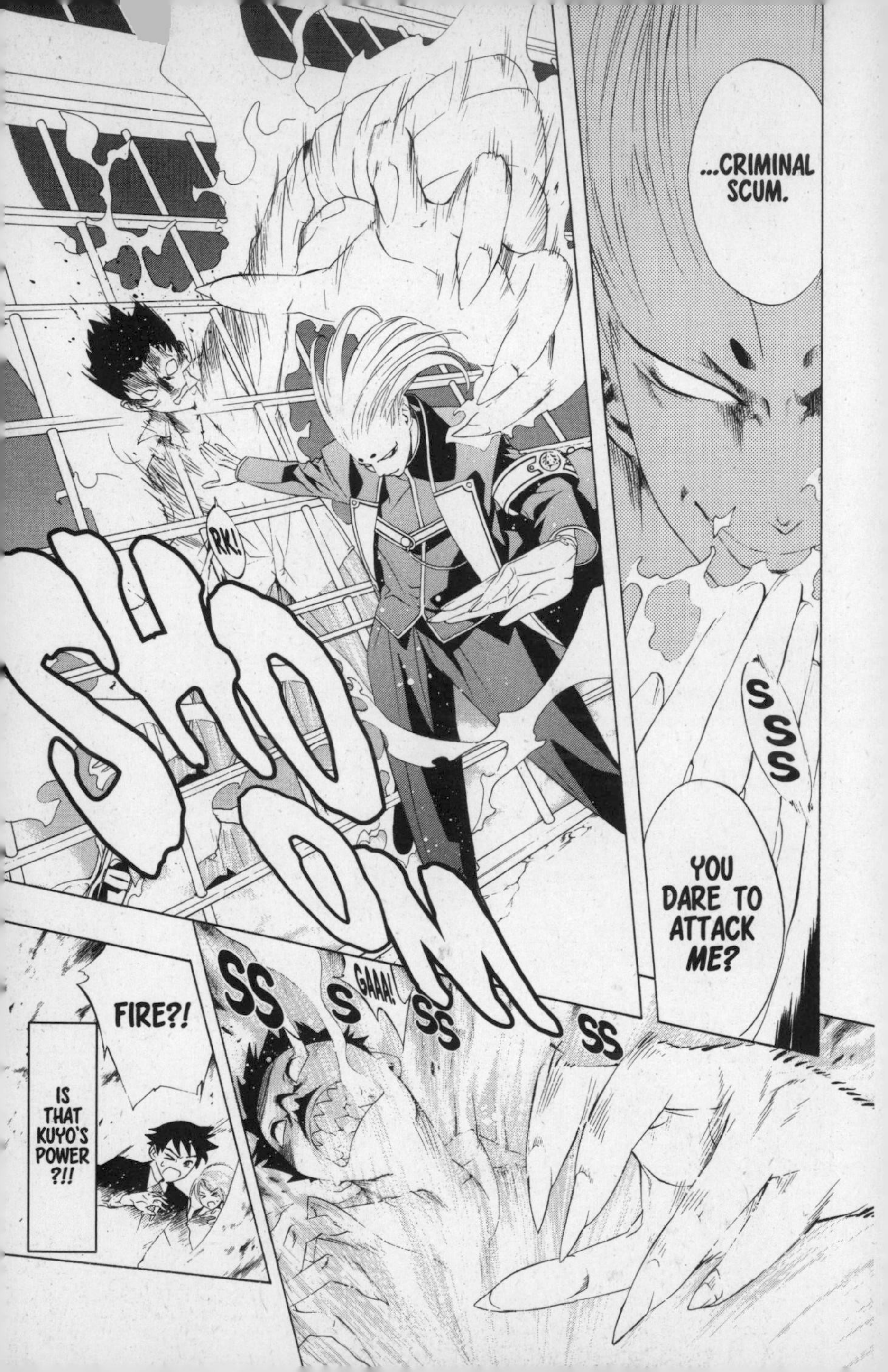
...CRIMINAL SCUM.
SSS
YOU DARE TO ATTACK ME?
RK!
SHOOM
SS
S
GAAA!
SS
SS
FIRE?!
IS THAT KUYO'S POWER ?!!

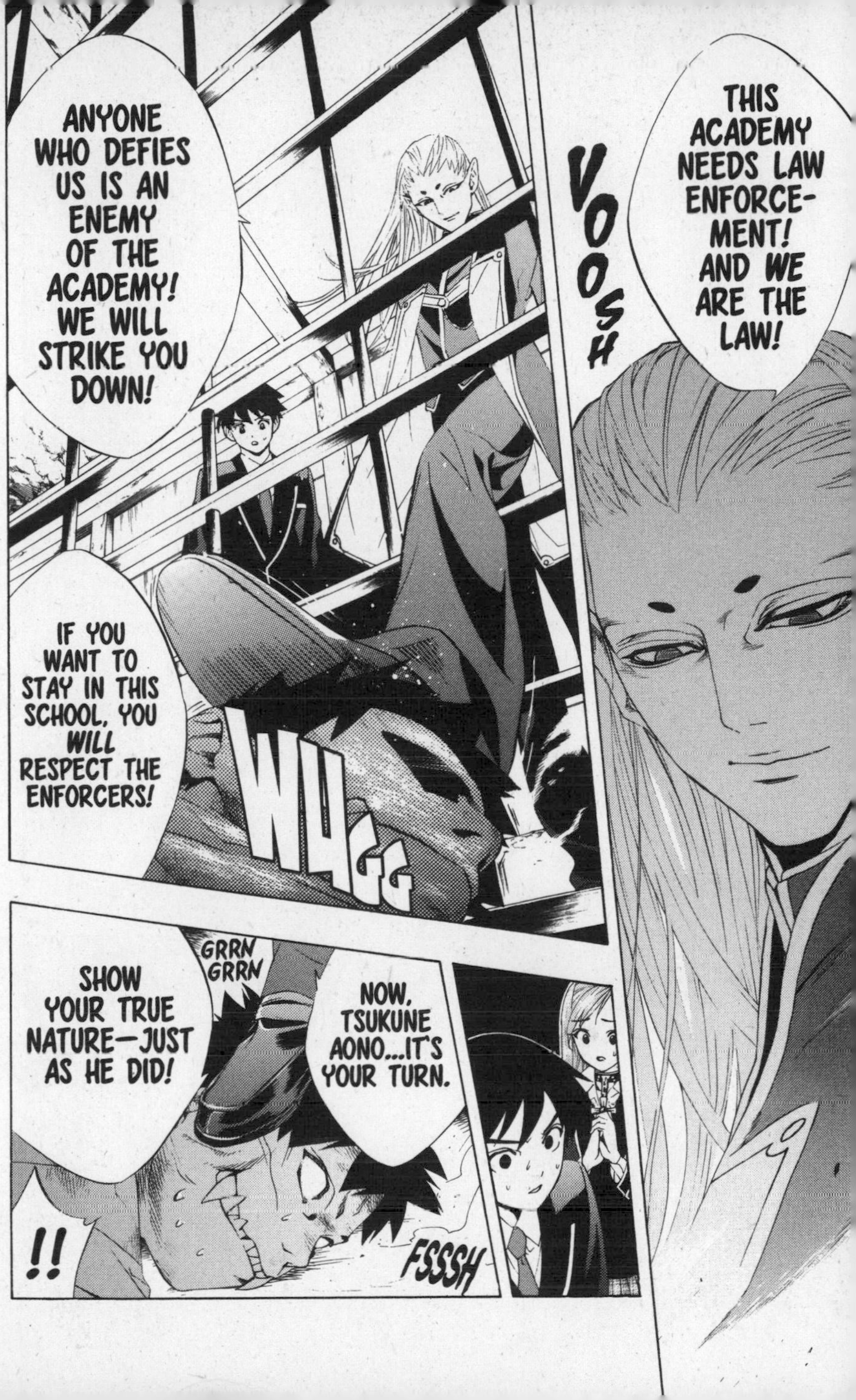
THIS ACADEMY NEEDS LAW ENFORCEMENT! AND WE ARE THE LAW!
VOOSH
ANYONE WHO DEFIES US IS AN ENEMY OF THE ACADEMY! WE WILL STRIKE YOU DOWN!
IF YOU WANT TO STAY IN THIS SCHOOL, YOU WILL RESPECT THE ENFORCERS!
WHUGG
NOW, TSUKUNE AONO...IT'S YOUR TURN.
FSSSH
GRRN GRRN
SHOW YOUR TRUE NATURE—JUST AS HE DID!
!!

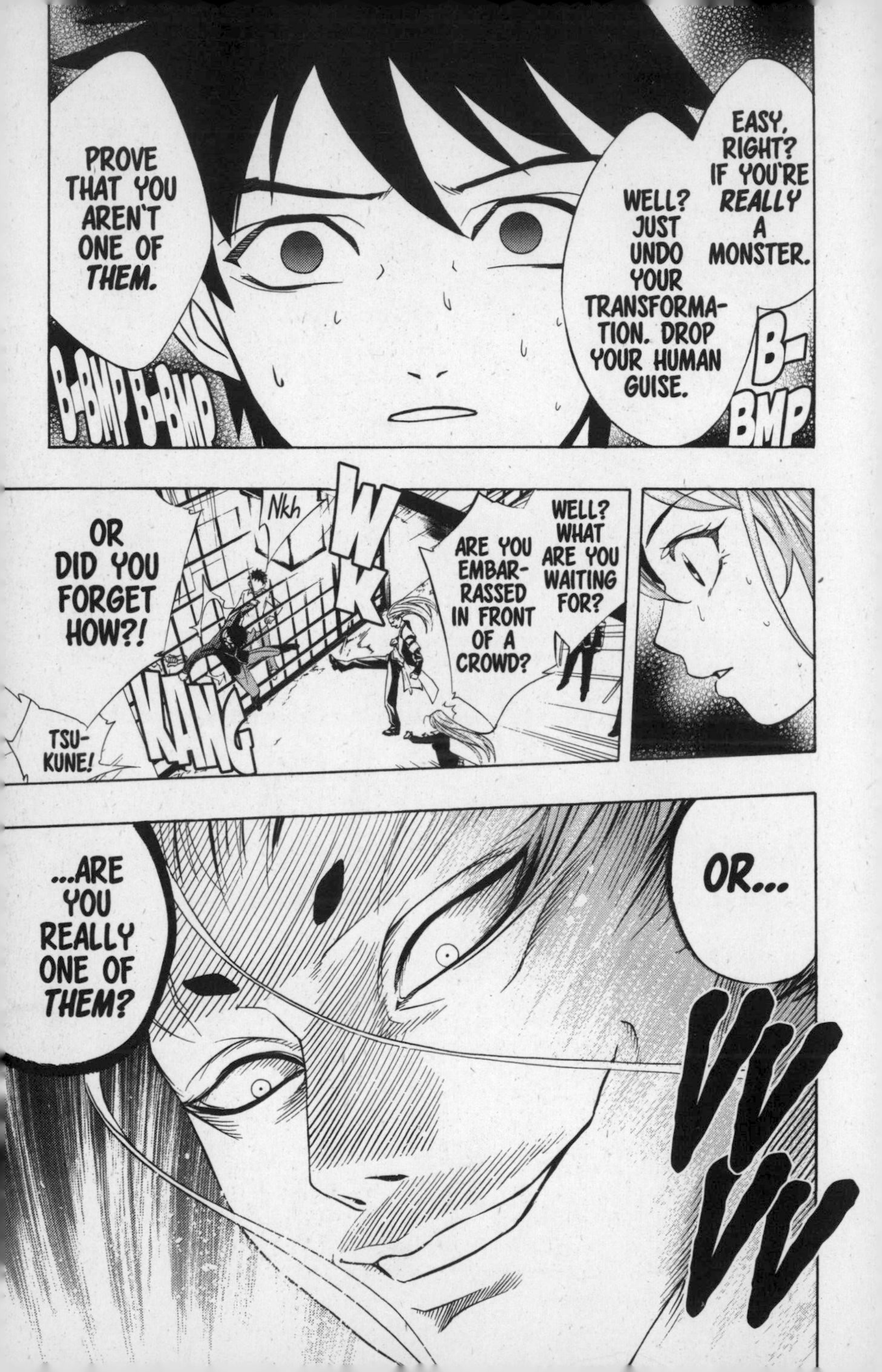
EASY, RIGHT? IF YOU'RE REALLY A MONSTER.
WELL? JUST UNDO YOUR TRANSFORMATION. DROP YOUR HUMAN GUISE.
B-BMP
PROVE THAT YOU AREN'T ONE OF THEM.
B-BMP B-BMP
WELL? WHAT ARE YOU WAITING FOR?
ARE YOU EMBARRASSED IN FRONT OF A CROWD?
WK
Nkh
OR DID YOU FORGET HOW?!
KANG
TSU-KUNE!
OR...
...ARE YOU REALLY ONE OF THEM?

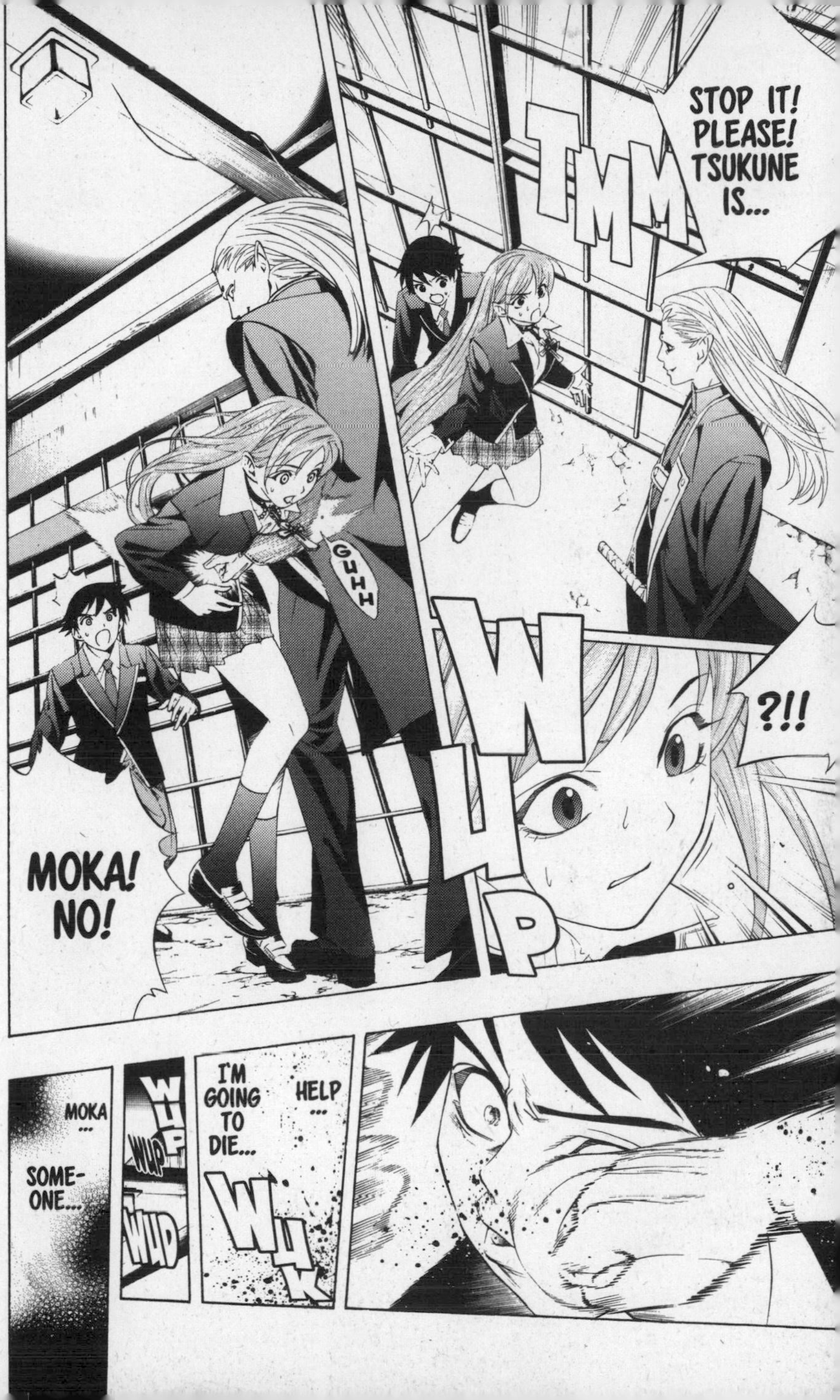
TMM
STOP IT! PLEASE! TSUKUNE IS...
WHUP
?!!
GUHH
MOKA! NO!
HELP...
I'M GOING TO DIE...
WHUK
WUP
WUP
WUD
MOKA...
SOME-ONE...

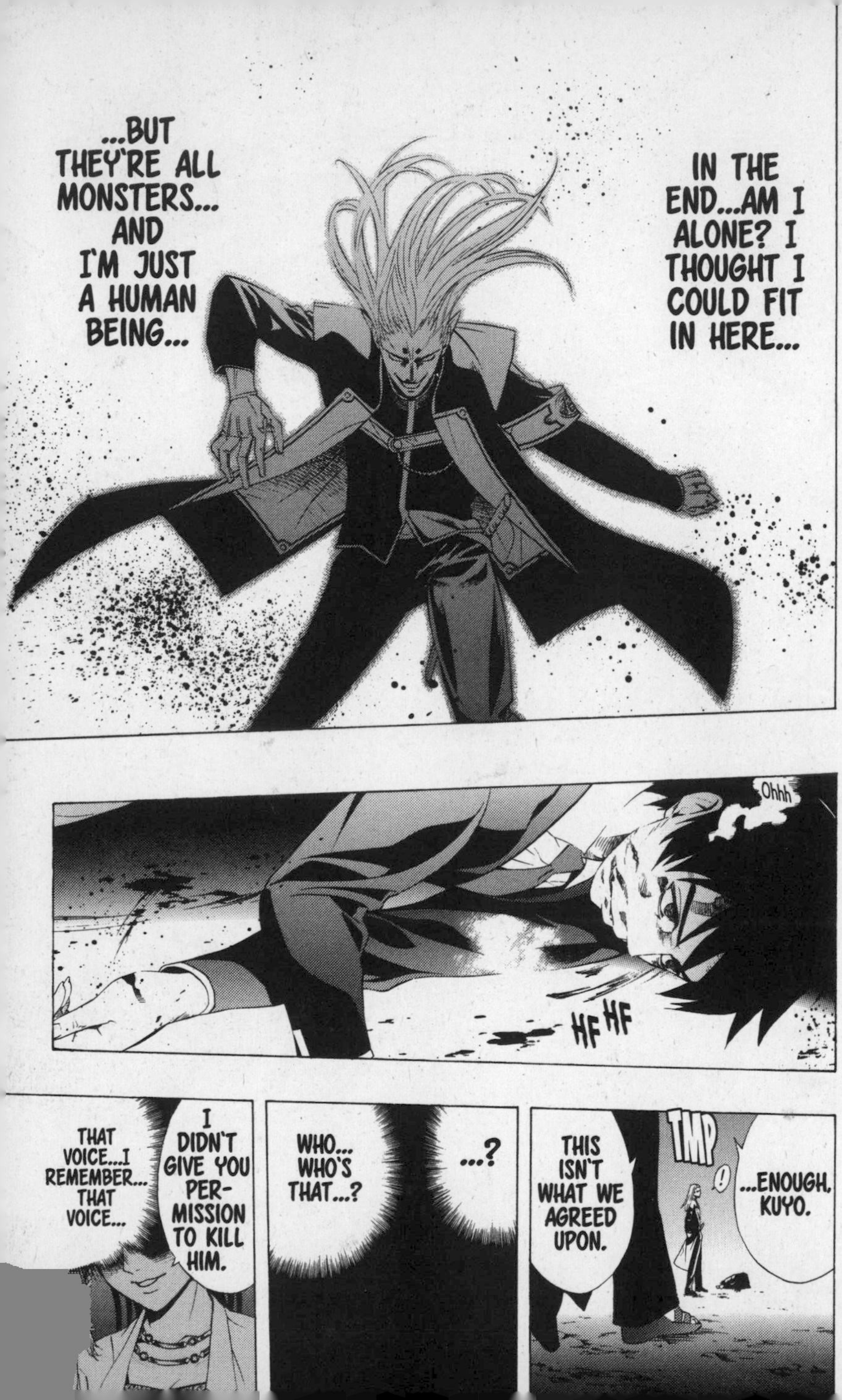
IN THE END...AM I ALONE? I THOUGHT I COULD FIT IN HERE...
...BUT THEY'RE ALL MONSTERS... AND I'M JUST A HUMAN BEING...
Ohhh
HF HF
TMP
!
...ENOUGH, KUYO.
THIS ISN'T WHAT WE AGREED UPON.
...?
WHO... WHO'S THAT...?
I DIDN'T GIVE YOU PER-MISSION TO KILL HIM.
THAT VOICE...I REMEMBER... THAT VOICE...

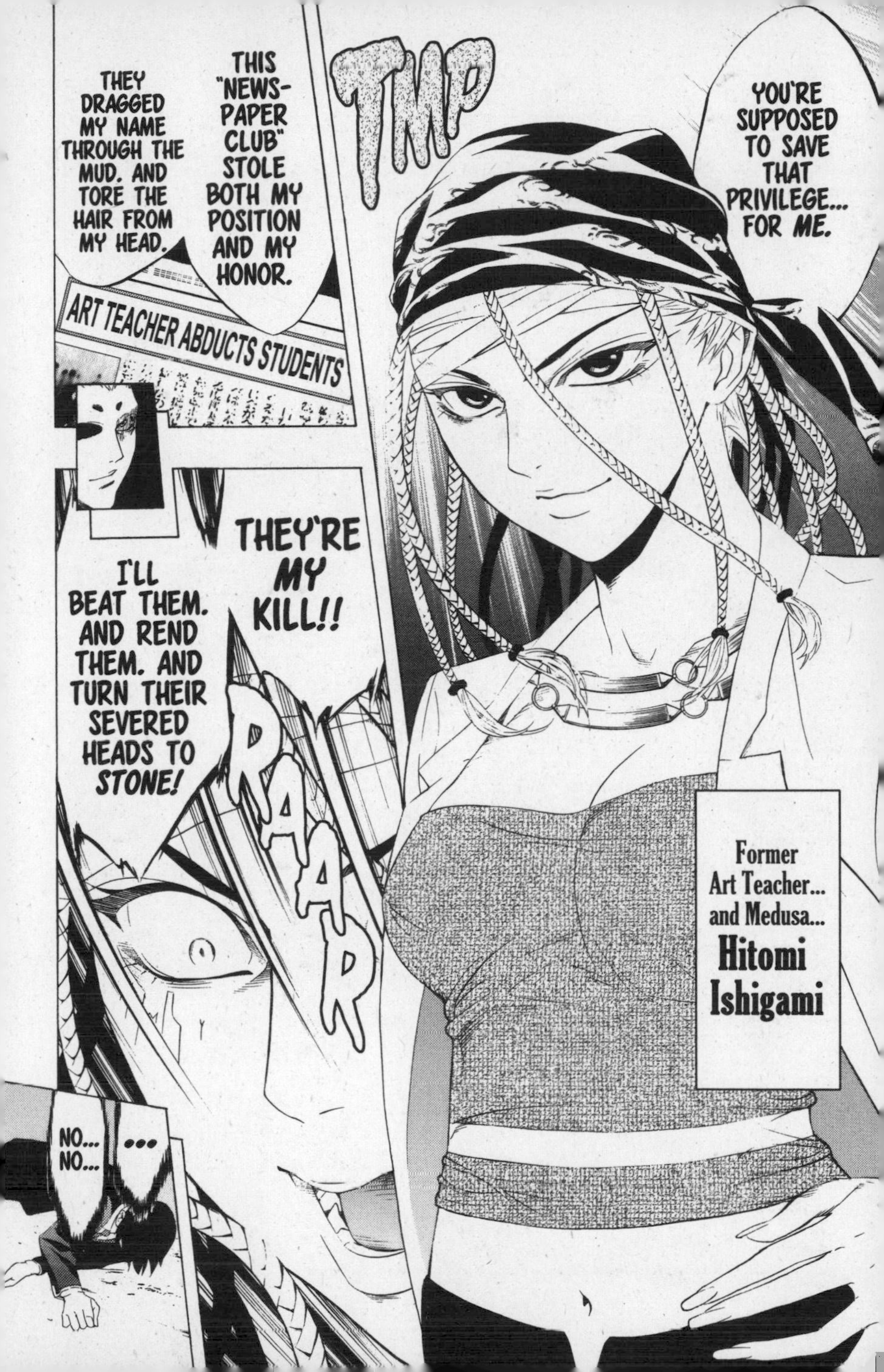
TMP
YOU'RE SUPPOSED TO SAVE THAT PRIVILEGE... FOR *ME*.
Former Art Teacher... and Medusa... Hitomi Ishigami
THIS "NEWSPAPER CLUB" STOLE BOTH MY POSITION AND MY HONOR.
THEY DRAGGED MY NAME THROUGH THE MUD. AND TORE THE HAIR FROM MY HEAD.
ART TEACHER ABDUCTS STUDENTS
THEY'RE *MY* KILL!!
I'LL BEAT THEM. AND REND THEM. AND TURN THEIR SEVERED HEADS TO *STONE*!
PAAR
...
NO... NO...

READ THIS WAY

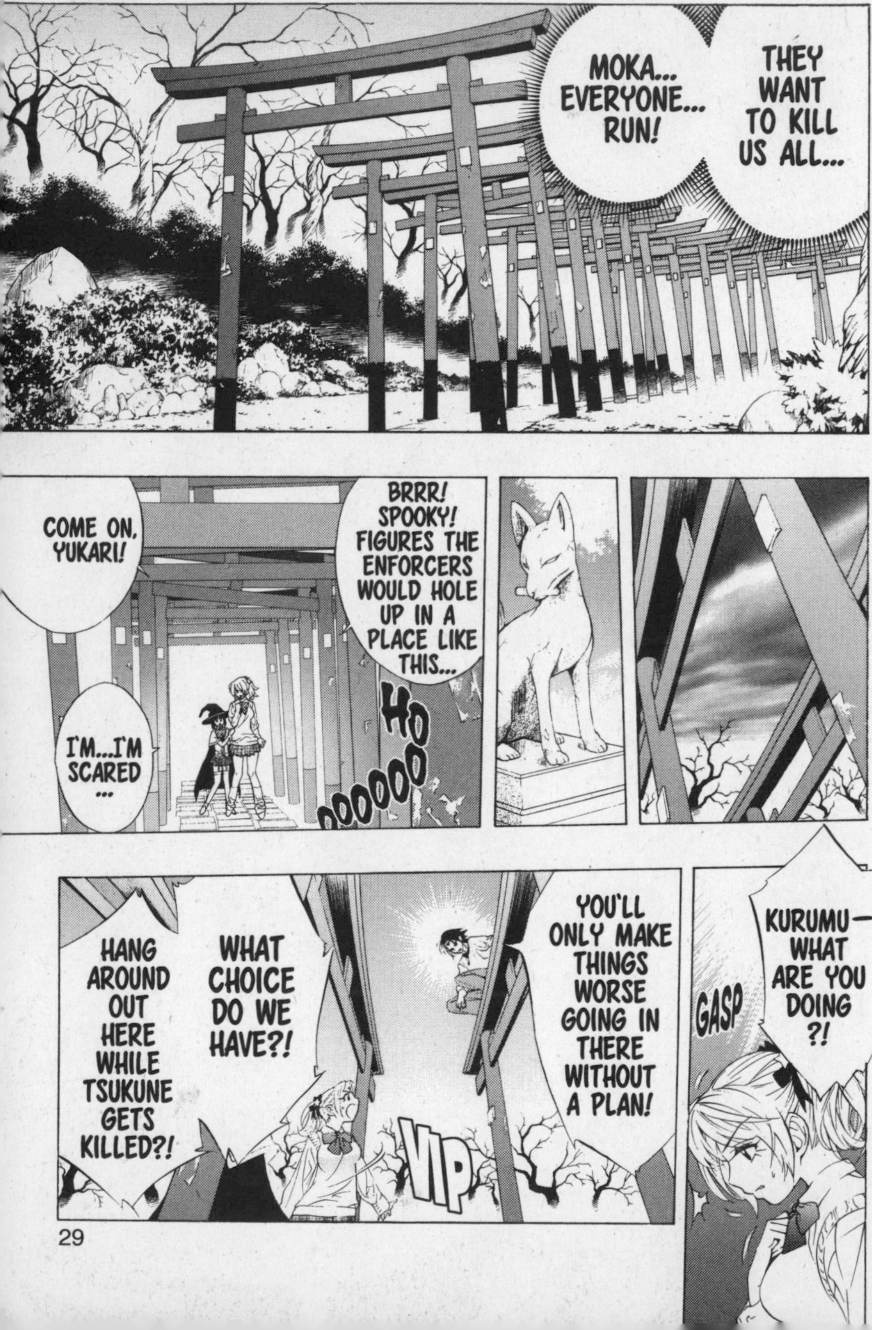

MOKA... EVERYONE... RUN!
THEY WANT TO KILL US ALL...
BRRR! SPOOKY! FIGURES THE ENFORCERS WOULD HOLE UP IN A PLACE LIKE THIS...
COME ON, YUKARI!
HOOOOOOO
I'M...I'M SCARED ...
KURUMU— WHAT ARE YOU DOING ?!
GASP
YOU'LL ONLY MAKE THINGS WORSE GOING IN THERE WITHOUT A PLAN!
WHAT CHOICE DO WE HAVE?!
HANG AROUND OUT HERE WHILE TSUKUNE GETS KILLED?!
VIP

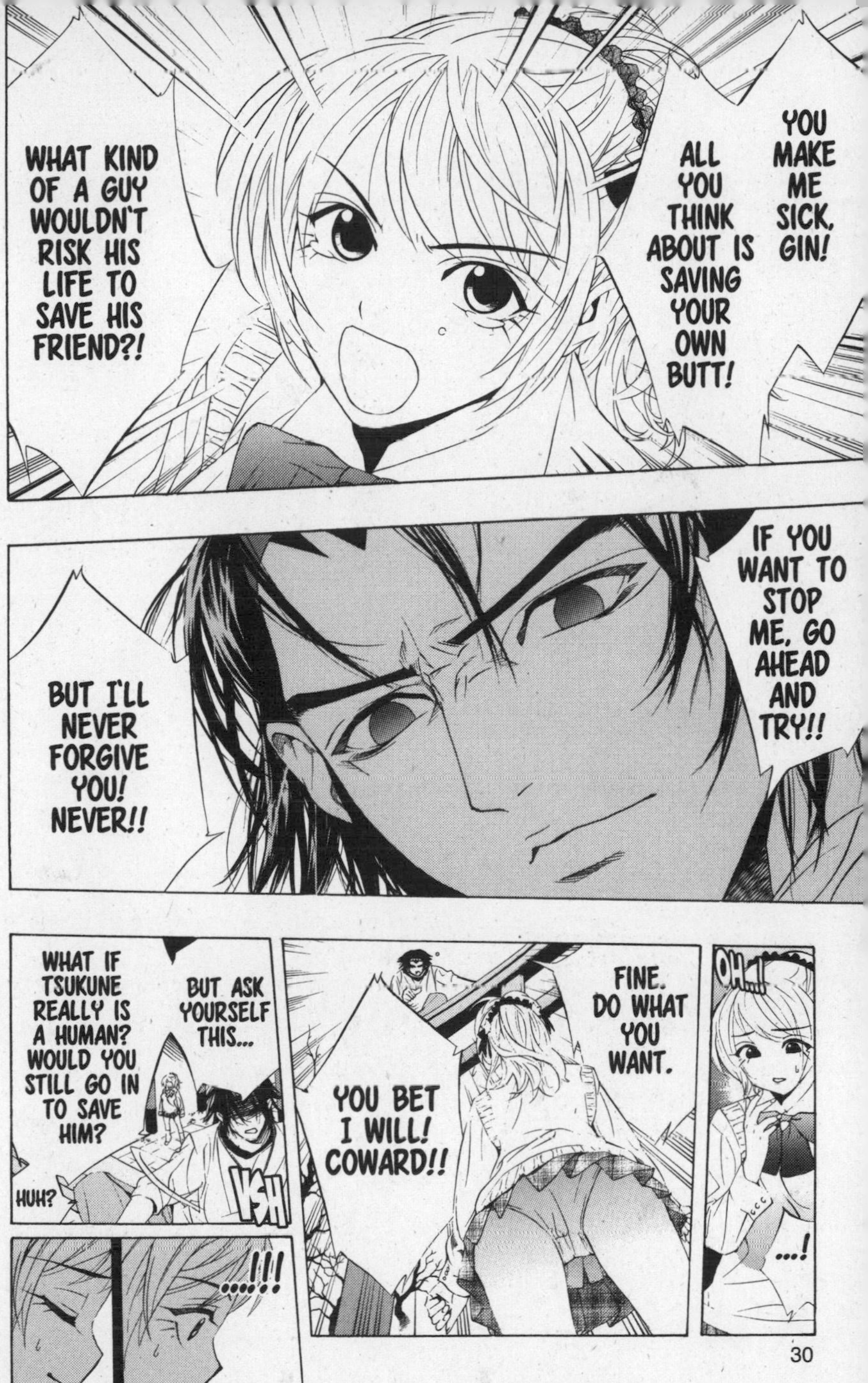
YOU MAKE ME SICK, GIN!
ALL YOU THINK ABOUT IS SAVING YOUR OWN BUTT!
WHAT KIND OF A GUY WOULDN'T RISK HIS LIFE TO SAVE HIS FRIEND?!
IF YOU WANT TO STOP ME, GO AHEAD AND TRY!!
BUT I'LL NEVER FORGIVE YOU! NEVER!!
OH...!
...!
FINE. DO WHAT YOU WANT.
YOU BET I WILL! COWARD!!
BUT ASK YOURSELF THIS...
WHAT IF TSUKUNE REALLY IS A HUMAN? WOULD YOU STILL GO IN TO SAVE HIM?
VSH
HUH?
...!!!

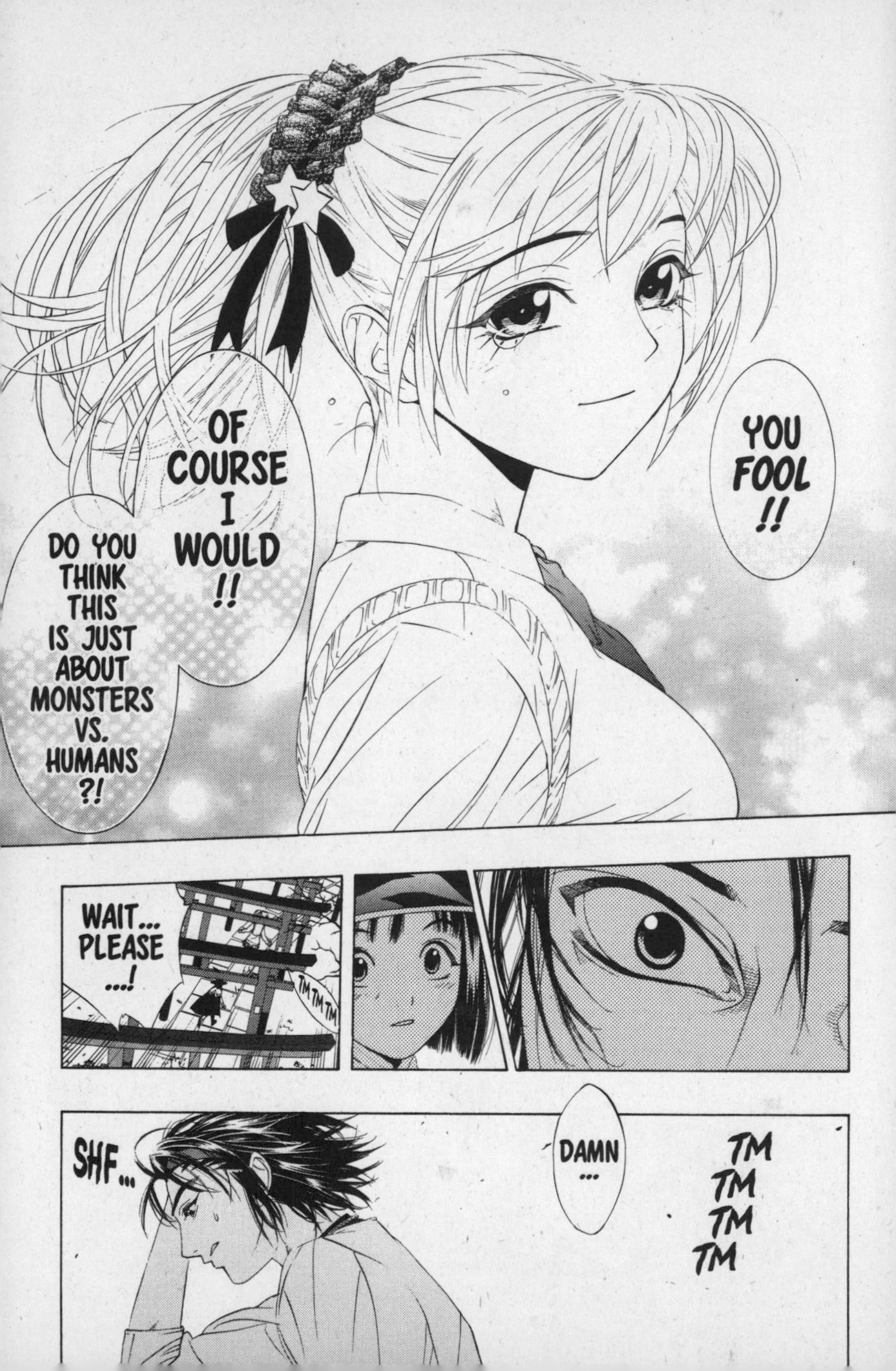
YOU FOOL!!
OF COURSE I WOULD!!
DO YOU THINK THIS IS JUST ABOUT MONSTERS VS. HUMANS?!
WAIT... PLEASE ...!
TM TM TM
TM TM TM TM
DAMN ...
SHF...

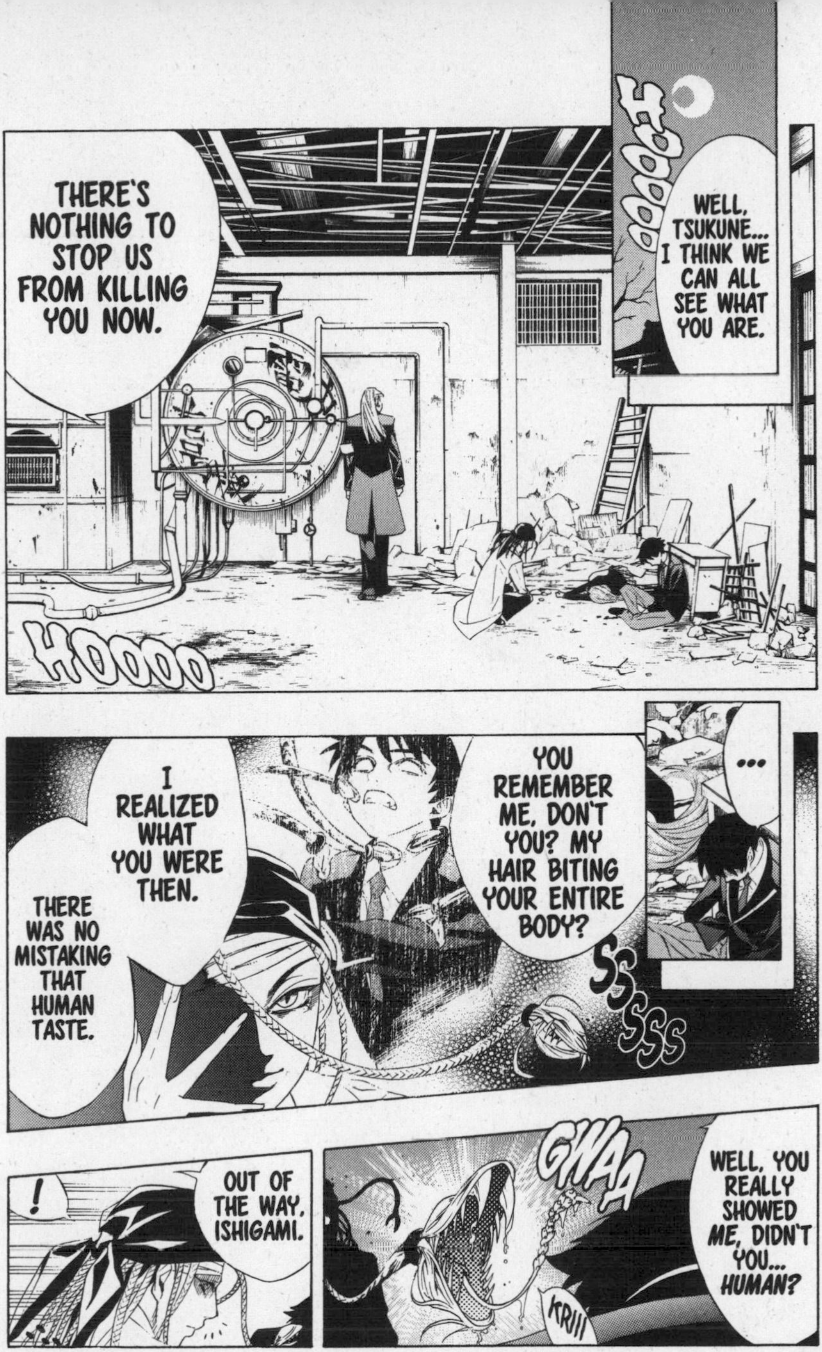
HOOOOO
WELL, TSUKUNE... I THINK WE CAN ALL SEE WHAT YOU ARE.
THERE'S NOTHING TO STOP US FROM KILLING YOU NOW.
HOOOO
...
YOU REMEMBER ME, DON'T YOU? MY HAIR BITING YOUR ENTIRE BODY?
SSSSSS
I REALIZED WHAT YOU WERE THEN.
THERE WAS NO MISTAKING THAT HUMAN TASTE.
GWAA
WELL, YOU REALLY SHOWED ME, DIDN'T YOU... HUMAN?
KRIII
OUT OF THE WAY, ISHIGAMI.
!

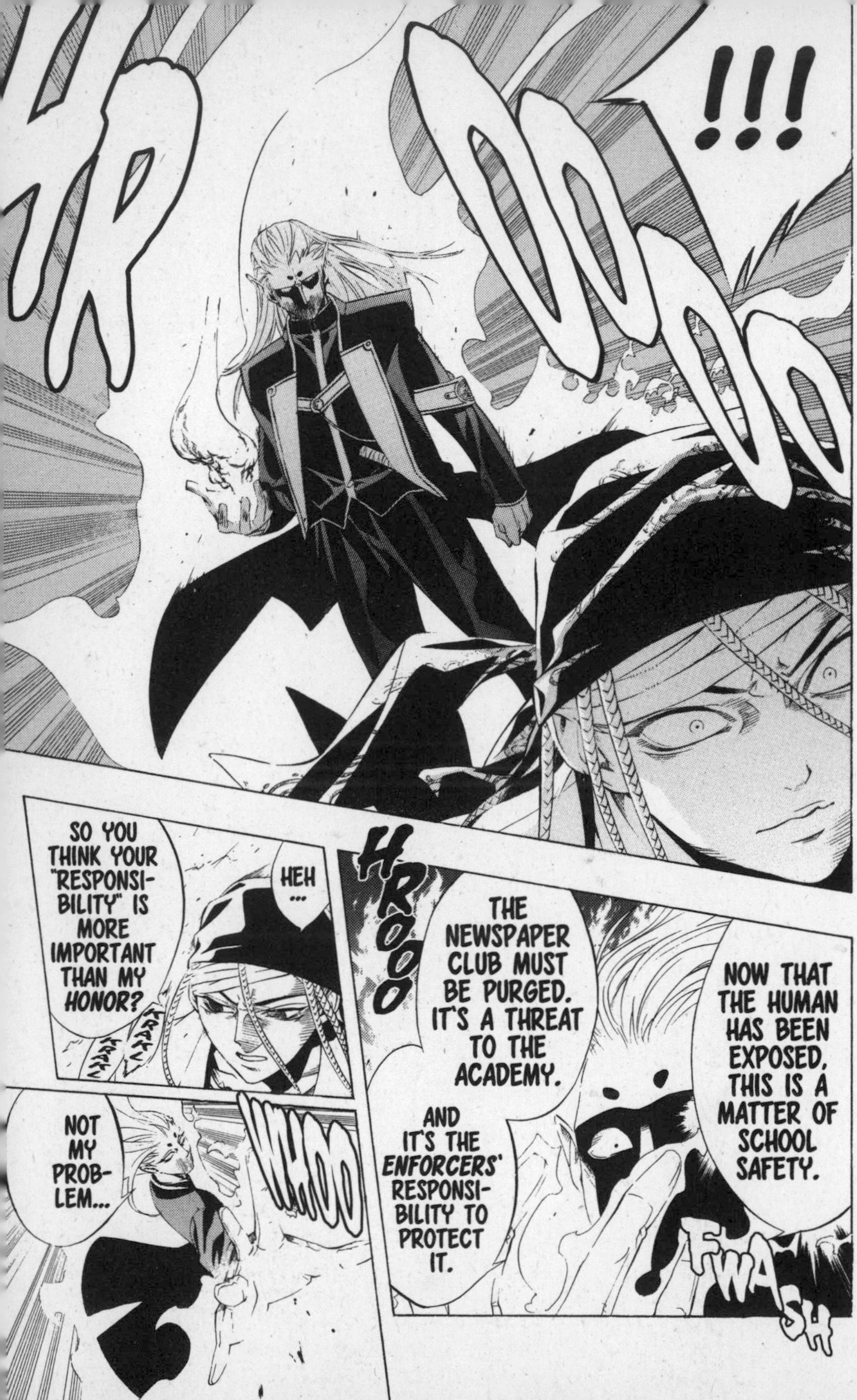
NOW THAT THE HUMAN HAS BEEN EXPOSED, THIS IS A MATTER OF SCHOOL SAFETY.
THE NEWSPAPER CLUB MUST BE PURGED. IT'S A THREAT TO THE ACADEMY.
AND IT'S THE *ENFORCERS'* RESPONSI-BILITY TO PROTECT IT.
FWASH
HROOOO
HEH...
SO YOU THINK YOUR "RESPONSI-BILITY" IS MORE IMPORTANT THAN MY *HONOR*?
NOT MY PROB-LEM...

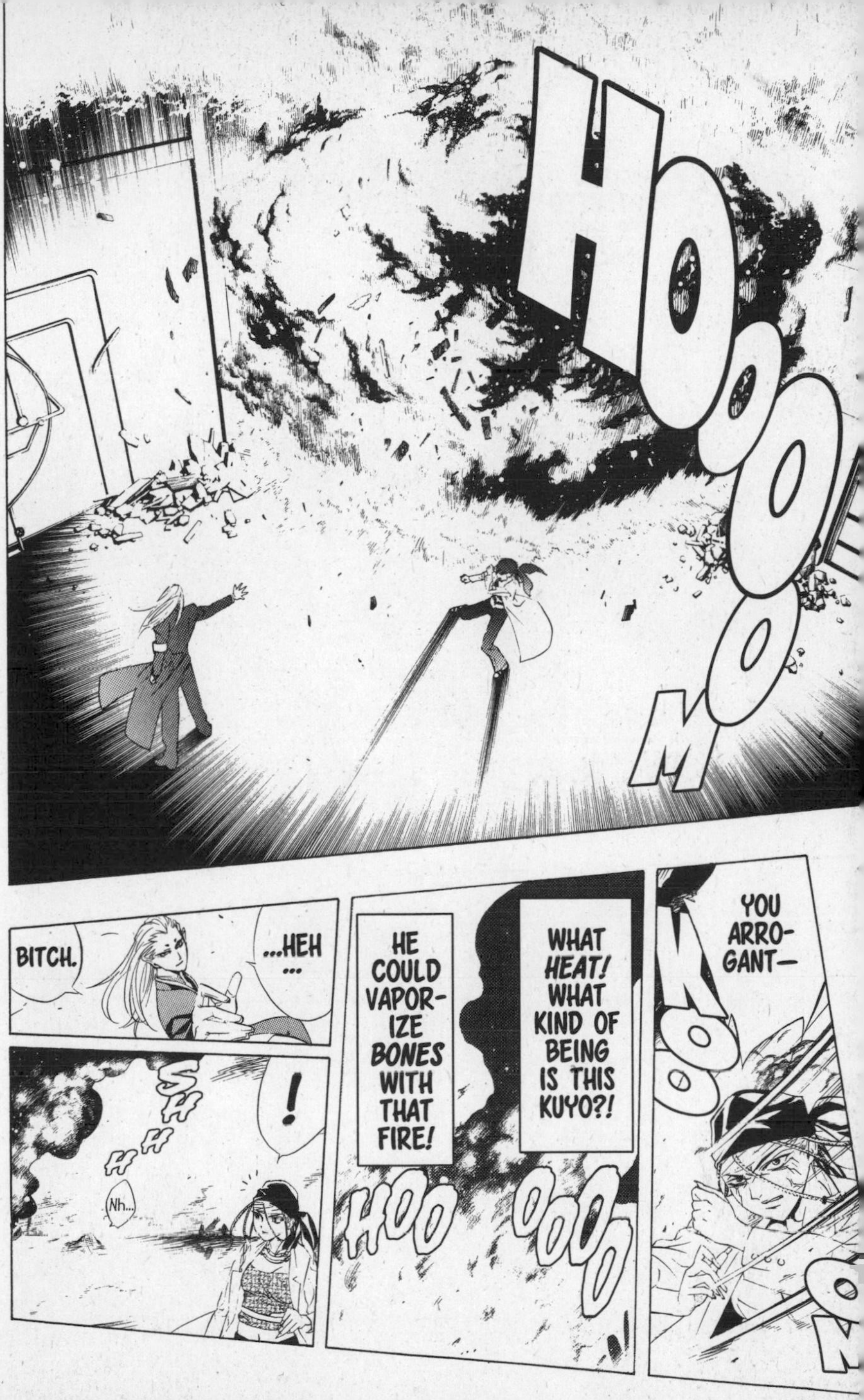
HOOOOM
YOU ARROGANT—
WHAT HEAT! WHAT KIND OF BEING IS THIS KUYO?!
HE COULD VAPORIZE BONES WITH THAT FIRE!
HOOOOOO
...HEH ...
BITCH.
!
SHHH
Nh...

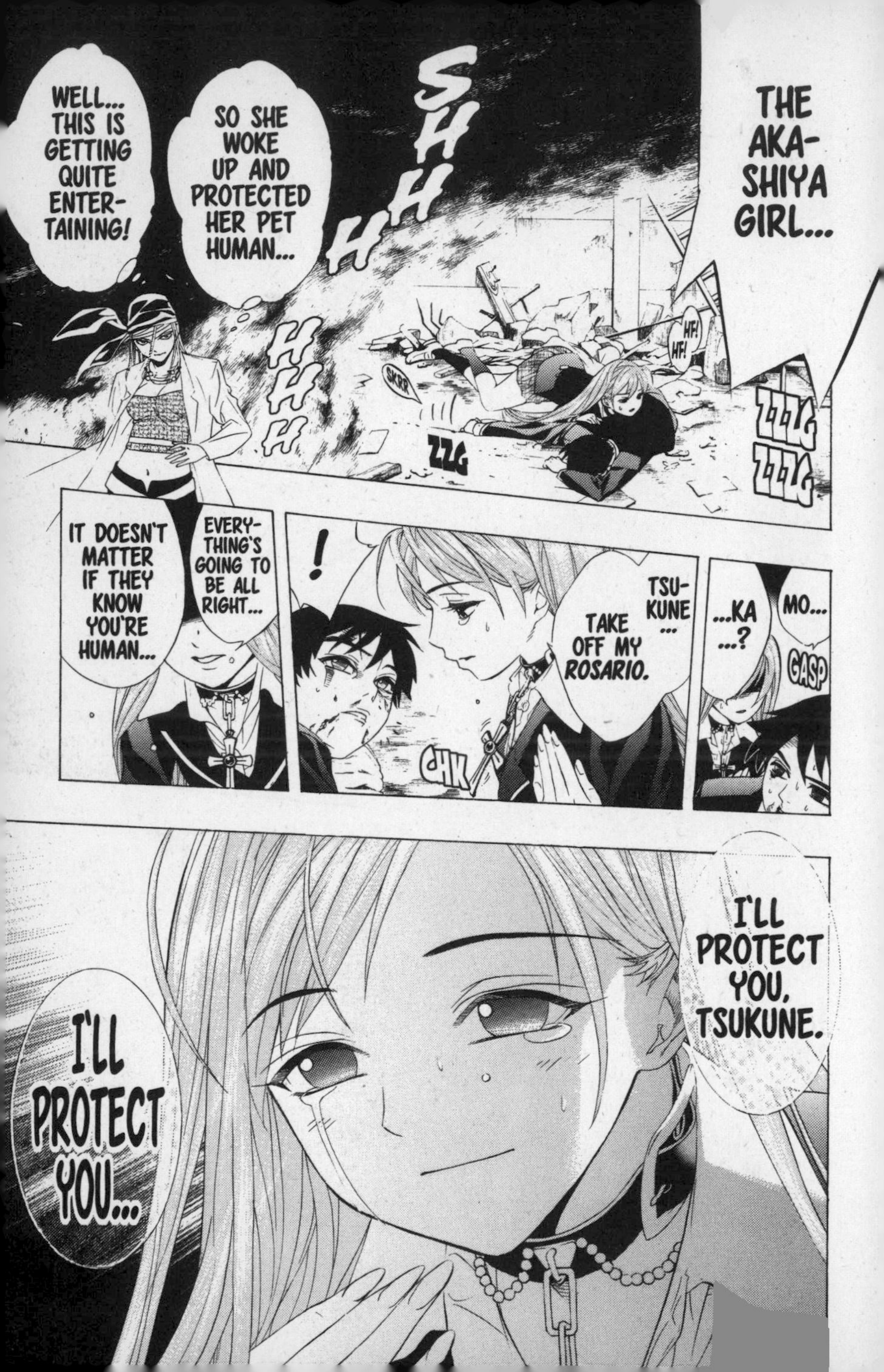
THE AKA-SHIYA GIRL...
ZZZG ZZZG
HF! HF!
SKRR
ZZG
SHHH
HHHH
SO SHE WOKE UP AND PROTECTED HER PET HUMAN...
WELL... THIS IS GETTING QUITE ENTER-TAINING!
MO...
GASP
...KA ...?
TSU-KUNE ...
TAKE OFF MY ROSARIO.
!
CHK
EVERY-THING'S GOING TO BE ALL RIGHT...
IT DOESN'T MATTER IF THEY KNOW YOU'RE HUMAN...
I'LL PROTECT YOU, TSUKUNE.
I'LL PROTECT YOU...

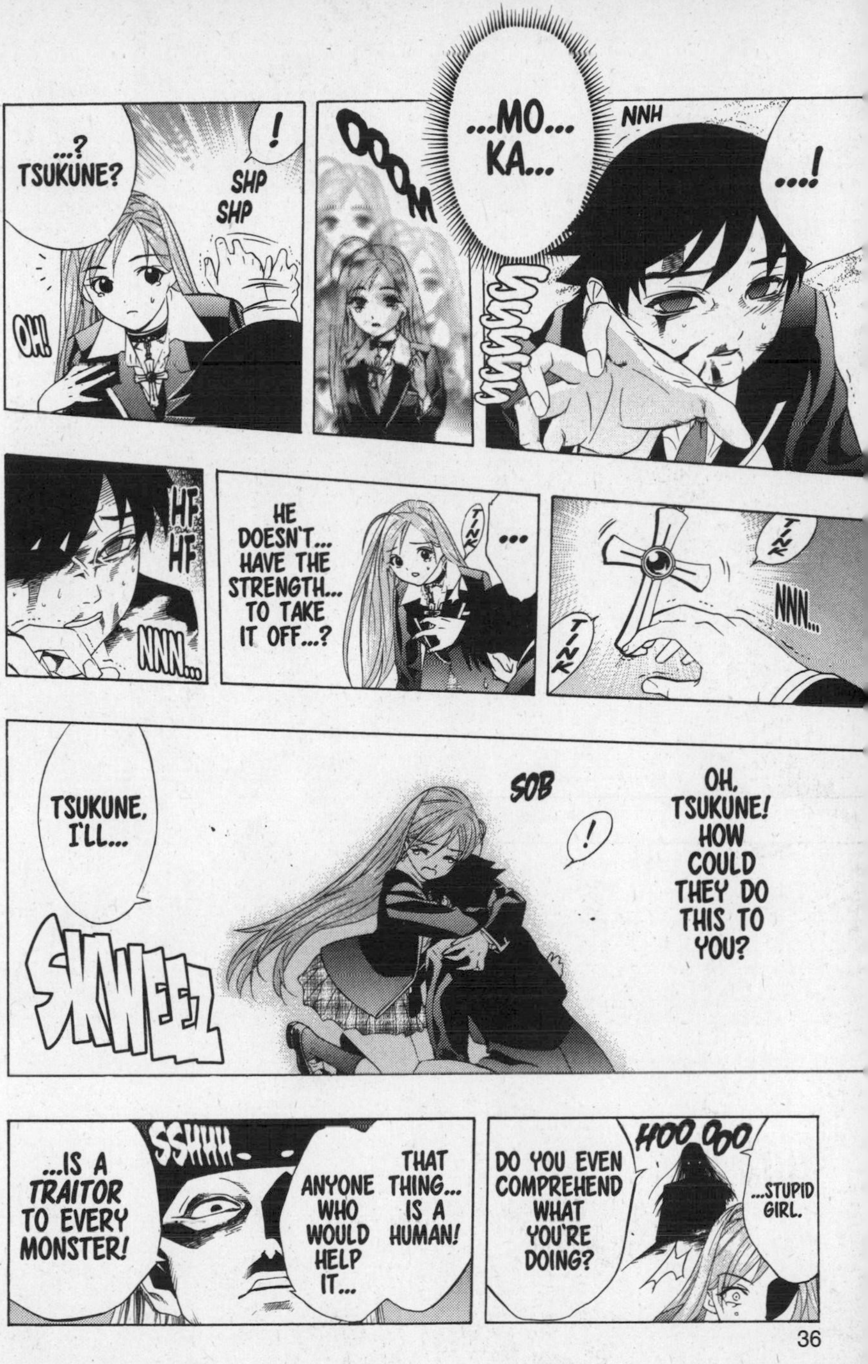
NNH
...!
...MO... KA...
SSSSS
OOOOM
!
SHP SHP
...? TSUKUNE?
OH!
TINK
NNN...
TINK
...
TINK
HE DOESN'T... HAVE THE STRENGTH... TO TAKE IT OFF...?
HF HF
NNN...
OH, TSUKUNE! HOW COULD THEY DO THIS TO YOU?
SOB
!
TSUKUNE, I'LL...
SKWEEZ
...STUPID GIRL.
HOO OOO
DO YOU EVEN COMPREHEND WHAT YOU'RE DOING?
THAT THING... IS A HUMAN!
ANYONE WHO WOULD HELP IT...
SSHHH
...IS A TRAITOR TO EVERY MONSTER!

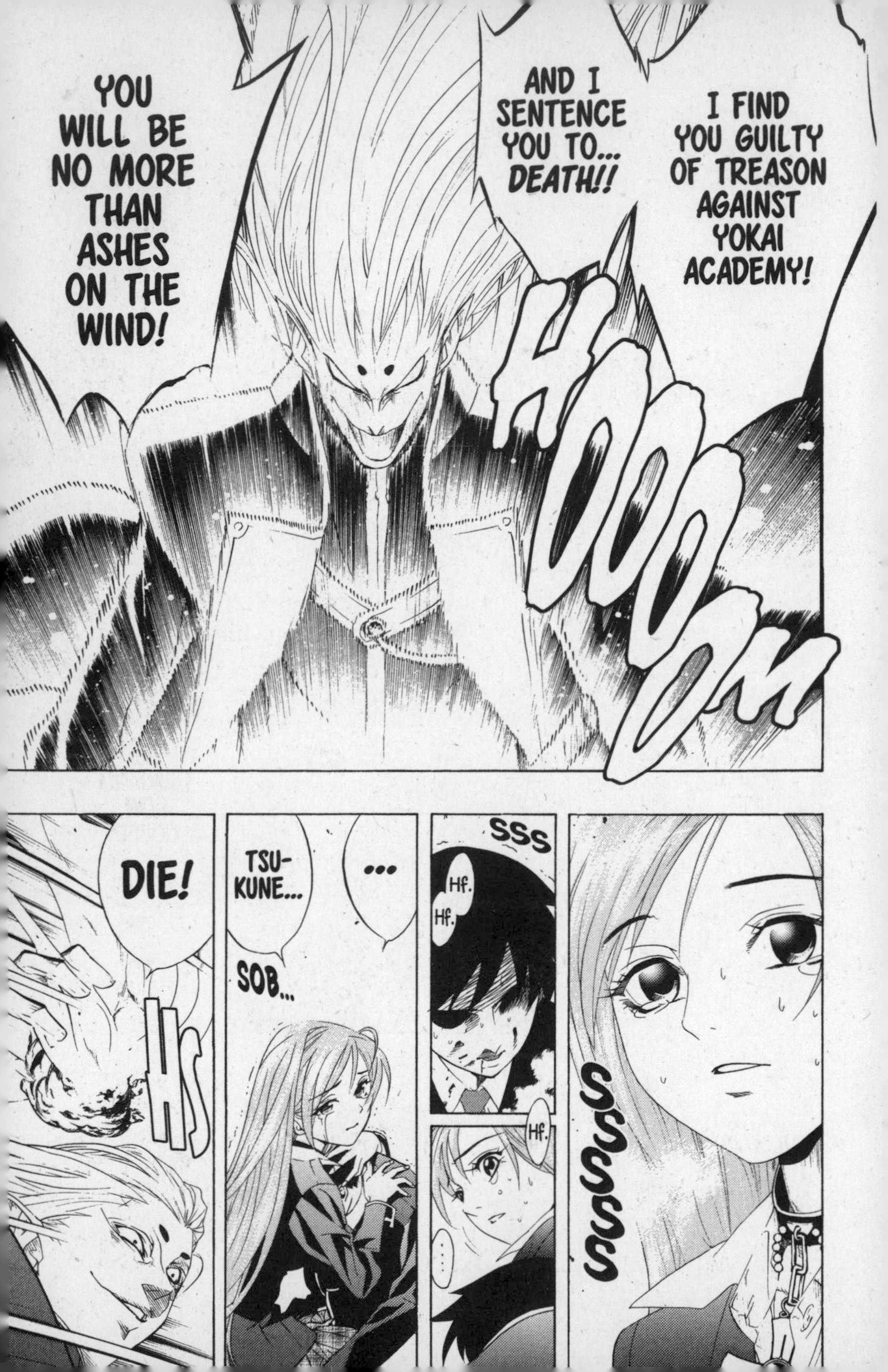
I FIND YOU GUILTY OF TREASON AGAINST YOKAI ACADEMY!
AND I SENTENCE YOU TO... DEATH!!
HOOOOM
YOU WILL BE NO MORE THAN ASHES ON THE WIND!
SSSSSS
SSS
Hf.
Hf.
Hf.
...
...
TSU-KUNE...
SOB...
DIE!
HS

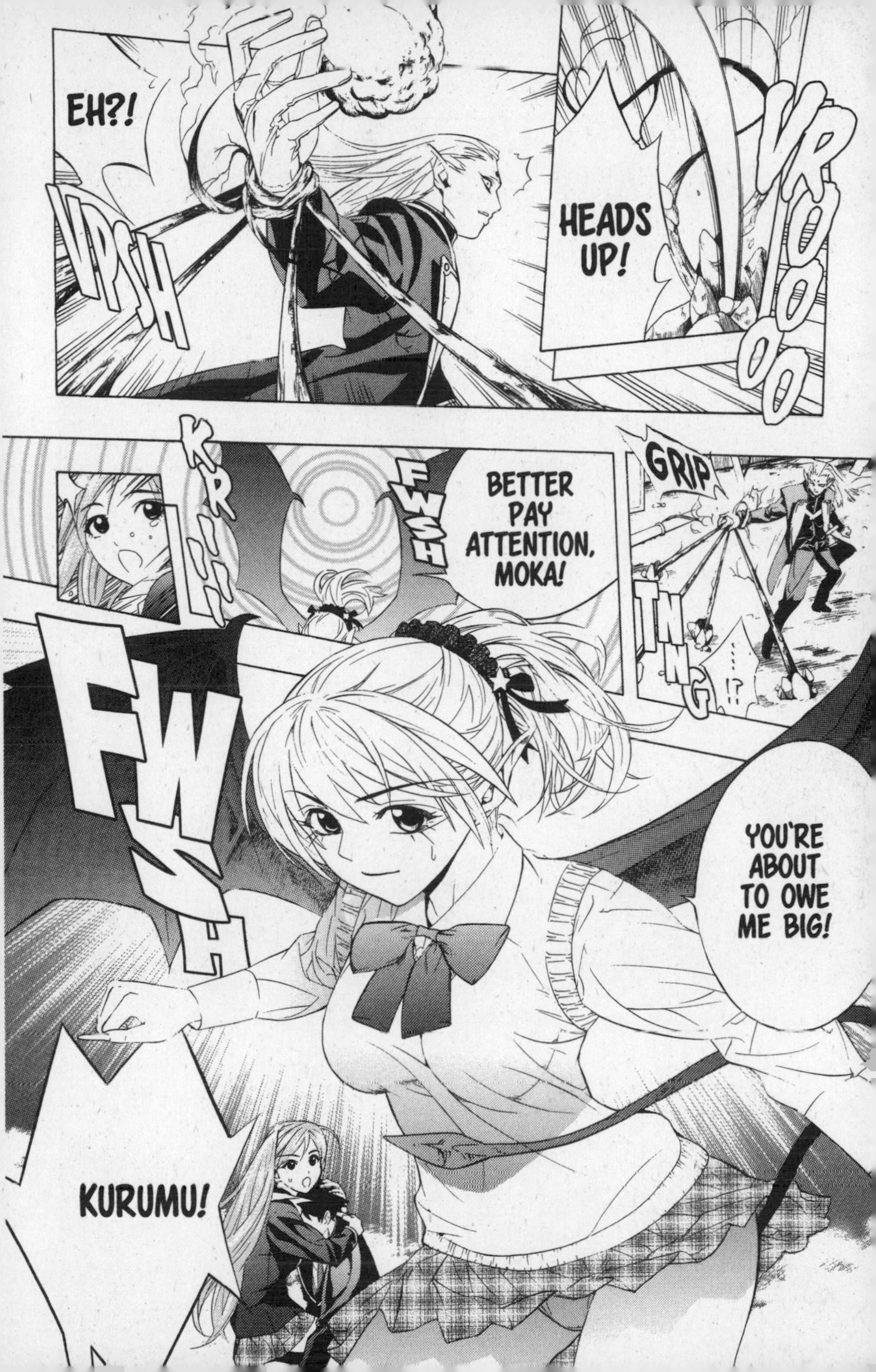
VROOOO
HEADS UP!
EH?!
VPSH
GRIP
TNNG
...!?
BETTER PAY ATTENTION, MOKA!
FWSH
KRIIII
YOU'RE ABOUT TO OWE ME BIG!
FWSH
KURUMU!

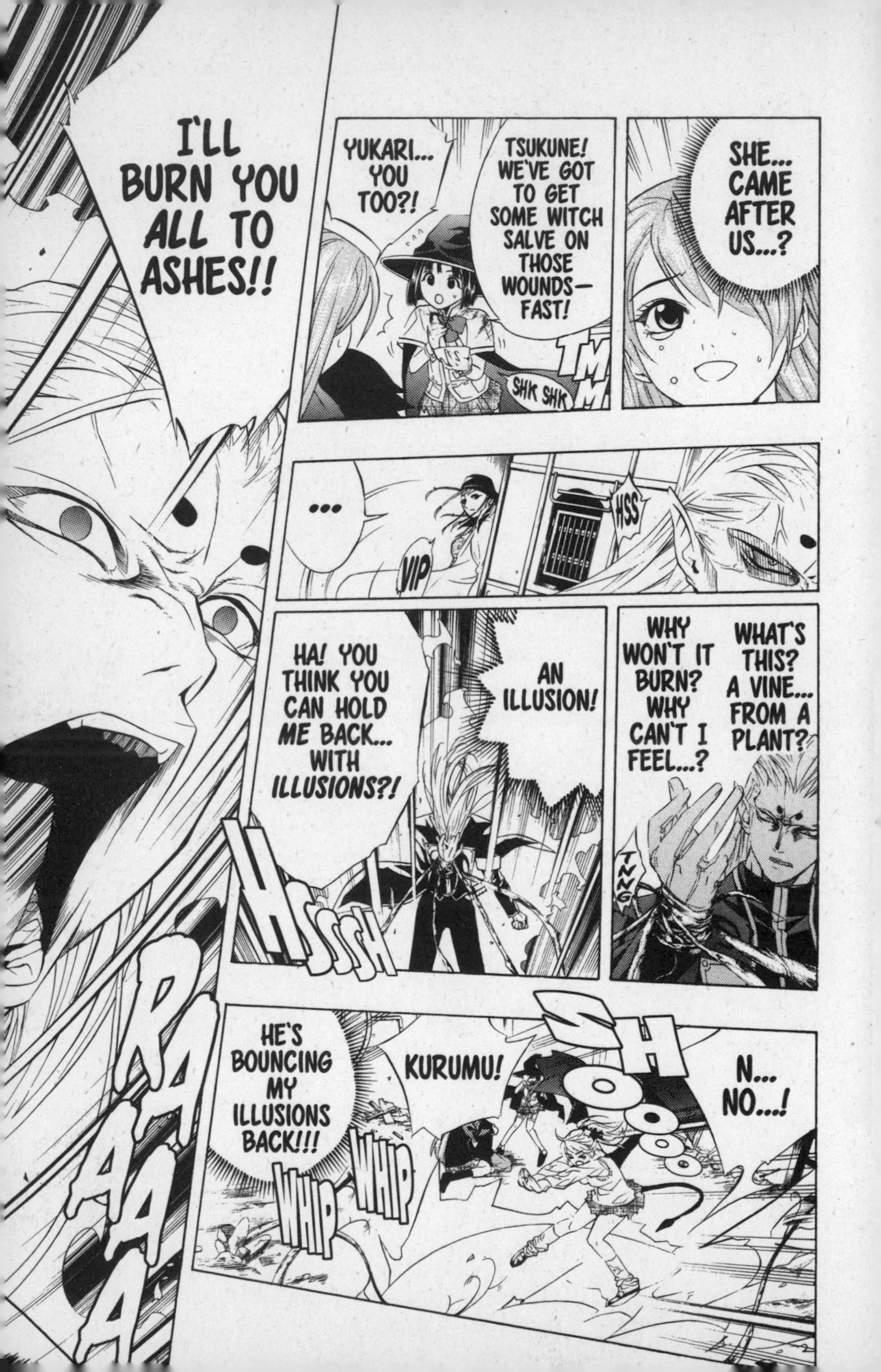
SHE... CAME AFTER US...?
TSUKUNE! WE'VE GOT TO GET SOME WITCH SALVE ON THOSE WOUNDS—FAST!
YUKARI... YOU TOO?!
TMM
SHK SHK
HSS
VIP
...
WHAT'S THIS? A VINE... FROM A PLANT?
WHY WON'T IT BURN? WHY CAN'T I FEEL...?
TNNG
AN ILLUSION!
HA! YOU THINK YOU CAN HOLD ME BACK... WITH ILLUSIONS?!
HISSSH
N... NO...!
SHOOOOO
KURUMU!
HE'S BOUNCING MY ILLUSIONS BACK!!!
WHIP
WHIP
I'LL BURN YOU ALL TO ASHES!!
RAAAA

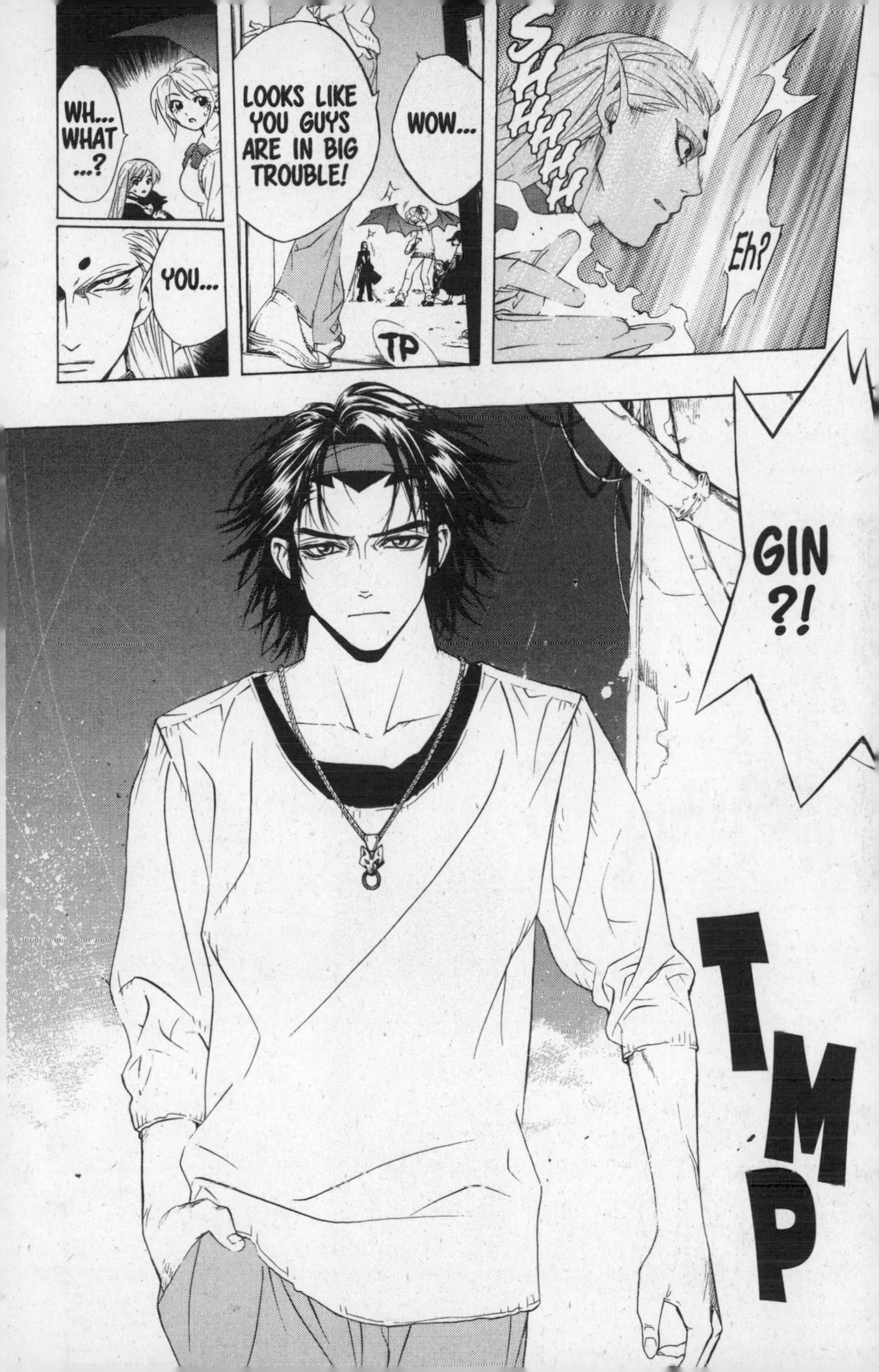
SHHHH
Eh?
WOW...
LOOKS LIKE YOU GUYS ARE IN BIG TROUBLE!
TP
WH... WHAT ...?
YOU...
GIN ?!
TMP

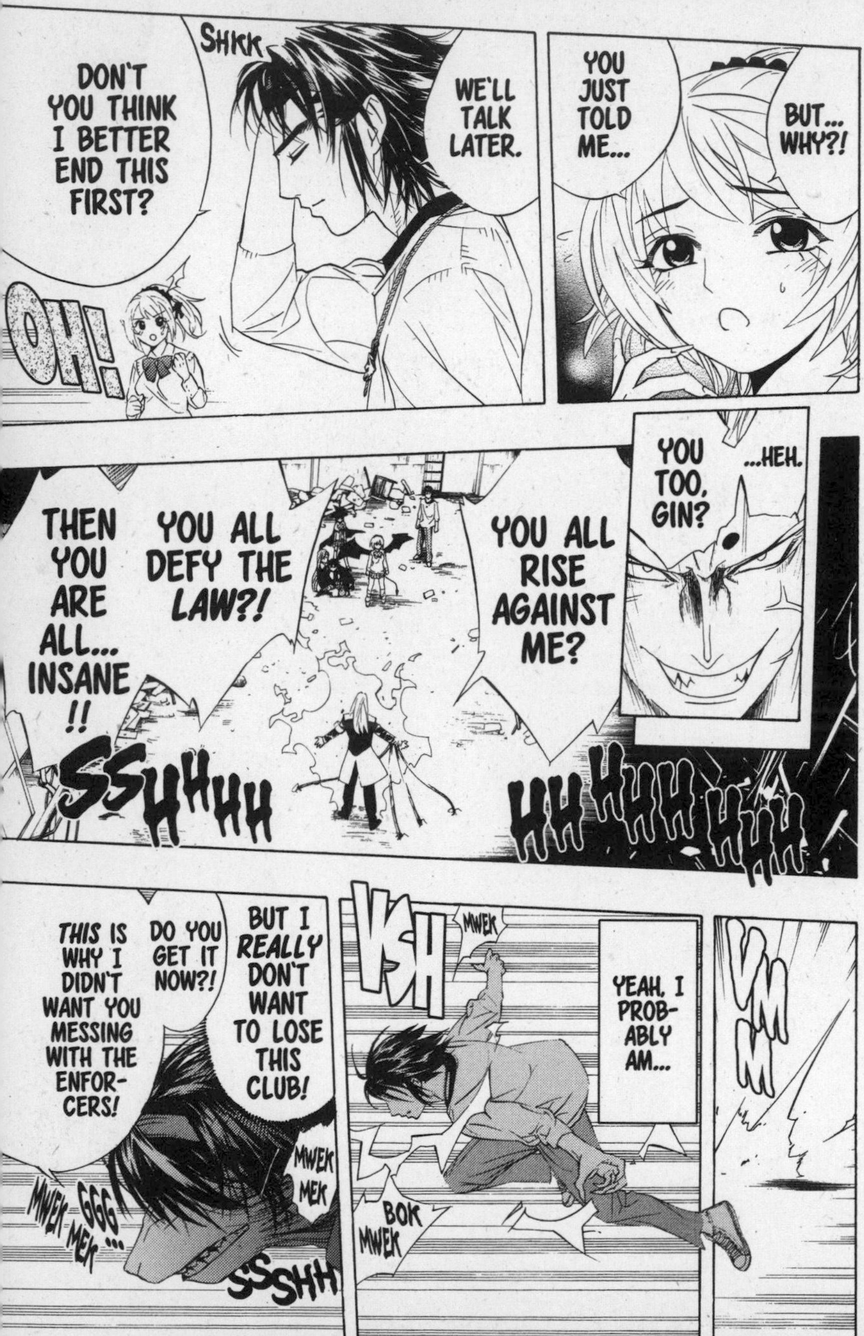
BUT... WHY?!
YOU JUST TOLD ME...
WE'LL TALK LATER.
SHKK
DON'T YOU THINK I BETTER END THIS FIRST?
OH!
...HEH.
YOU TOO, GIN?
YOU ALL RISE AGAINST ME?
YOU ALL DEFY THE *LAW*?!
THEN YOU ARE ALL... INSANE !!
SSHHHH
HHHHHHHHH
VSH
MWEK
YEAH, I PROBABLY AM...
BOK MWEK
BUT I *REALLY* DON'T WANT TO LOSE THIS CLUB!
DO YOU GET IT NOW?!
THIS IS WHY I DIDN'T WANT YOU MESSING WITH THE ENFORCERS!
MWEK MEK
GGG...
MWEK MEK
SSSHH

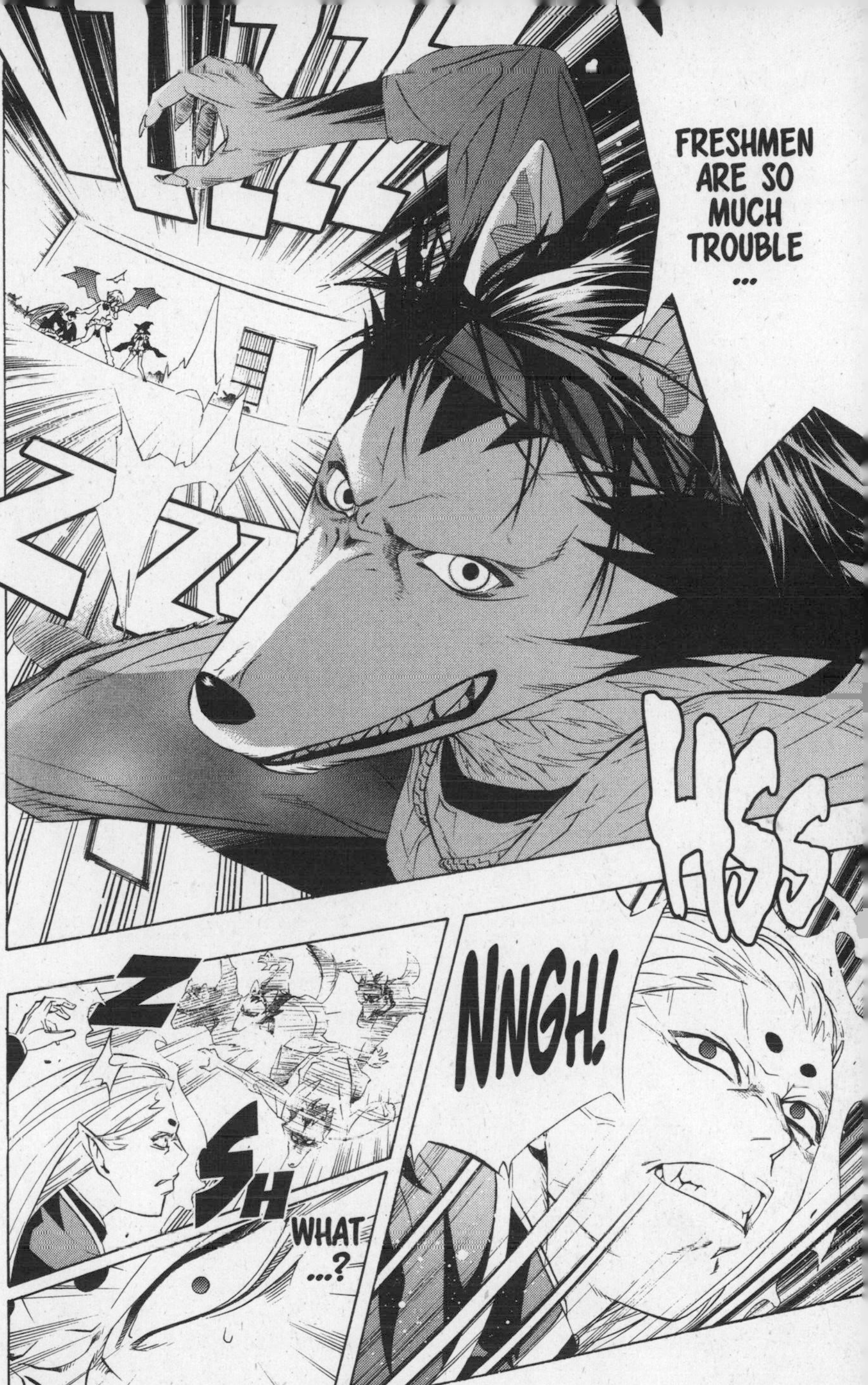
FRESHMEN ARE SO MUCH TROUBLE ...
HSS
NNGH!
Z
SH
WHAT ...?

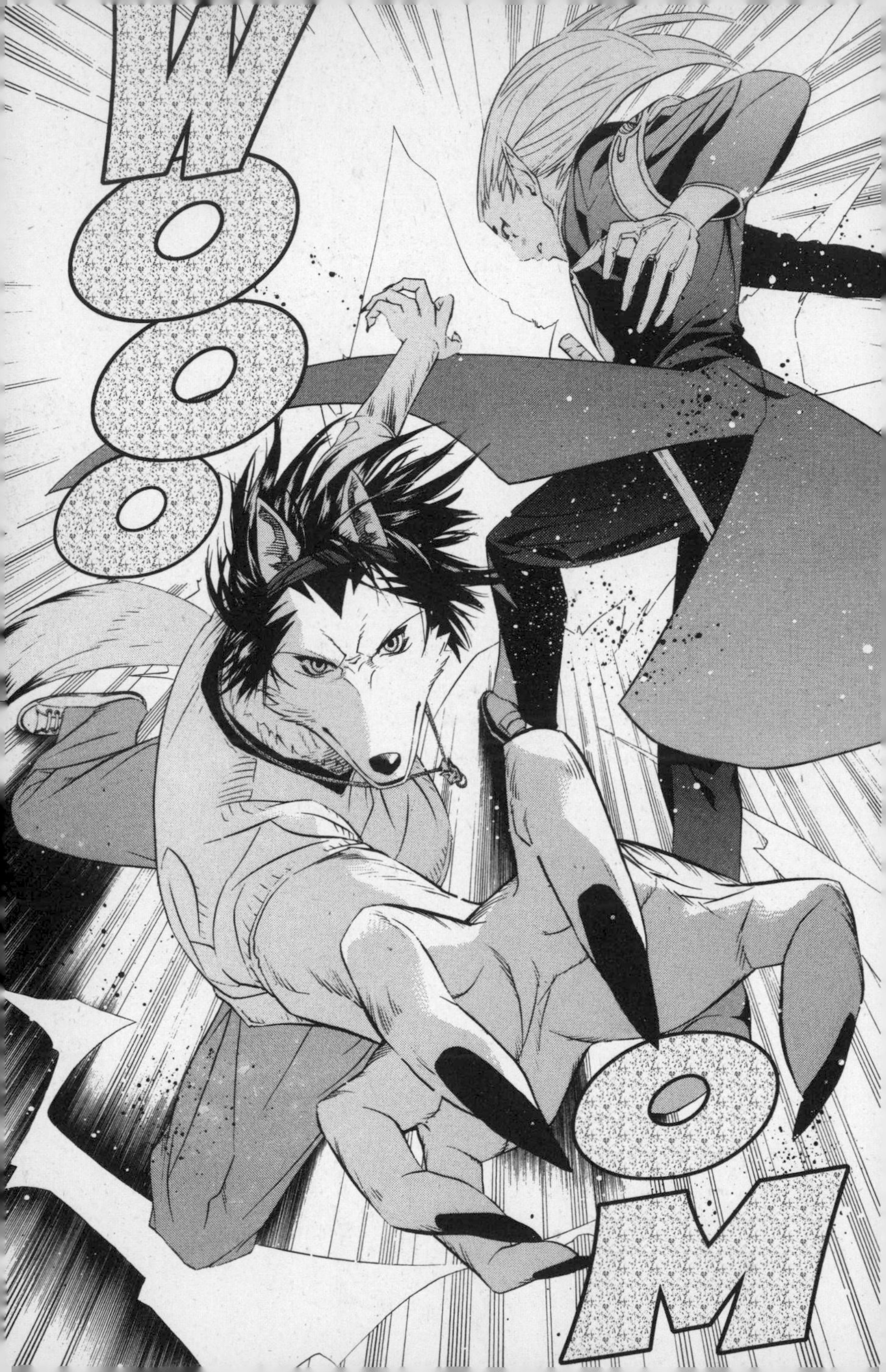
WOOOOM

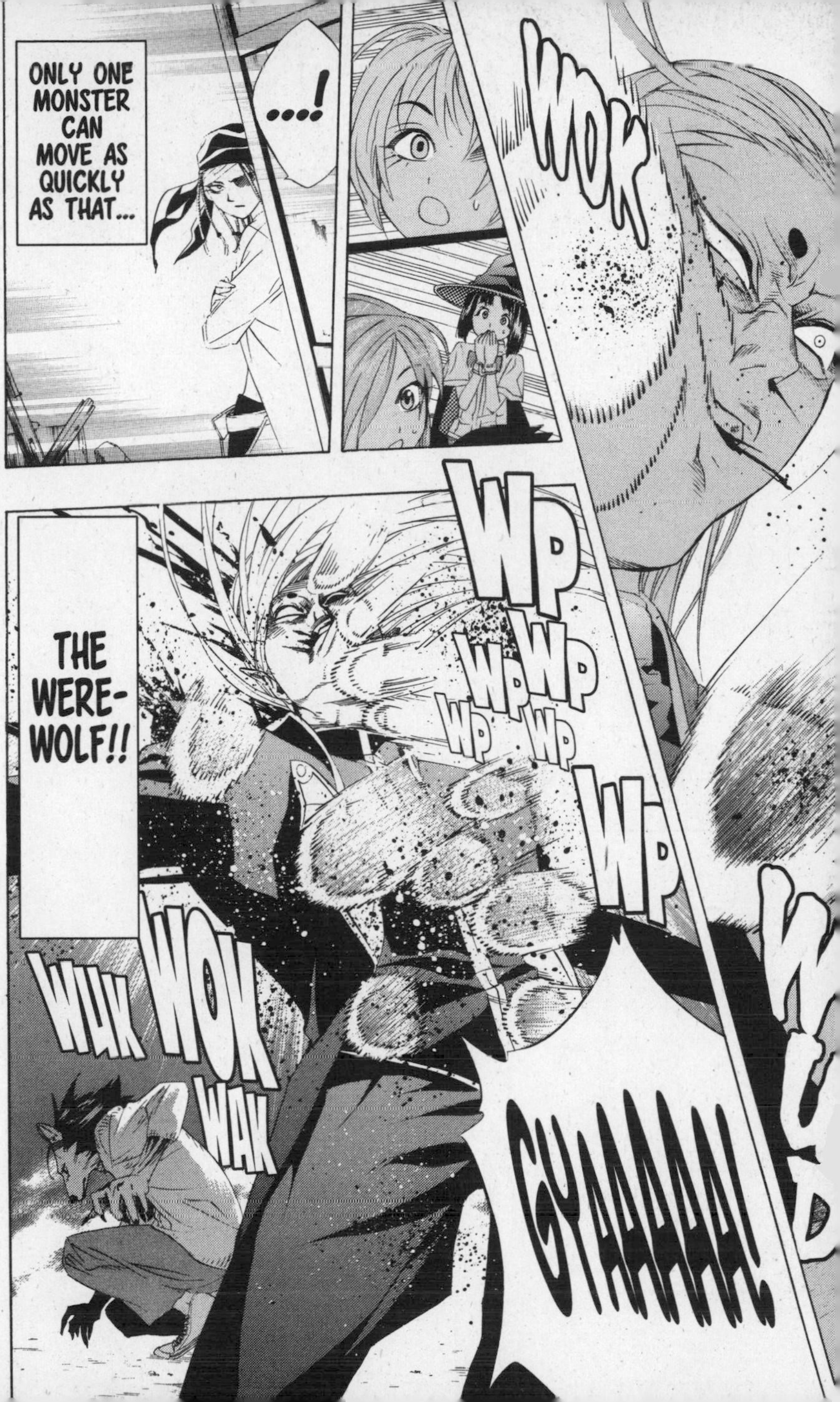
WOK
GYAAAAA!
...!
ONLY ONE MONSTER CAN MOVE AS QUICKLY AS THAT...
WP
WP WP
WP WP
WP
THE WERE-WOLF!!
WOK
WUK
WAK

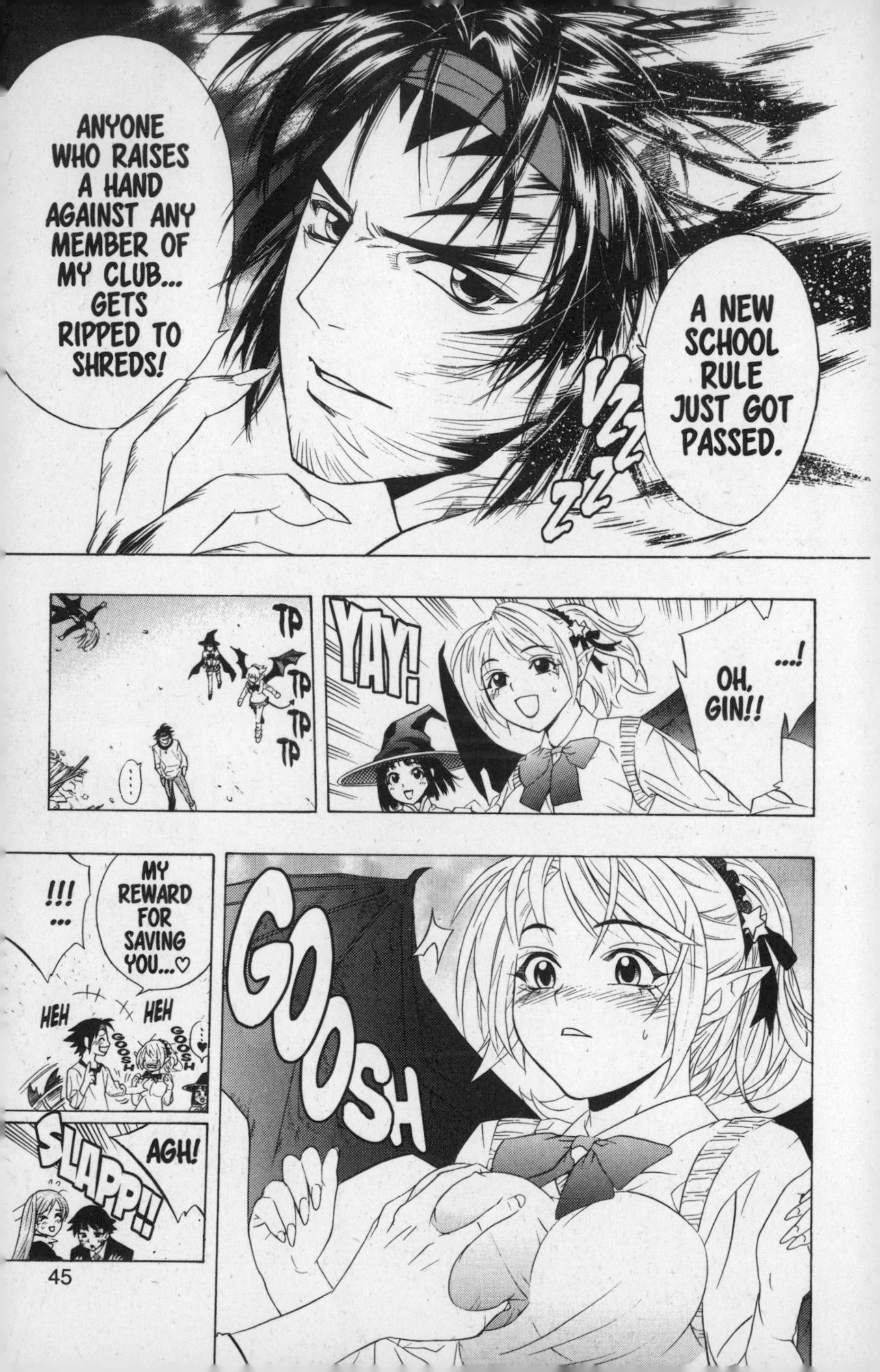
A NEW SCHOOL RULE JUST GOT PASSED.
VZZZZ
ANYONE WHO RAISES A HAND AGAINST ANY MEMBER OF MY CLUB... GETS RIPPED TO SHREDS!
...!
OH, GIN!!
YAY!
TP
TP
TP
TP
...
GOOSH
MY REWARD FOR SAVING YOU...♡
!!! ...
HEH
HEH
GOOSH
GOOSH
...♥
AGH!
SLAPP!!

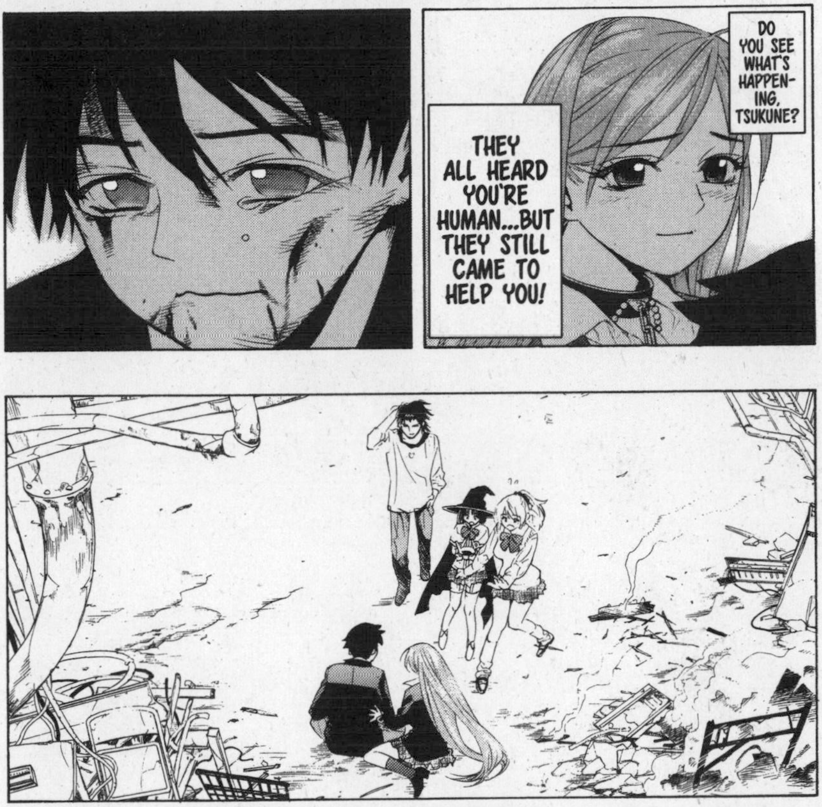

DO YOU SEE WHAT'S HAPPENING, TSUKUNE?
THEY ALL HEARD YOU'RE HUMAN...BUT THEY STILL CAME TO HELP YOU!
...
OKAY... THAT DIDN'T HAVE THE EFFECT I WAS HOPING FOR...
SHKK SHKK
VERY IMPRESSIVE, CHILDREN. NOW...
TMP
...LET'S SEE WHAT HAPPENS WHEN YOUR OPPONENT GROWS UP!
BRRR

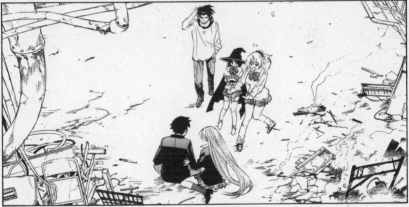

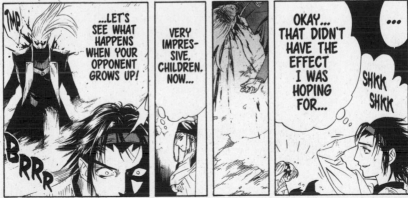

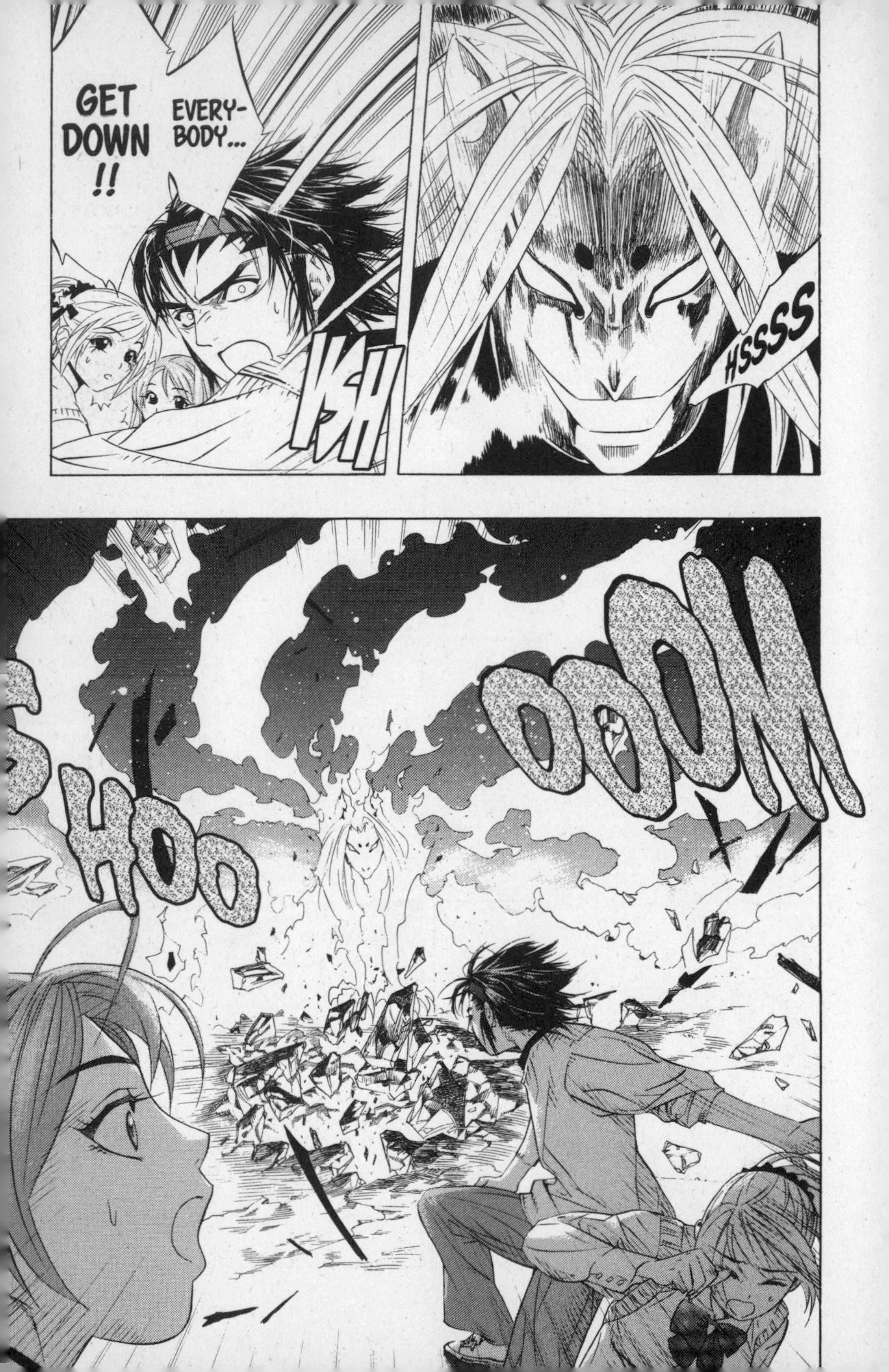
HSSSS
EVERY-BODY...
GET DOWN !!
VSH
SHOO
OOOM

10 : The Gamble

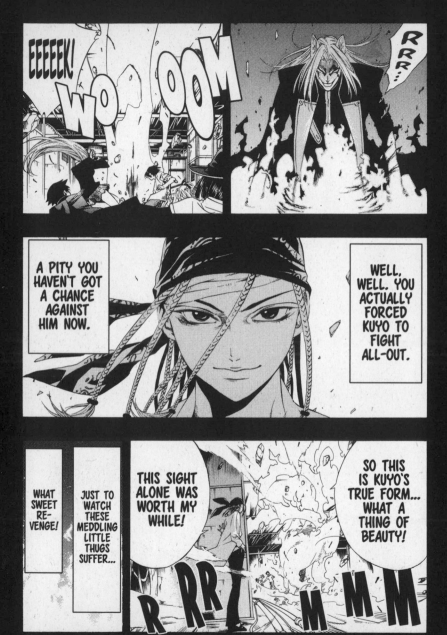

RRR...
EEEEEK!
WOOOM
WELL, WELL. YOU ACTUALLY FORCED KUYO TO FIGHT ALL-OUT.
A PITY YOU HAVEN'T GOT A CHANCE AGAINST HIM NOW.
SO THIS IS KUYO'S TRUE FORM... WHAT A THING OF BEAUTY!
THIS SIGHT ALONE WAS WORTH MY WHILE!
RRRMMM
JUST TO WATCH THESE MEDDLING LITTLE THUGS SUFFER...
WHAT SWEET RE-VENGE!

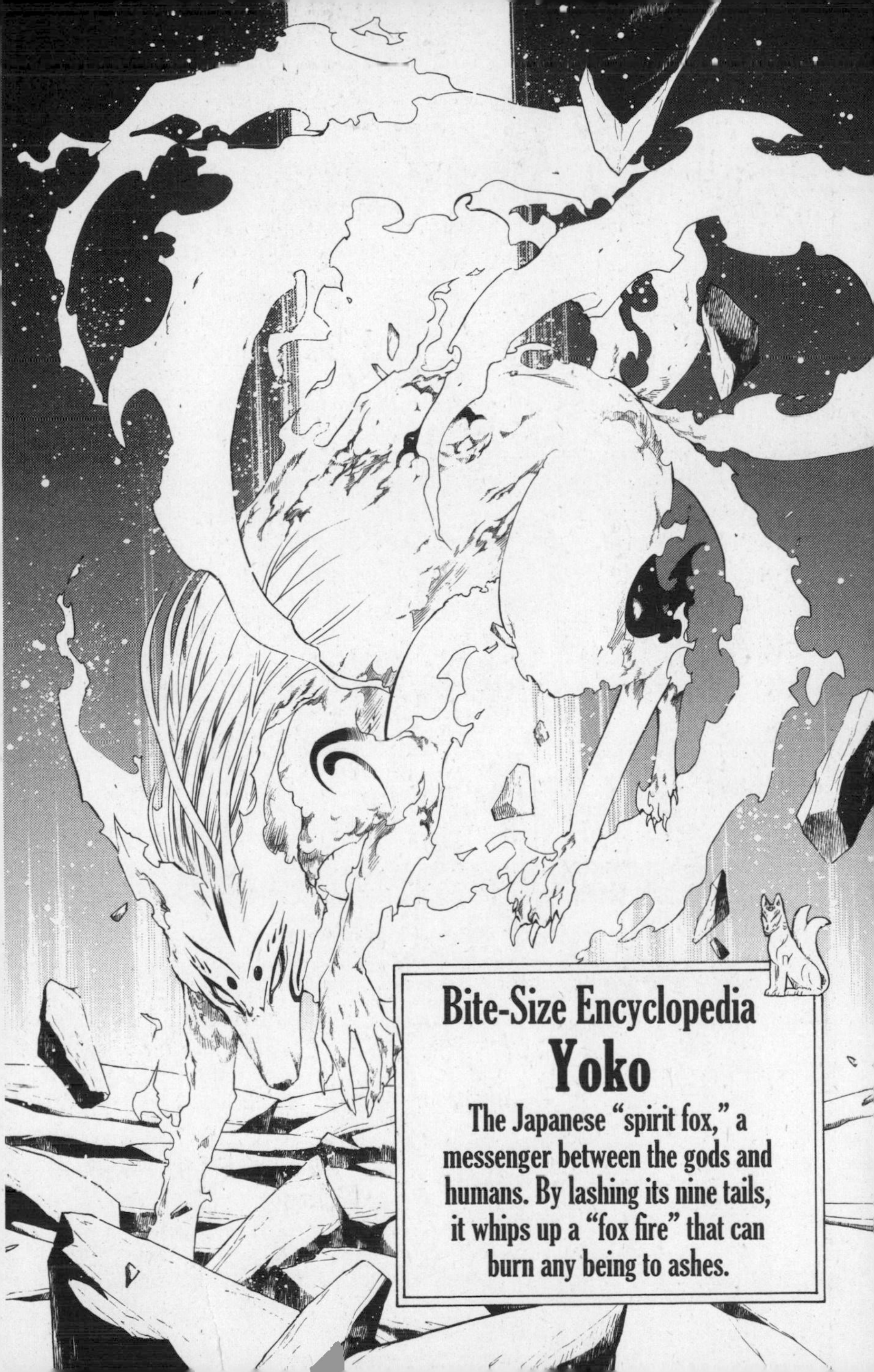
Bite-Size Encyclopedia
Yoko
The Japanese "spirit fox," a messenger between the gods and humans. By lashing its nine tails, it whips up a "fox fire" that can burn any being to ashes.

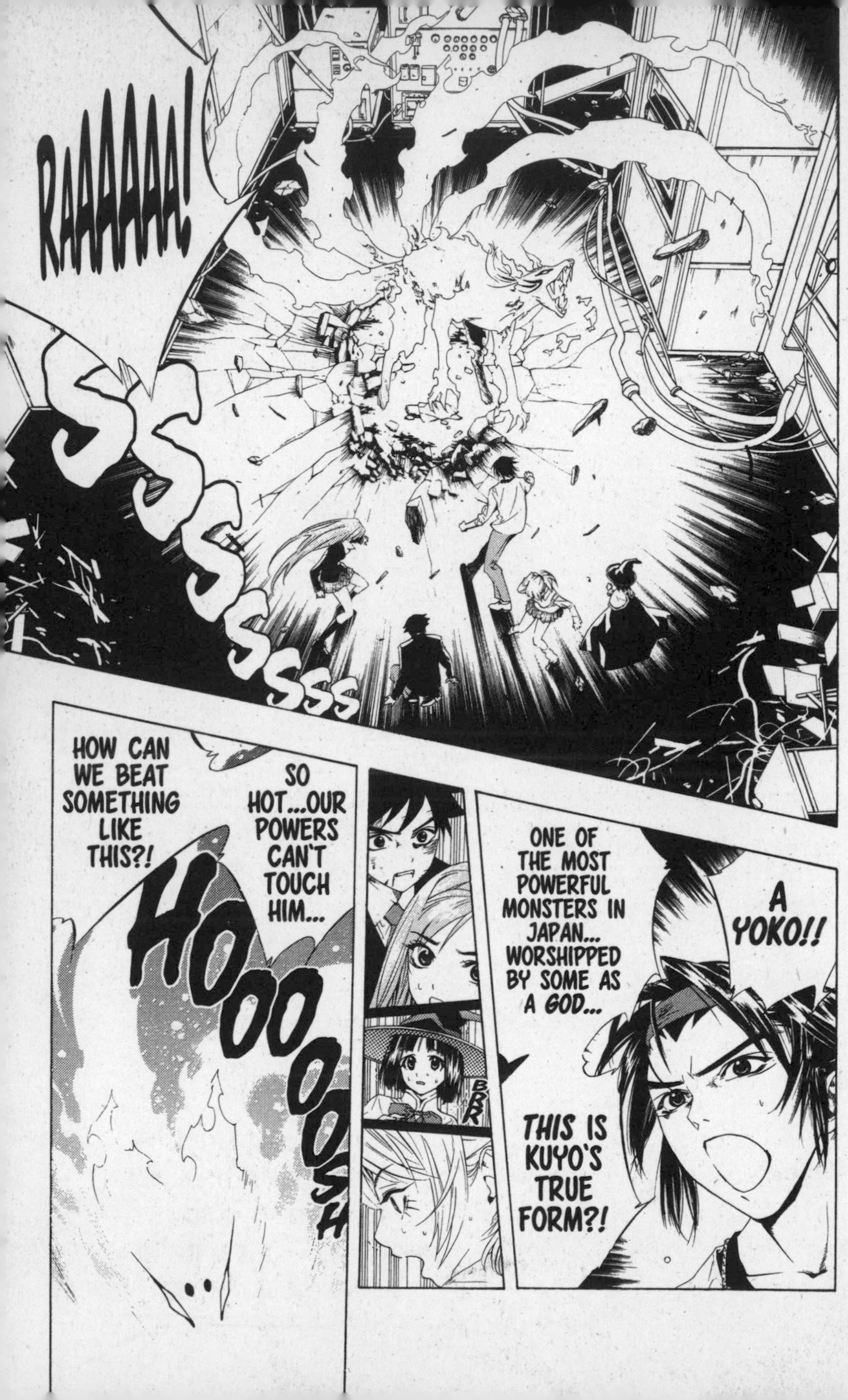
RAAAAA!
SSSSSSSSS
A YOKO!!
ONE OF THE MOST POWERFUL MONSTERS IN JAPAN... WORSHIPPED BY SOME AS A GOD...
THIS IS KUYO'S TRUE FORM?!
BRR
SO HOT...OUR POWERS CAN'T TOUCH HIM...
HOW CAN WE BEAT SOMETHING LIKE THIS?!
HOOOOOSH

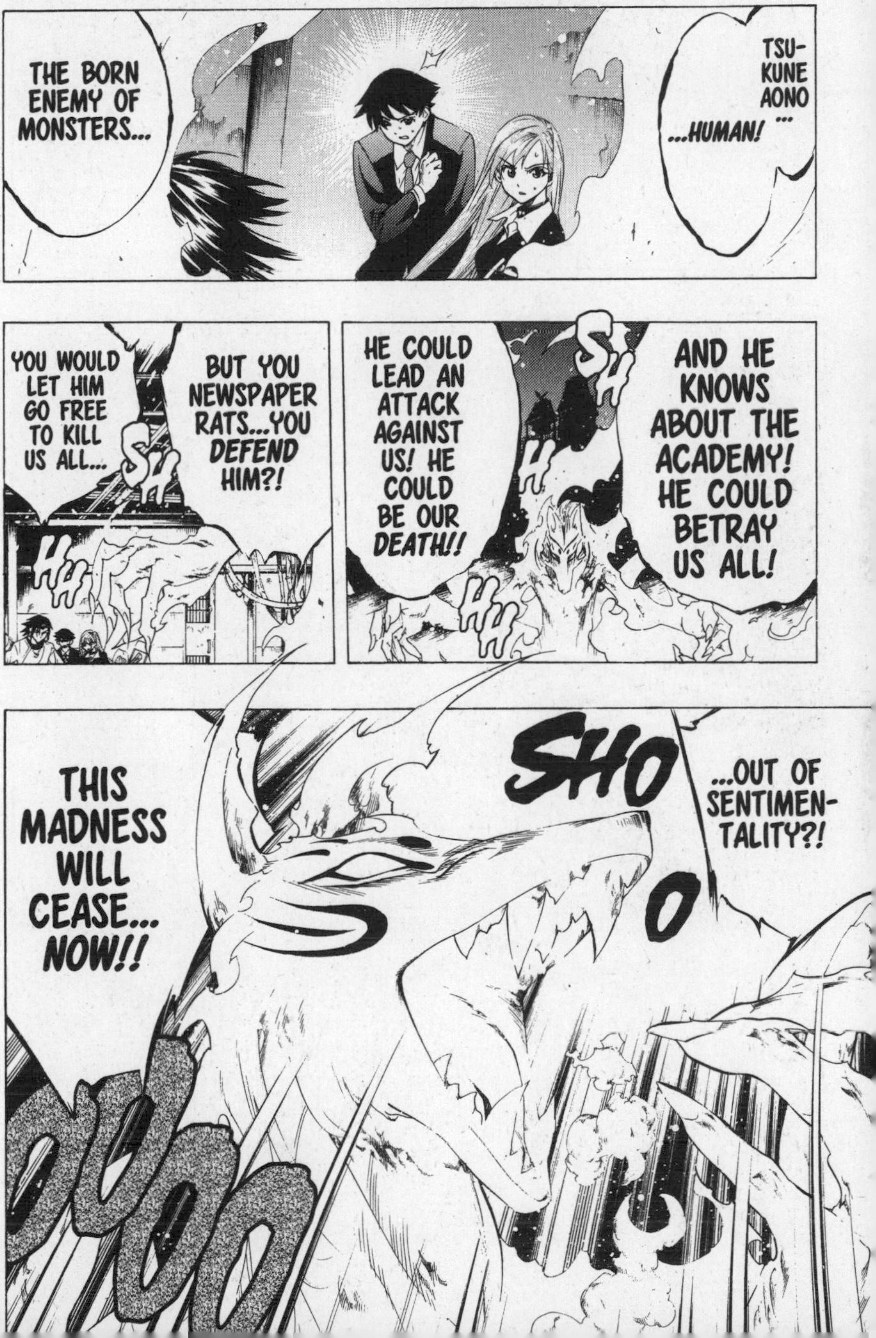
TSU-KUNE AONO ...
...HUMAN!
THE BORN ENEMY OF MONSTERS...
SH
AND HE KNOWS ABOUT THE ACADEMY! HE COULD BETRAY US ALL!
HE COULD LEAD AN ATTACK AGAINST US! HE COULD BE OUR DEATH!!
HH
BUT YOU NEWSPAPER RATS...YOU DEFEND HIM?!
YOU WOULD LET HIM GO FREE TO KILL US ALL...
SH
HH
...OUT OF SENTIMEN-TALITY?!
SHO
O
THIS MADNESS WILL CEASE... NOW!!

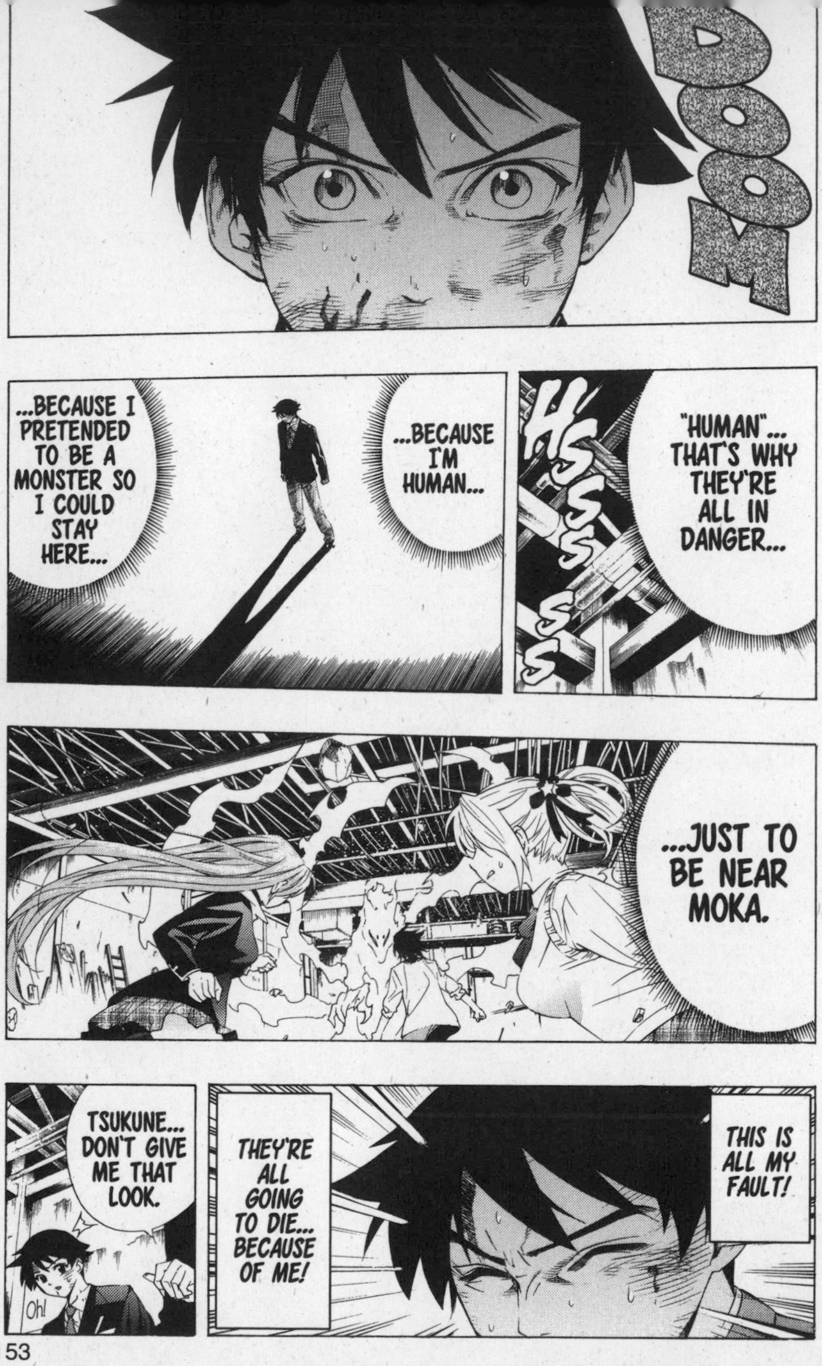
DOOOM
"HUMAN"... THAT'S WHY THEY'RE ALL IN DANGER...
HSSSSS
...BECAUSE I'M HUMAN...
...BECAUSE I PRETENDED TO BE A MONSTER SO I COULD STAY HERE...
...JUST TO BE NEAR MOKA.
THIS IS ALL MY FAULT!
THEY'RE ALL GOING TO DIE... BECAUSE OF ME!
TSUKUNE... DON'T GIVE ME THAT LOOK.
Oh!

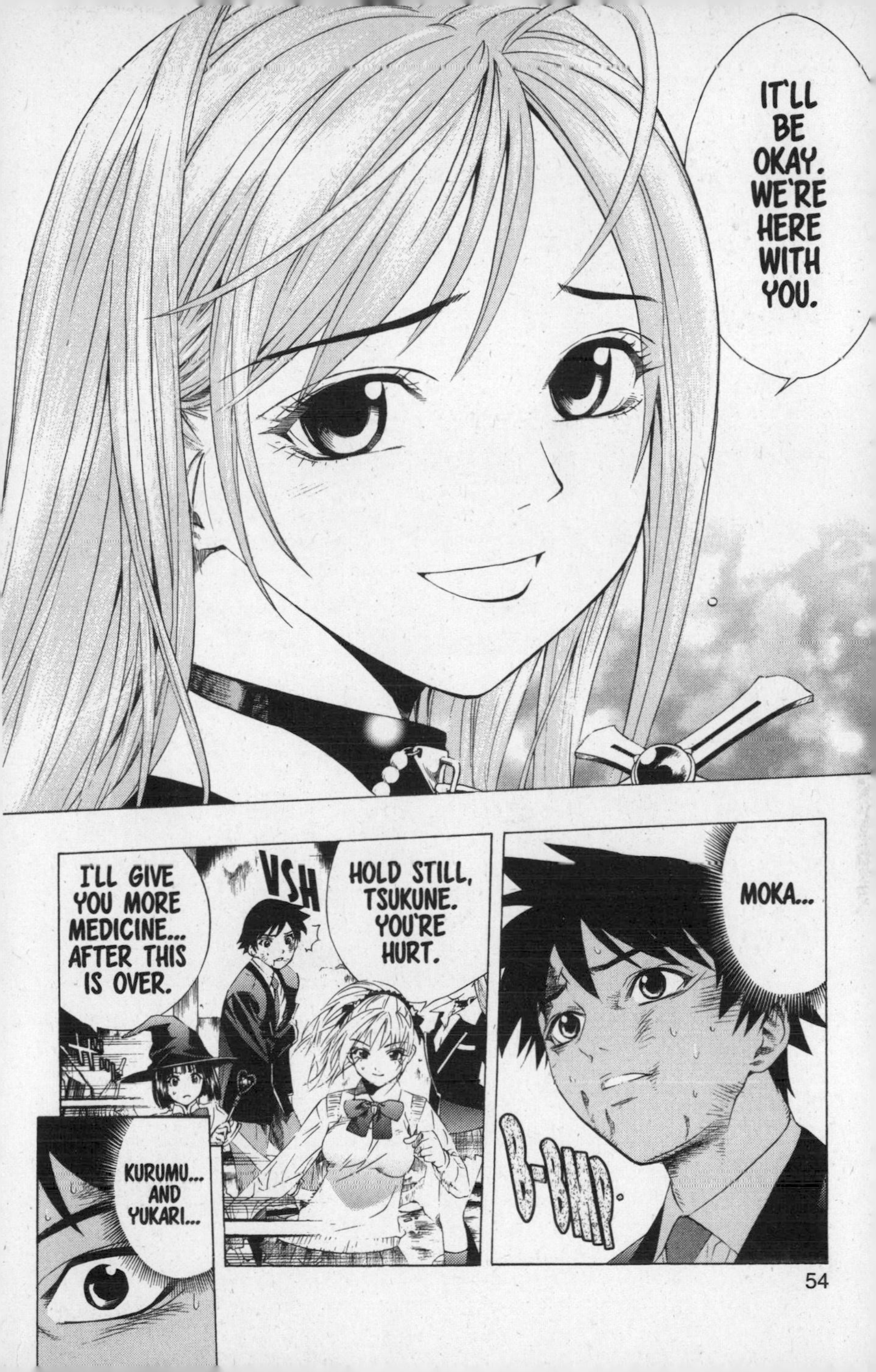
IT'LL BE OKAY. WE'RE HERE WITH YOU.
MOKA...
HOLD STILL, TSUKUNE. YOU'RE HURT.
VSH
I'LL GIVE YOU MORE MEDICINE... AFTER THIS IS OVER.
KURUMU... AND YUKARI...

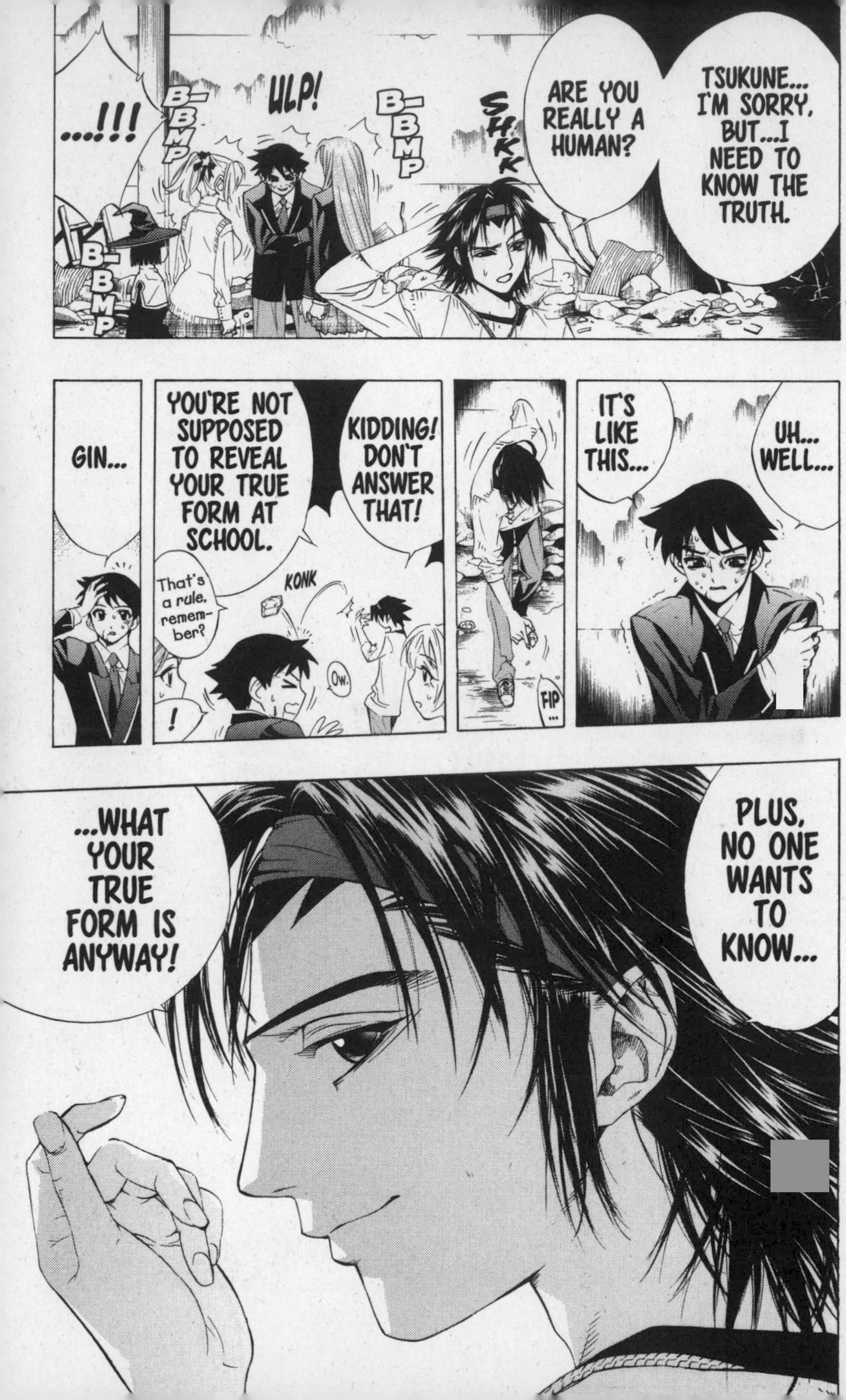
TSUKUNE... I'M SORRY, BUT...I NEED TO KNOW THE TRUTH.
ARE YOU REALLY A HUMAN?
SHKK
B-BMP
ULP!
B-BMP
...!!!
B-BMP
UH... WELL...
IT'S LIKE THIS...
FIP...
KIDDING! DON'T ANSWER THAT!
YOU'RE NOT SUPPOSED TO REVEAL YOUR TRUE FORM AT SCHOOL.
KONK
That's a rule, remember?
Ow.
!
GIN...
PLUS, NO ONE WANTS TO KNOW...
...WHAT YOUR TRUE FORM IS ANYWAY!

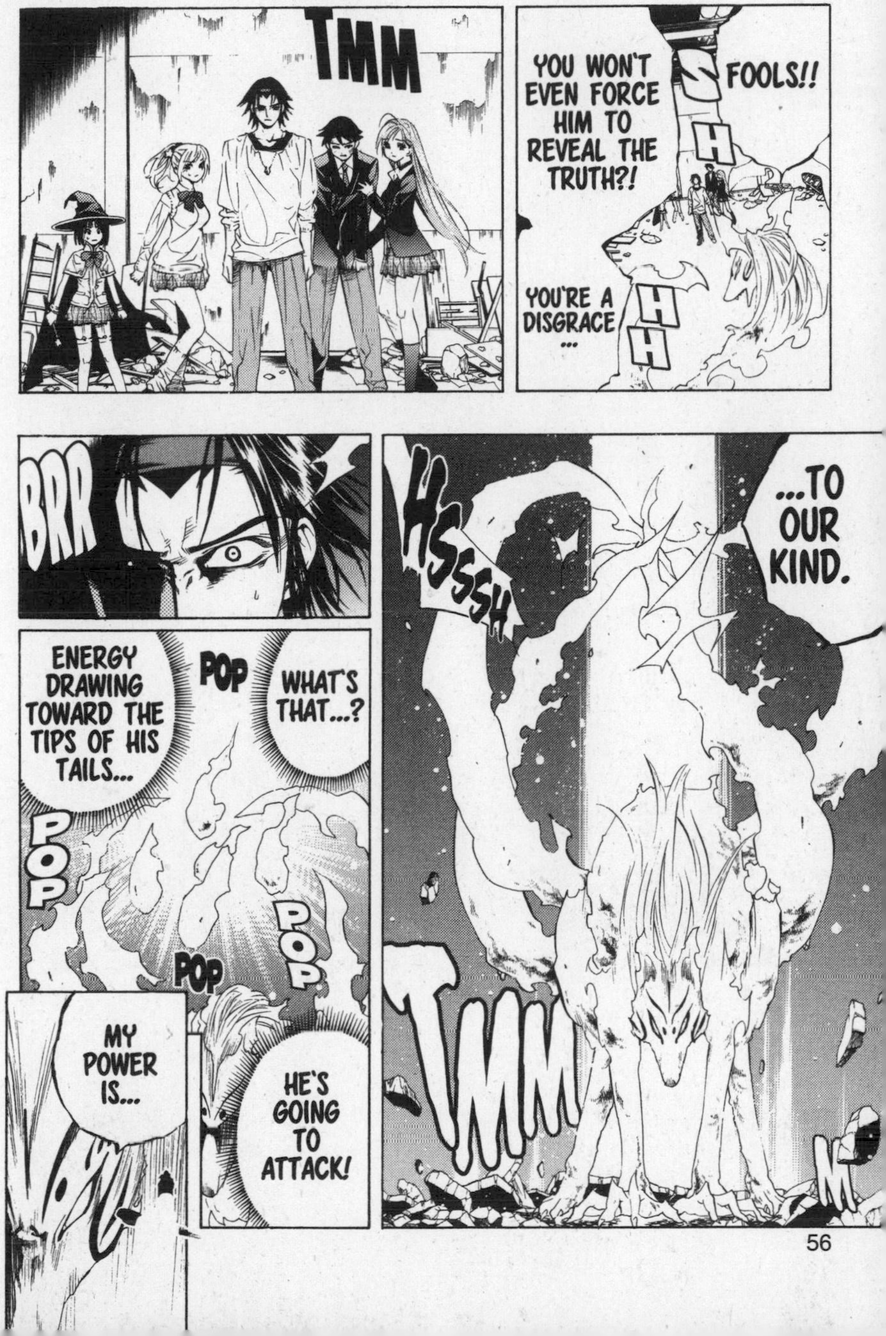
FOOLS!!
YOU WON'T EVEN FORCE HIM TO REVEAL THE TRUTH?!
SHHH
YOU'RE A DISGRACE...
TMM
...TO OUR KIND.
HSSSH
TMMM
BRR
WHAT'S THAT...?
POP
ENERGY DRAWING TOWARD THE TIPS OF HIS TAILS...
POP
POP
POP
POP
HE'S GOING TO ATTACK!
MY POWER IS...

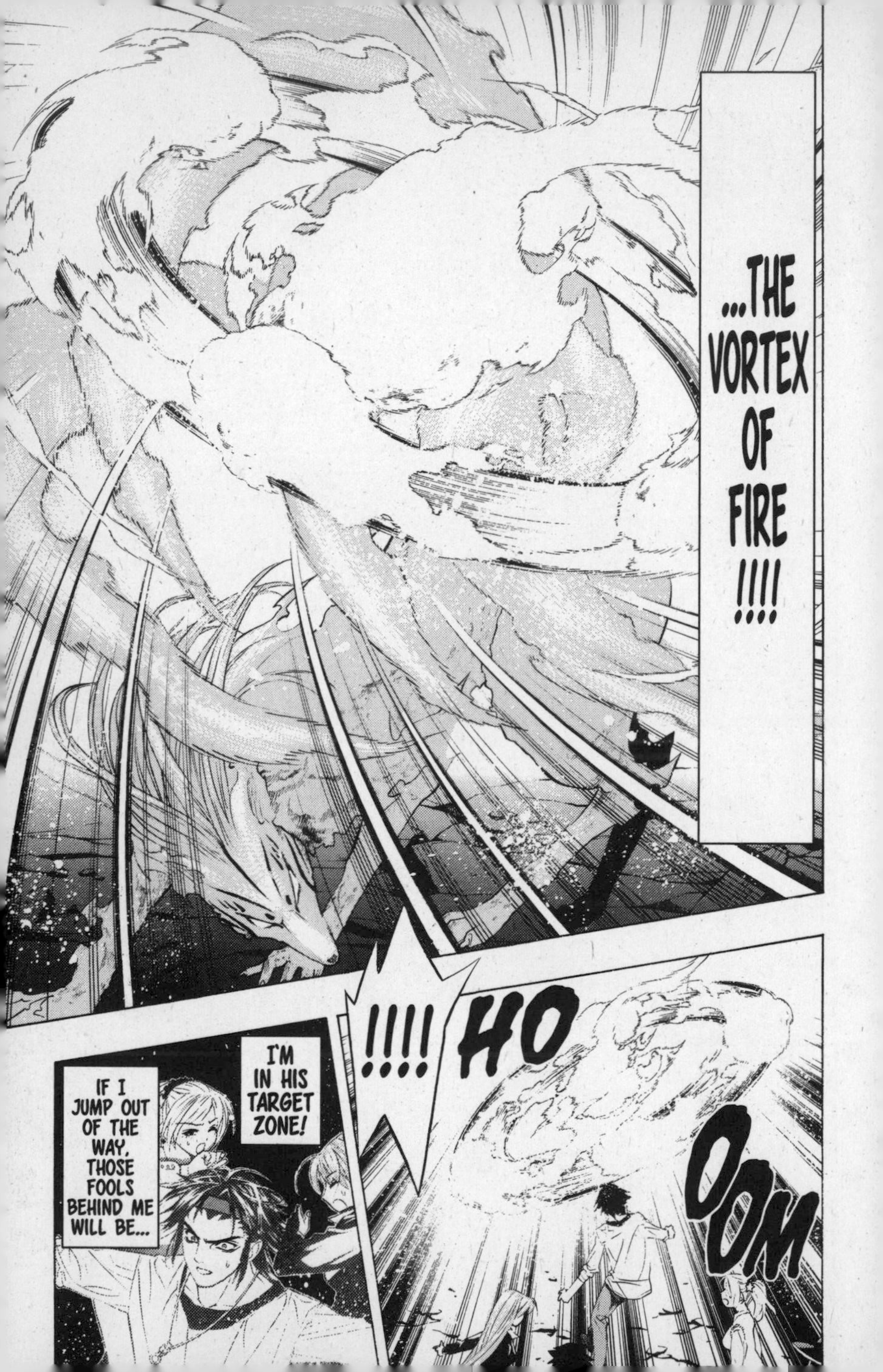
...THE VORTEX OF FIRE !!!!
!!!!
HO OOM
I'M IN HIS TARGET ZONE!
IF I JUMP OUT OF THE WAY, THOSE FOOLS BEHIND ME WILL BE...

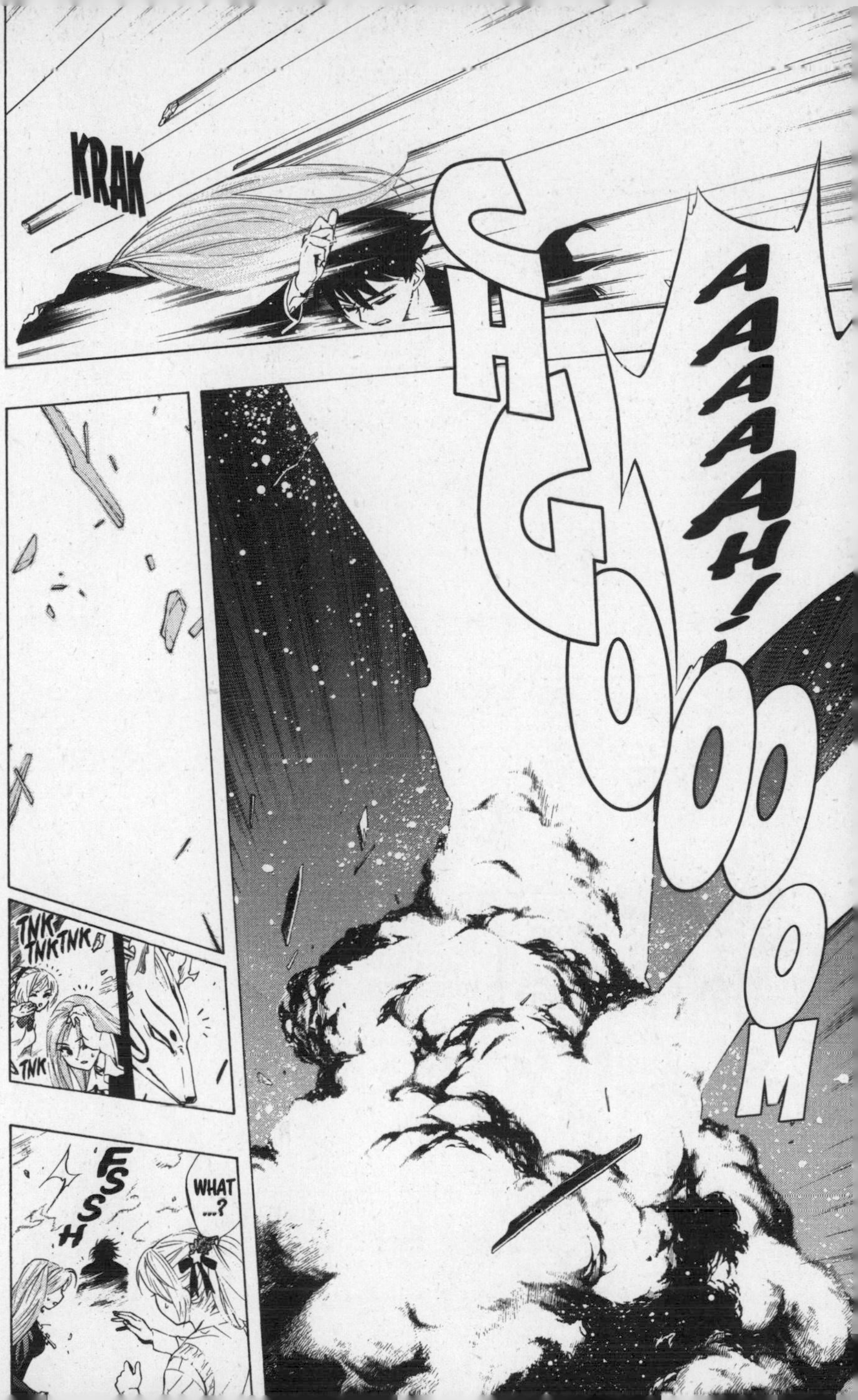

AAAAAH!
KRAK
CHGOOOOOM
TNK TNKTNK
TNK
FSSH
WHAT ...?

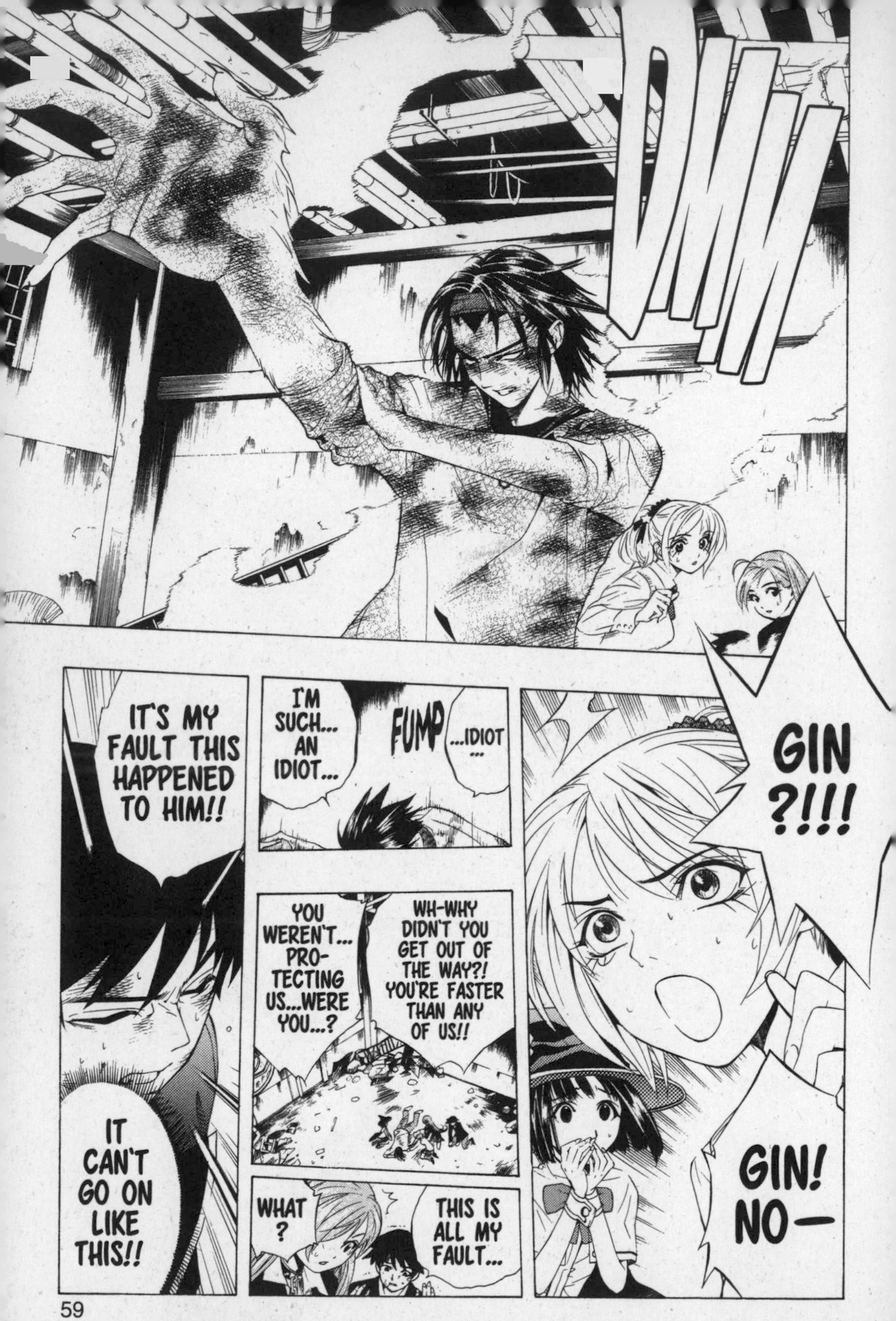
GIN ?!!!
GIN! NO—
I'M SUCH... AN IDIOT...
FUMP
...IDIOT ...
WH-WHY DIDN'T YOU GET OUT OF THE WAY?! YOU'RE FASTER THAN ANY OF US!!
YOU WEREN'T... PRO-TECTING US...WERE YOU...?
THIS IS ALL MY FAULT...
WHAT ?
IT'S MY FAULT THIS HAPPENED TO HIM!!
IT CAN'T GO ON LIKE THIS!!

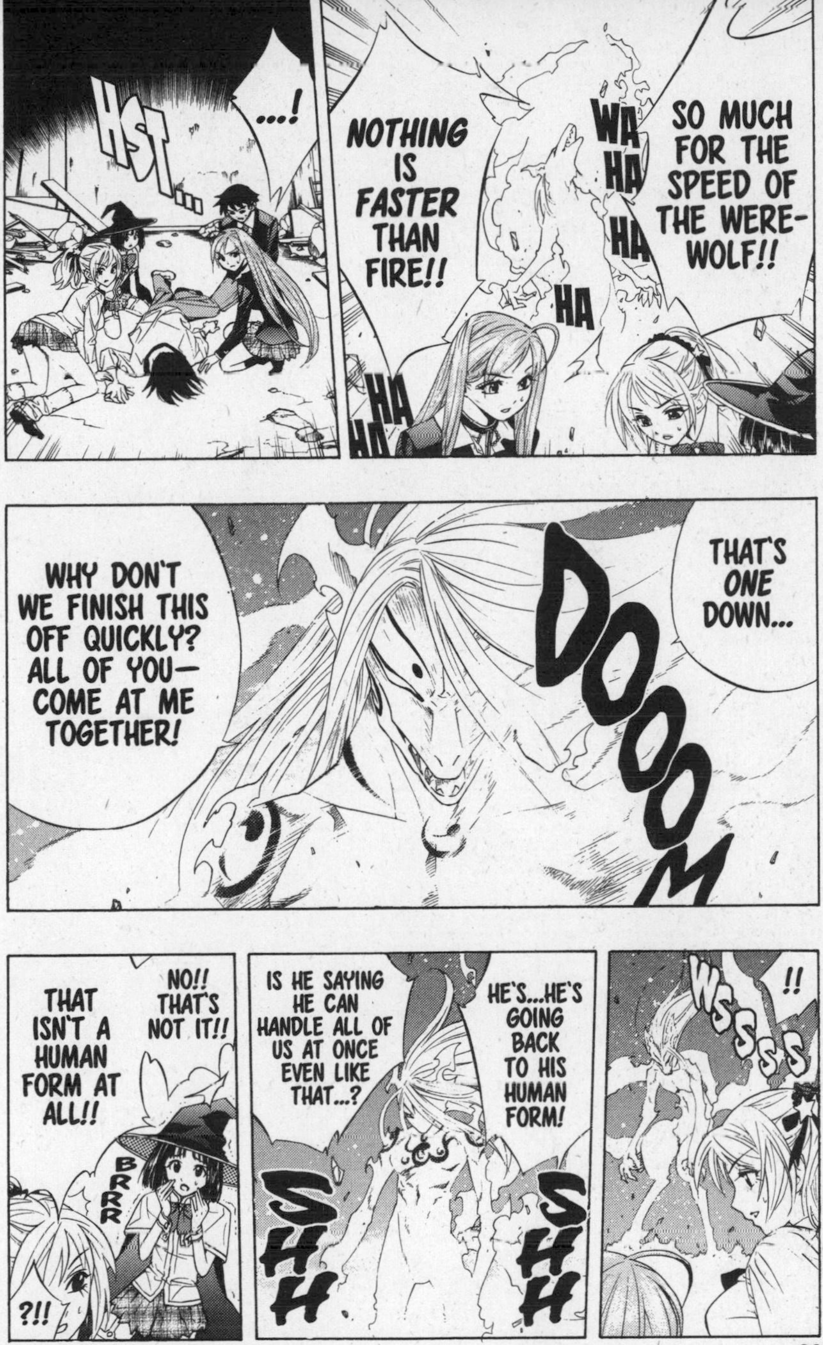
SO MUCH FOR THE SPEED OF THE WERE-WOLF!!
WA HA HA HA HA HA
NOTHING IS FASTER THAN FIRE!!
...!
HST...
THAT'S ONE DOWN...
DOOOOM
WHY DON'T WE FINISH THIS OFF QUICKLY? ALL OF YOU— COME AT ME TOGETHER!
!!
WSSSSS
HE'S...HE'S GOING BACK TO HIS HUMAN FORM!
SHH
SHH
IS HE SAYING HE CAN HANDLE ALL OF US AT ONCE EVEN LIKE THAT...?
NO!! THAT'S NOT IT!!
THAT ISN'T A HUMAN FORM AT ALL!!
BRRR
?!!

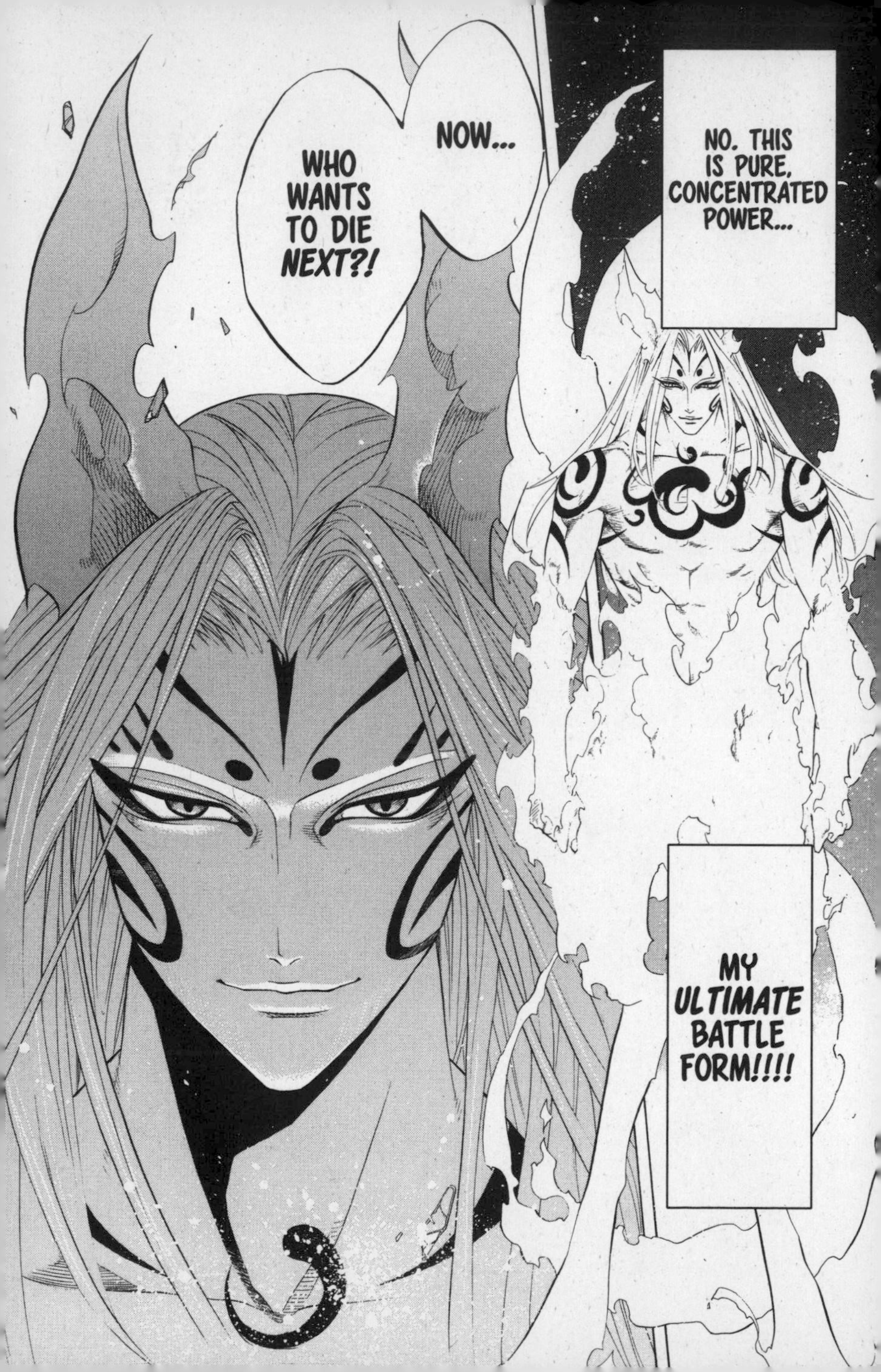
NO. THIS IS PURE, CONCENTRATED POWER...
MY ULTIMATE BATTLE FORM!!!!
NOW...
WHO WANTS TO DIE NEXT?!

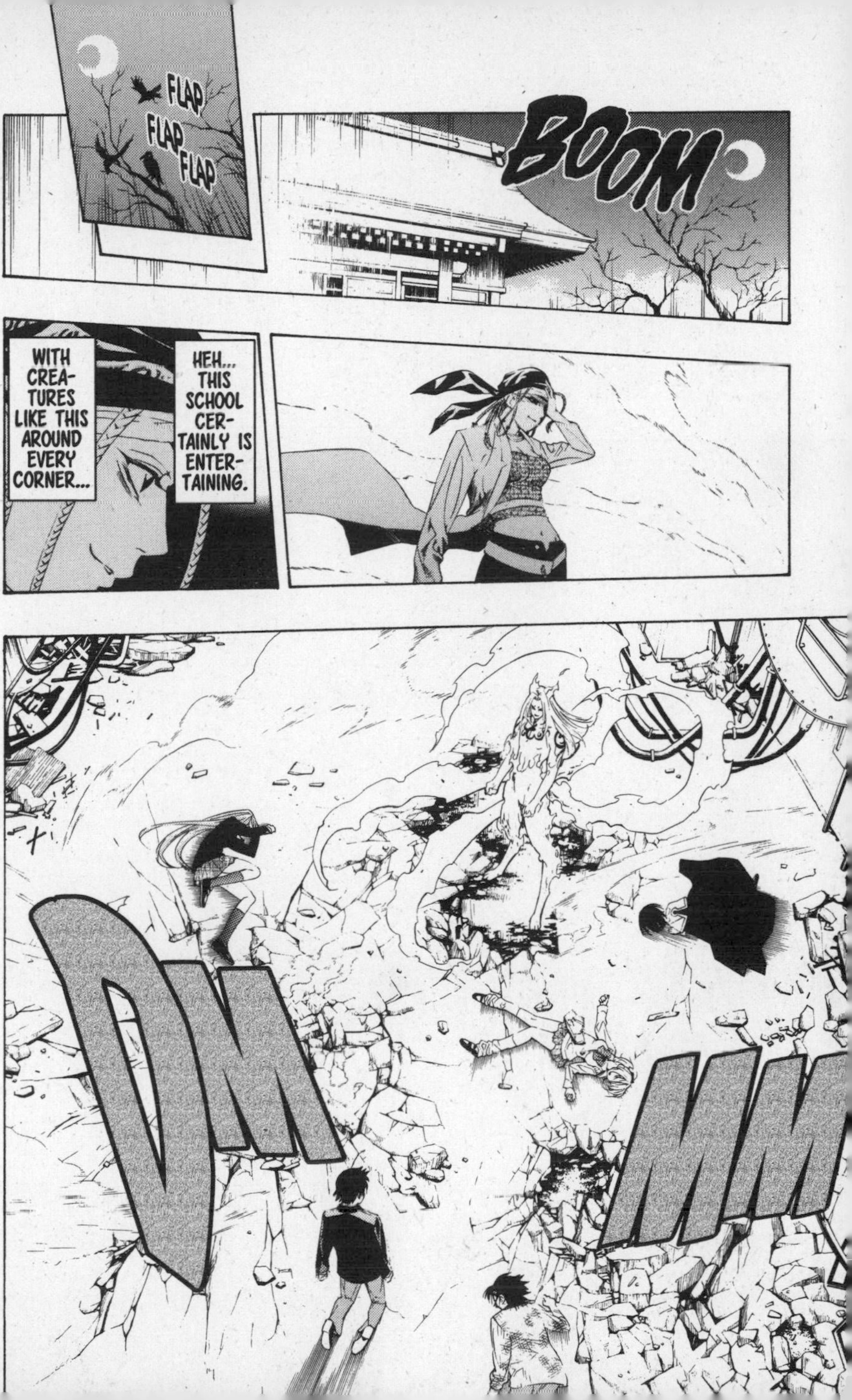
BOOM
FLAP FLAP FLAP
HEH... THIS SCHOOL CERTAINLY IS ENTERTAINING.
WITH CREATURES LIKE THIS AROUND EVERY CORNER...
DMMM

READ THIS WAY

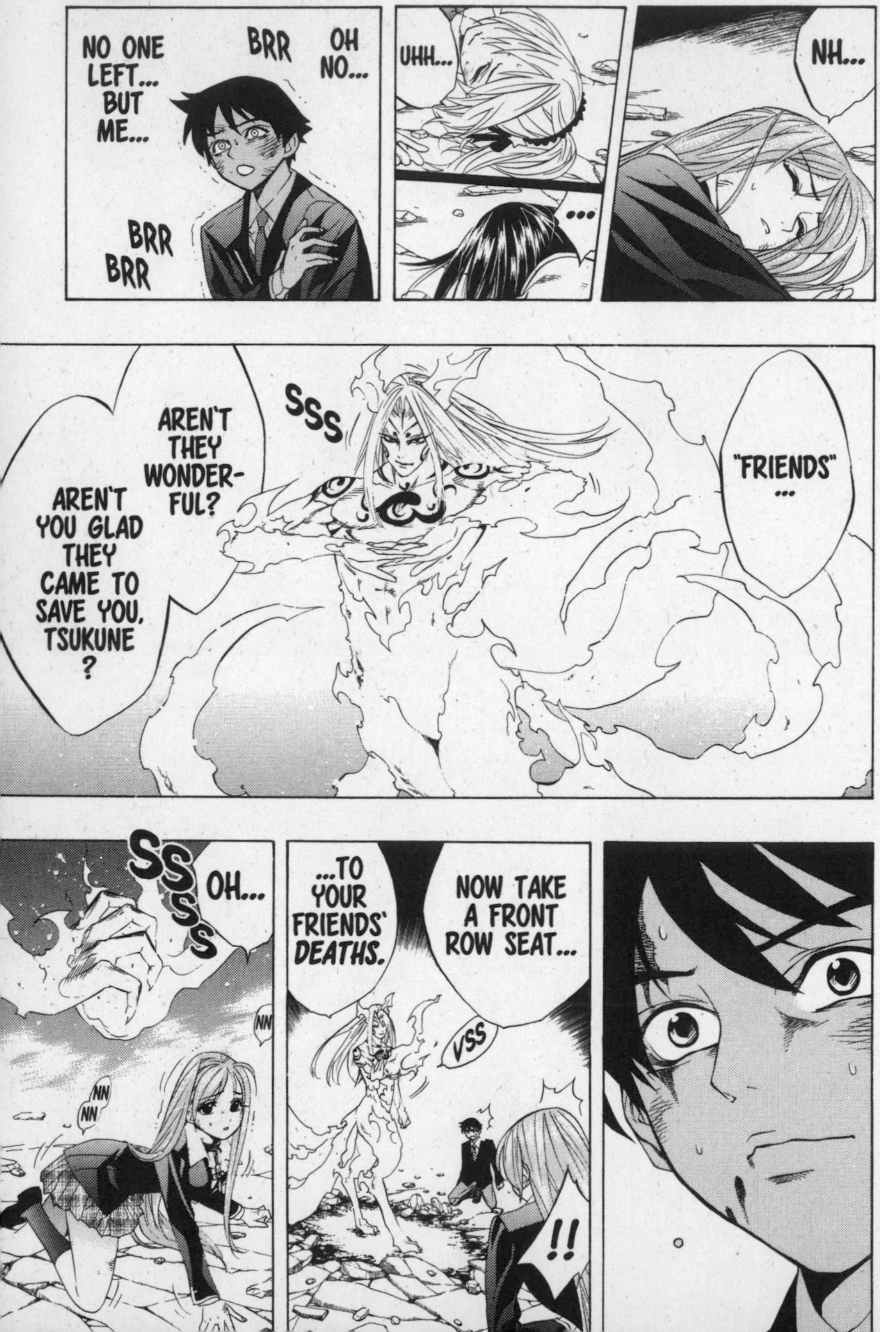
NH...
UHH...
...
OH NO...
BRR
NO ONE LEFT... BUT ME...
BRR BRR
"FRIENDS" ...
AREN'T THEY WONDERFUL?
SSS
AREN'T YOU GLAD THEY CAME TO SAVE YOU, TSUKUNE?
NOW TAKE A FRONT ROW SEAT...
...TO YOUR FRIENDS' DEATHS.
VSS
!!
OH...
SSSS
NN
NN NN

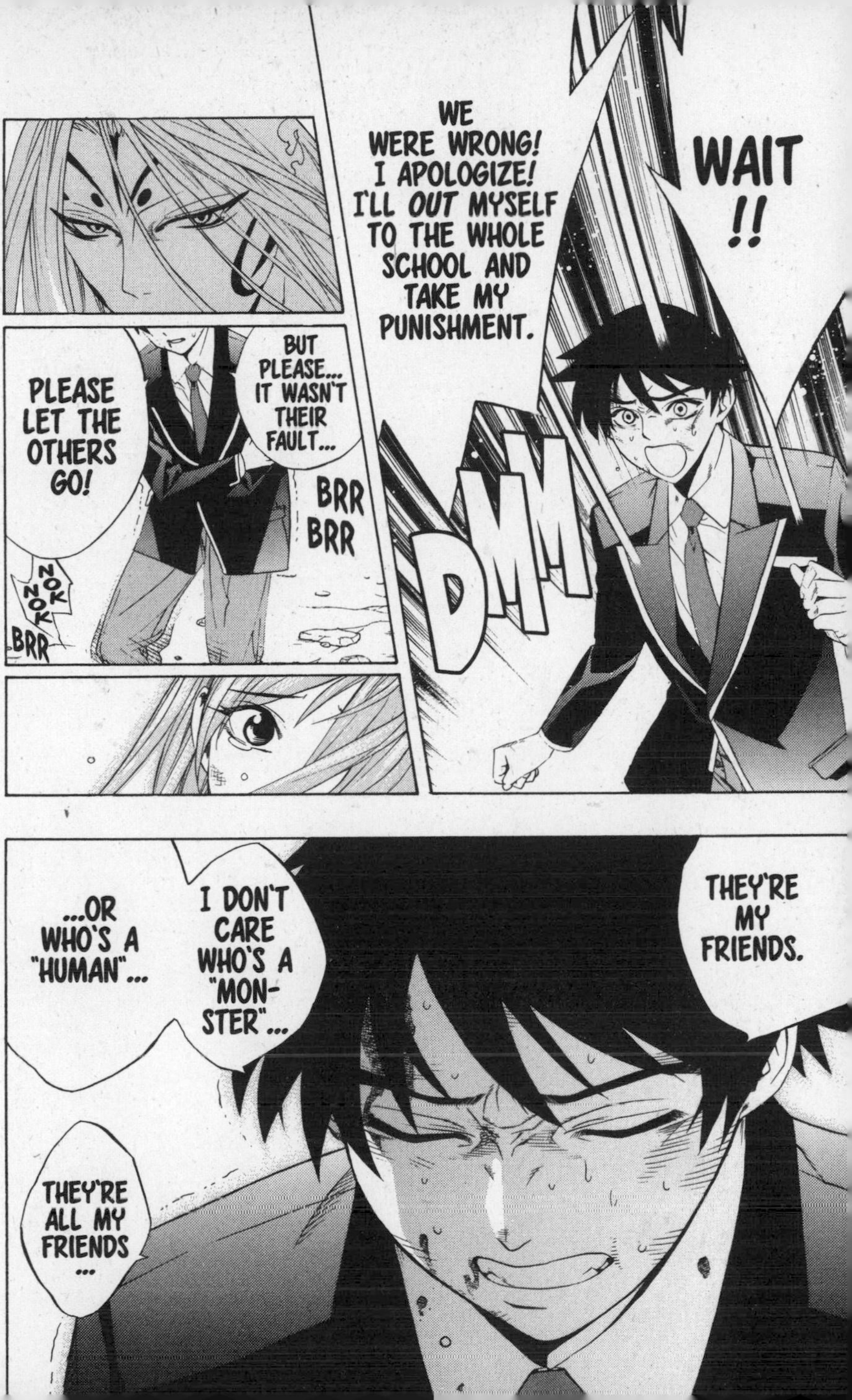
WAIT !!
WE WERE WRONG! I APOLOGIZE! I'LL *OUT* MYSELF TO THE WHOLE SCHOOL AND TAKE MY PUNISHMENT.
DMM
BUT PLEASE... IT WASN'T THEIR FAULT...
PLEASE LET THE OTHERS GO!
BRR BRR
NOK NOK
BRR
THEY'RE MY FRIENDS.
I DON'T CARE WHO'S A "MON-STER"...
...OR WHO'S A "HUMAN"...
THEY'RE ALL MY FRIENDS ...

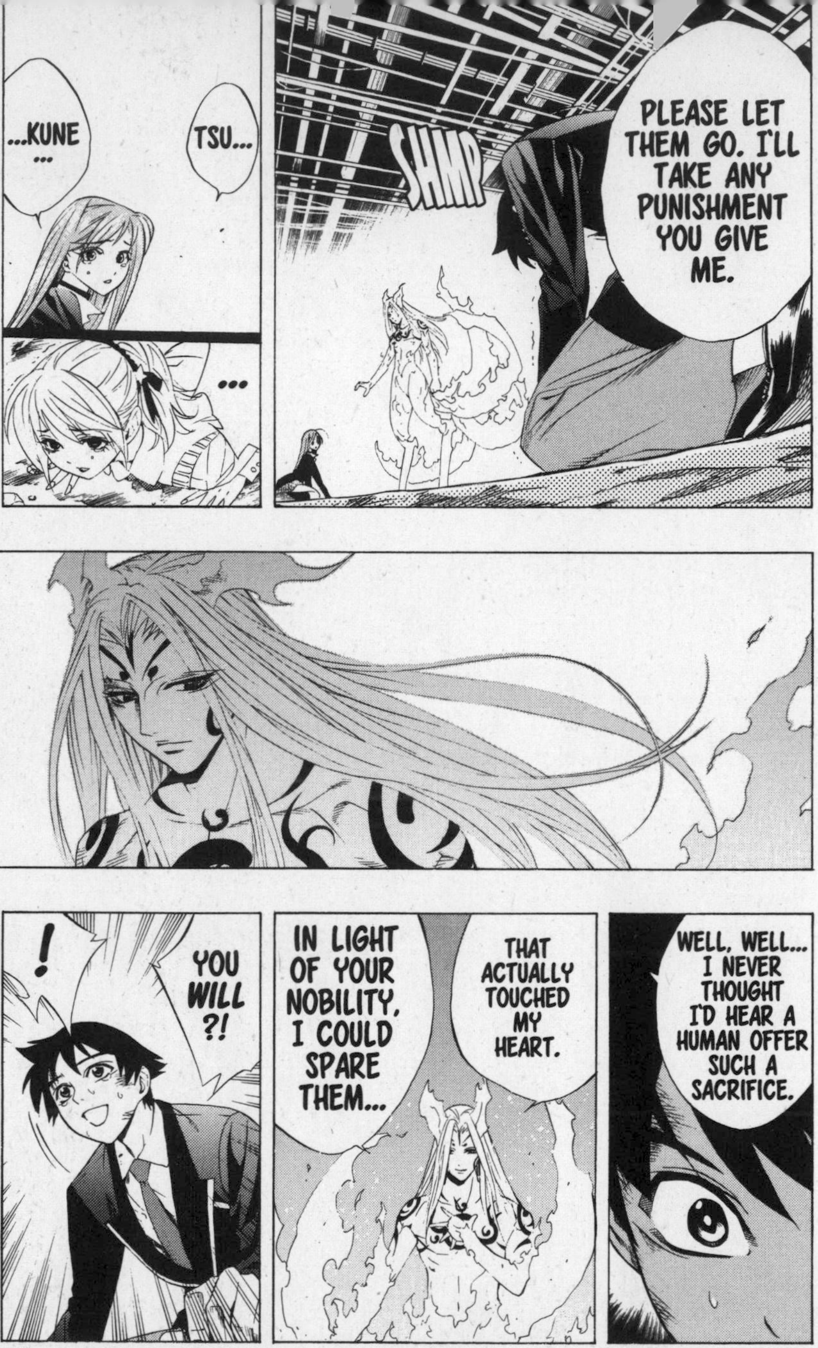
SHMP
PLEASE LET THEM GO. I'LL TAKE ANY PUNISHMENT YOU GIVE ME.
TSU...
...KUNE ...
...
WELL, WELL... I NEVER THOUGHT I'D HEAR A HUMAN OFFER SUCH A SACRIFICE.
THAT ACTUALLY TOUCHED MY HEART.
IN LIGHT OF YOUR NOBILITY, I COULD SPARE THEM...
YOU WILL ?!
!

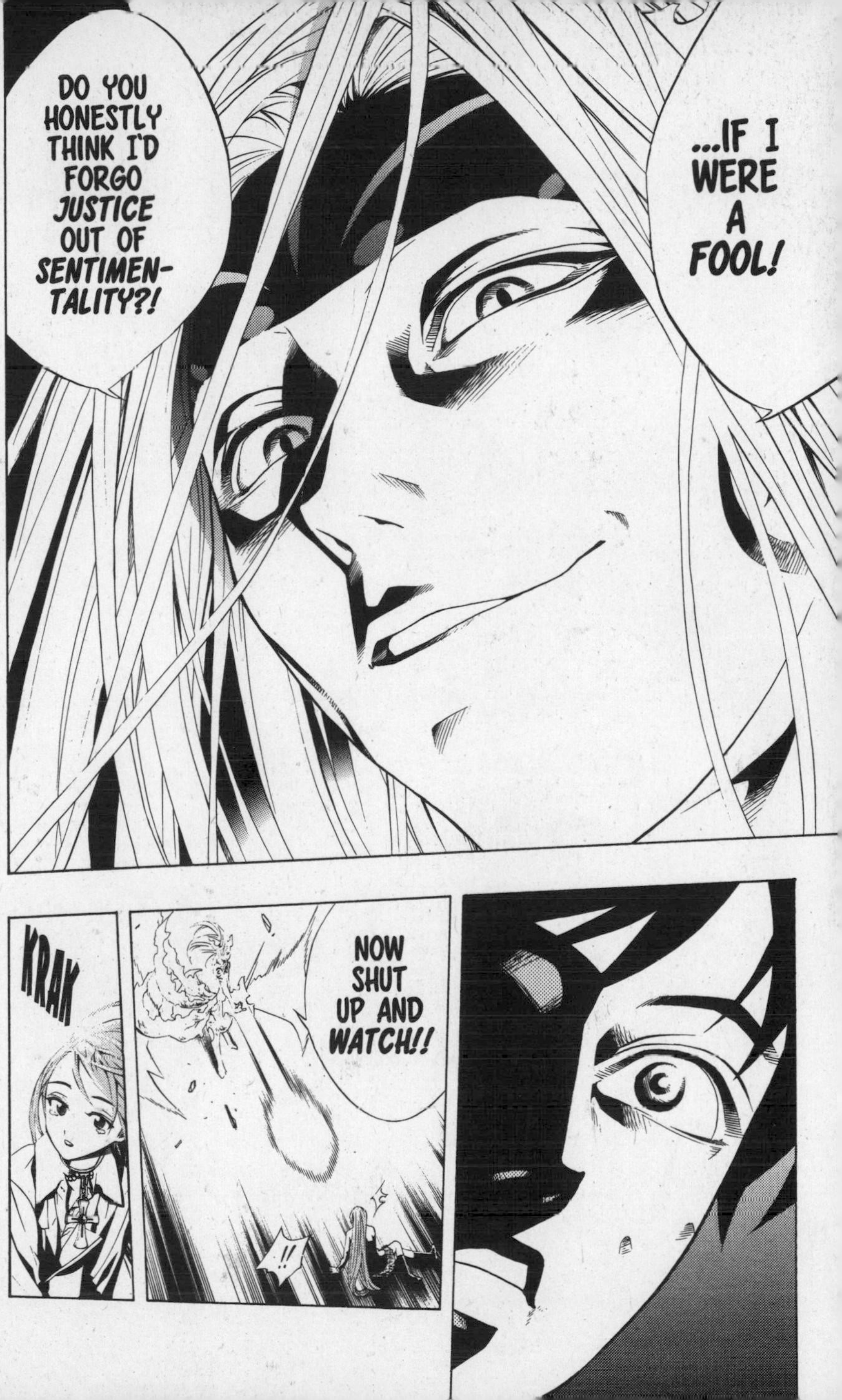
DO YOU HONESTLY THINK I'D FORGO JUSTICE OUT OF SENTIMENTALITY?!
...IF I WERE A FOOL!
NOW SHUT UP AND WATCH!!
!!
KRAK

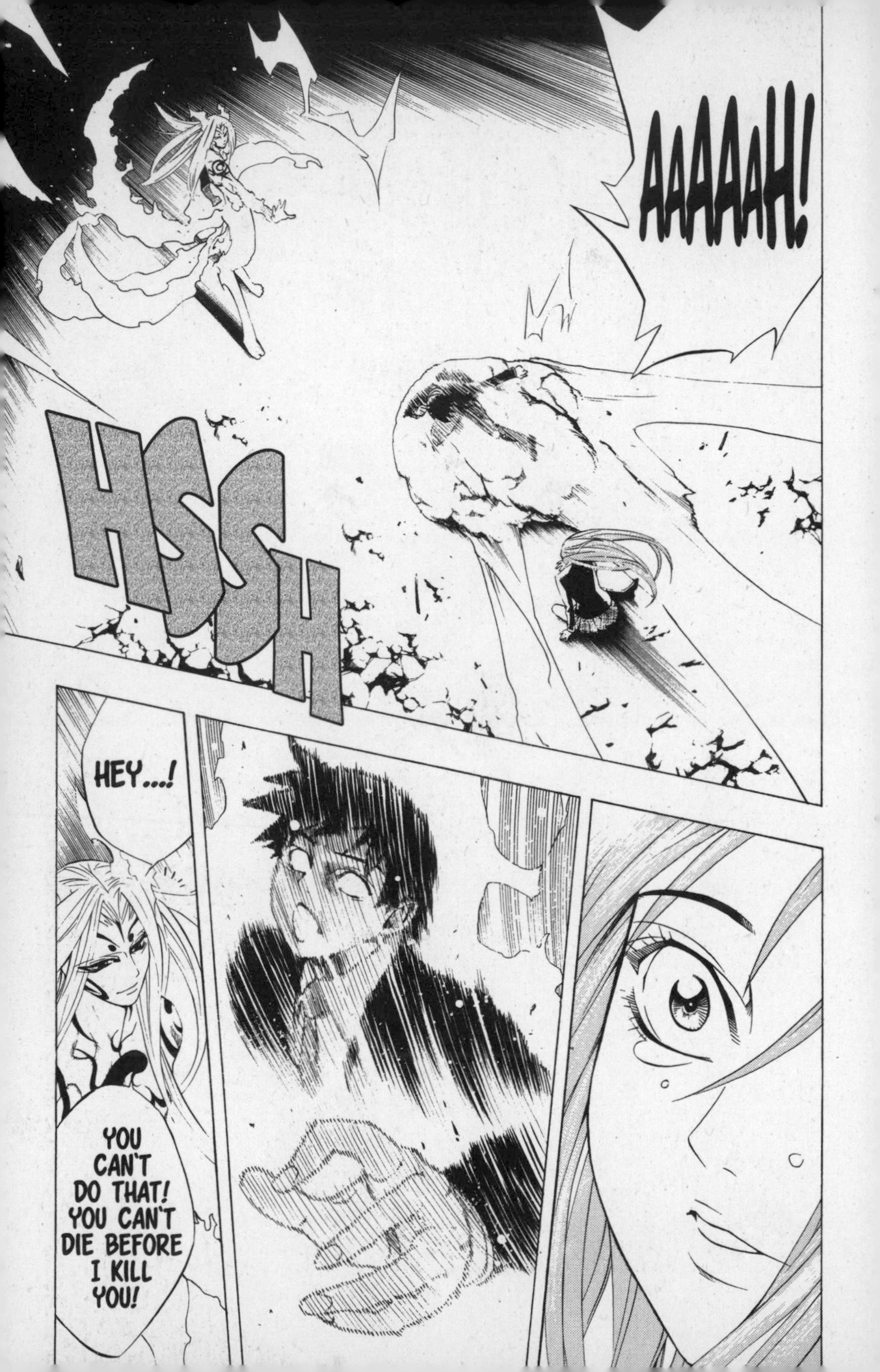
AAAAAH!
HSSSH
HEY...!
YOU CAN'T DO THAT! YOU CAN'T DIE BEFORE I KILL YOU!

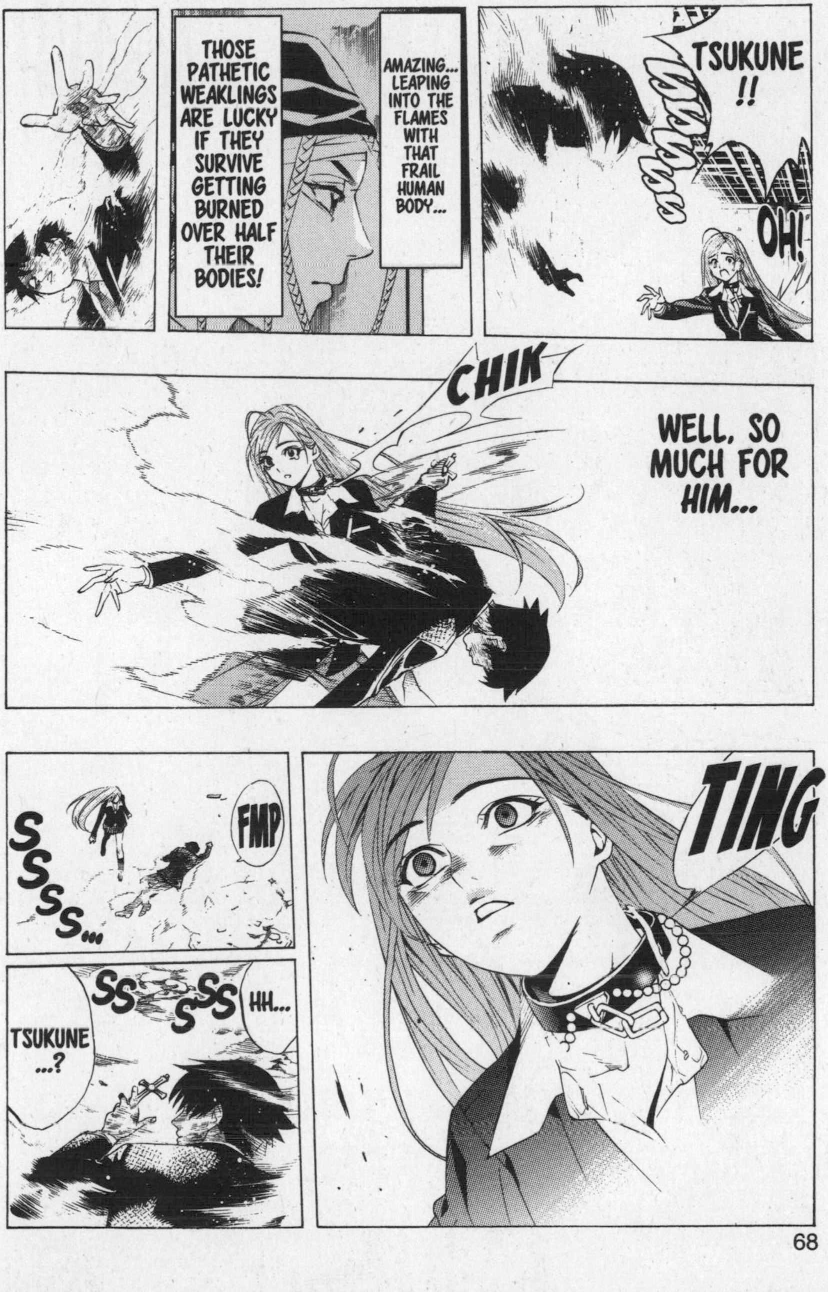

TSUKUNE !!
OH!
AMAZING... LEAPING INTO THE FLAMES WITH THAT FRAIL HUMAN BODY...
THOSE PATHETIC WEAKLINGS ARE LUCKY IF THEY SURVIVE GETTING BURNED OVER HALF THEIR BODIES!
CHIK
WELL, SO MUCH FOR HIM...
TING
FMP
SSSS...
SSSSSHH...
TSUKUNE ...?

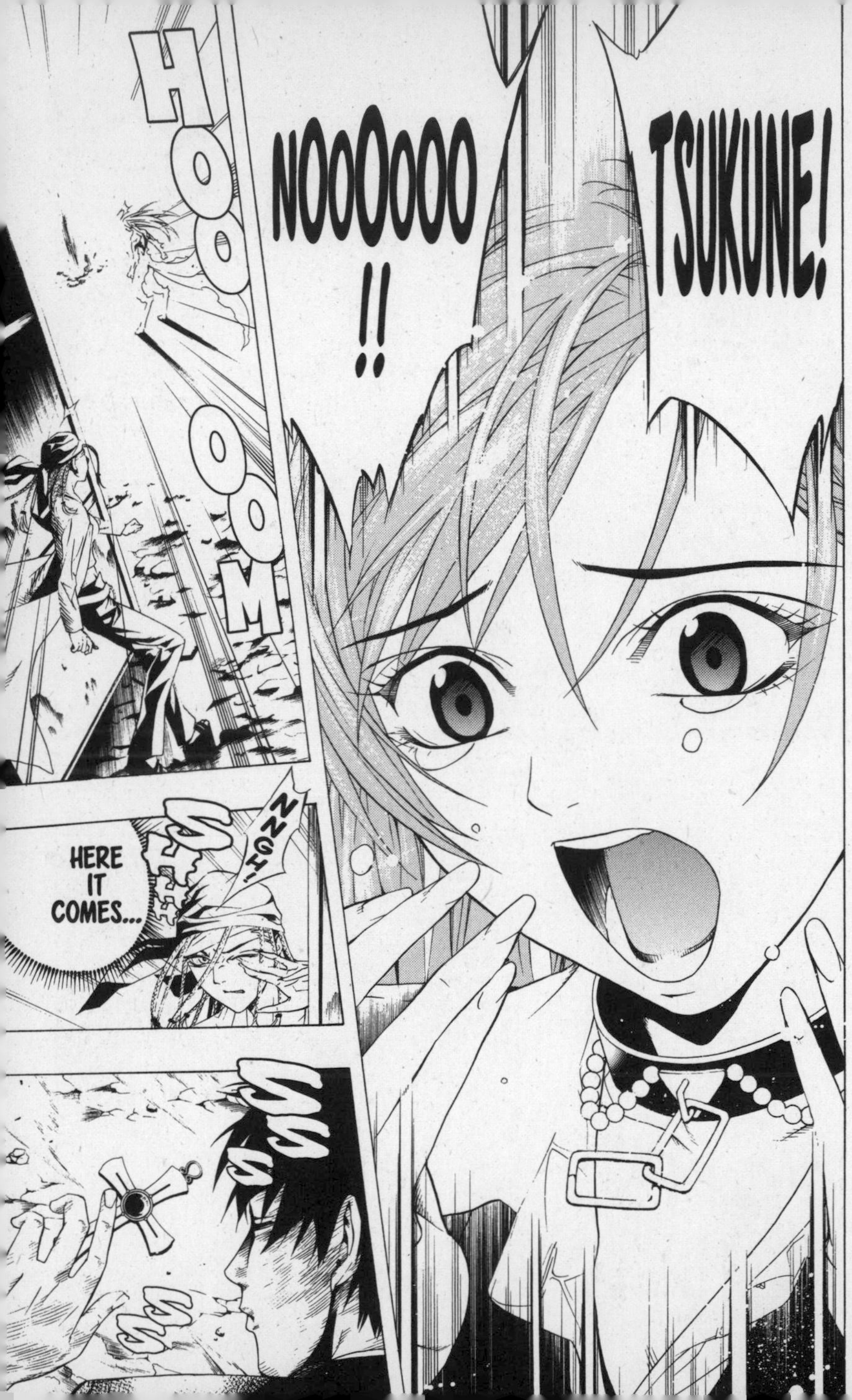
TSUKUNE!
NOOOOOO!!
HOOOOOOOM
NNGH!
HERE IT COMES...
SSS
SS

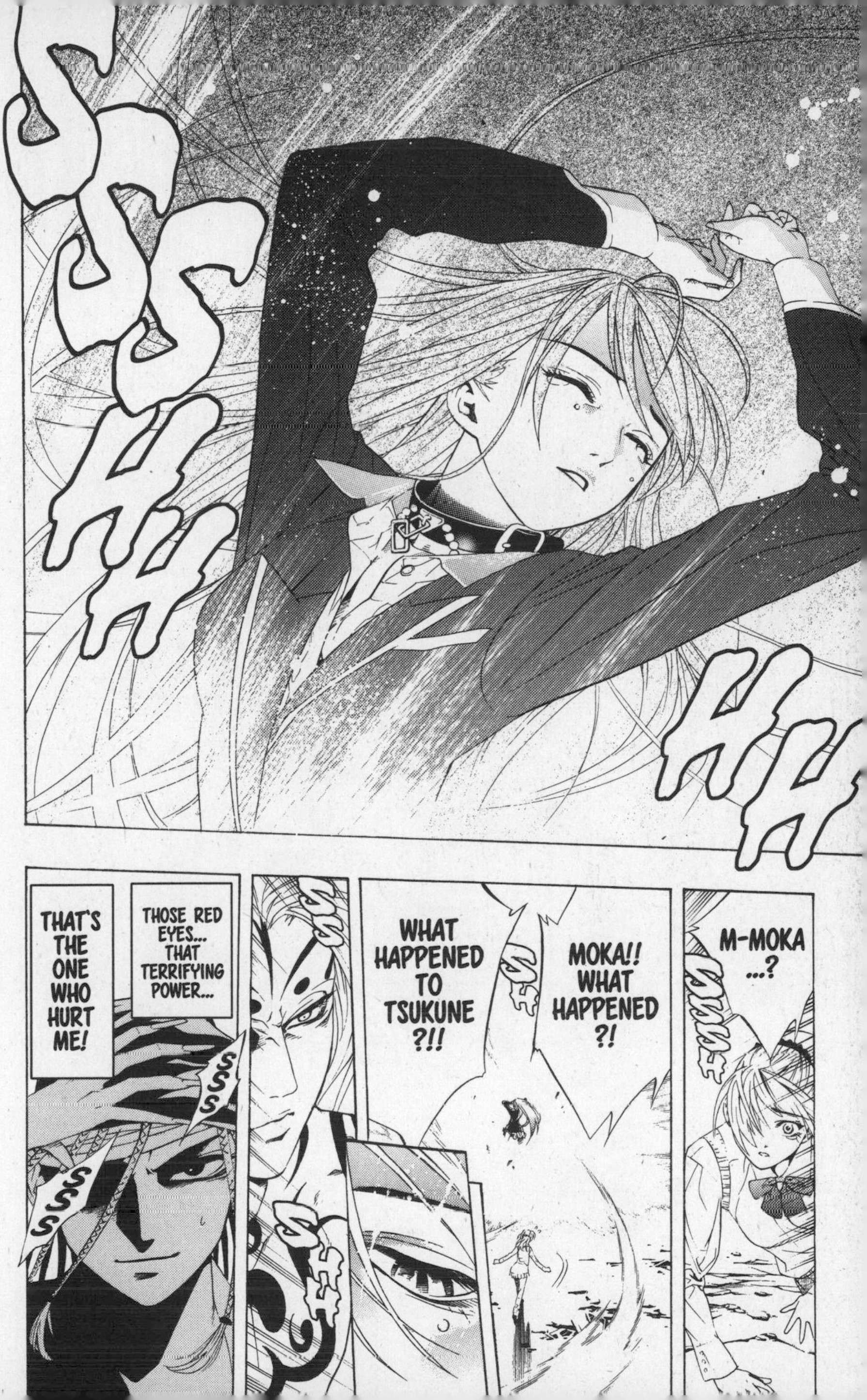
M-MOKA ...?
MOKA!! WHAT HAPPENED ?!
WHAT HAPPENED TO TSUKUNE ?!!
THOSE RED EYES... THAT TERRIFYING POWER...
THAT'S THE ONE WHO HURT ME!

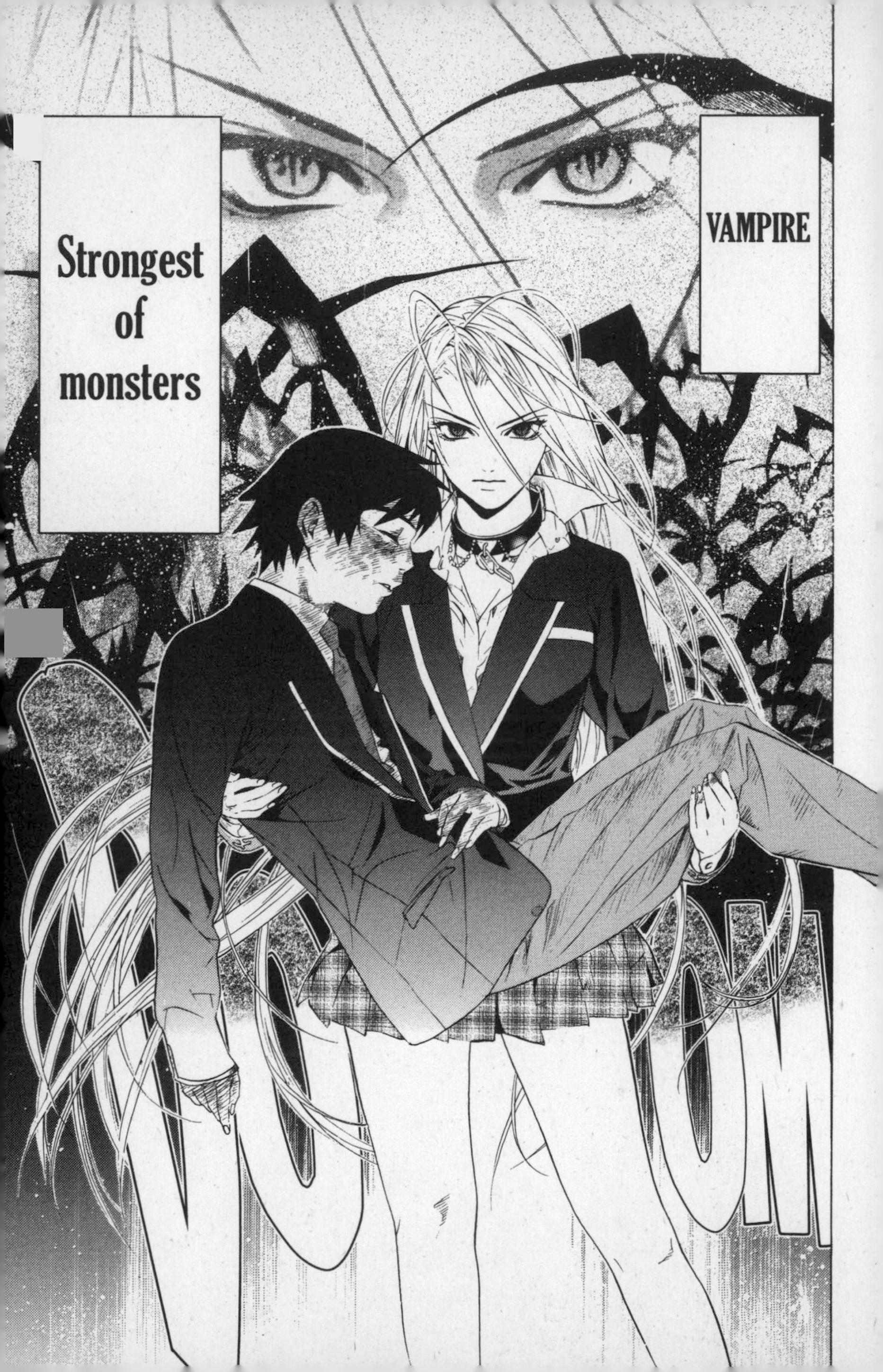
VAMPIRE
Strongest of monsters

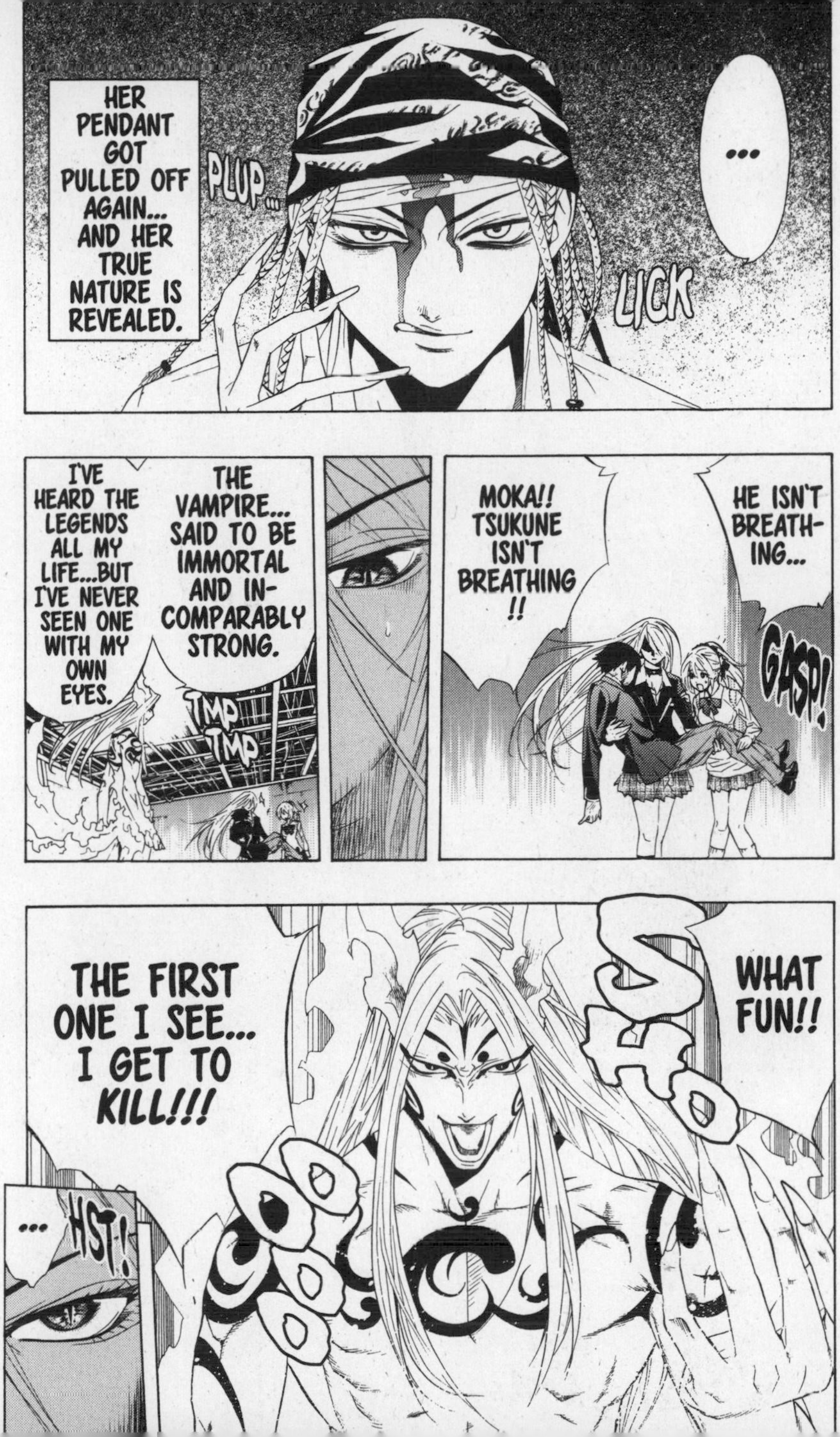
...
HER PENDANT GOT PULLED OFF AGAIN... AND HER TRUE NATURE IS REVEALED.
PLUP...
LICK
HE ISN'T BREATH-ING...
MOKA!! TSUKUNE ISN'T BREATHING!!
GASP!
THE VAMPIRE... SAID TO BE IMMORTAL AND IN-COMPARABLY STRONG.
I'VE HEARD THE LEGENDS ALL MY LIFE...BUT I'VE NEVER SEEN ONE WITH MY OWN EYES.
TMP TMP
WHAT FUN!!
SHO
THE FIRST ONE I SEE... I GET TO *KILL!!!*
HST!
...

READ THIS WAY

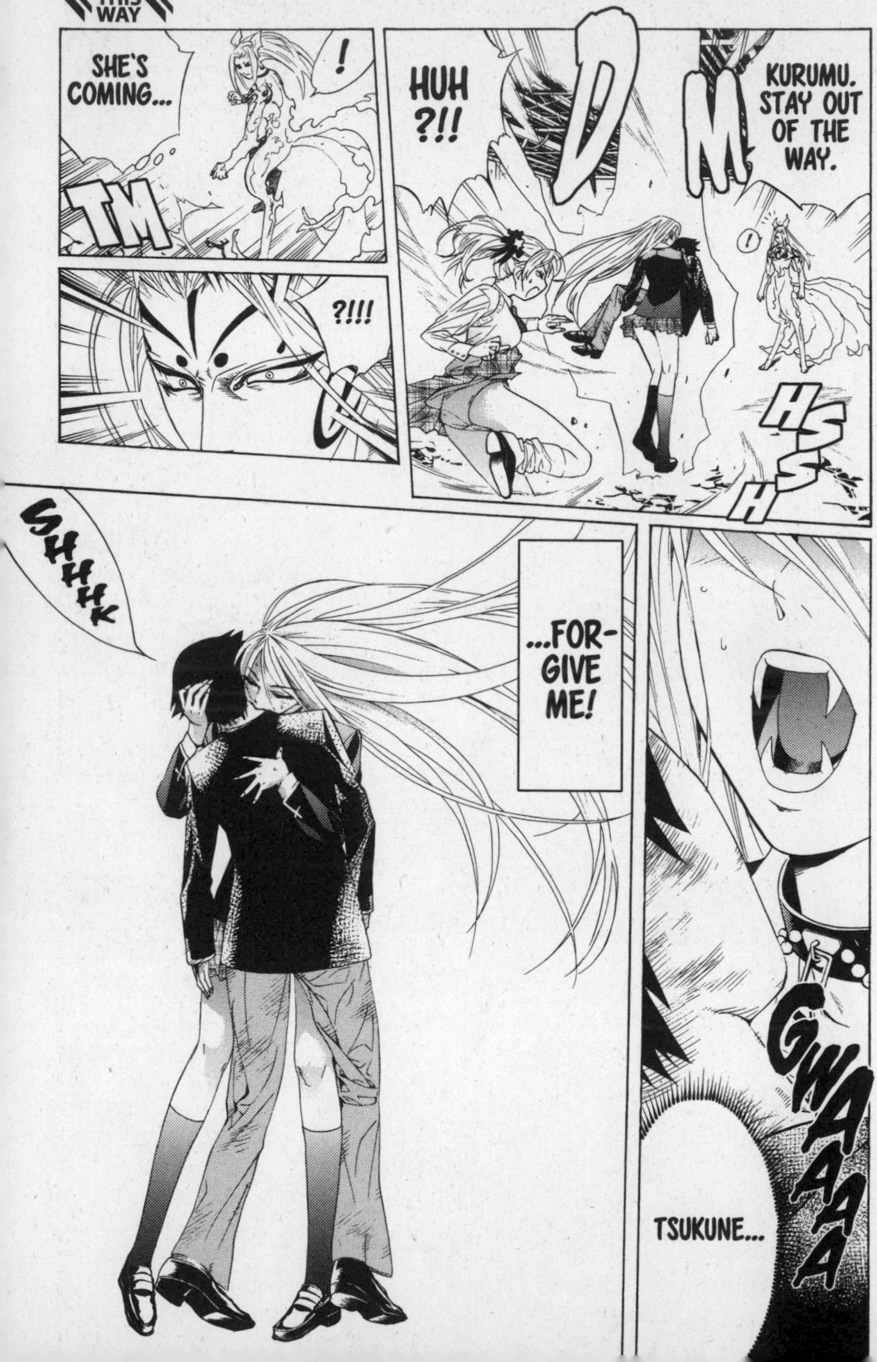
KURUMU. STAY OUT OF THE WAY.
DM
HUH ?!!
!
HSSH
!
SHE'S COMING...
TM
?!!!
TSUKUNE...
GWAAAAA
...FOR-GIVE ME!
SHHHK

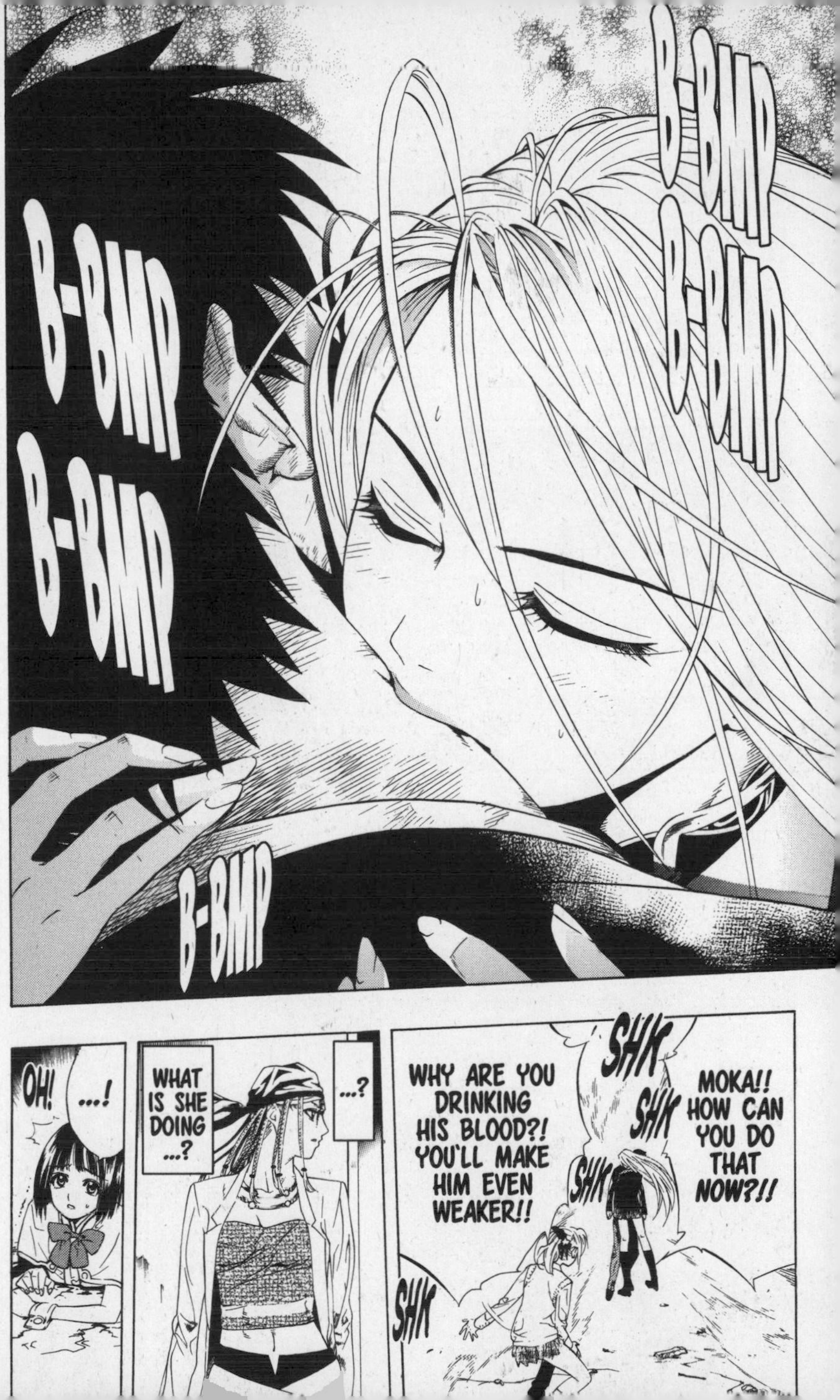
B-BMP
B-BMP
B-BMP
B-BMP
B-BMP
MOKA!! HOW CAN YOU DO THAT NOW?!!
SHK
SHK
WHY ARE YOU DRINKING HIS BLOOD?! YOU'LL MAKE HIM EVEN WEAKER!!
SHK
SHK
...?
WHAT IS SHE DOING ...?
...!
OH!

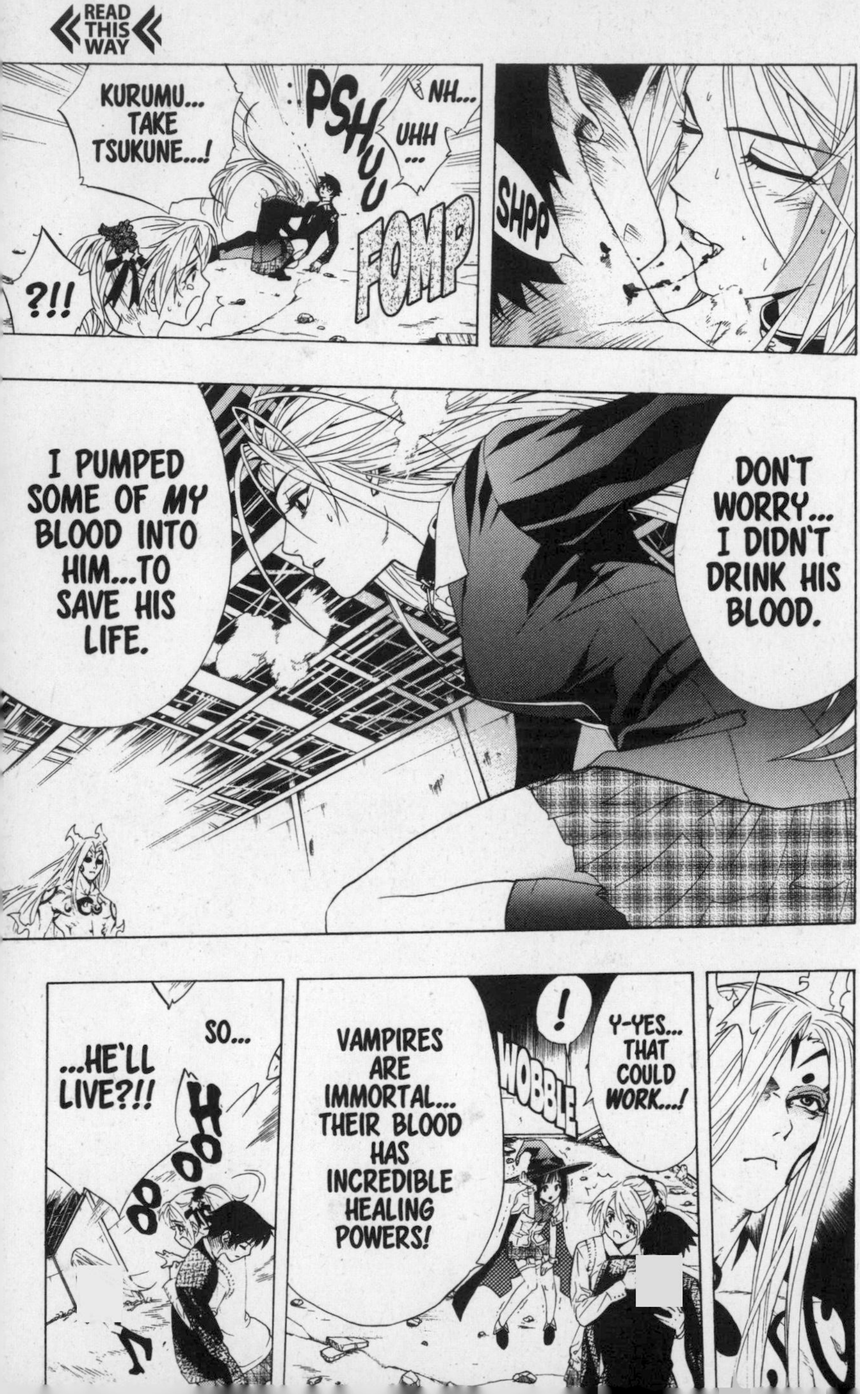
READ THIS WAY
SHPP
NH...
UHH...
PSHUU
KURUMU... TAKE TSUKUNE...!
FOMP
?!!
DON'T WORRY... I DIDN'T DRINK HIS BLOOD.
I PUMPED SOME OF MY BLOOD INTO HIM...TO SAVE HIS LIFE.
Y-YES... THAT COULD WORK...!
!
WOBBLE
VAMPIRES ARE IMMORTAL... THEIR BLOOD HAS INCREDIBLE HEALING POWERS!
SO...
...HE'LL LIVE?!!
HOOOOO

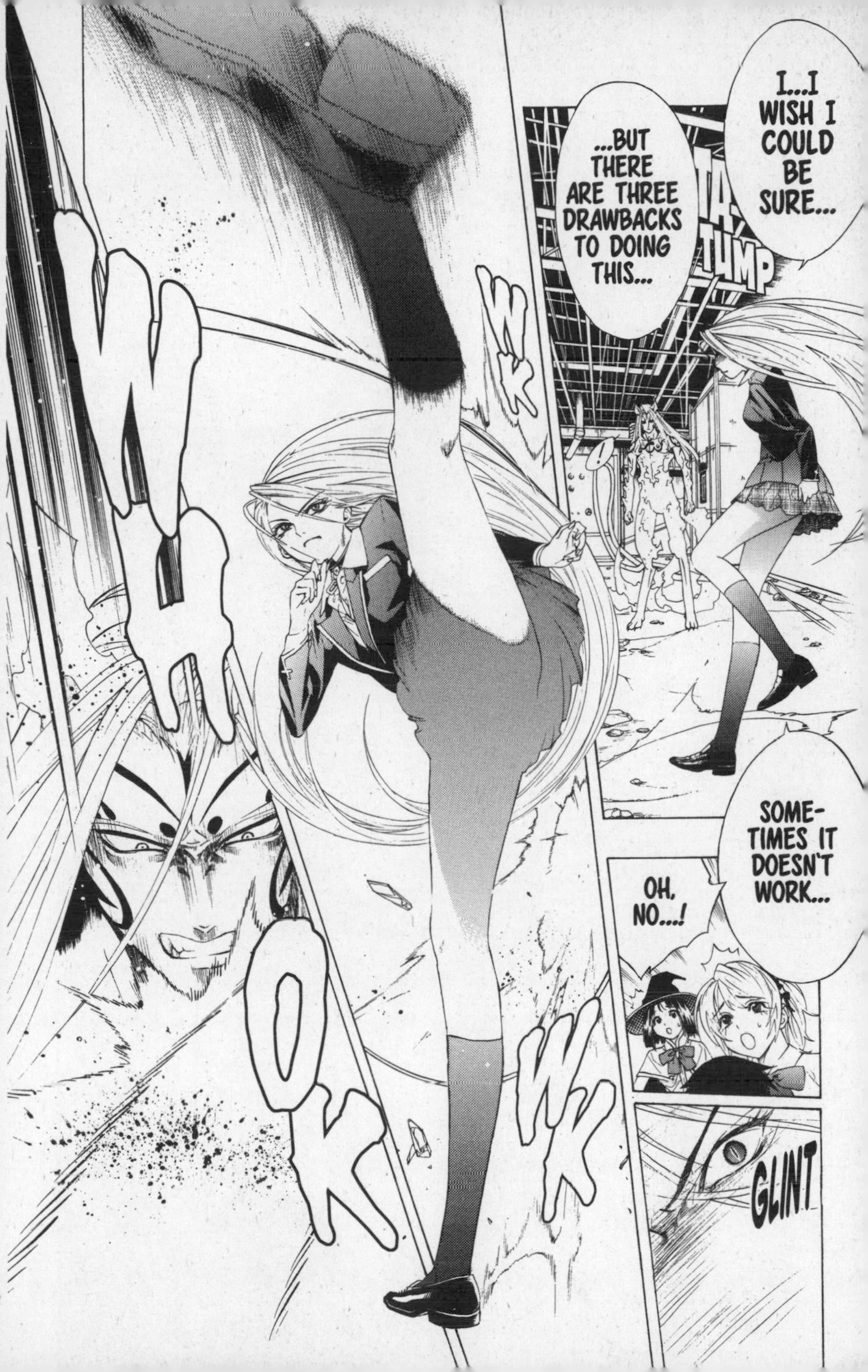
I...I WISH I COULD BE SURE...
...BUT THERE ARE THREE DRAWBACKS TO DOING THIS...
TA TUMP
SOME-TIMES IT DOESN'T WORK...
OH, NO...!
GLINT

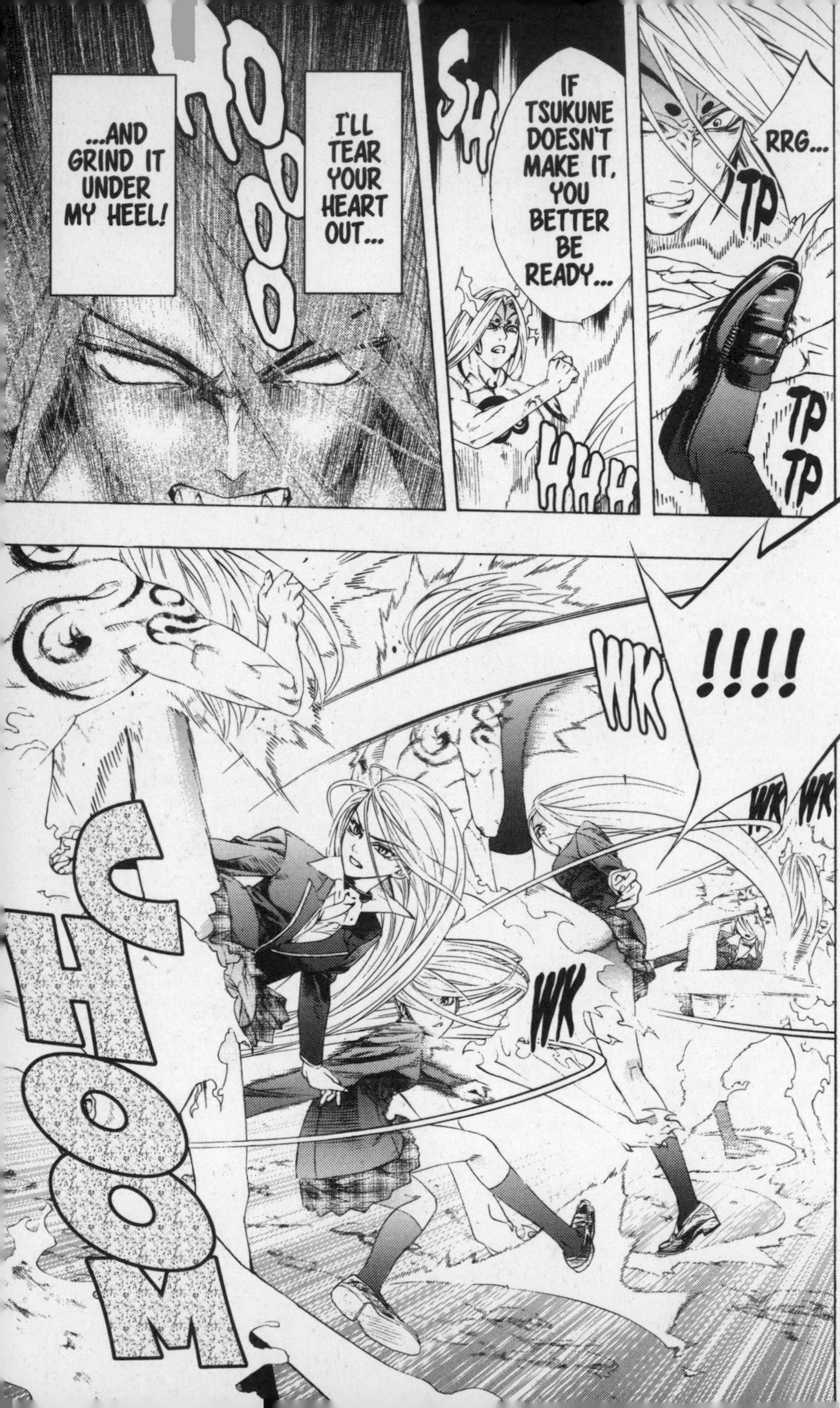
RRG...
TP
TP
TP
SH
IF TSUKUNE DOESN'T MAKE IT, YOU BETTER BE READY...
HHH
I'LL TEAR YOUR HEART OUT...
...AND GRIND IT UNDER MY HEEL!
WK
!!!!
WK
WK
WK

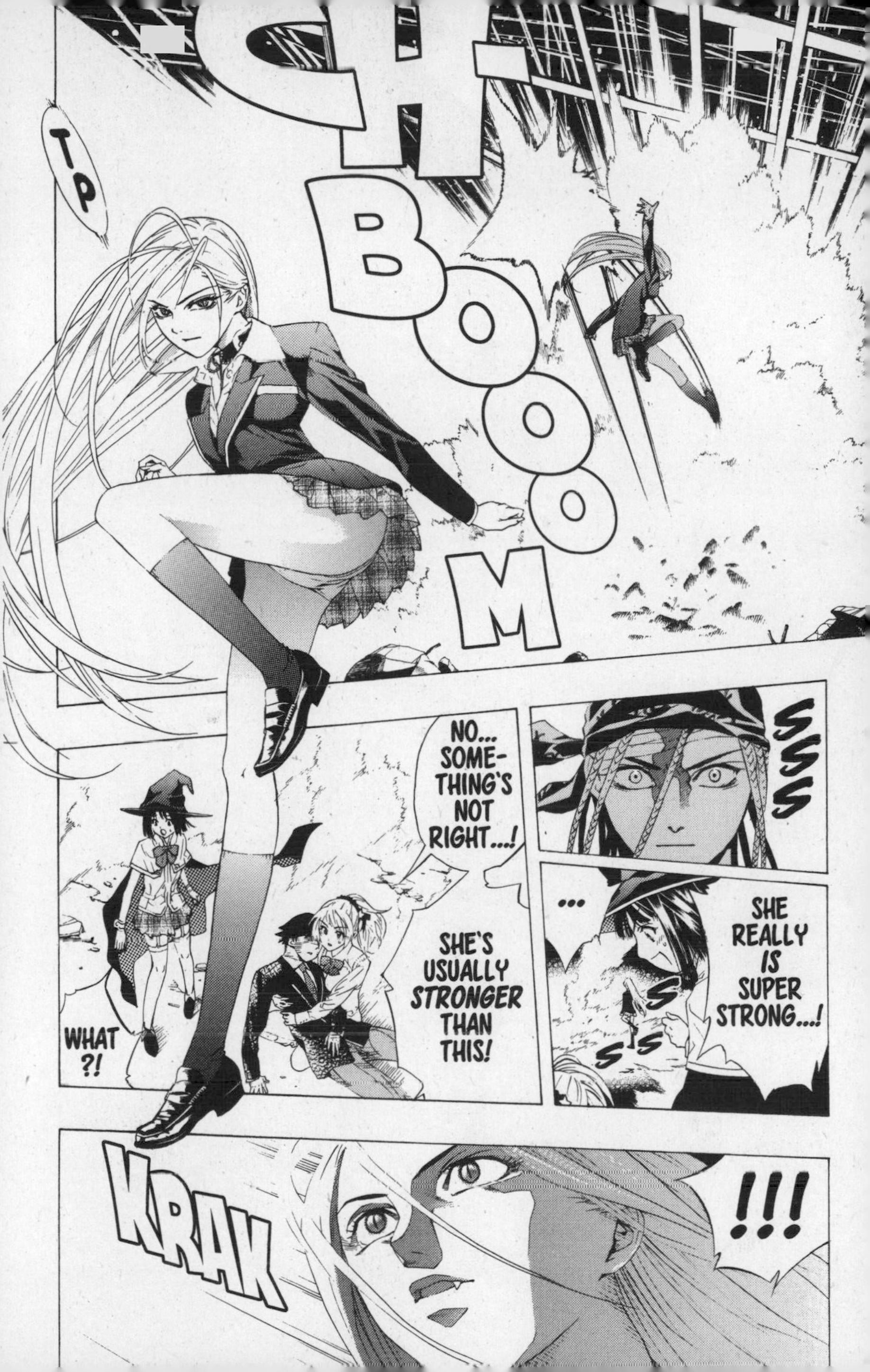
CH-
BOOOOM
TP
SSS
...
SHE REALLY IS SUPER STRONG...!
SSS
NO... SOME-THING'S NOT RIGHT...!
SHE'S USUALLY STRONGER THAN THIS!
WHAT?!
!!!
KRAK

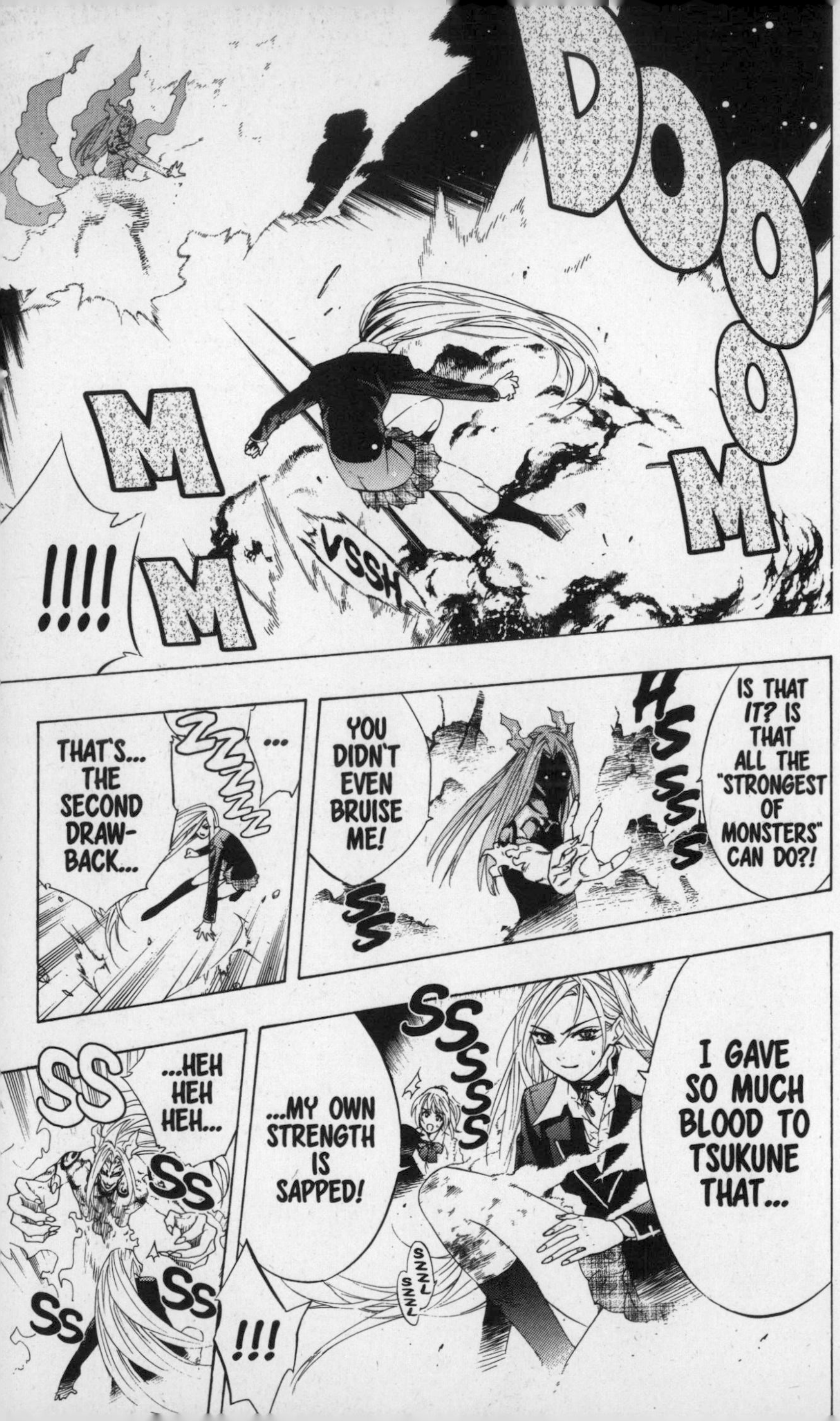
DOOOOM
MM
VSSH
!!!!
HSSSSS
SS
IS THAT IT? IS THAT ALL THE "STRONGEST OF MONSTERS" CAN DO?!
YOU DIDN'T EVEN BRUISE ME!
...
THAT'S... THE SECOND DRAW-BACK...
SSSSSS
I GAVE SO MUCH BLOOD TO TSUKUNE THAT...
...MY OWN STRENGTH IS SAPPED!
SZZL SZZL
!!!
SS
...HEH HEH HEH...
SS
SS
SS

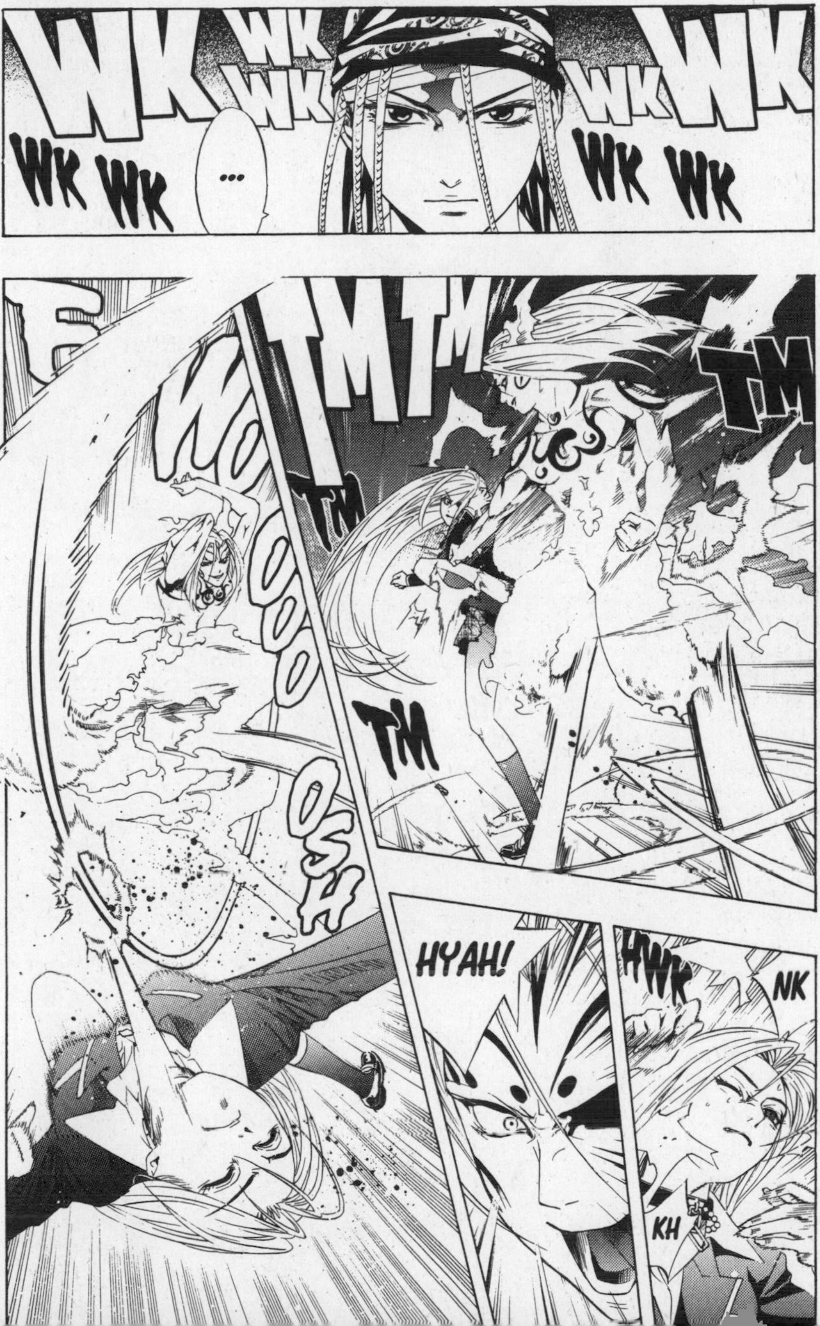
WK WK WK WK
WK WK WK WK
WK WK WK WK
...
TM TM TM TM TM
TM
NK
HWK
KH
HYAH!
WHOOOOOOSH

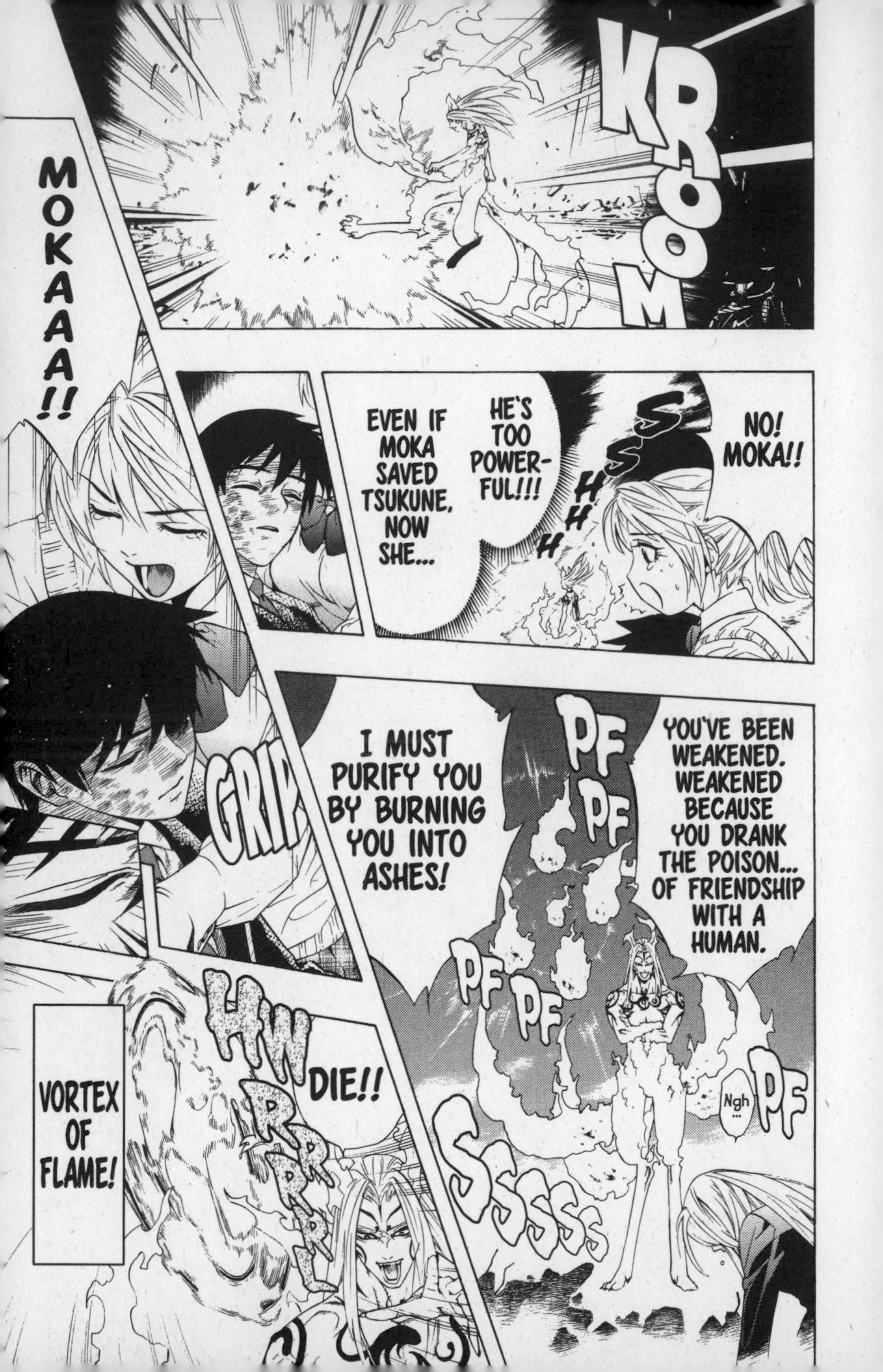
KROOOM
NO! MOKA!!
SSHHHH
HE'S TOO POWER-FUL!!!
EVEN IF MOKA SAVED TSUKUNE, NOW SHE...
MOKAAAA!!
YOU'VE BEEN WEAKENED. WEAKENED BECAUSE YOU DRANK THE POISON... OF FRIENDSHIP WITH A HUMAN.
PF PF
I MUST PURIFY YOU BY BURNING YOU INTO ASHES!
Ngh...
PF
PF PF
SSSSSS
GRIP
HWRRRRL
DIE!!
VORTEX OF FLAME!

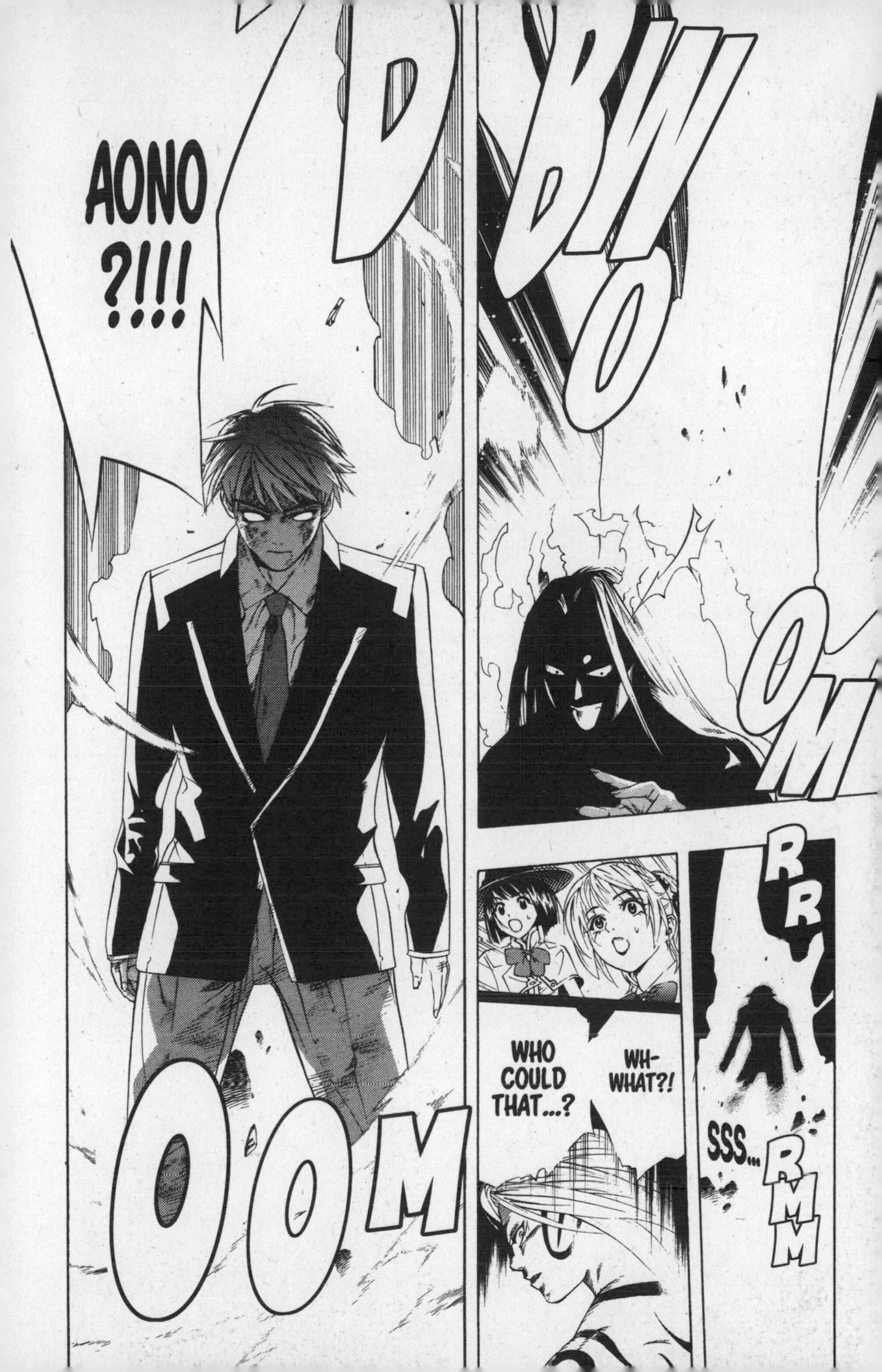
RRRMM
SSS...
WH- WHAT?!
WHO COULD THAT...?
AONO ?!!!

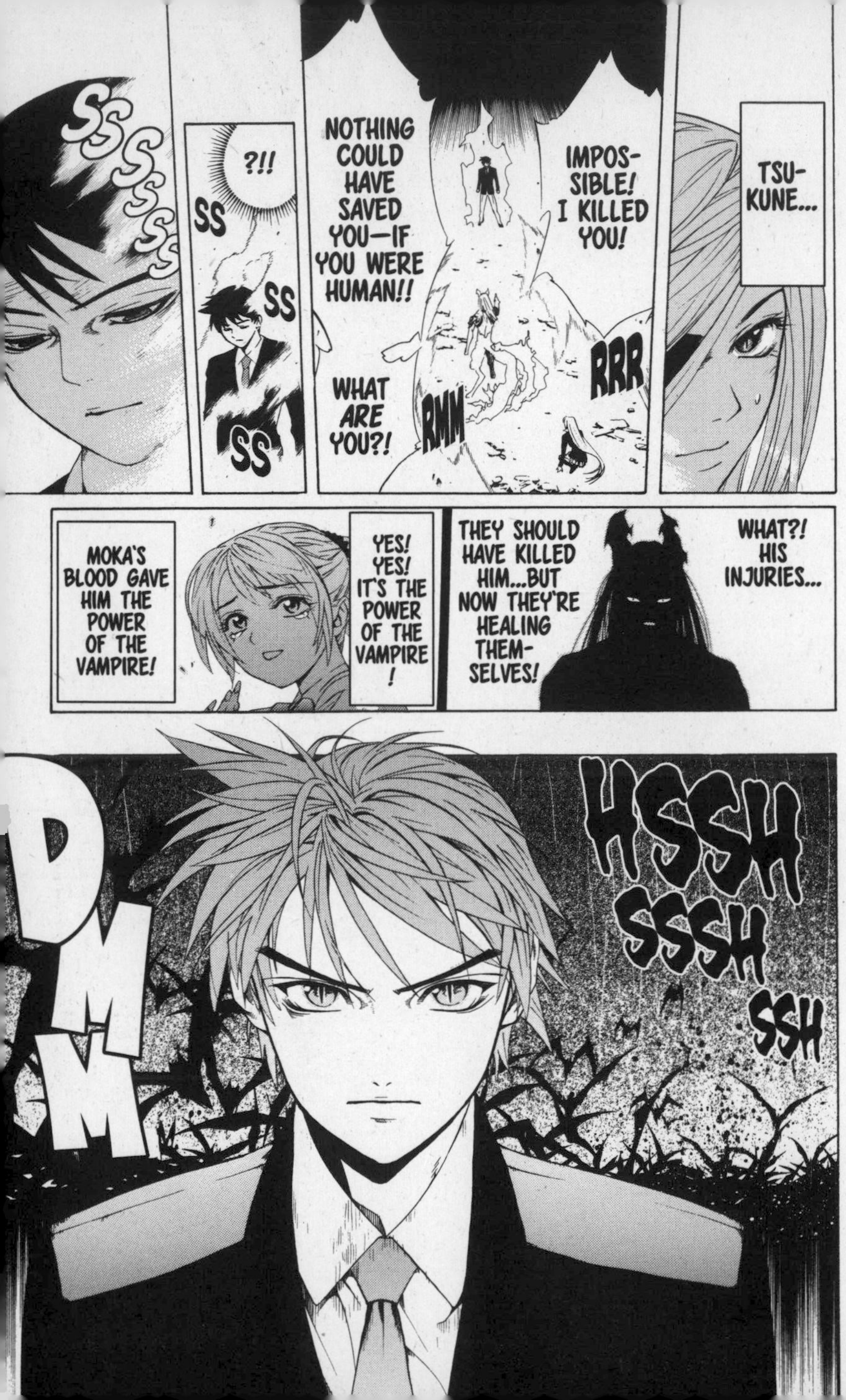
TSU-
KUNE...
IMPOS-
SIBLE!
I KILLED
YOU!
NOTHING
COULD
HAVE
SAVED
YOU—IF
YOU WERE
HUMAN!!
RRR
RMM
WHAT
ARE
YOU?!
?!!
SS
SS
SS
SSSSSS
WHAT?!
HIS
INJURIES...
THEY SHOULD
HAVE KILLED
HIM...BUT
NOW THEY'RE
HEALING
THEM-
SELVES!
YES!
YES!
IT'S THE
POWER
OF THE
VAMPIRE
!
MOKA'S
BLOOD GAVE
HIM THE
POWER
OF THE
VAMPIRE!
HSSH
SSSH
SSH
DMMM

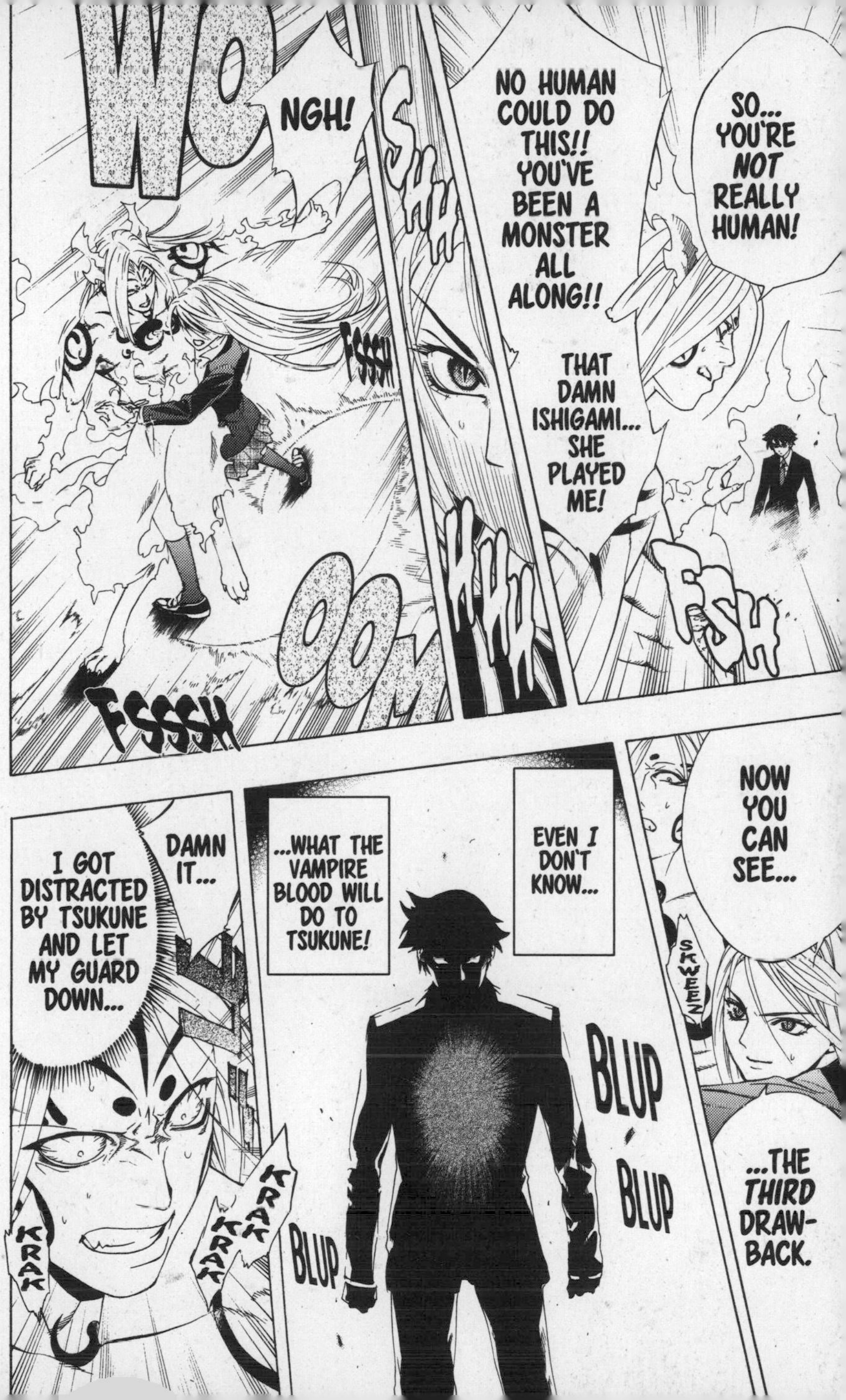
SO... YOU'RE *NOT* REALLY HUMAN!
FSH
NO HUMAN COULD DO THIS!! YOU'VE BEEN A MONSTER ALL ALONG!!
THAT DAMN ISHIGAMI... SHE PLAYED ME!
SHHHHHH
NGH!
WOOOM
FSSSH
FSSSH
NOW YOU CAN SEE...
SKWEEZ
...THE *THIRD* DRAW-BACK.
EVEN *I* DON'T KNOW...
...WHAT THE VAMPIRE BLOOD WILL DO TO TSUKUNE!
BLUP
BLUP
BLUP
DAMN IT...
I GOT DISTRACTED BY TSUKUNE AND LET MY GUARD DOWN...
KRAK
KRAK
KRAK

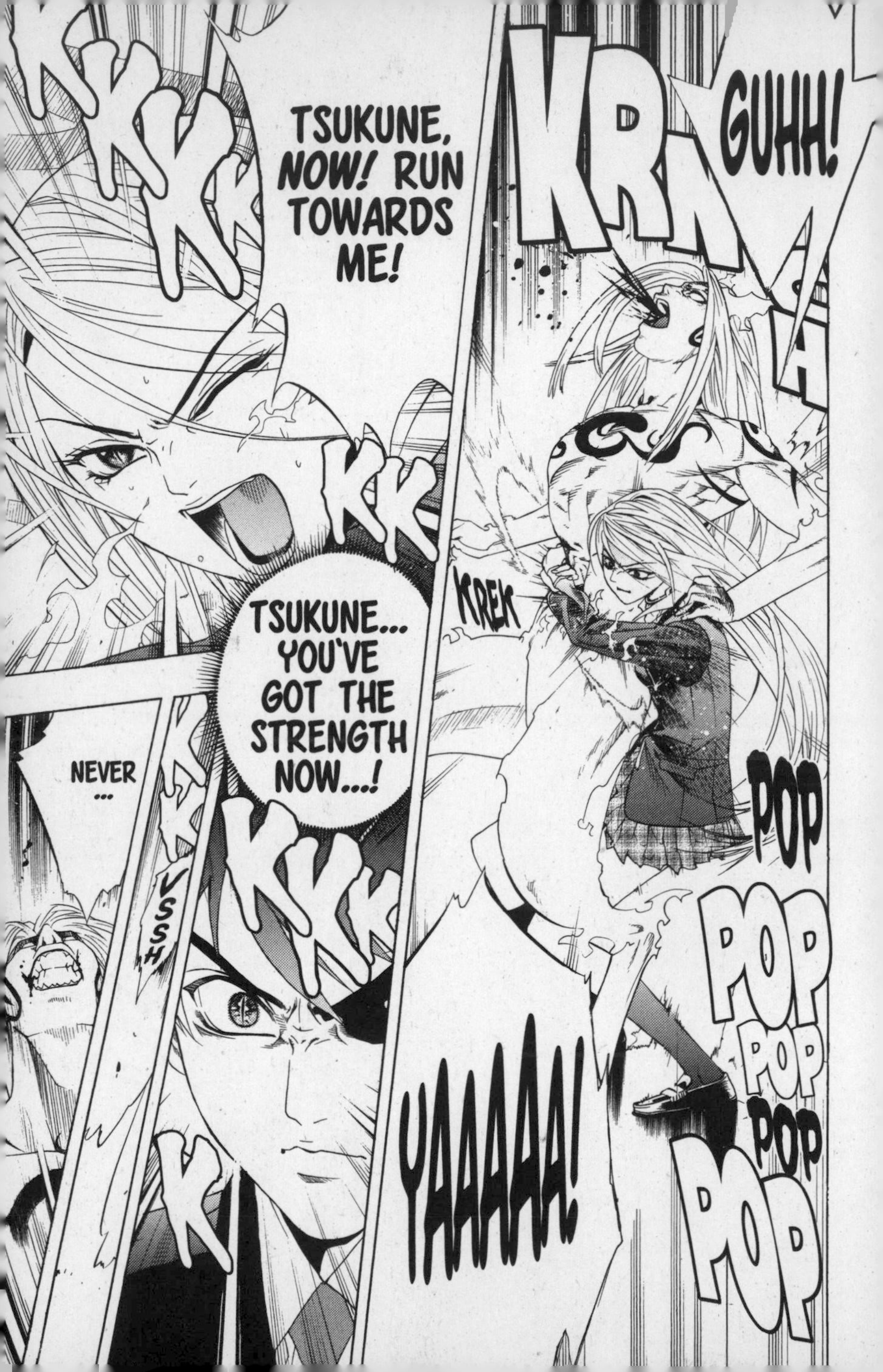
GUHH!
KREK
POP
POP
POP
POP
POP
YAAAAA!
TSUKUNE, NOW! RUN TOWARDS ME!
KKK
KK
TSUKUNE... YOU'VE GOT THE STRENGTH NOW...!
NEVER ...
VSSH
KKK
KK

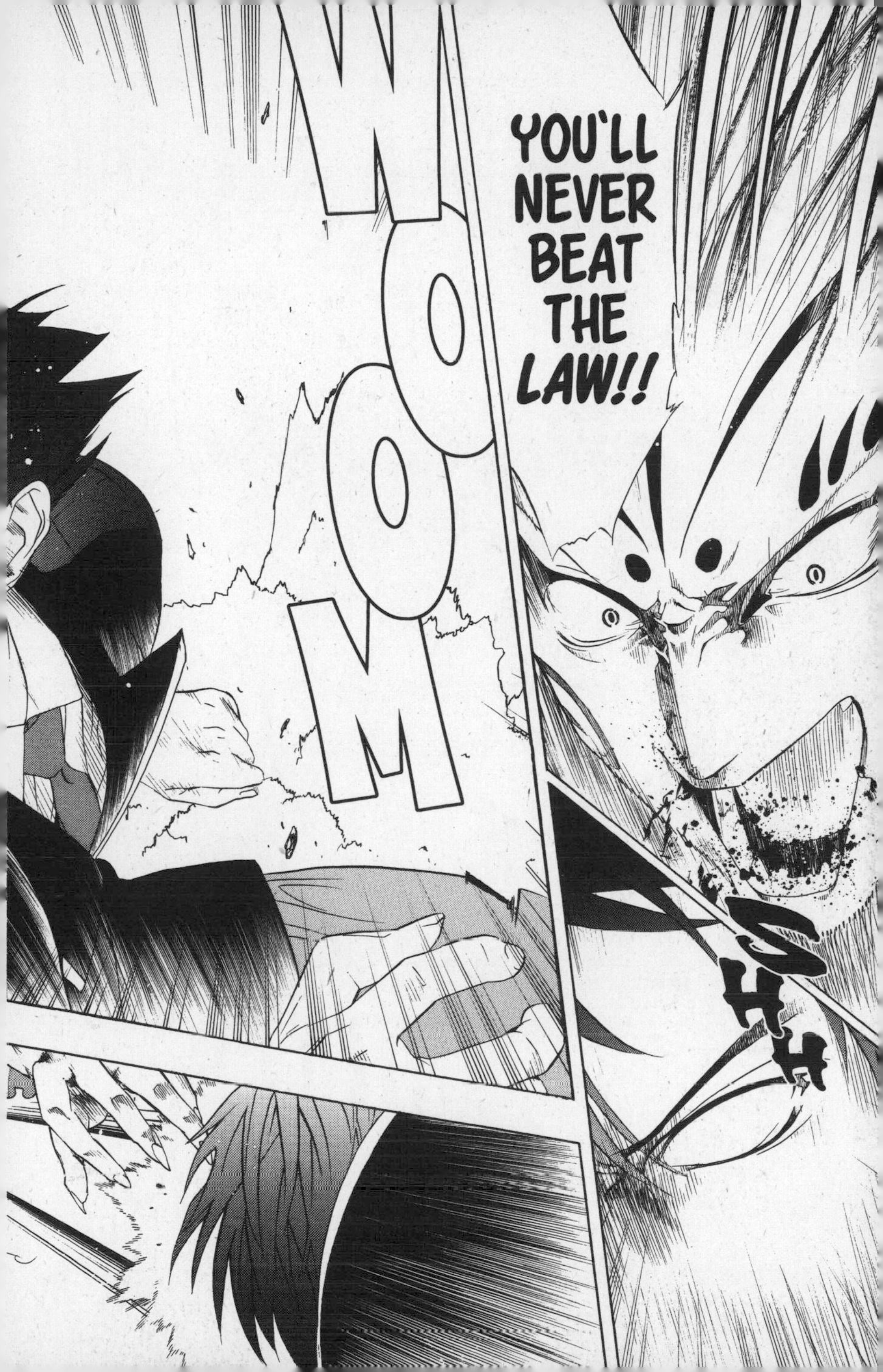
YOU'LL NEVER BEAT THE LAW!!

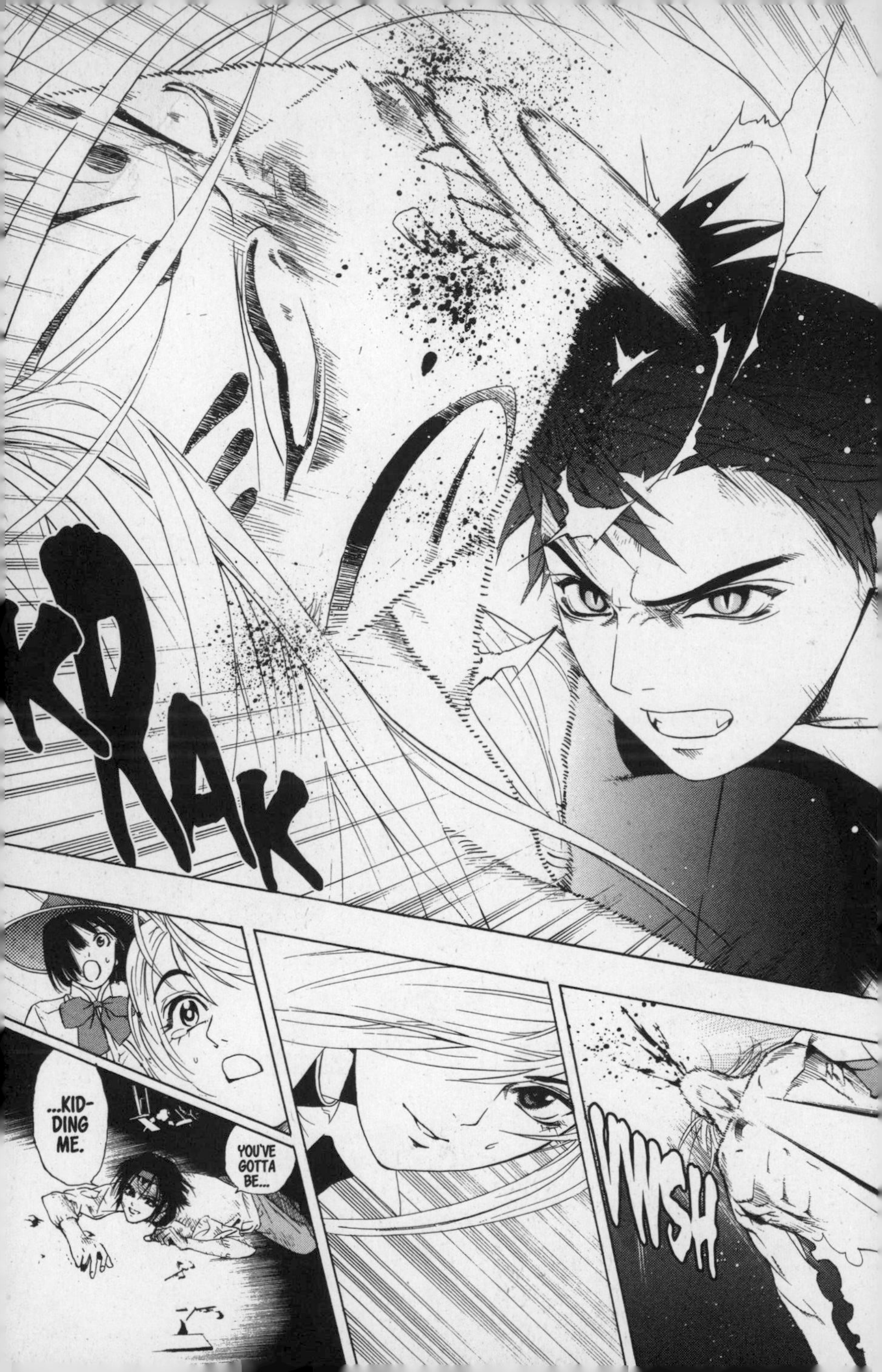
KRAK
VWSH
YOU'VE GOTTA BE...
...KID-DING ME.

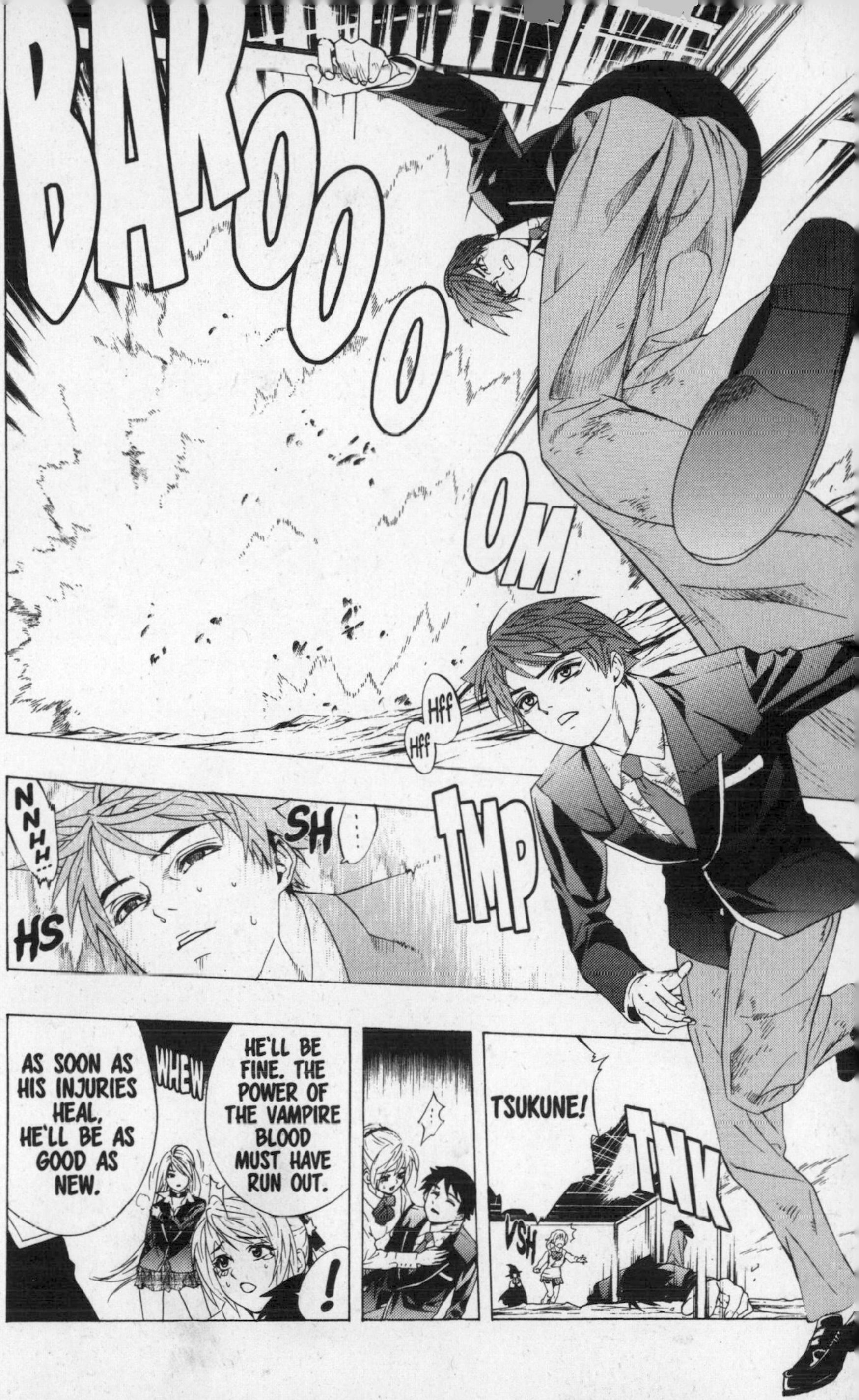
BAKOOOOOOM
Hff
Hff
TMP
SH
...
NNHH!!
HS
TSUKUNE!
TNK
VSH
!..
HE'LL BE FINE. THE POWER OF THE VAMPIRE BLOOD MUST HAVE RUN OUT.
WHEW
AS SOON AS HIS INJURIES HEAL, HE'LL BE AS GOOD AS NEW.
!

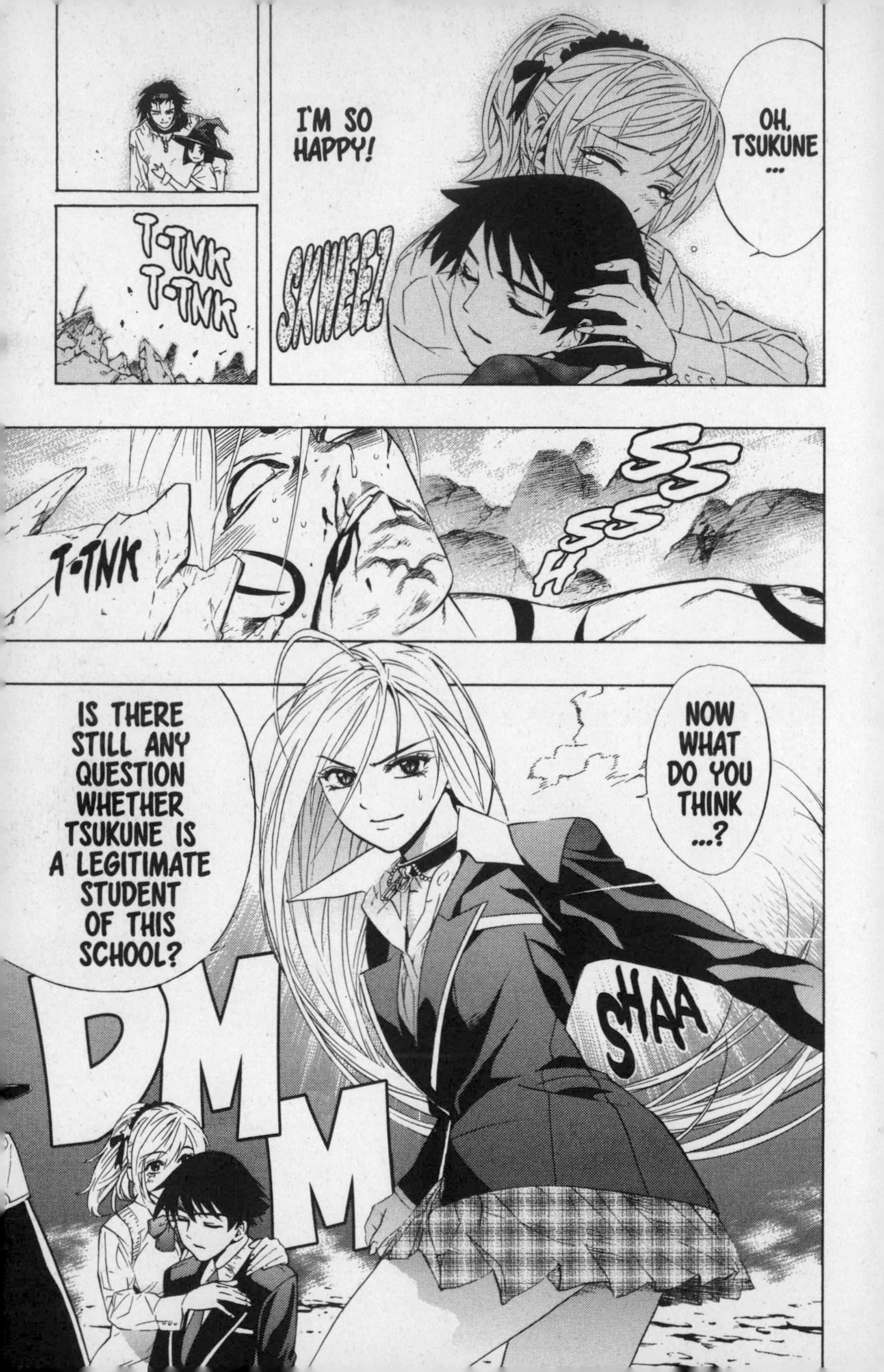
OH, TSUKUNE ...
I'M SO HAPPY!
SKWEEZ
T-TNK T-TNK
SSSSH
T-TNK
NOW WHAT DO YOU THINK ...?
IS THERE STILL ANY QUESTION WHETHER TSUKUNE IS A LEGITIMATE STUDENT OF THIS SCHOOL?
SHAA
DMMM

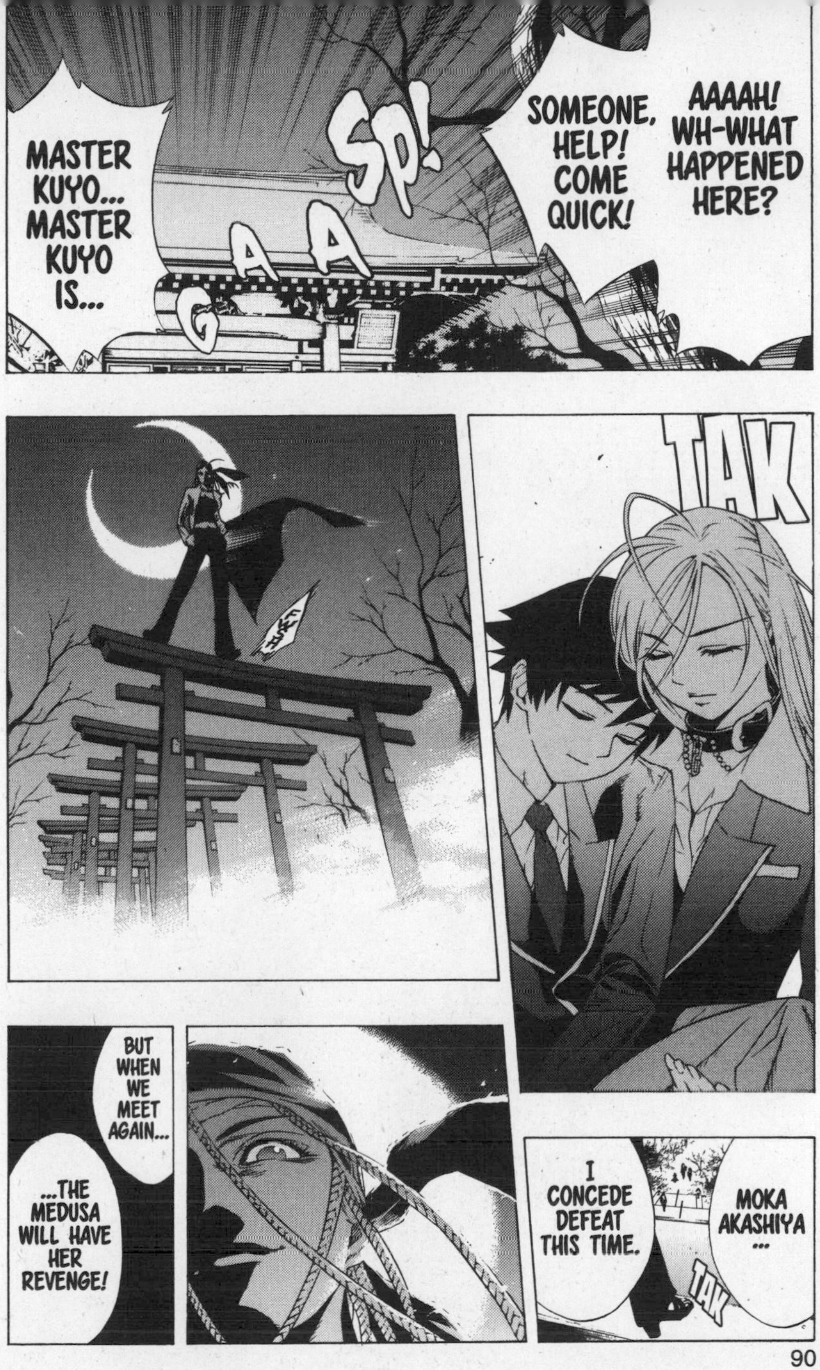
AAAAH! WH-WHAT HAPPENED HERE?
SOMEONE, HELP! COME QUICK!
GAASP!
MASTER KUYO... MASTER KUYO IS...
TAK
MOKA AKASHIYA ...
I CONCEDE DEFEAT THIS TIME.
TAK
BUT WHEN WE MEET AGAIN...
...THE MEDUSA WILL HAVE HER REVENGE!

11: Blood

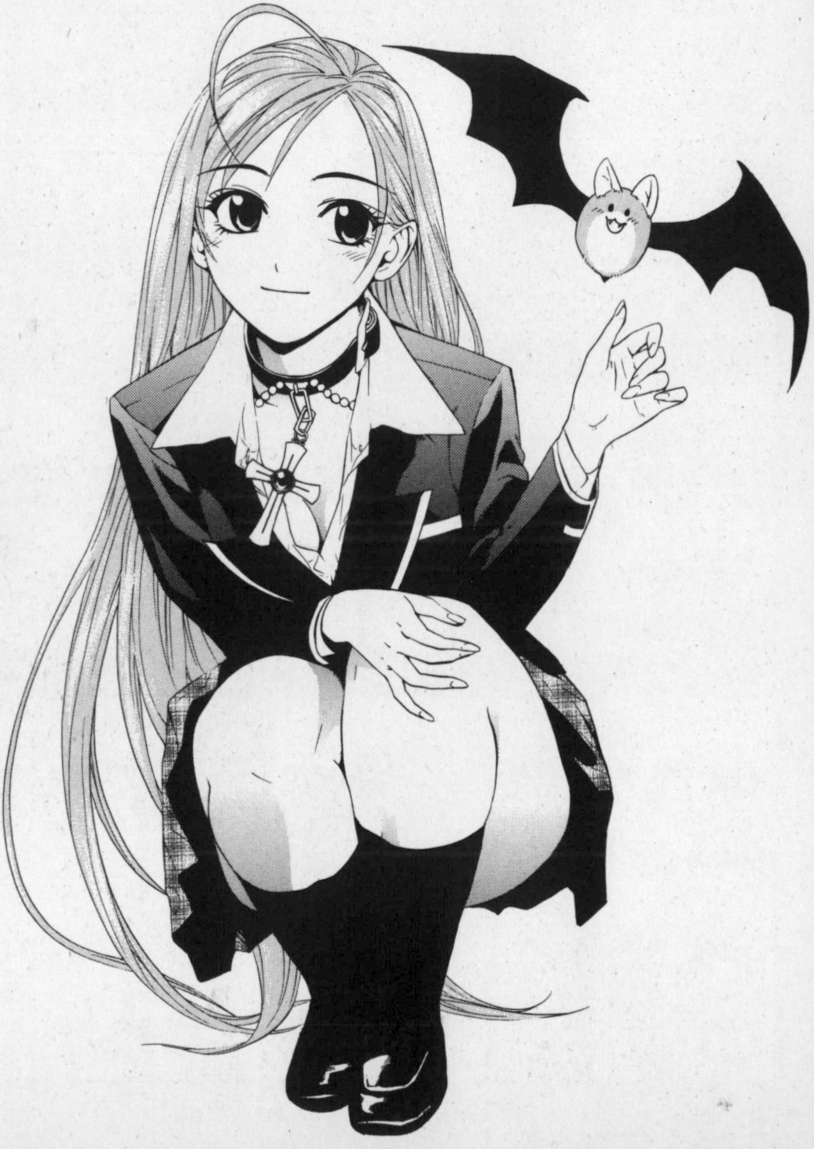

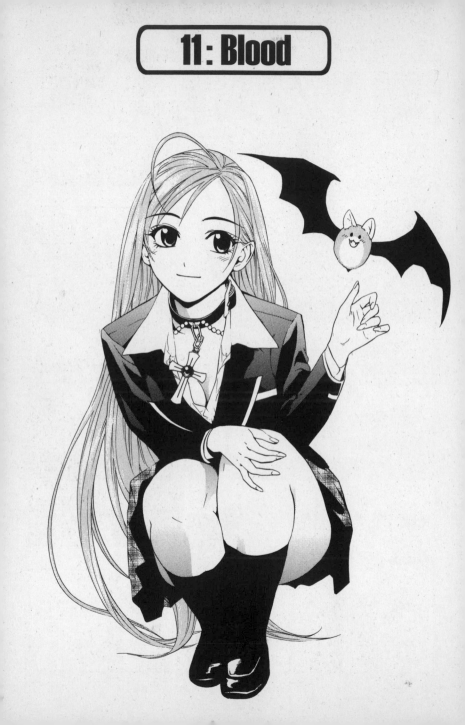

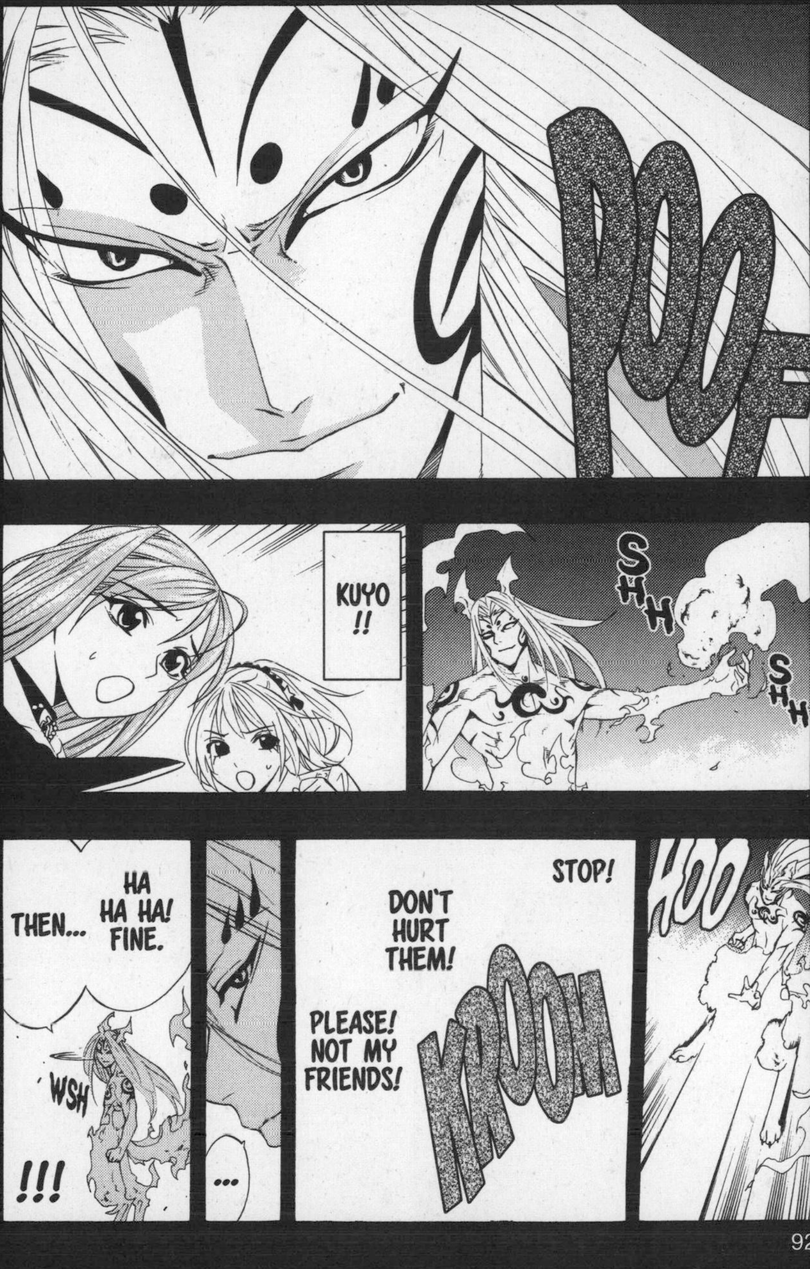
POOF
SHH
SHH
KUYO !!
HOO
STOP!
DON'T HURT THEM!
KROOOM
PLEASE! NOT MY FRIENDS!
...
HA HA HA! FINE.
THEN...
WSH
!!!

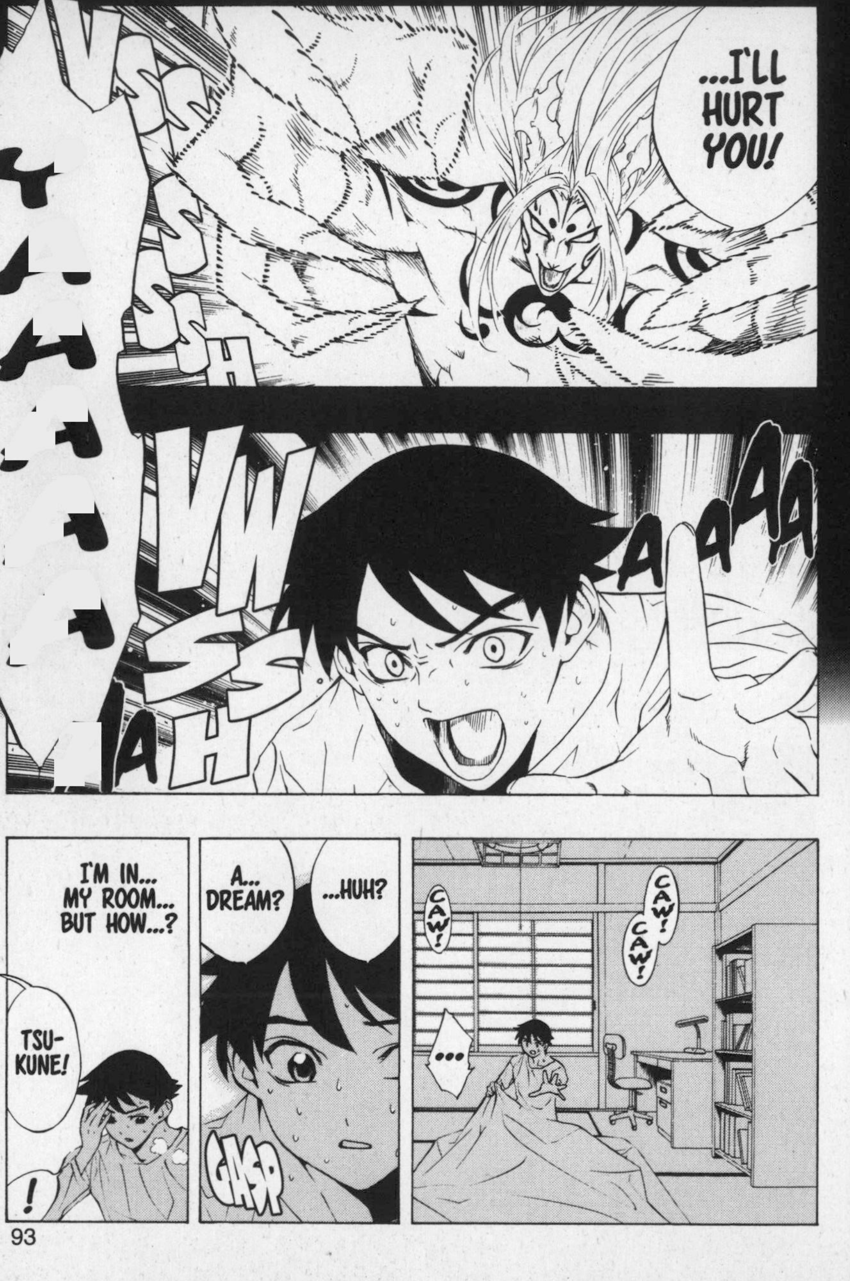
...I'LL HURT YOU!
VWSSH
AAAAA
CAW! CAW!
CAW!
...
...HUH?
A... DREAM?
GASP
I'M IN... MY ROOM... BUT HOW...?
TSU-KUNE!
!

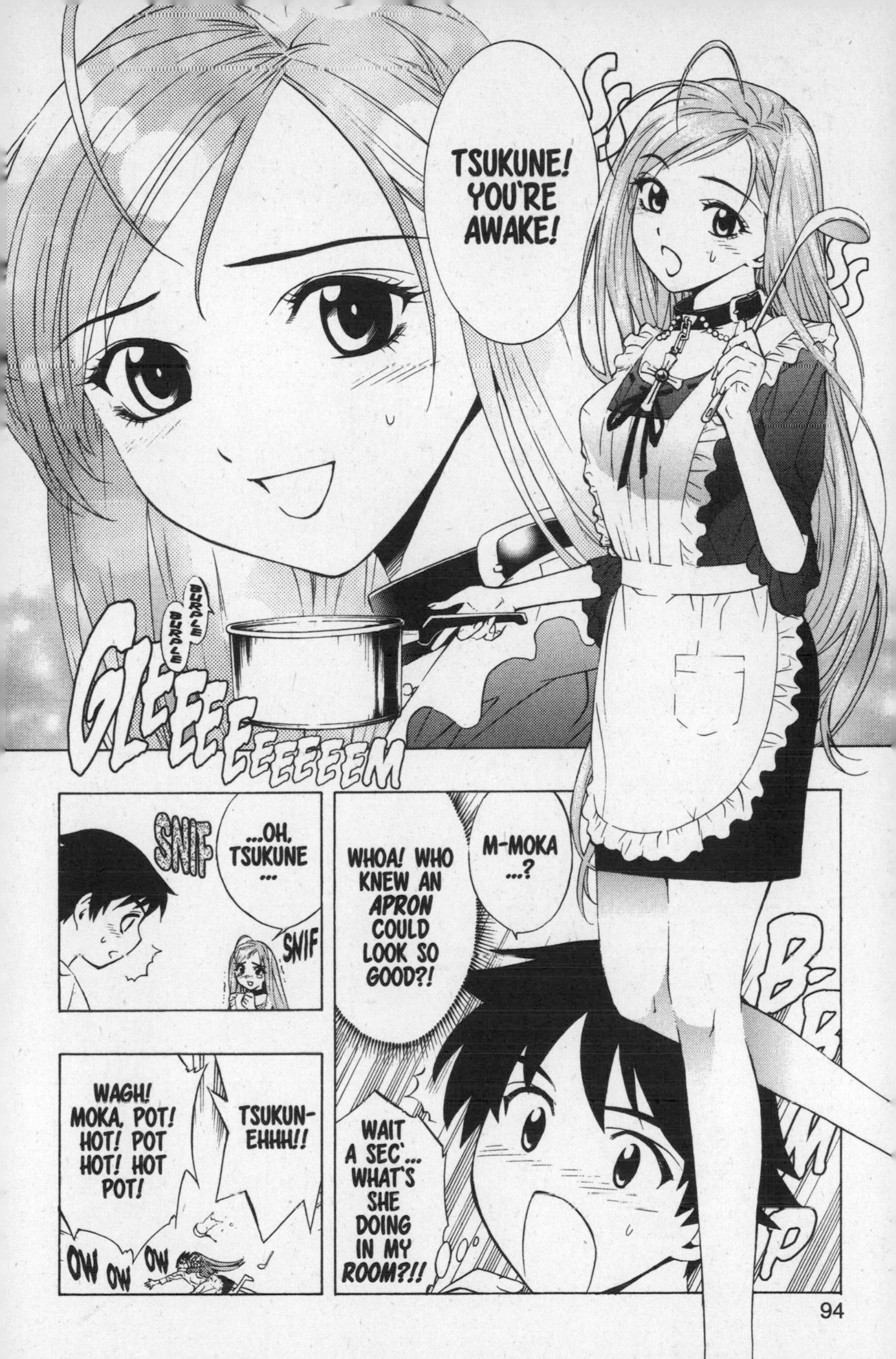
TSUKUNE! YOU'RE AWAKE!
BURPLE
BURPLE
GLEEEEEEEEEM
M-MOKA ...?
WHOA! WHO KNEW AN APRON COULD LOOK SO GOOD?!
WAIT A SEC'... WHAT'S SHE DOING IN MY ROOM?!!
SNIF
...OH, TSUKUNE ...
SNIF
TSUKUN-EHHH!!
WAGH! MOKA, POT! HOT! POT HOT! HOT POT!
OW OW OW

READ THIS WAY

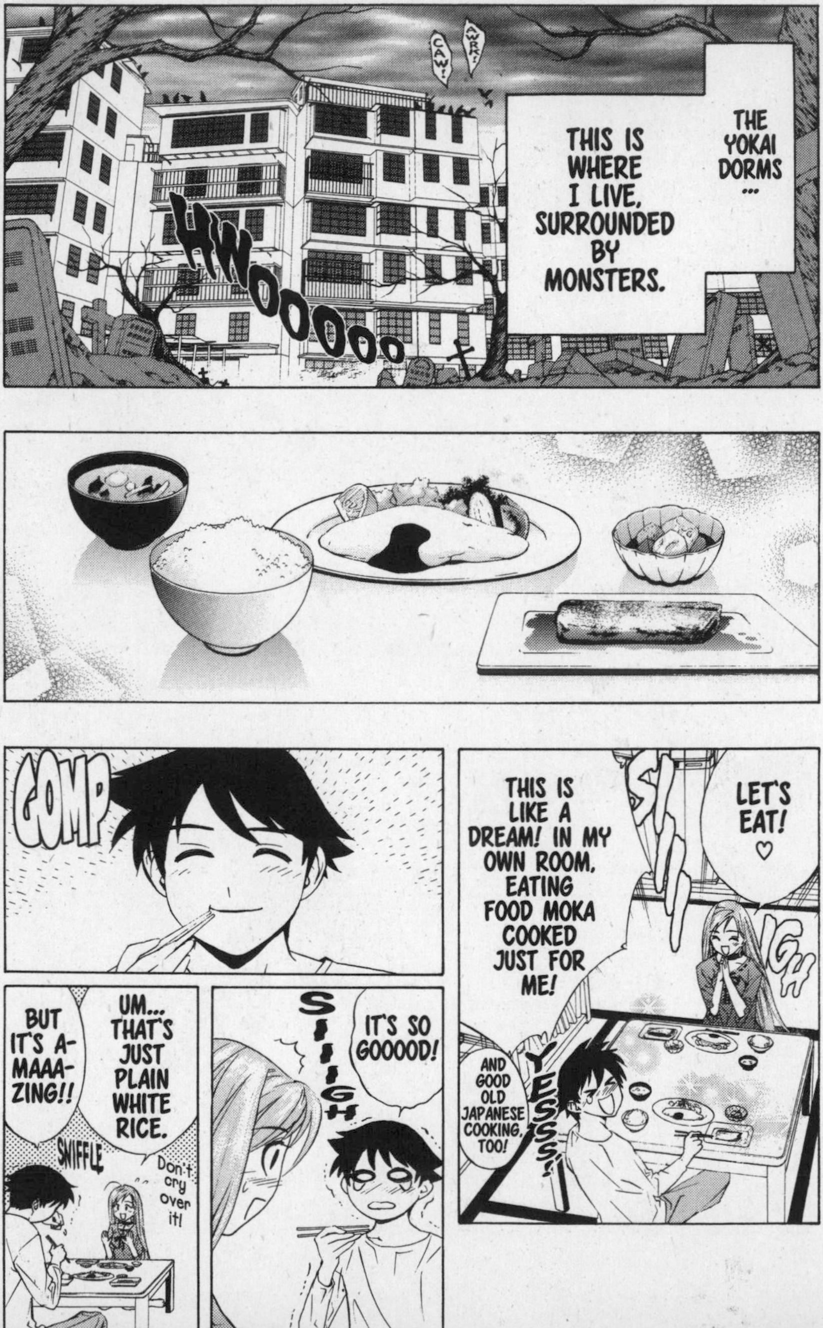
AWRK!
CAW!
THE YOKAI DORMS...
THIS IS WHERE I LIVE, SURROUNDED BY MONSTERS.
HWOOOOOO
LET'S EAT! ♡
SIGH
THIS IS LIKE A DREAM! IN MY OWN ROOM, EATING FOOD MOKA COOKED JUST FOR ME!
YESSS!
AND GOOD OLD JAPANESE COOKING, TOO!
GOMP
IT'S SO GOOOOD!
SIGH
UM... THAT'S JUST PLAIN WHITE RICE.
BUT IT'S A-MAAAZING!!
SNIFFLE
Don't cry over it!

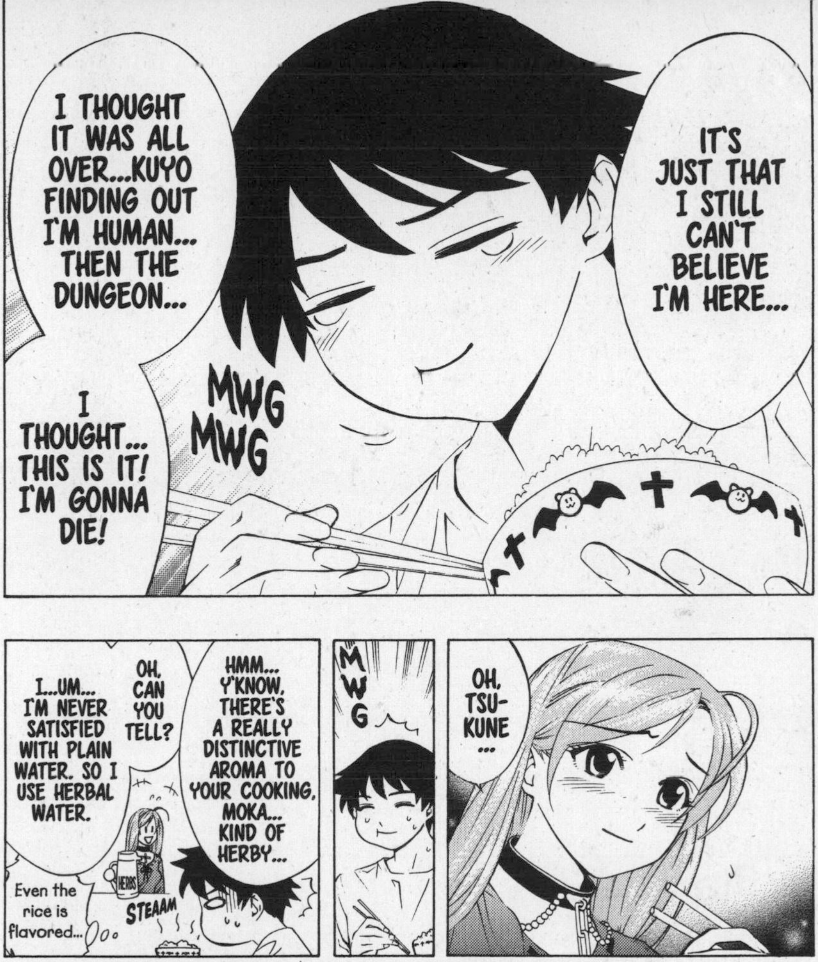
IT'S JUST THAT I STILL CAN'T BELIEVE I'M HERE...
I THOUGHT IT WAS ALL OVER...KUYO FINDING OUT I'M HUMAN... THEN THE DUNGEON...
MWG MWG
I THOUGHT... THIS IS IT! I'M GONNA DIE!
OH, TSU-KUNE...
MWG
HMM... Y'KNOW, THERE'S A REALLY DISTINCTIVE AROMA TO YOUR COOKING, MOKA... KIND OF HERBY...
OH, CAN YOU TELL?
I...UM... I'M NEVER SATISFIED WITH PLAIN WATER. SO I USE HERBAL WATER.
HERBS
STEAAM
Even the rice is flavored...

*NOTE: VAMPIRES CAN'T TOLERATE PURE WATER (SEE VOL. 1).

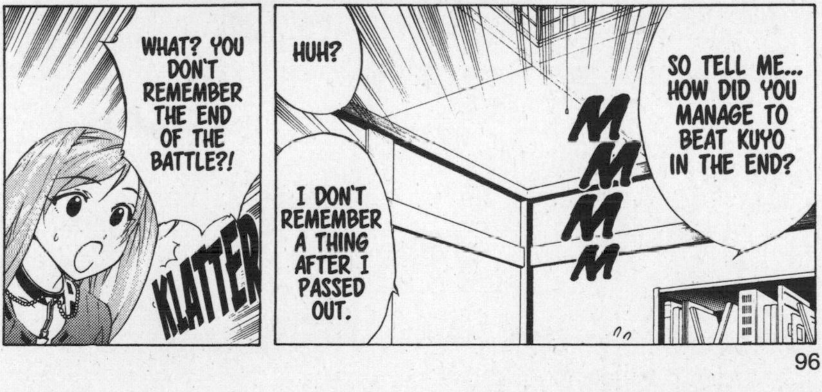
SO TELL ME... HOW DID YOU MANAGE TO BEAT KUYO IN THE END?
HUH?
I DON'T REMEMBER A THING AFTER I PASSED OUT.
M.M.M.M.M
WHAT? YOU DON'T REMEMBER THE END OF THE BATTLE?!
KLATTER

READ THIS WAY

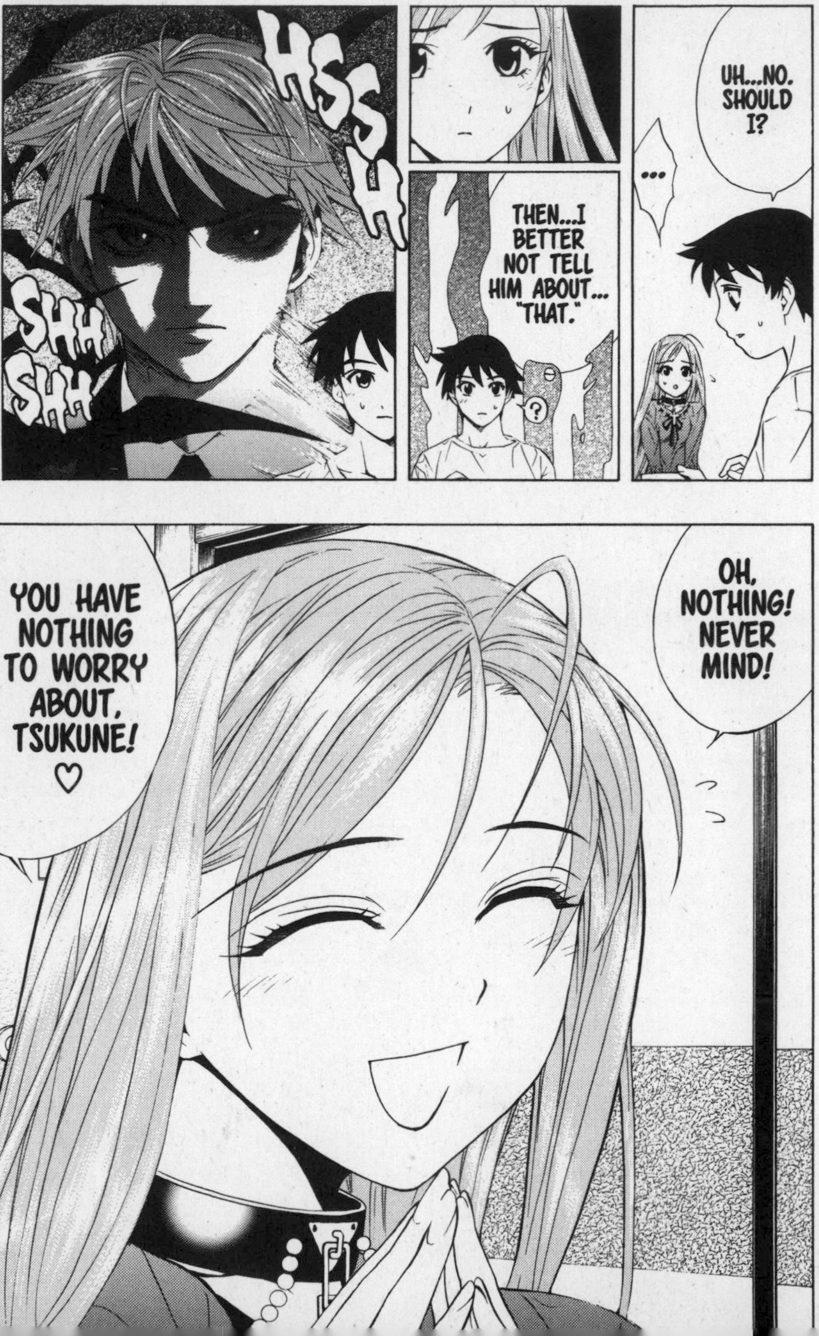
UH...NO. SHOULD I?
...
THEN...I BETTER NOT TELL HIM ABOUT... "THAT."
?
HSSSH
SHH SHH
OH, NOTHING! NEVER MIND!
YOU HAVE NOTHING TO WORRY ABOUT, TSUKUNE! ♡

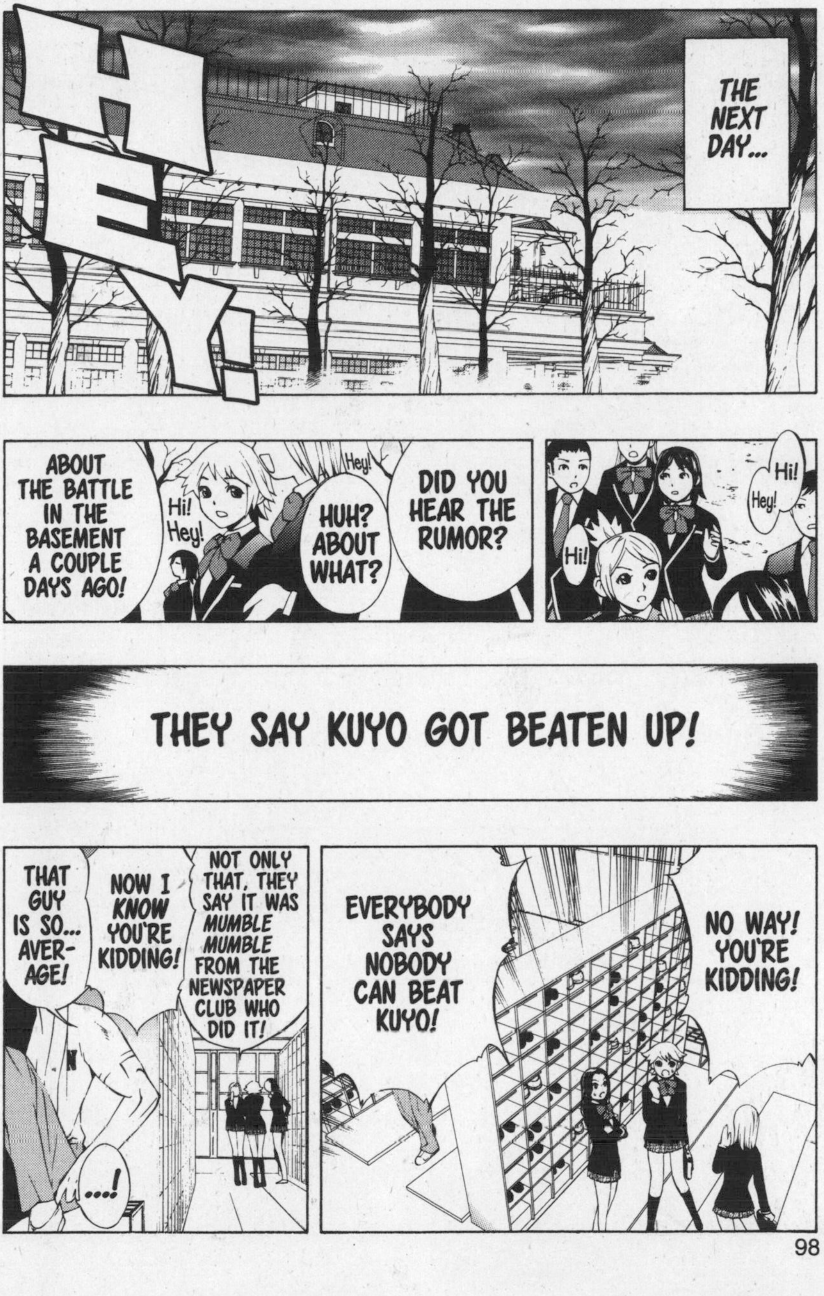
THE NEXT DAY...
HEY!
Hi!
Hey!
Hi!
DID YOU HEAR THE RUMOR?
Hey!
HUH? ABOUT WHAT?
Hi! Hey!
ABOUT THE BATTLE IN THE BASEMENT A COUPLE DAYS AGO!
THEY SAY KUYO GOT BEATEN UP!
NO WAY! YOU'RE KIDDING!
EVERYBODY SAYS NOBODY CAN BEAT KUYO!
NOT ONLY THAT, THEY SAY IT WAS MUMBLE MUMBLE FROM THE NEWSPAPER CLUB WHO DID IT!
NOW I KNOW YOU'RE KIDDING!
THAT GUY IS SO... AVER-AGE!
...!

READ THIS WAY

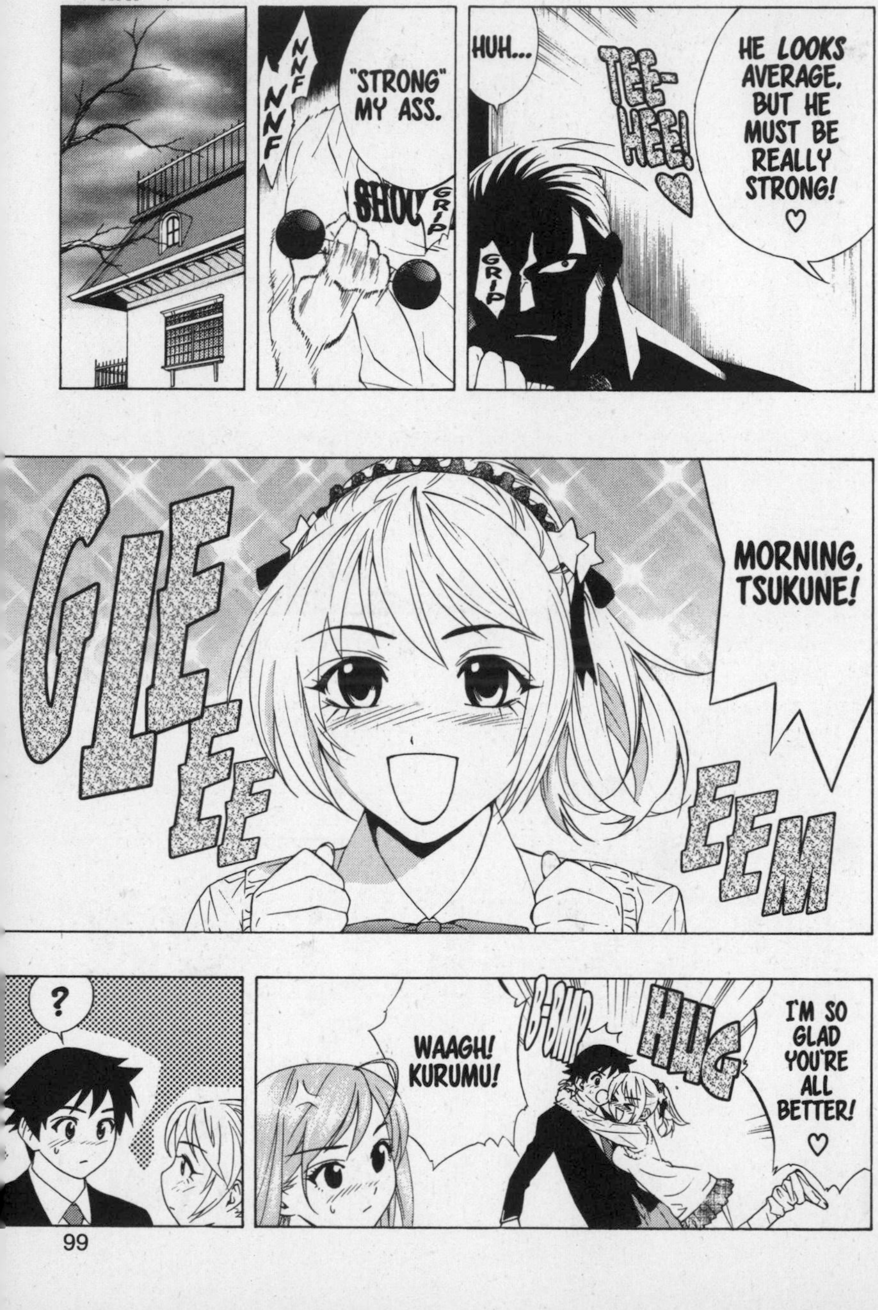
HE LOOKS AVERAGE, BUT HE MUST BE REALLY STRONG! ♡
TEE-HEE! ♡
HUH...
GRIP
"STRONG" MY ASS.
NNF NNF
SHOO
GRIP
MORNING, TSUKUNE!
GLEEEEEEM
I'M SO GLAD YOU'RE ALL BETTER! ♡
HUG
WAAGH! KURUMU!
?

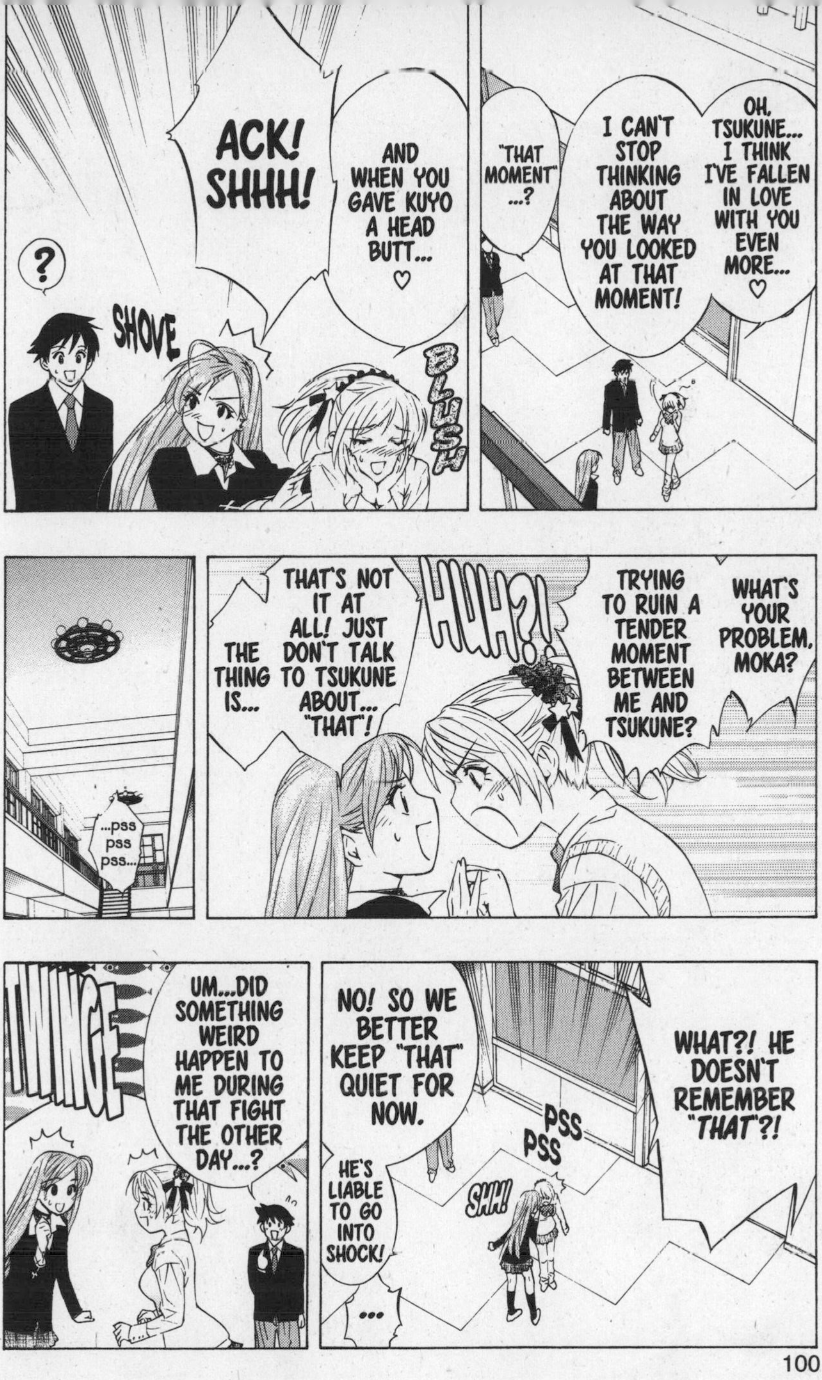
OH, TSUKUNE... I THINK I'VE FALLEN IN LOVE WITH YOU EVEN MORE... ♡
I CAN'T STOP THINKING ABOUT THE WAY YOU LOOKED AT THAT MOMENT!
"THAT MOMENT" ...?
AND WHEN YOU GAVE KUYO A HEAD BUTT... ♡
BLUSH
ACK! SHHH!
SHOVE
?
WHAT'S YOUR PROBLEM, MOKA?
TRYING TO RUIN A TENDER MOMENT BETWEEN ME AND TSUKUNE?
HUH?!
THAT'S NOT IT AT ALL! JUST DON'T TALK TO TSUKUNE ABOUT... "THAT"!
THE THING IS...
...pss pss pss...
WHAT?! HE DOESN'T REMEMBER "THAT"?!
PSS PSS
SHH!
NO! SO WE BETTER KEEP "THAT" QUIET FOR NOW.
HE'S LIABLE TO GO INTO SHOCK!
...
UM...DID SOMETHING WEIRD HAPPEN TO ME DURING THAT FIGHT THE OTHER DAY...?
TWINGE

READ THIS WAY

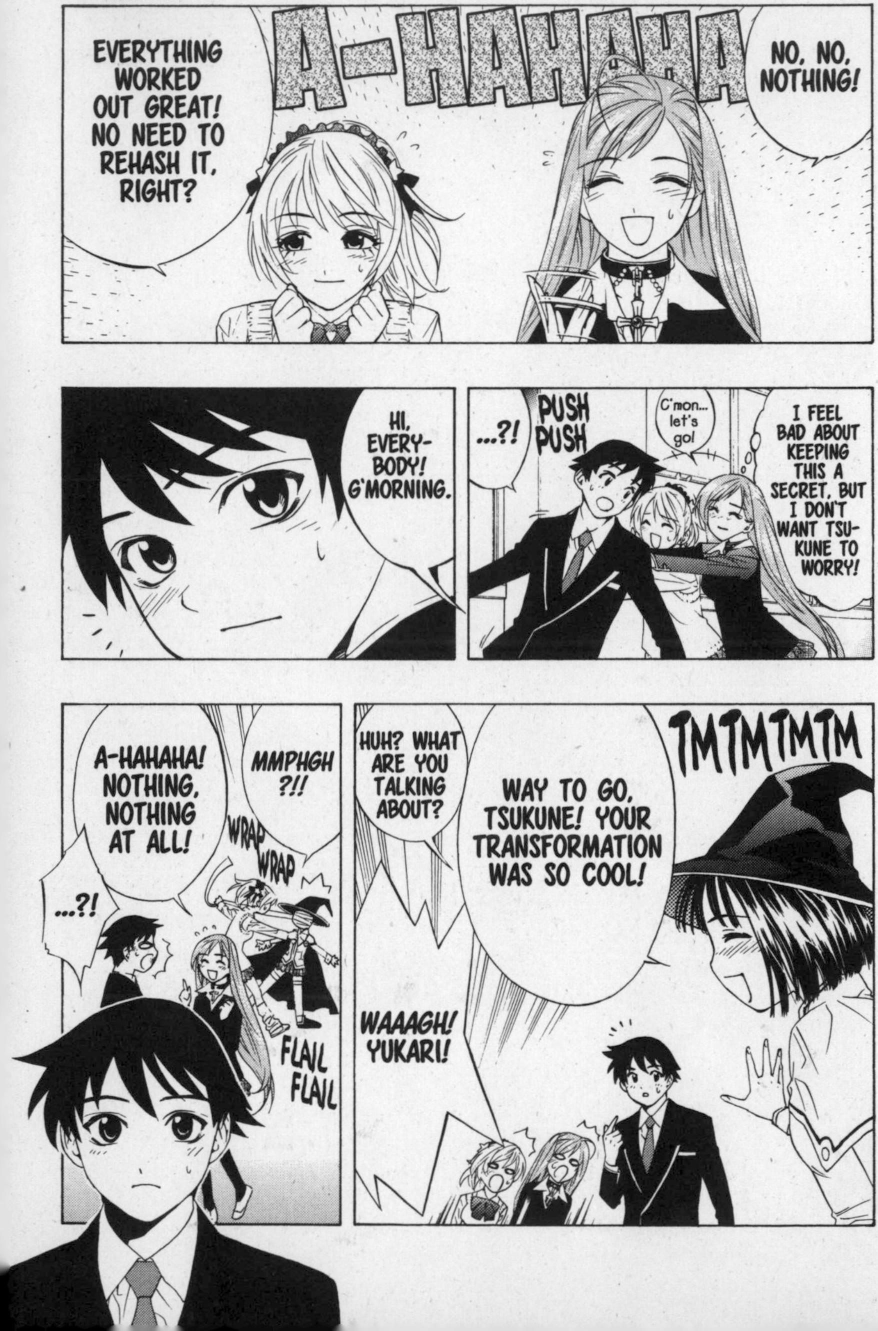
NO, NO, NOTHING!
A-HAHAHA
EVERYTHING WORKED OUT GREAT! NO NEED TO REHASH IT, RIGHT?
I FEEL BAD ABOUT KEEPING THIS A SECRET, BUT I DON'T WANT TSUKUNE TO WORRY!
C'mon... let's go!
PUSH PUSH
...?!
HI, EVERYBODY! G'MORNING.
TMTMTMTM
WAY TO GO, TSUKUNE! YOUR TRANSFORMATION WAS SO COOL!
HUH? WHAT ARE YOU TALKING ABOUT?
WAAAGH! YUKARI!
MMPHGH ?!!
A-HAHAHA! NOTHING, NOTHING AT ALL!
WRAP WRAP
...?!
FLAIL FLAIL

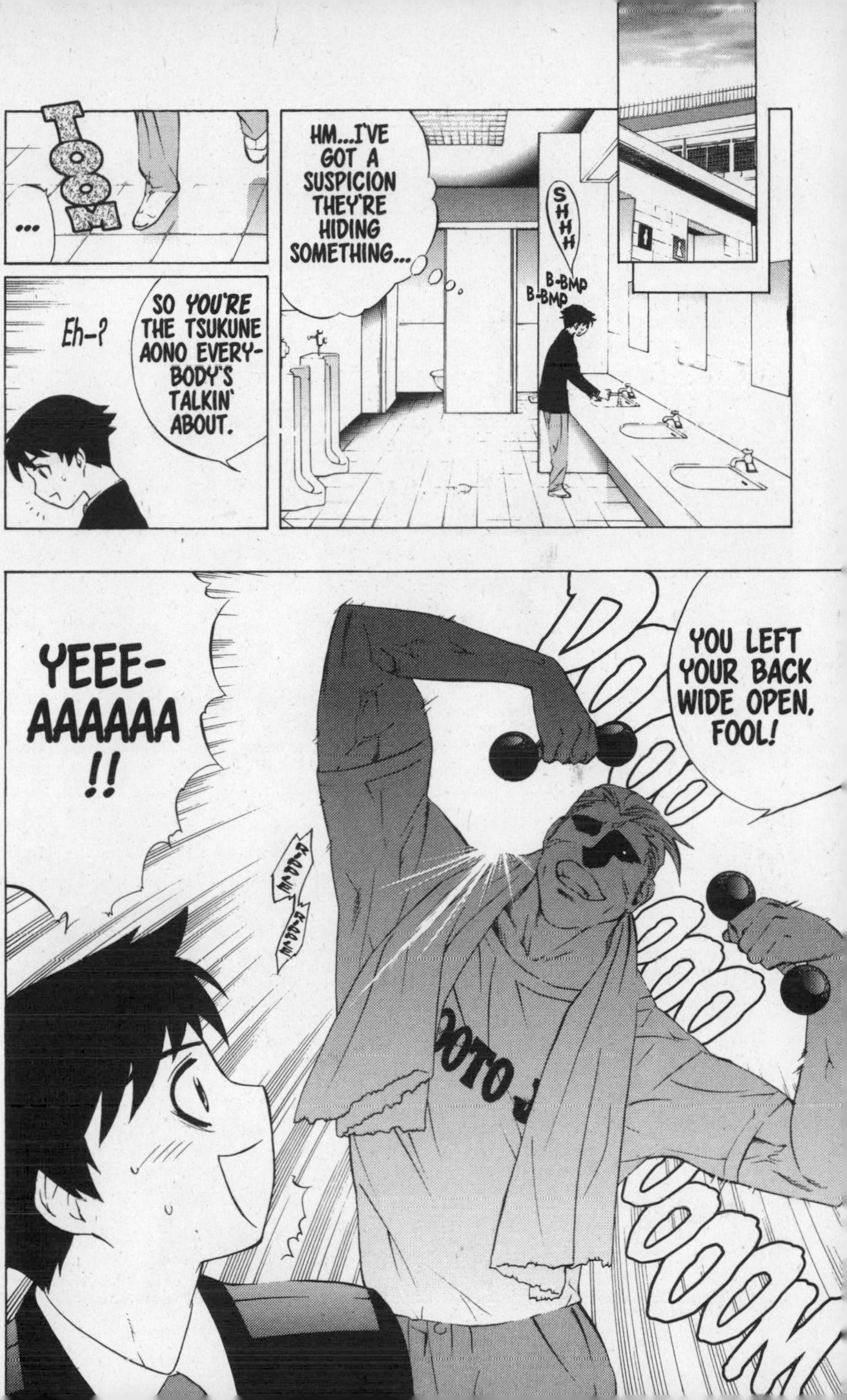
SHHH
B-BMP B-BMP
HM...I'VE GOT A SUSPICION THEY'RE HIDING SOMETHING...
TOOM
...
SO YOU'RE THE TSUKUNE AONO EVERY-BODY'S TALKIN' ABOUT.
Eh-?
YOU LEFT YOUR BACK WIDE OPEN, FOOL!
DOOOOOOOOOOOOOM
RIDDLE RIDDLE
YEEE-AAAAAA!!

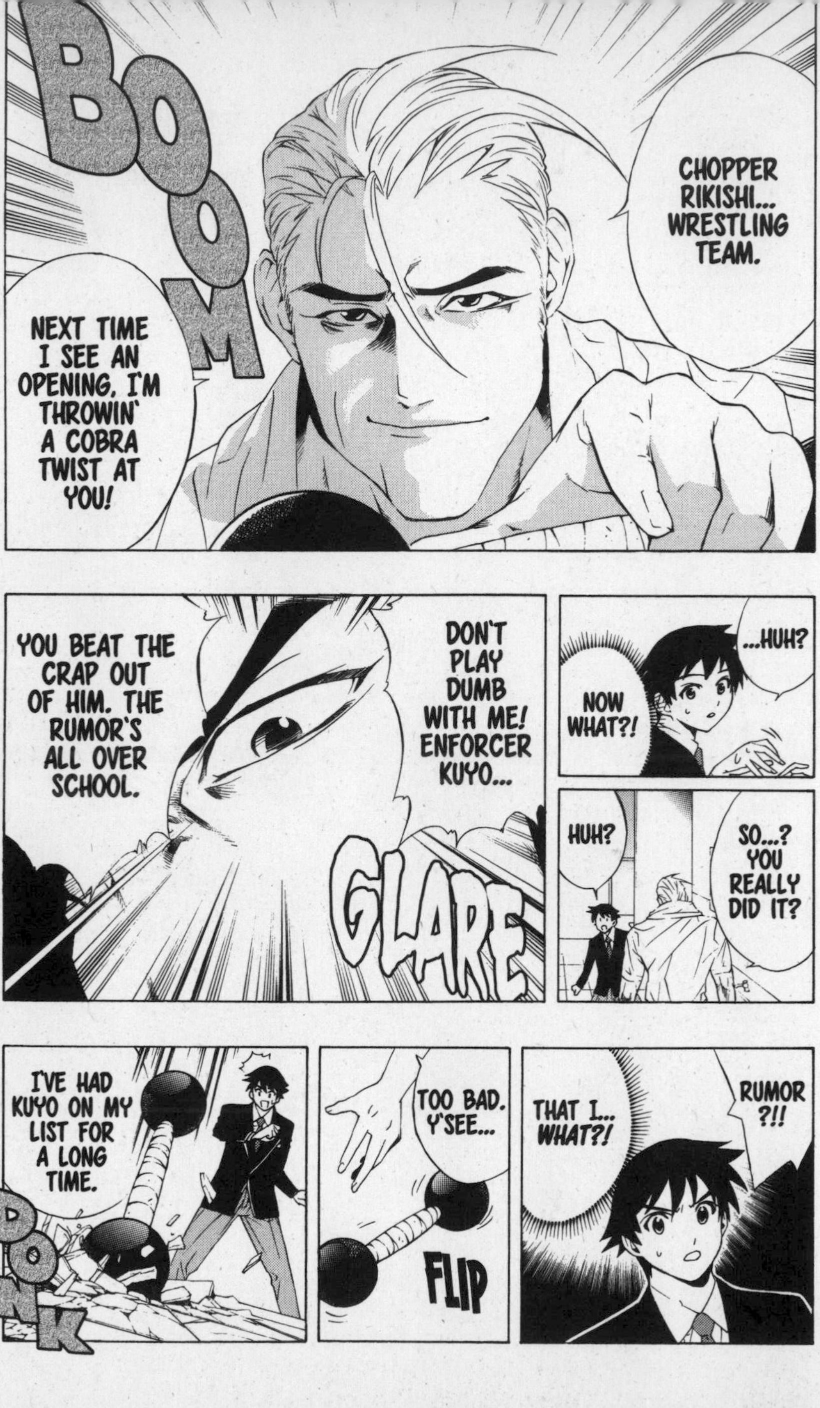
CHOPPER RIKISHI... WRESTLING TEAM.
BOOM
NEXT TIME I SEE AN OPENING, I'M THROWIN' A COBRA TWIST AT YOU!
...HUH?
NOW WHAT?!
SO...? YOU REALLY DID IT?
HUH?
DON'T PLAY DUMB WITH ME! ENFORCER KUYO...
GLARE
YOU BEAT THE CRAP OUT OF HIM. THE RUMOR'S ALL OVER SCHOOL.
RUMOR?!!
THAT I... WHAT?!
TOO BAD. Y'SEE...
FLIP
I'VE HAD KUYO ON MY LIST FOR A LONG TIME.
DONK

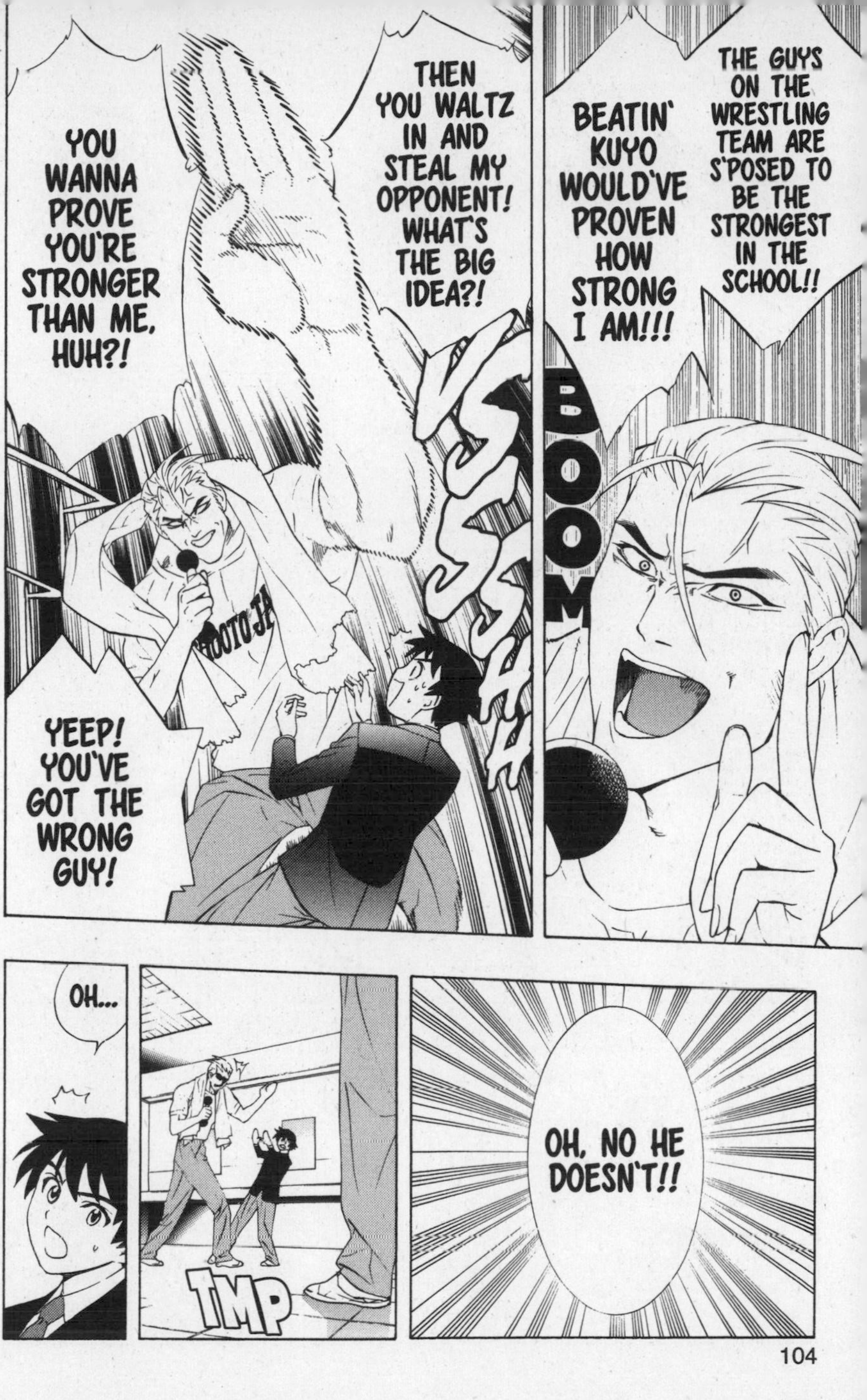
THE GUYS ON THE WRESTLING TEAM ARE S'POSED TO BE THE STRONGEST IN THE SCHOOL!!
BEATIN' KUYO WOULD'VE PROVEN HOW STRONG I AM!!!
BOOM
THEN YOU WALTZ IN AND STEAL MY OPPONENT! WHAT'S THE BIG IDEA?!
YOU WANNA PROVE YOU'RE STRONGER THAN ME, HUH?!
YEEP! YOU'VE GOT THE WRONG GUY!
OH, NO HE DOESN'T!!
TMP
OH...

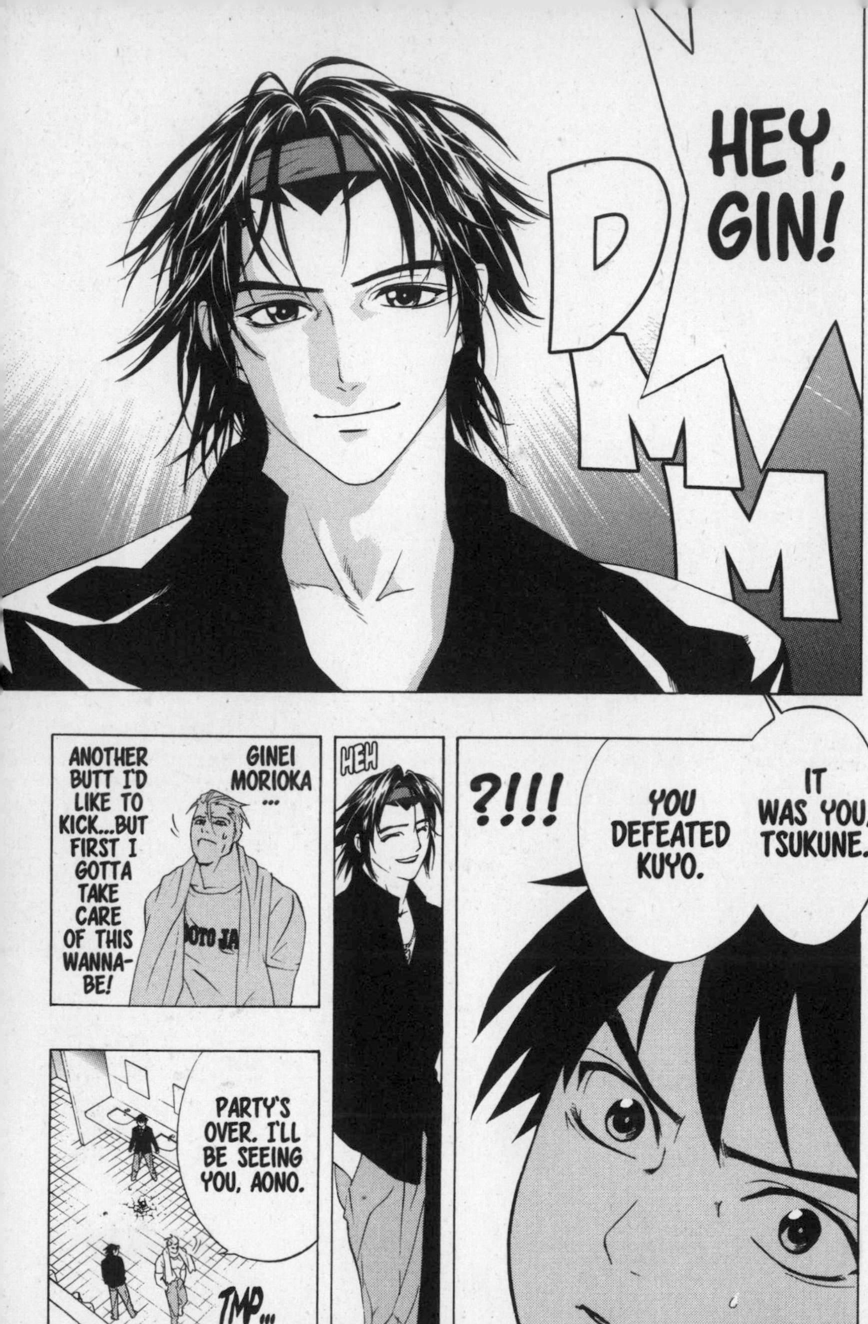
HEY, GIN!
DMMM
IT WAS YOU, TSUKUNE.
YOU DEFEATED KUYO.
?!!!
HEH
GINEI MORIOKA...
ANOTHER BUTT I'D LIKE TO KICK...BUT FIRST I GOTTA TAKE CARE OF THIS WANNA-BE!
PARTY'S OVER. I'LL BE SEEING YOU, AONO.
TMP...

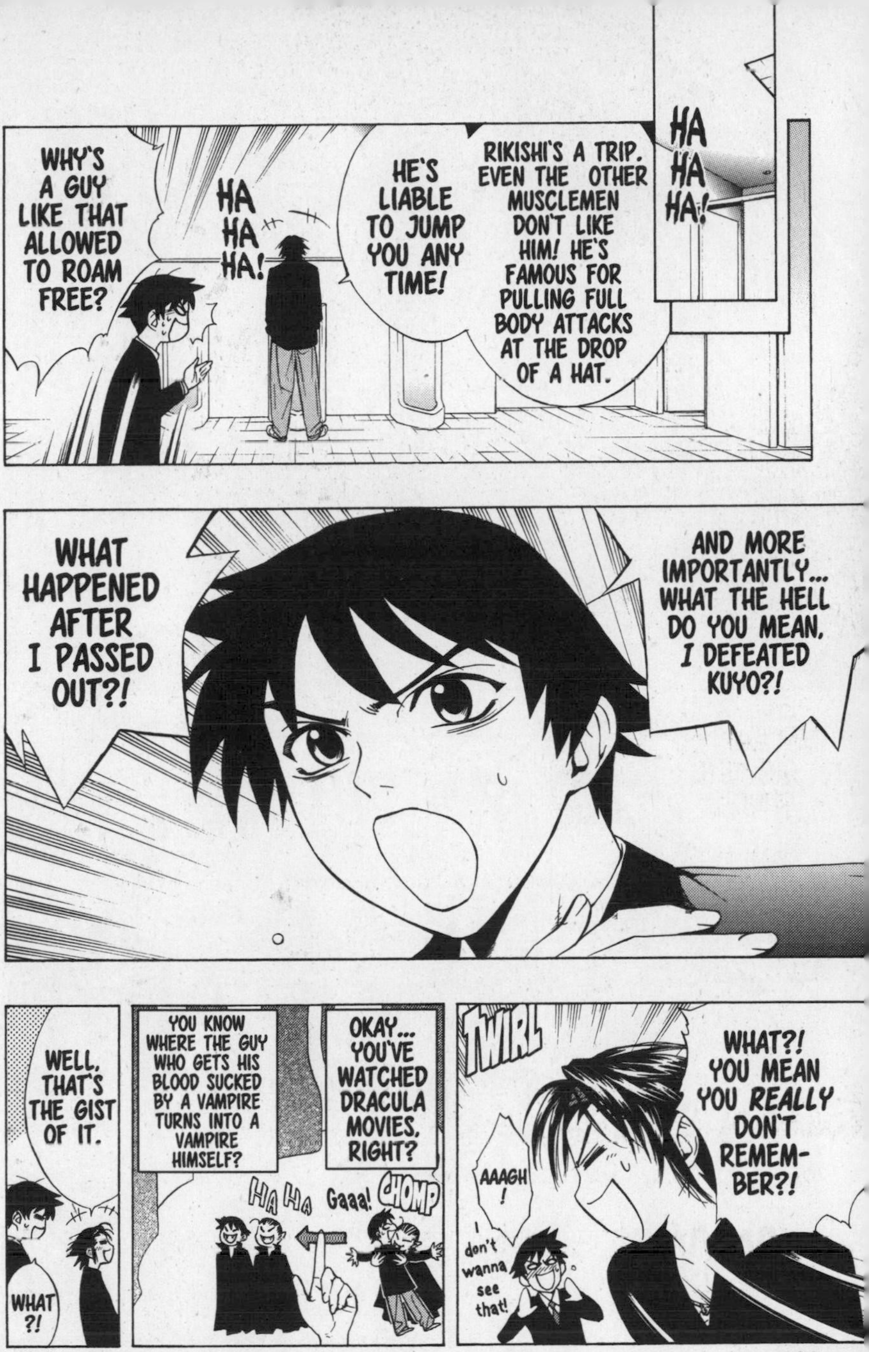
HA HA HA!
RIKISHI'S A TRIP. EVEN THE OTHER MUSCLEMEN DON'T LIKE HIM! HE'S FAMOUS FOR PULLING FULL BODY ATTACKS AT THE DROP OF A HAT.
HE'S LIABLE TO JUMP YOU ANY TIME!
HA HA HA!
WHY'S A GUY LIKE THAT ALLOWED TO ROAM FREE?
AND MORE IMPORTANTLY... WHAT THE HELL DO YOU MEAN, *I* DEFEATED KUYO?!
WHAT HAPPENED AFTER I PASSED OUT?!
TWIRL
WHAT?! YOU MEAN YOU *REALLY* DON'T REMEM-BER?!
AAAGH!
I don't wanna see that!
OKAY... YOU'VE WATCHED DRACULA MOVIES, RIGHT?
YOU KNOW WHERE THE GUY WHO GETS HIS BLOOD SUCKED BY A VAMPIRE TURNS INTO A VAMPIRE HIMSELF?
CHOMP
Gaaa!
HA HA
WELL, THAT'S THE GIST OF IT.
WHAT?!

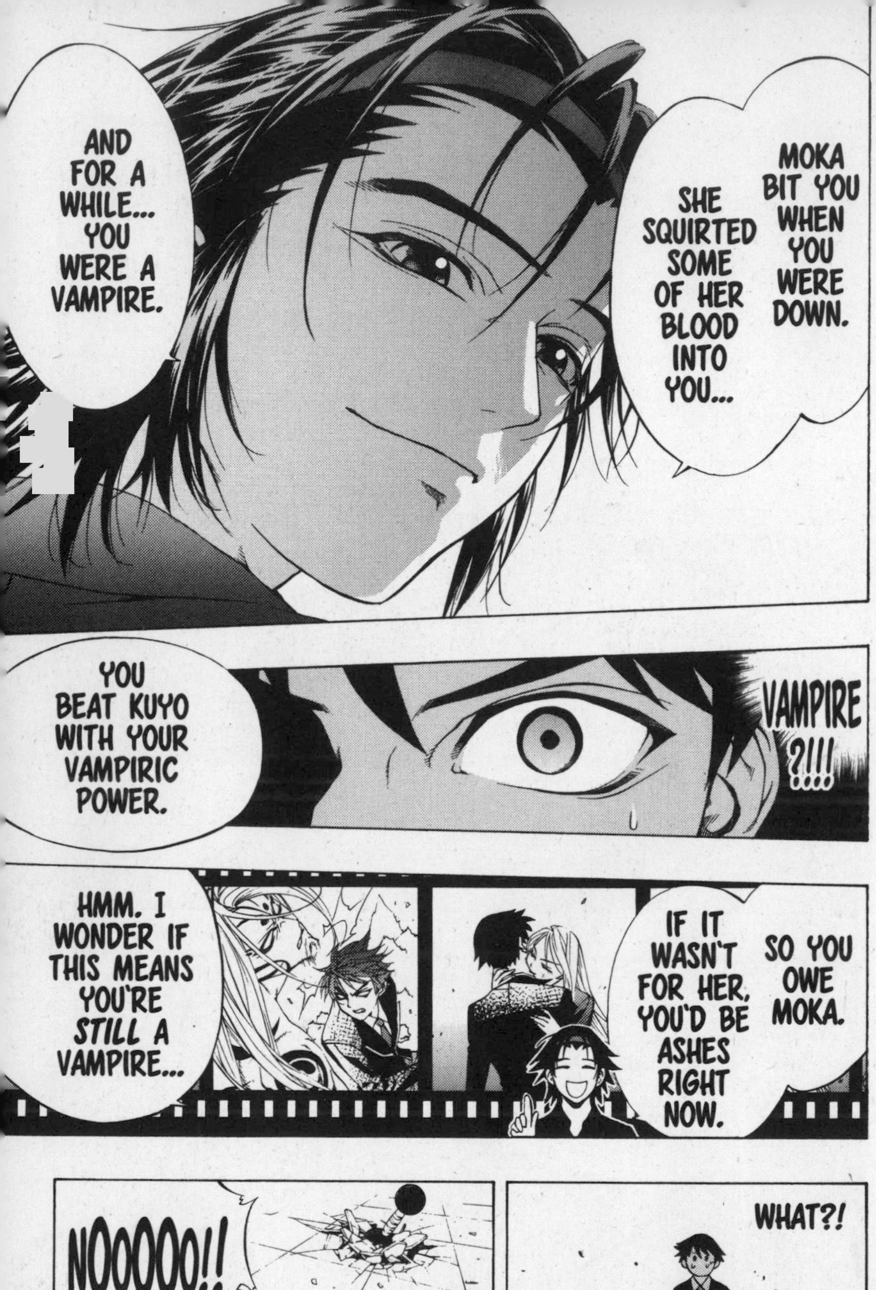
MOKA BIT YOU WHEN YOU WERE DOWN.
SHE SQUIRTED SOME OF HER BLOOD INTO YOU...
AND FOR A WHILE... YOU WERE A VAMPIRE.
VAMPIRE ?!!!
YOU BEAT KUYO WITH YOUR VAMPIRIC POWER.
SO YOU OWE MOKA.
IF IT WASN'T FOR HER, YOU'D BE ASHES RIGHT NOW.
HMM. I WONDER IF THIS MEANS YOU'RE *STILL* A VAMPIRE...
WHAT?!
NOOOOO!!

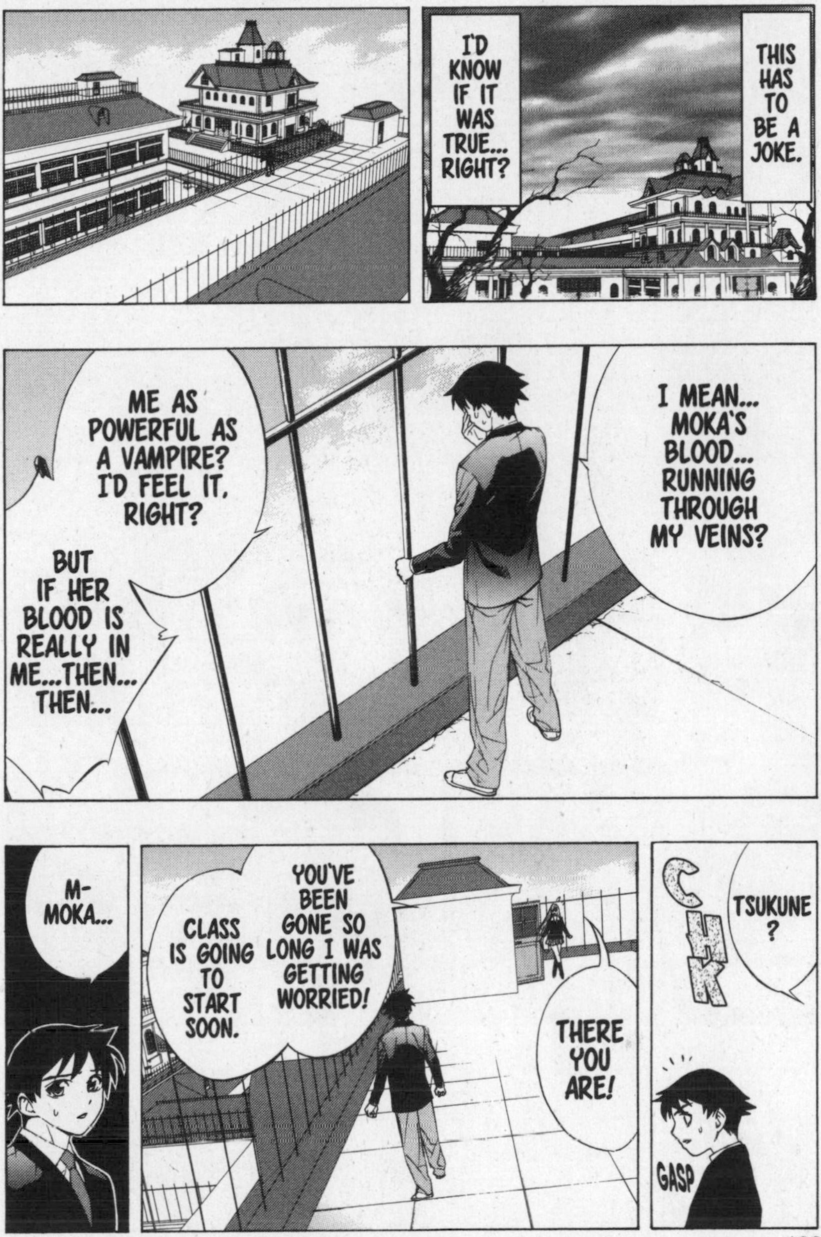
THIS HAS TO BE A JOKE.
I'D KNOW IF IT WAS TRUE... RIGHT?
I MEAN... MOKA'S BLOOD... RUNNING THROUGH MY VEINS?
ME AS POWERFUL AS A VAMPIRE? I'D FEEL IT, RIGHT?
BUT IF HER BLOOD IS REALLY IN ME...THEN... THEN...
CHK
TSUKUNE?
GASP
THERE YOU ARE!
YOU'VE BEEN GONE SO LONG I WAS GETTING WORRIED!
CLASS IS GOING TO START SOON.
M-MOKA...

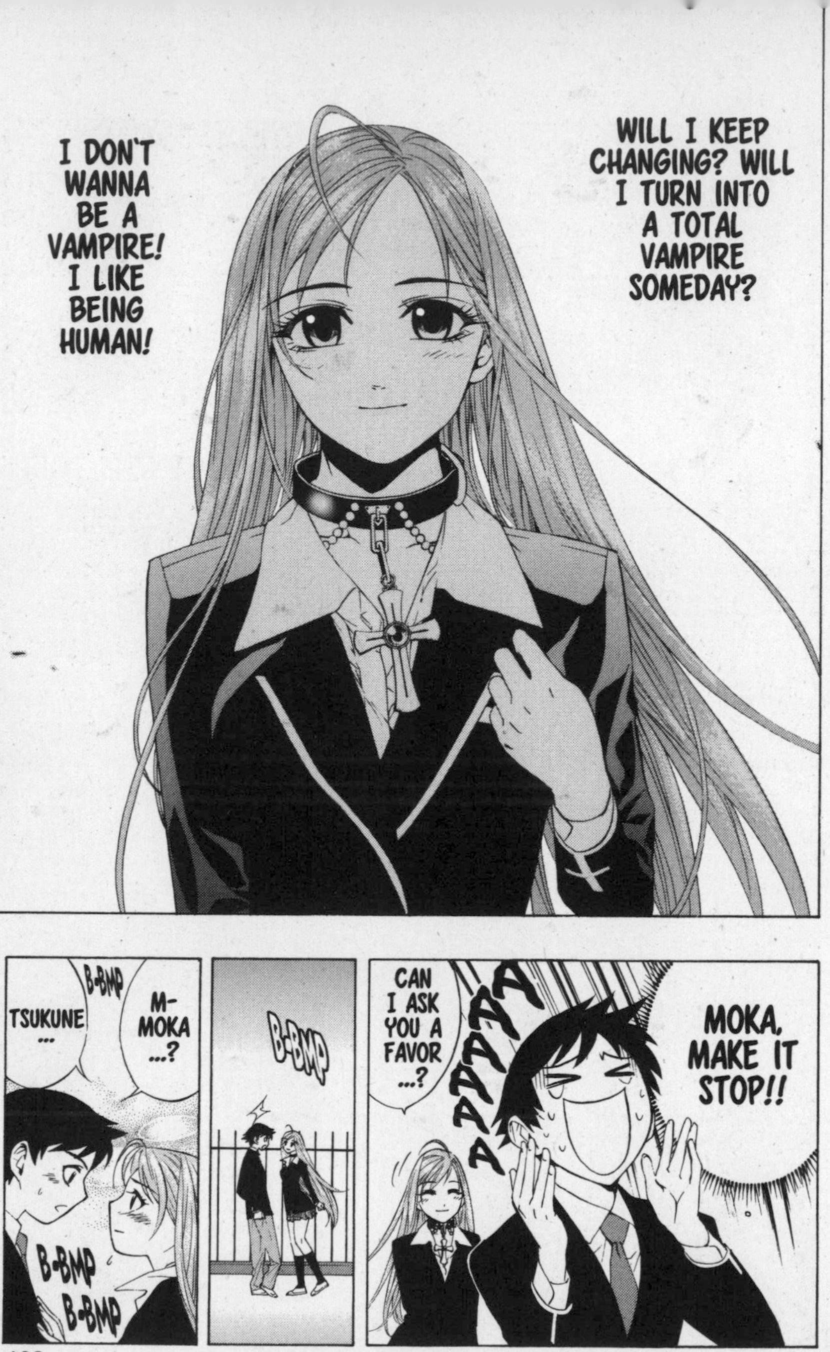
WILL I KEEP CHANGING? WILL I TURN INTO A TOTAL VAMPIRE SOMEDAY?
I DON'T WANNA BE A VAMPIRE! I LIKE BEING HUMAN!
MOKA, MAKE IT STOP!!
AAAAAA
CAN I ASK YOU A FAVOR ...?
B-BMP
M-MOKA ...?
B-BMP
TSUKUNE ...
B-BMP
B-BMP

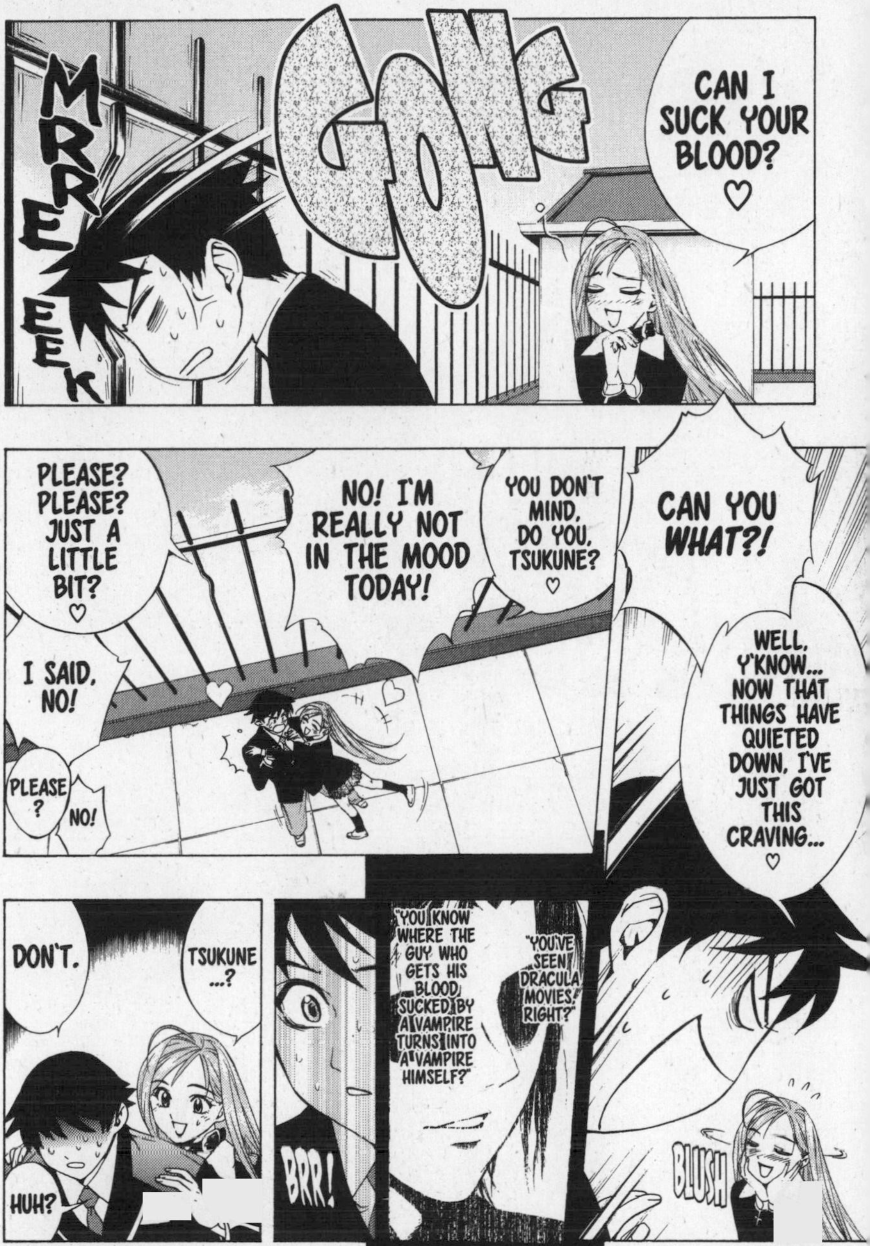

CAN I SUCK YOUR BLOOD? ♡
GONG
MRREEEK
CAN YOU WHAT?!
WELL, Y'KNOW... NOW THAT THINGS HAVE QUIETED DOWN, I'VE JUST GOT THIS CRAVING... ♡
YOU DON'T MIND, DO YOU, TSUKUNE? ♡
NO! I'M REALLY NOT IN THE MOOD TODAY!
PLEASE? PLEASE? JUST A LITTLE BIT? ♡
I SAID, NO!
NO!
PLEASE?
BLUSH
"YOU'VE SEEN DRACULA MOVIES, RIGHT?"
"YOU KNOW WHERE THE GUY WHO GETS HIS BLOOD SUCKED BY A VAMPIRE TURNS INTO A VAMPIRE HIMSELF?"
BRR!
TSUKUNE ...?
DON'T.
HUH?

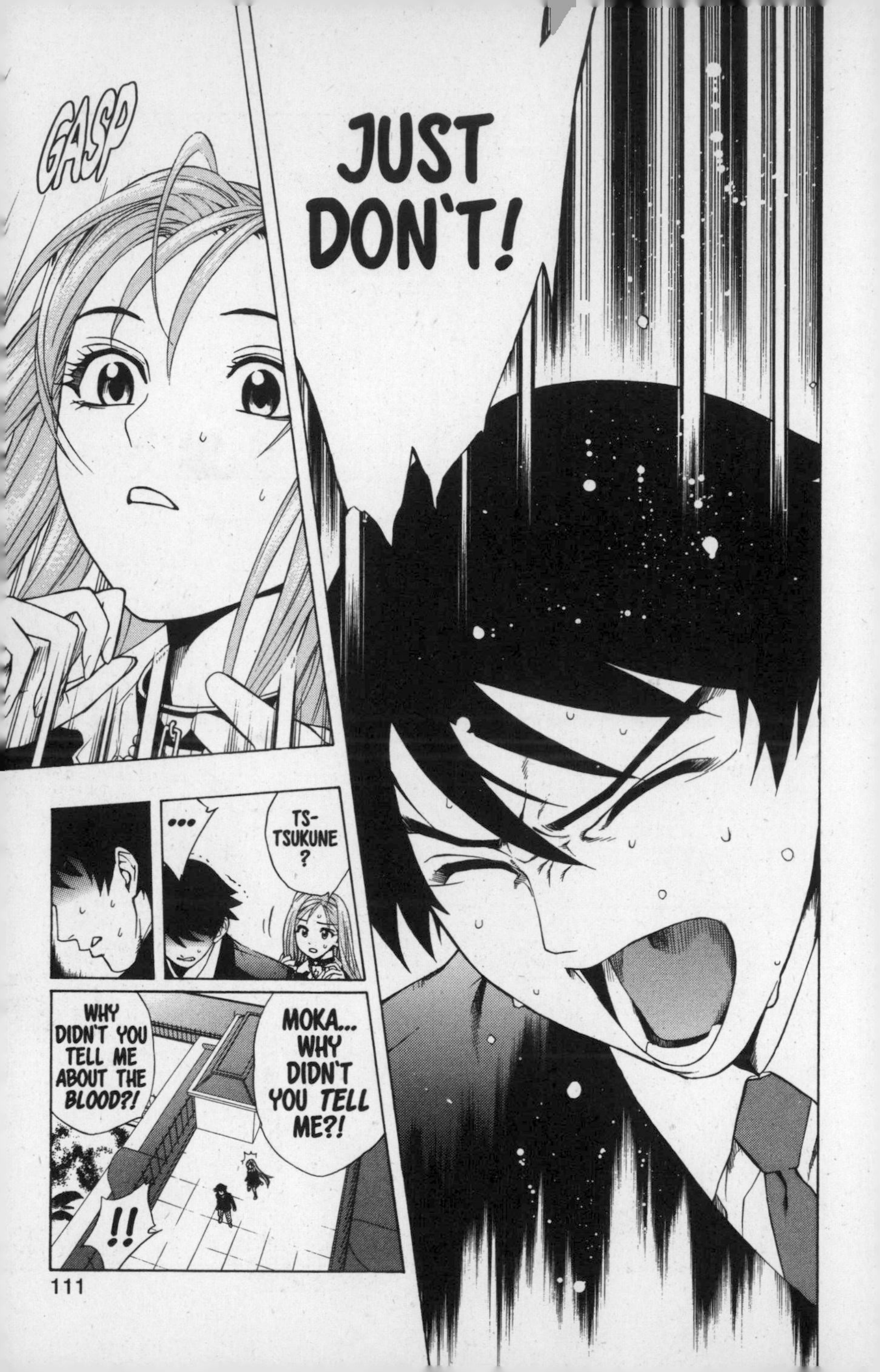
JUST DON'T!
GASP
TS-TSUKUNE?
...
MOKA... WHY DIDN'T YOU TELL ME?!
WHY DIDN'T YOU TELL ME ABOUT THE BLOOD?!
!!

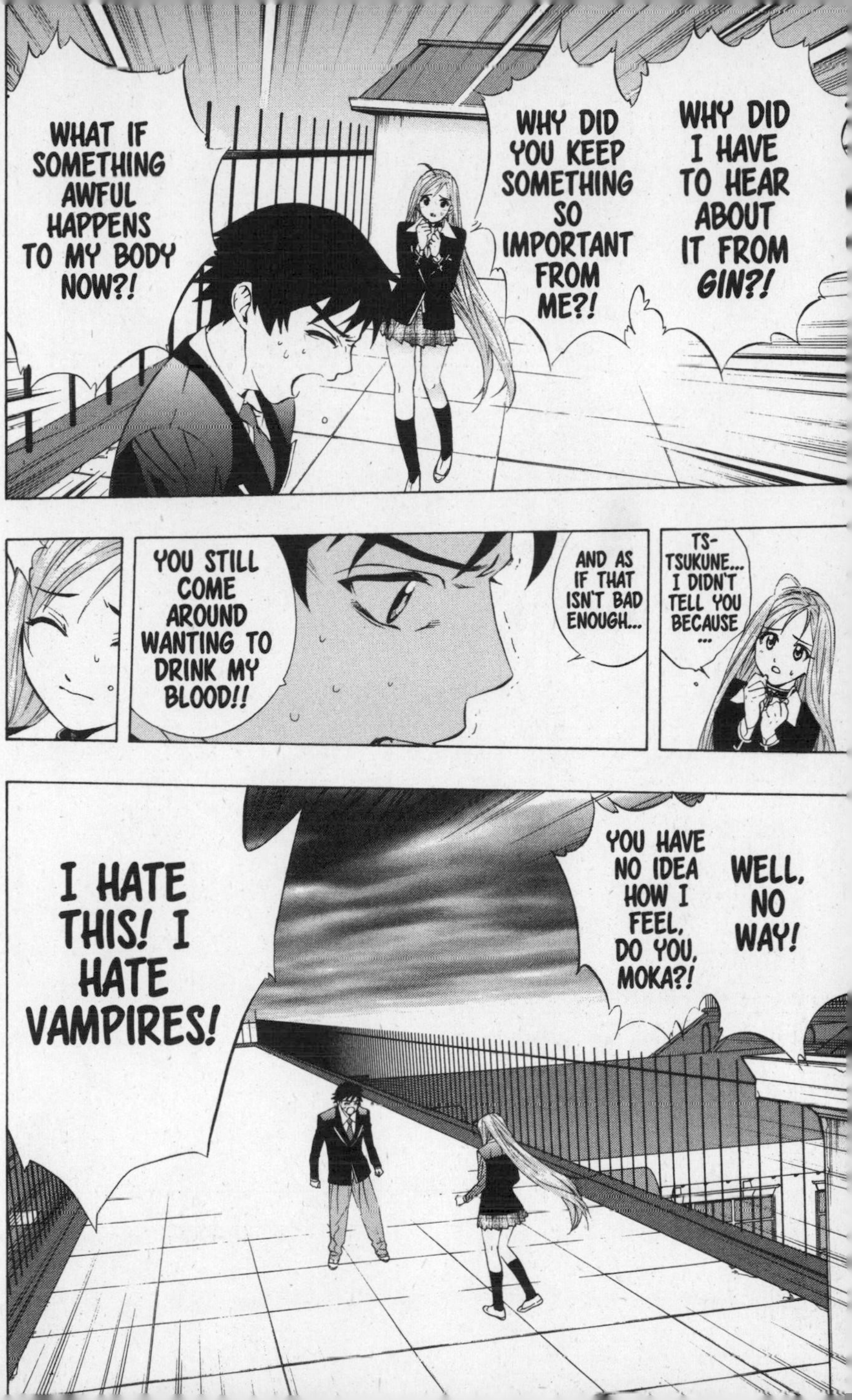
WHY DID I HAVE TO HEAR ABOUT IT FROM GIN?!
WHY DID YOU KEEP SOMETHING SO IMPORTANT FROM ME?!
WHAT IF SOMETHING AWFUL HAPPENS TO MY BODY NOW?!
TS-TSUKUNE... I DIDN'T TELL YOU BECAUSE ...
AND AS IF THAT ISN'T BAD ENOUGH...
YOU STILL COME AROUND WANTING TO DRINK MY BLOOD!!
WELL, NO WAY!
YOU HAVE NO IDEA HOW I FEEL, DO YOU, MOKA?!
I HATE THIS! I HATE VAMPIRES!

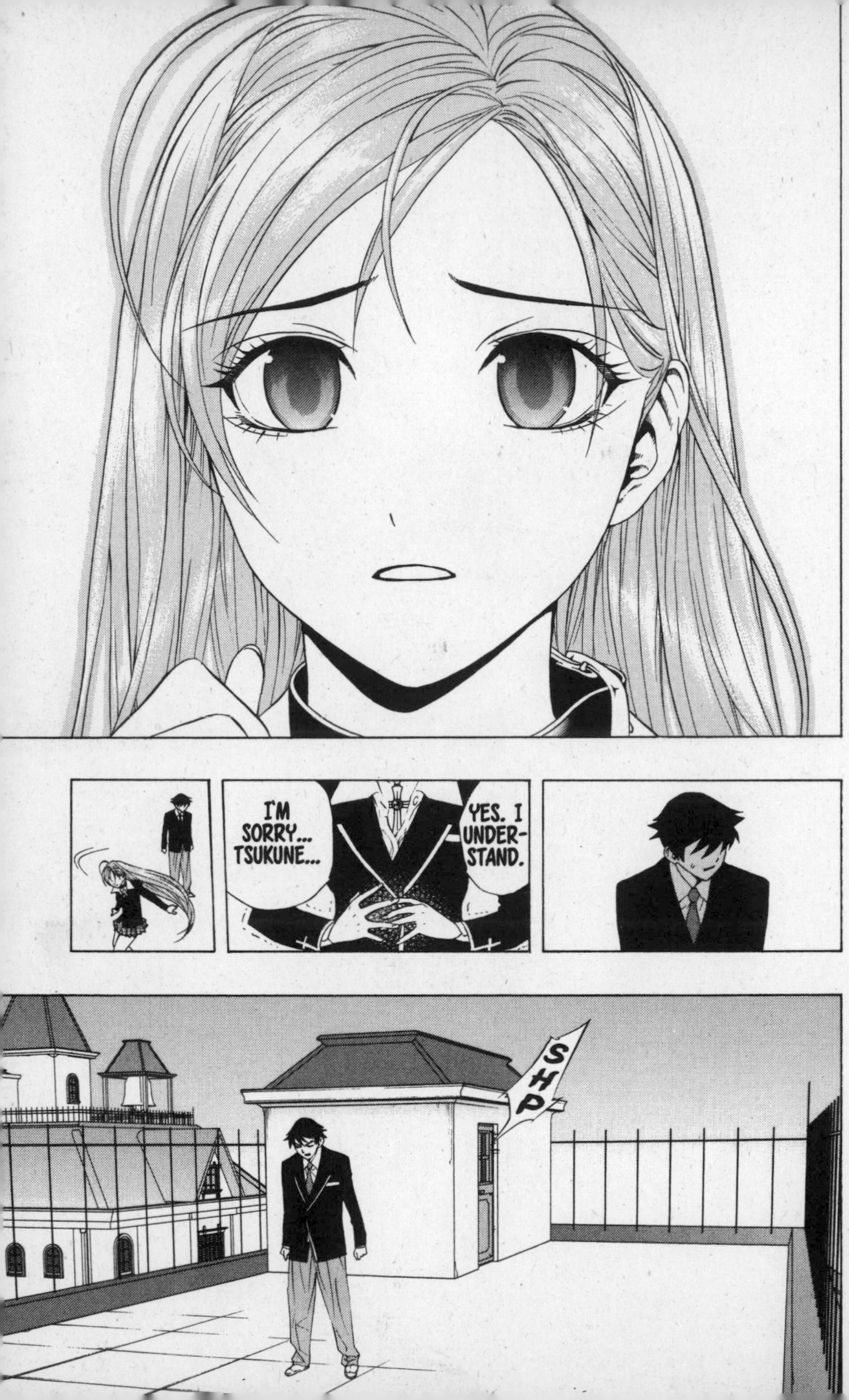
YES. I UNDER-STAND.
I'M SORRY... TSUKUNE...
SHP

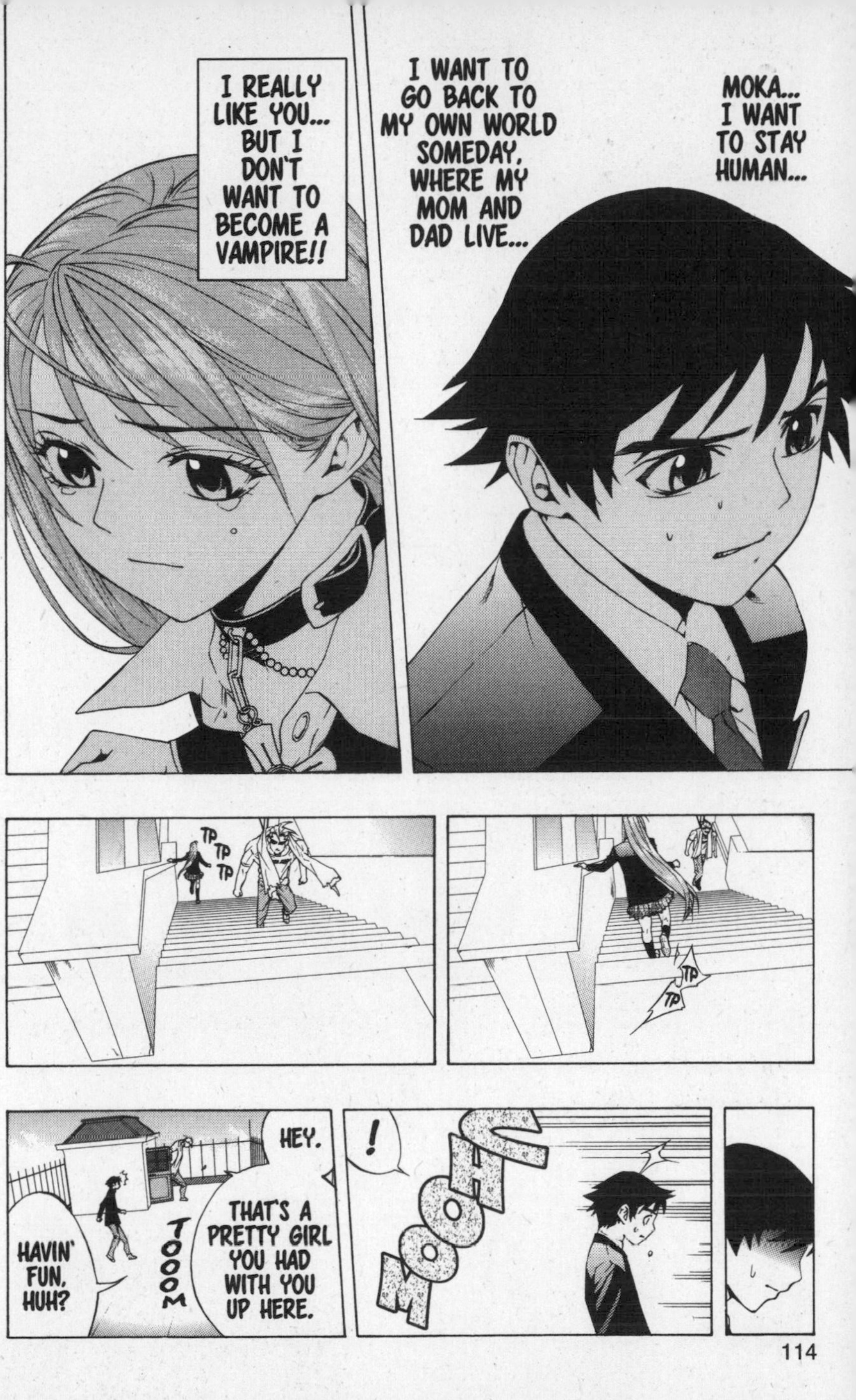
MOKA... I WANT TO STAY HUMAN...
I WANT TO GO BACK TO MY OWN WORLD SOMEDAY, WHERE MY MOM AND DAD LIVE...
I REALLY LIKE YOU... BUT I DON'T WANT TO BECOME A VAMPIRE!!
TP TP
TP TP TP
!
WHOOSH
HEY.
THAT'S A PRETTY GIRL YOU HAD WITH YOU UP HERE.
TOOOM
HAVIN' FUN, HUH?

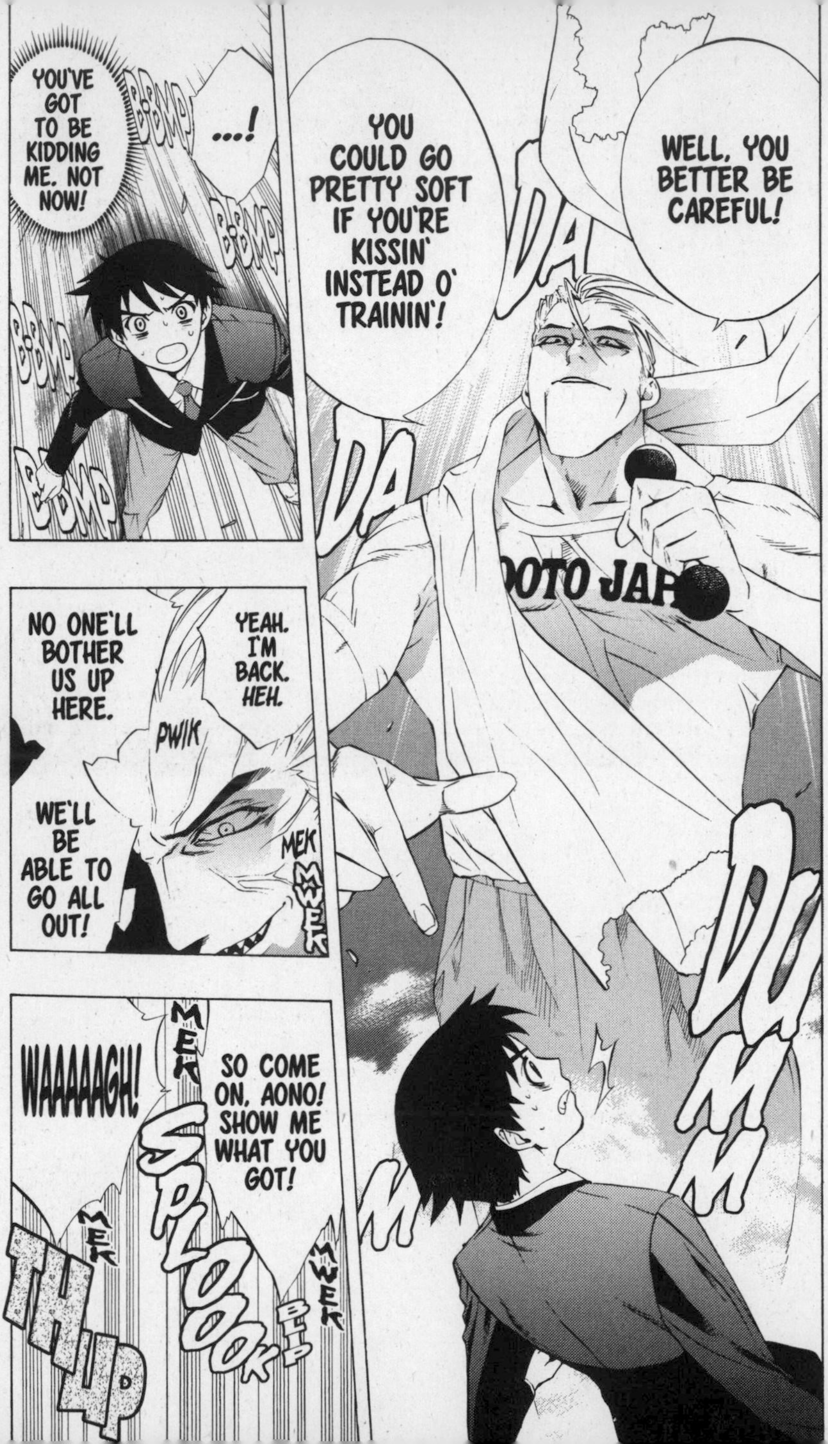
WELL, YOU BETTER BE CAREFUL!
YOU COULD GO PRETTY SOFT IF YOU'RE KISSIN' INSTEAD O' TRAININ'!
DA
DA
DA
DUMMM
...!
YOU'VE GOT TO BE KIDDING ME. NOT NOW!
BBBMP
BBBMP
BBBMP
BBBMP
BBBMP
YEAH. I'M BACK. HEH.
NO ONE'LL BOTHER US UP HERE.
PWIK
WE'LL BE ABLE TO GO ALL OUT!
MEK
MWEK
SO COME ON, AONO! SHOW ME WHAT YOU GOT!
MEK
WAAAAAGH!
SPLOOOK
MWEK
BLIP
MEK
THUP

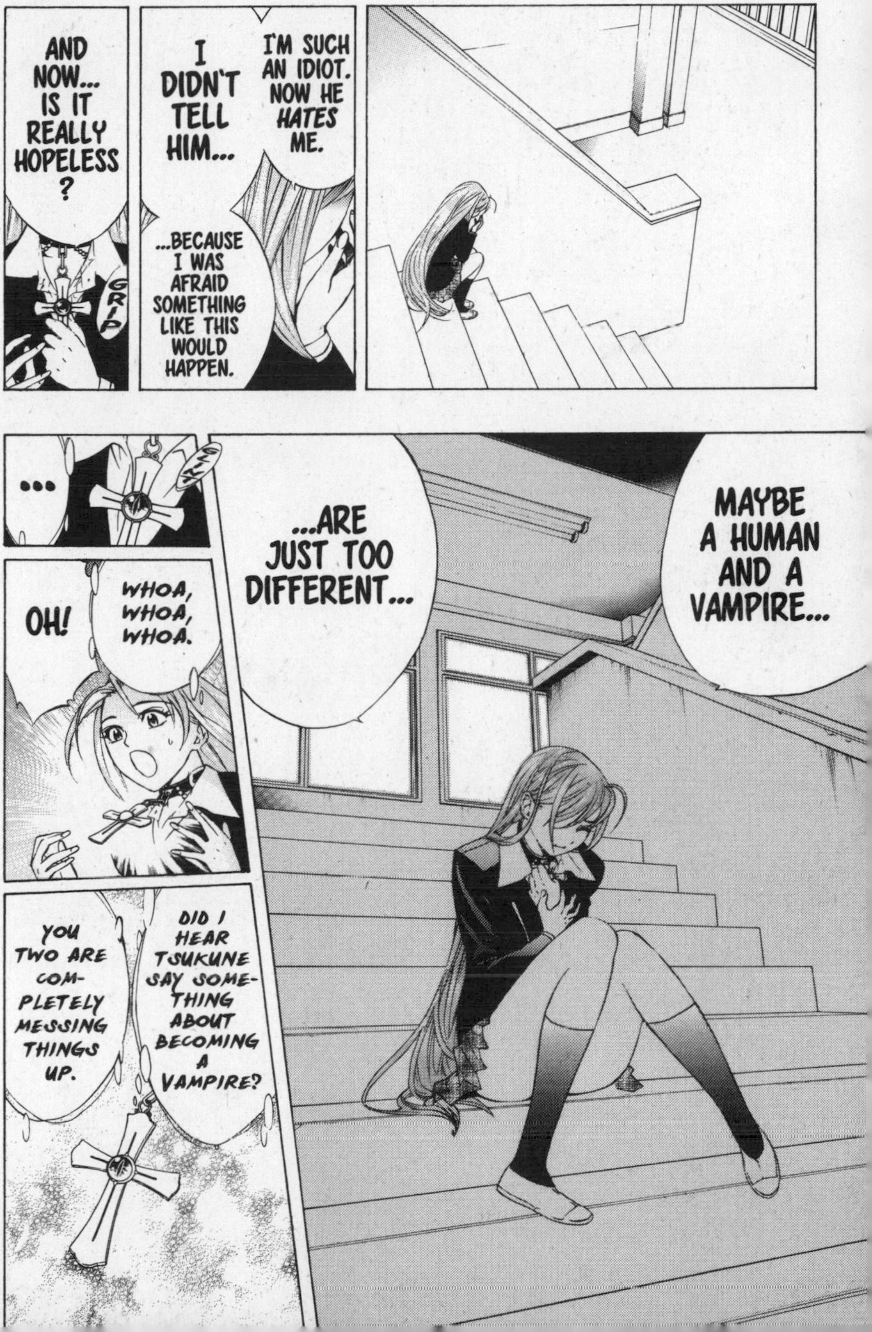
I'M SUCH AN IDIOT. NOW HE HATES ME.
I DIDN'T TELL HIM...
...BECAUSE I WAS AFRAID SOMETHING LIKE THIS WOULD HAPPEN.
AND NOW... IS IT REALLY HOPELESS?
GRIP
MAYBE A HUMAN AND A VAMPIRE...
...ARE JUST TOO DIFFERENT...
...
WHOA, WHOA, WHOA.
OH!
DID I HEAR TSUKUNE SAY SOME-THING ABOUT BECOMING A VAMPIRE?
YOU TWO ARE COM-PLETELY MESSING THINGS UP.

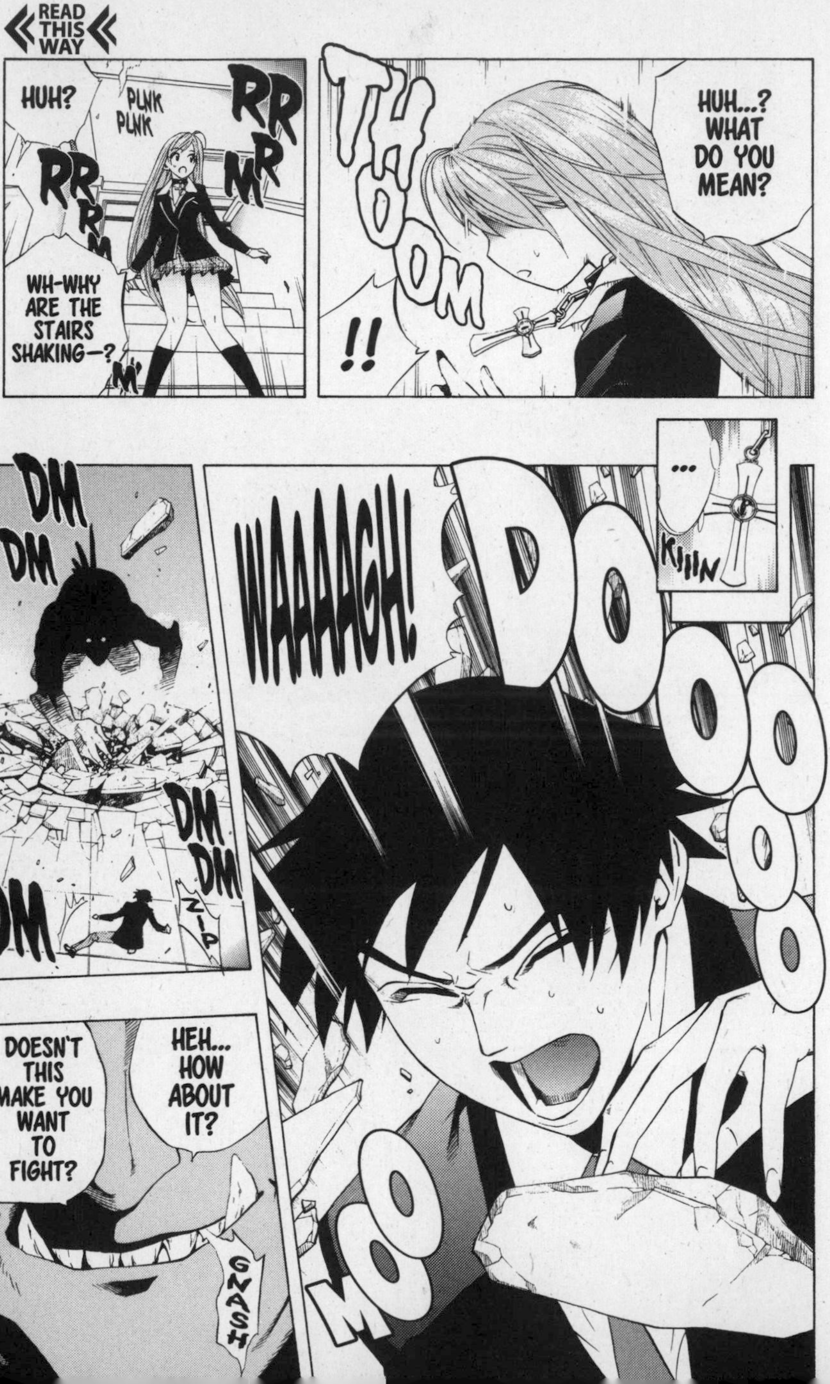
READ THIS WAY
THOOM
!!
HUH...? WHAT DO YOU MEAN?
RRRRM
HUH?
PLNK PLNK
RRRRM
WH-WHY ARE THE STAIRS SHAKING—?
M
...
KIIIN
WAAAAGH!
DOOOOOOOOM
DM DM
DM DM
DM
ZIP
HEH... HOW ABOUT IT?
DOESN'T THIS MAKE YOU WANT TO FIGHT?
GNASH

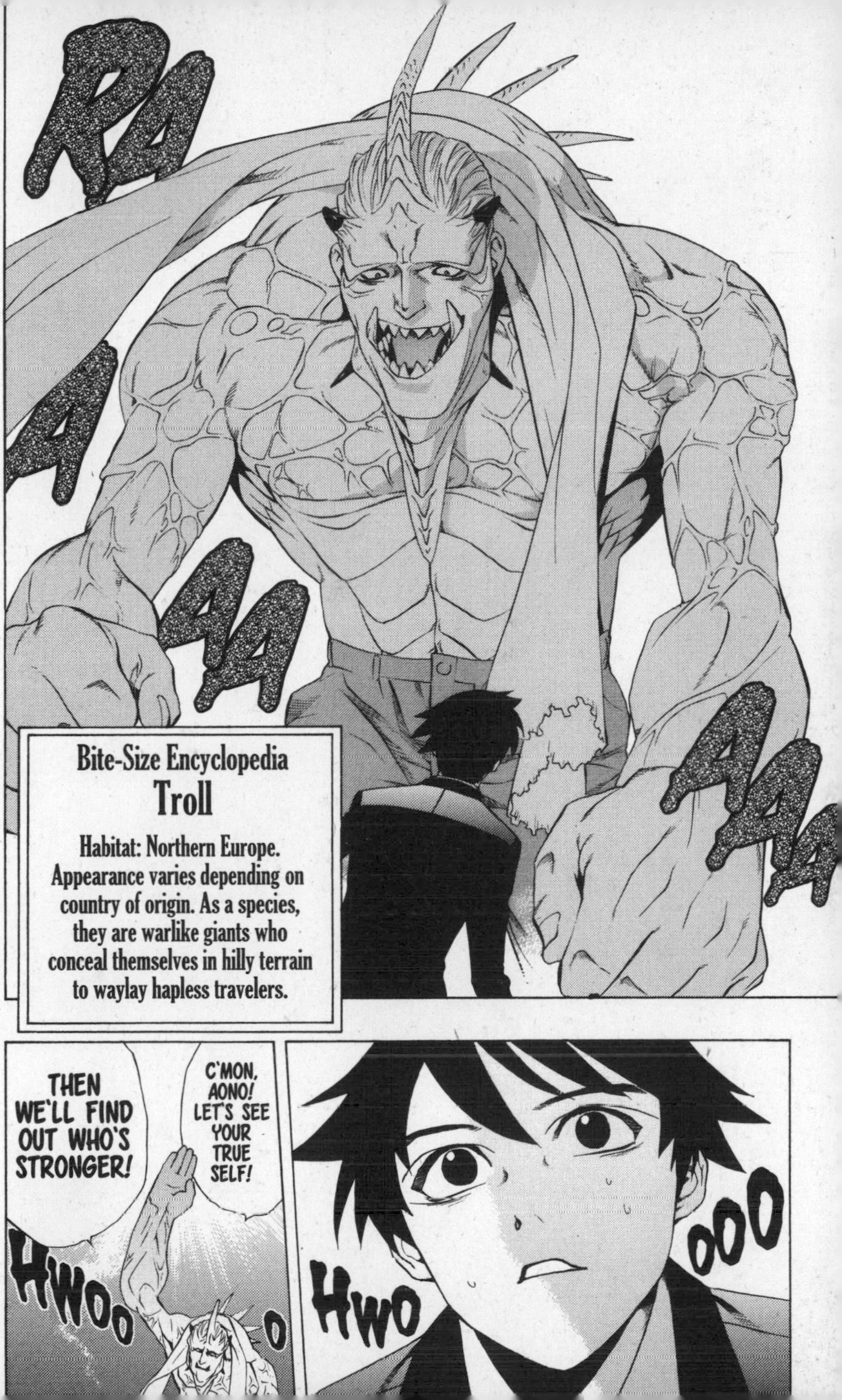
RAAAAAAAA
Bite-Size Encyclopedia
Troll
Habitat: Northern Europe. Appearance varies depending on country of origin. As a species, they are warlike giants who conceal themselves in hilly terrain to waylay hapless travelers.
HWOOOO
C'MON, AONO! LET'S SEE YOUR TRUE SELF!
THEN WE'LL FIND OUT WHO'S STRONGER!
HWOOO

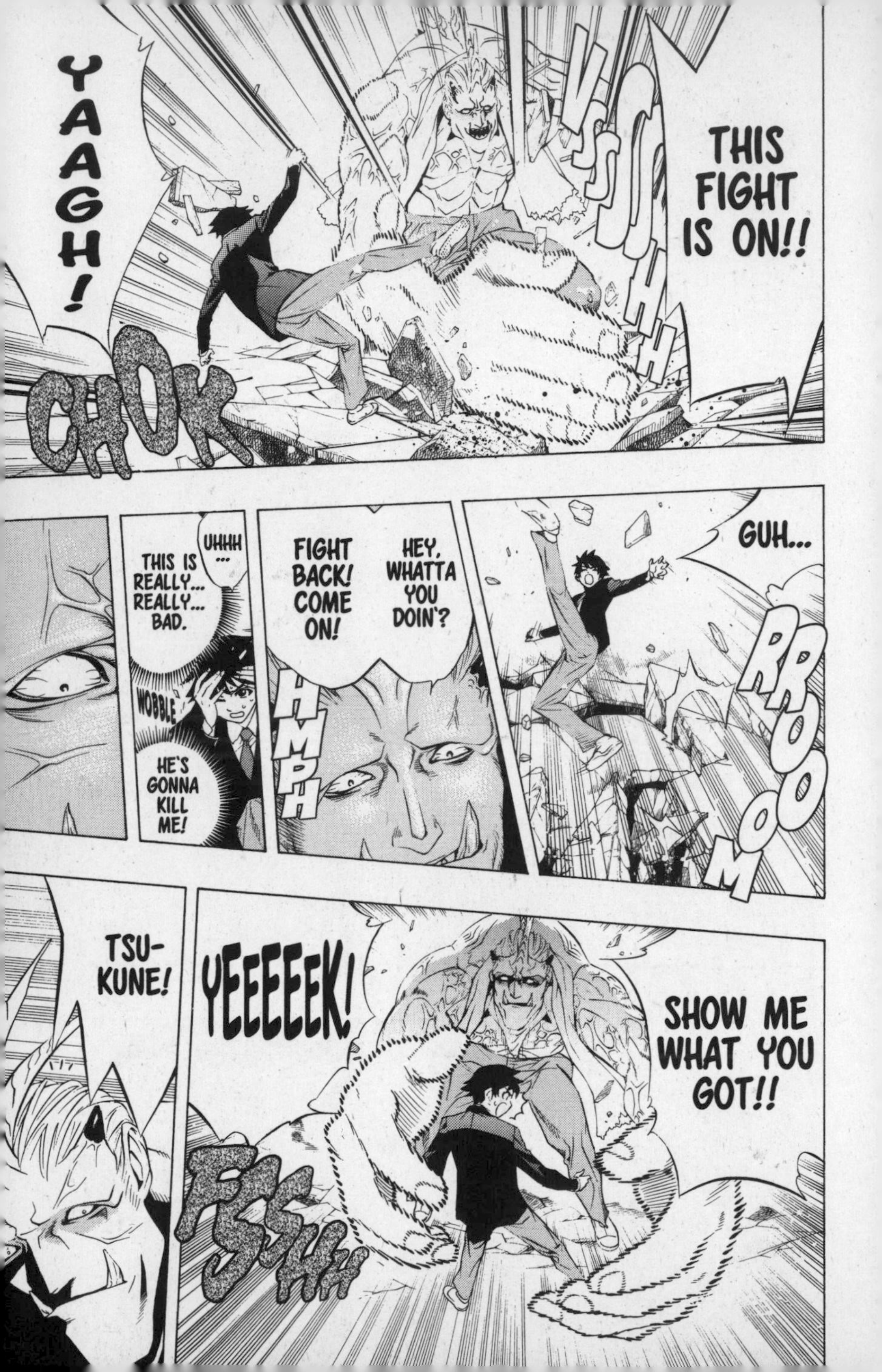

THIS FIGHT IS ON!!
VSSCHH
YAAGH!
CHOK
GUH...
RROOOM
HEY, WHATTA YOU DOIN'?
FIGHT BACK! COME ON!
HMPH
UHHH...
THIS IS REALLY... REALLY... BAD.
WOBBLE
HE'S GONNA KILL ME!
SHOW ME WHAT YOU GOT!!
YEEEEEK!
TSU-KUNE!
FSSHH

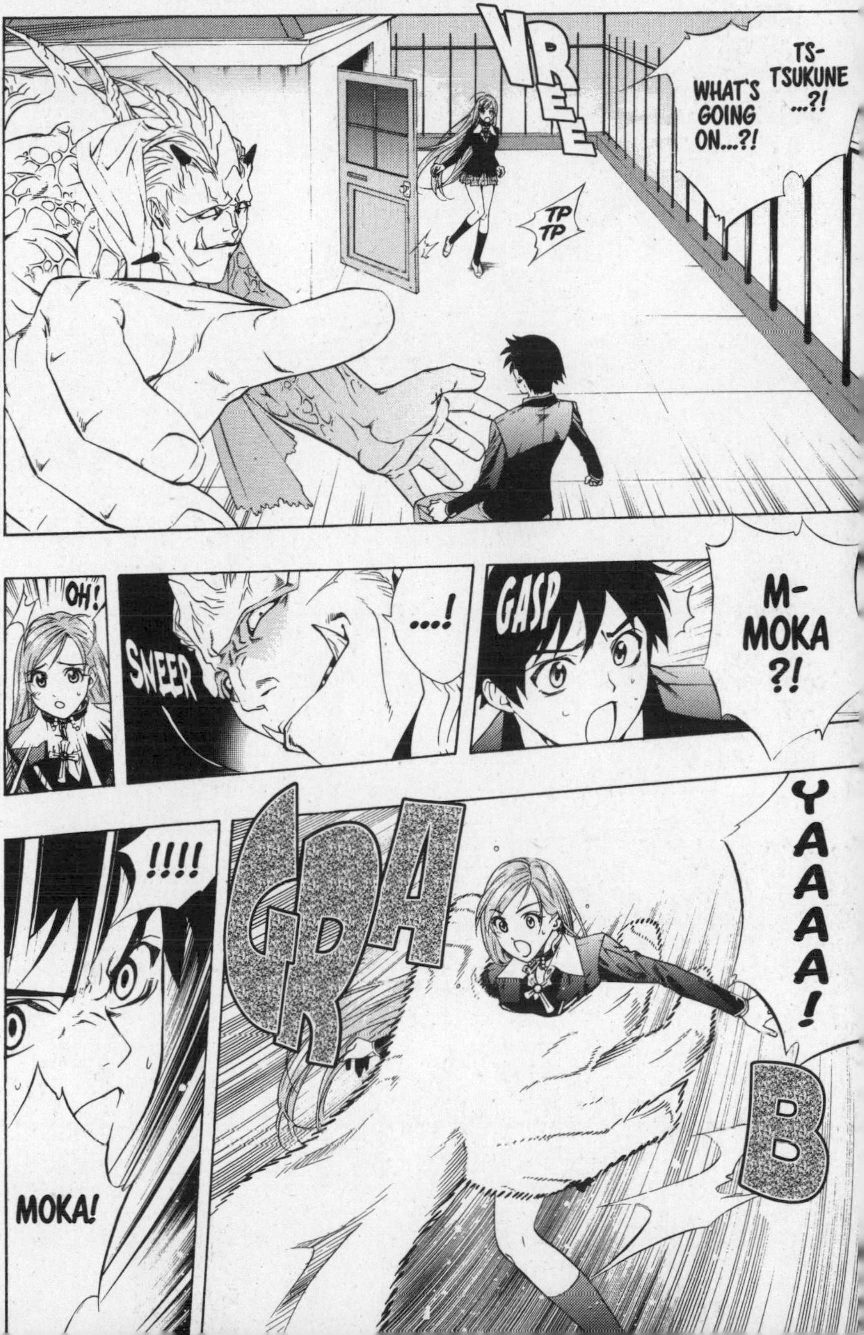
TS-TSUKUNE...?!
WHAT'S GOING ON...?!
VREEE
TP TP
M-MOKA?!
GASP
...!
SNEER
OH!
YAAAAA!
B
GRA
!!!!
MOKA!

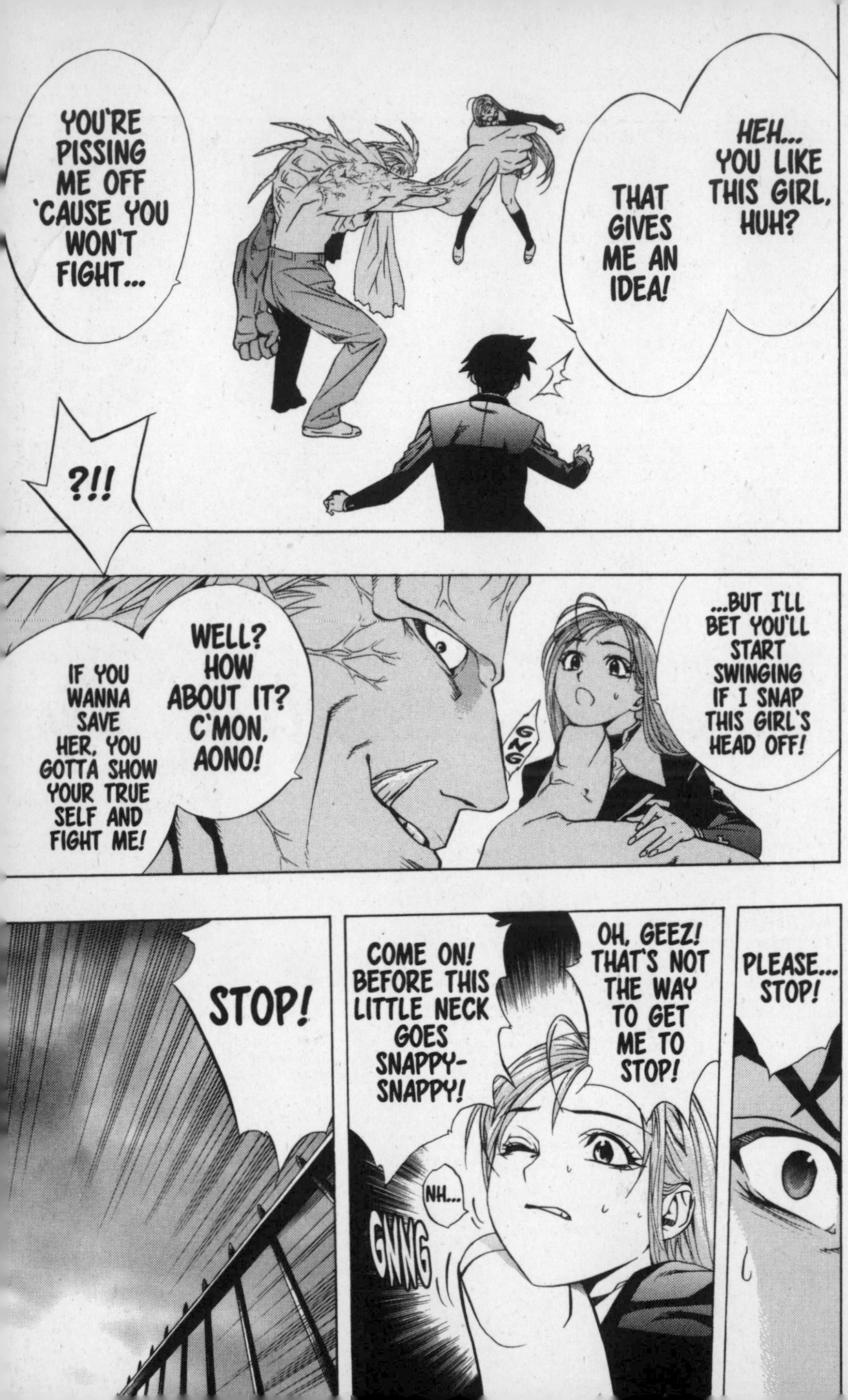
HEH... YOU LIKE THIS GIRL, HUH?
THAT GIVES ME AN IDEA!
YOU'RE PISSING ME OFF 'CAUSE YOU WON'T FIGHT...
?!!
...BUT I'LL BET YOU'LL START SWINGING IF I SNAP THIS GIRL'S HEAD OFF!
GNG
WELL? HOW ABOUT IT? C'MON, AONO!
IF YOU WANNA SAVE HER, YOU GOTTA SHOW YOUR TRUE SELF AND FIGHT ME!
PLEASE... STOP!
OH, GEEZ! THAT'S NOT THE WAY TO GET ME TO STOP!
COME ON! BEFORE THIS LITTLE NECK GOES SNAPPY-SNAPPY!
NH...
GNNG
STOP!

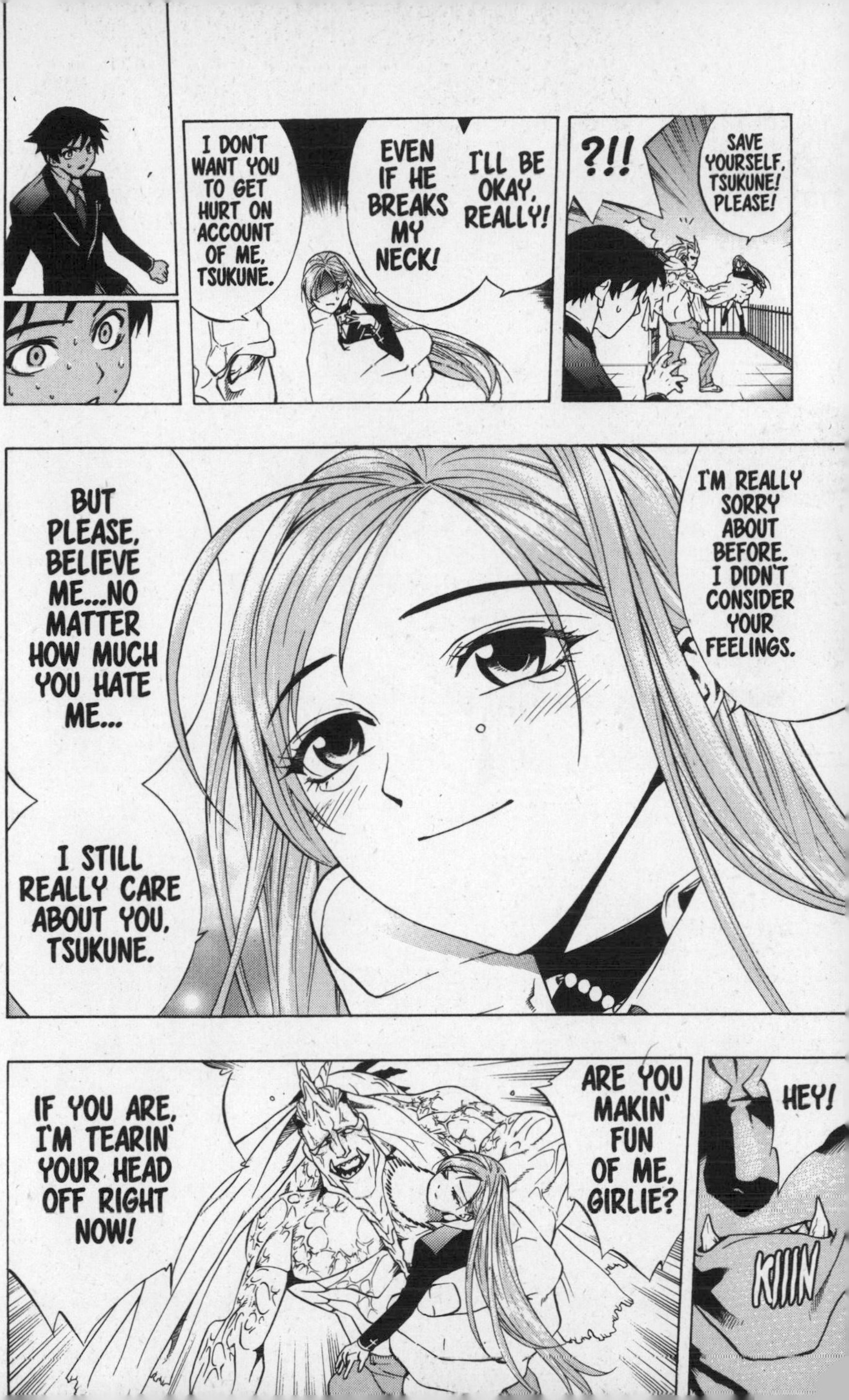
SAVE YOURSELF, TSUKUNE! PLEASE!
?!!
I'LL BE OKAY, REALLY!
EVEN IF HE BREAKS MY NECK!
I DON'T WANT YOU TO GET HURT ON ACCOUNT OF ME, TSUKUNE.
I'M REALLY SORRY ABOUT BEFORE. I DIDN'T CONSIDER YOUR FEELINGS.
BUT PLEASE, BELIEVE ME...NO MATTER HOW MUCH YOU HATE ME...
I STILL REALLY CARE ABOUT YOU, TSUKUNE.
HEY!
KIIIN
ARE YOU MAKIN' FUN OF ME, GIRLIE?
IF YOU ARE, I'M TEARIN' YOUR HEAD OFF RIGHT NOW!

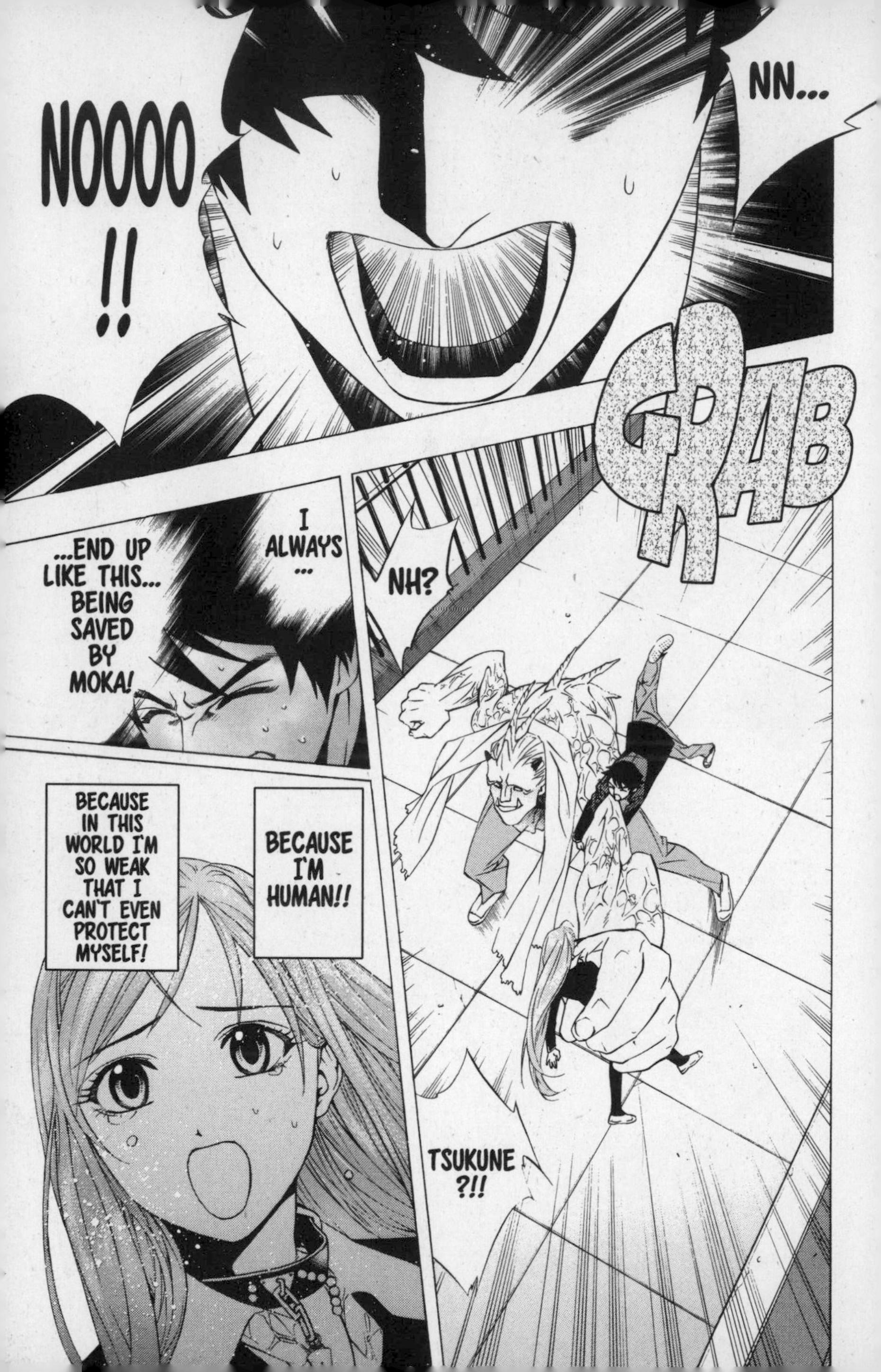
NN...
NOOOO!!
GRAB
NH?
TSUKUNE?!!
I ALWAYS...
...END UP LIKE THIS... BEING SAVED BY MOKA!
BECAUSE I'M HUMAN!!
BECAUSE IN THIS WORLD I'M SO WEAK THAT I CAN'T EVEN PROTECT MYSELF!

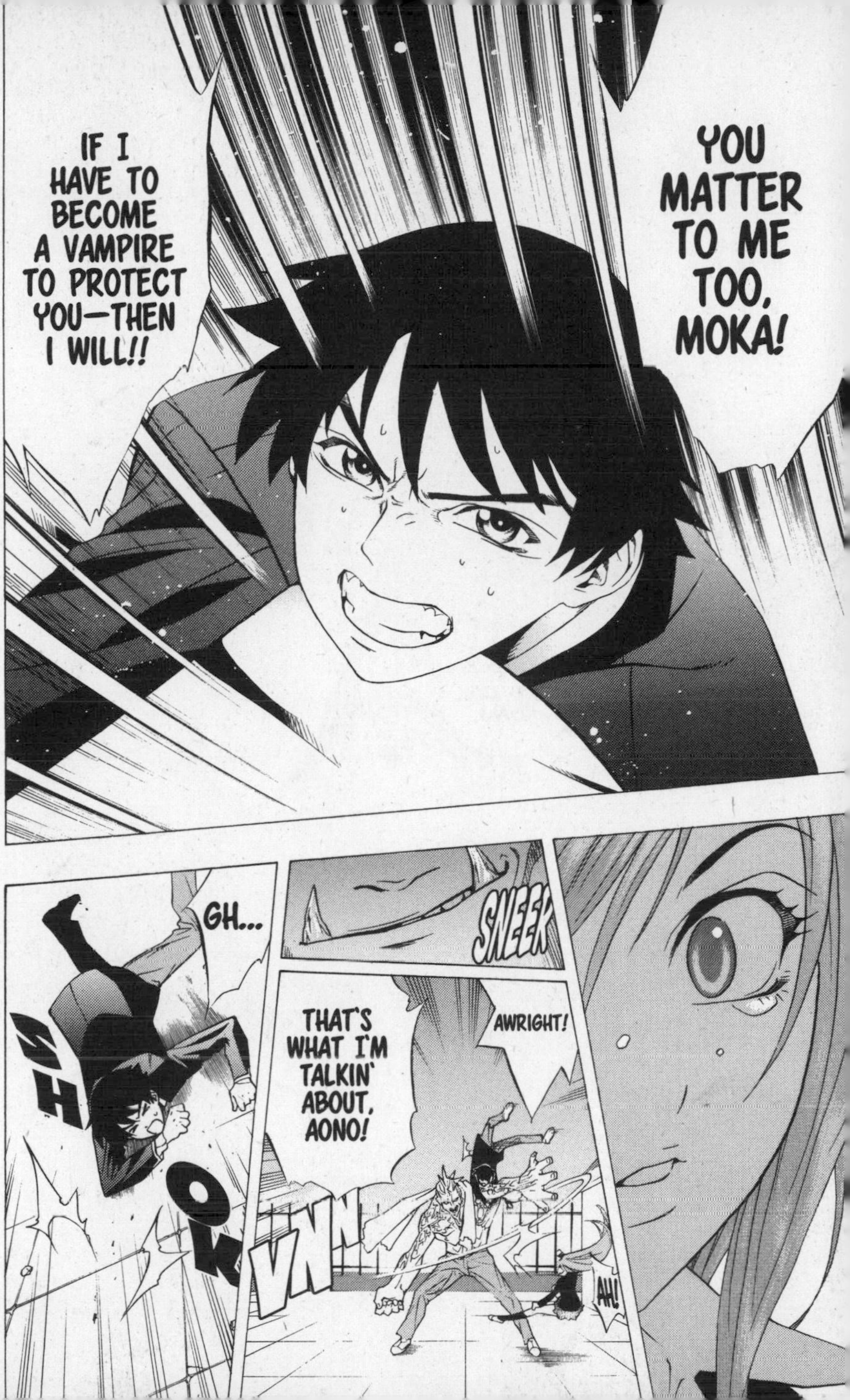
YOU MATTER TO ME TOO, MOKA!
IF I HAVE TO BECOME A VAMPIRE TO PROTECT YOU—THEN I WILL!!
SNEER
AWRIGHT!
THAT'S WHAT I'M TALKIN' ABOUT, AONO!
AH!
VNN
GH...
SHOK

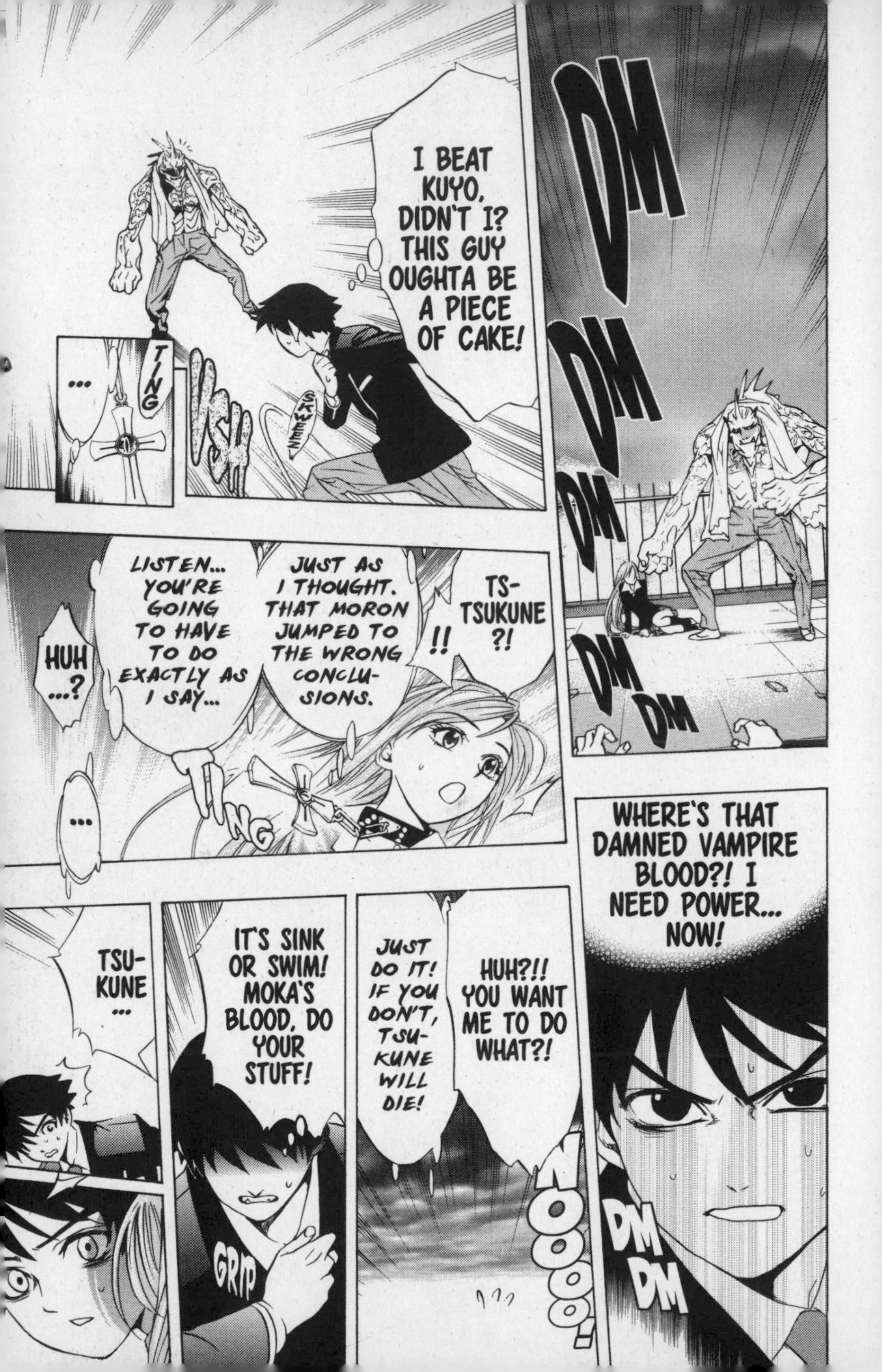
DM
DM
DM
DM
DM
DM
I BEAT KUYO, DIDN'T I? THIS GUY OUGHTA BE A PIECE OF CAKE!
SKWEEZ
TING
...
TS-TSUKUNE?!
!!
JUST AS I THOUGHT. THAT MORON JUMPED TO THE WRONG CONCLUSIONS.
LISTEN... YOU'RE GOING TO HAVE TO DO EXACTLY AS I SAY...
HUH ...?
...
WHERE'S THAT DAMNED VAMPIRE BLOOD?! I NEED POWER... NOW!
DM
DM
NOOOO
HUH?!! YOU WANT ME TO DO WHAT?!
JUST DO IT! IF YOU DON'T, TSUKUNE WILL DIE!
IT'S SINK OR SWIM! MOKA'S BLOOD, DO YOUR STUFF!
GRIP
TSU-KUNE ...

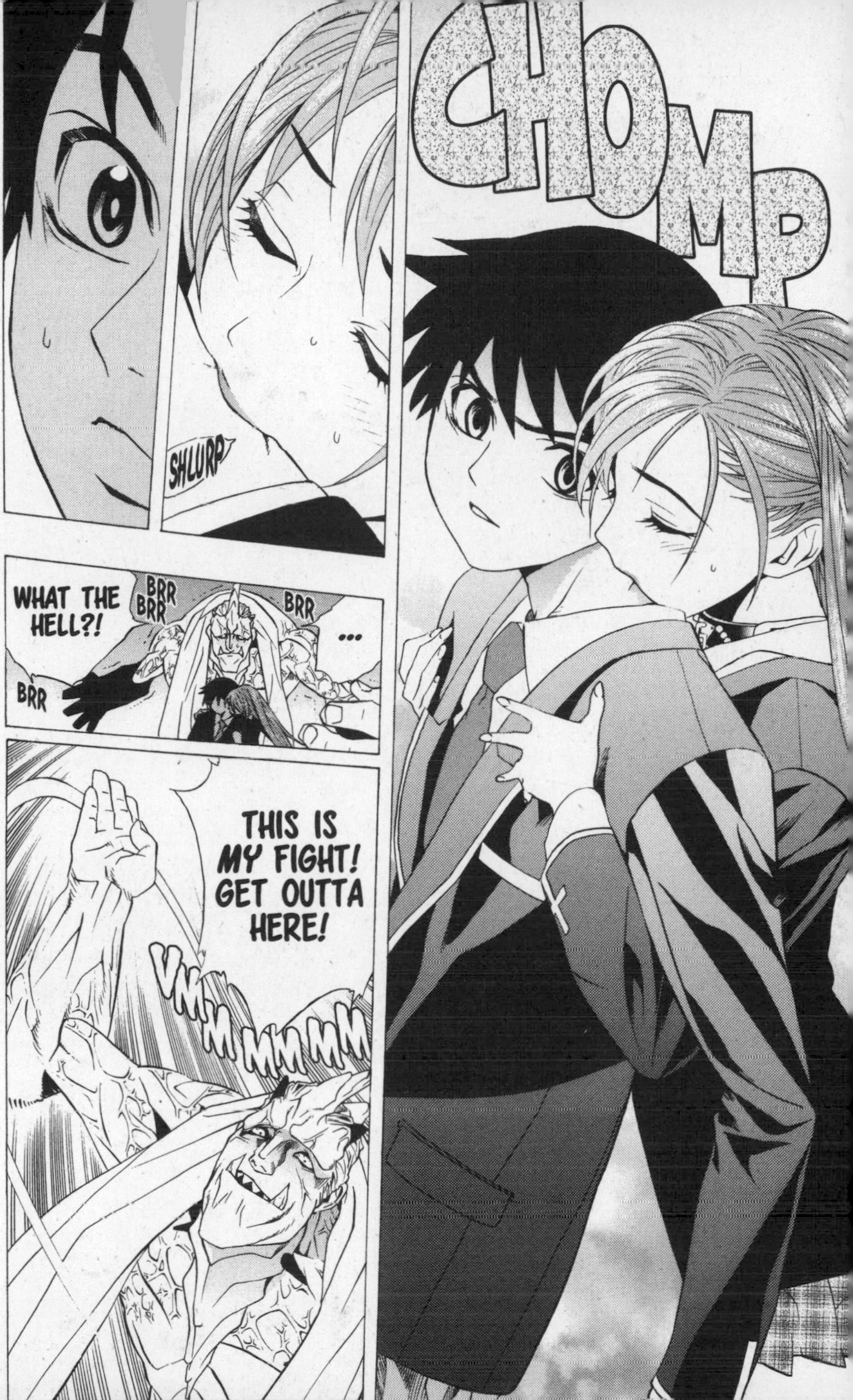
CHOMP
SHLURP
...
BRR
BRR BRR
WHAT THE HELL?!
BRR
THIS IS MY FIGHT! GET OUTTA HERE!
VMMMMMMM

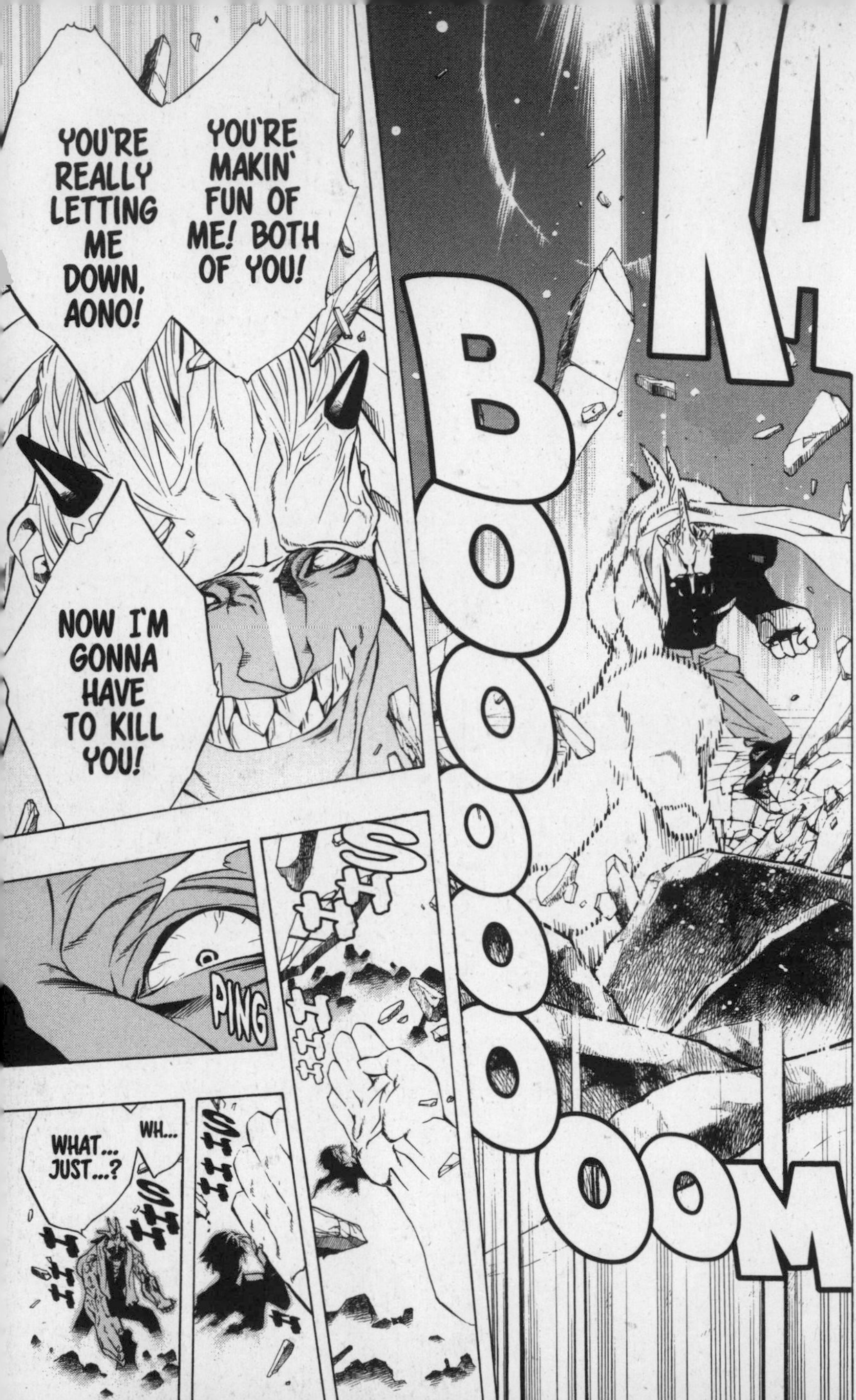
KA
BOOOOOOOOOM
YOU'RE MAKIN' FUN OF ME! BOTH OF YOU!
YOU'RE REALLY LETTING ME DOWN, AONO!
NOW I'M GONNA HAVE TO KILL YOU!
SHHH
SHHHH
PING
SHHHH
WH...
SHHH
WHAT... JUST...?
HHH

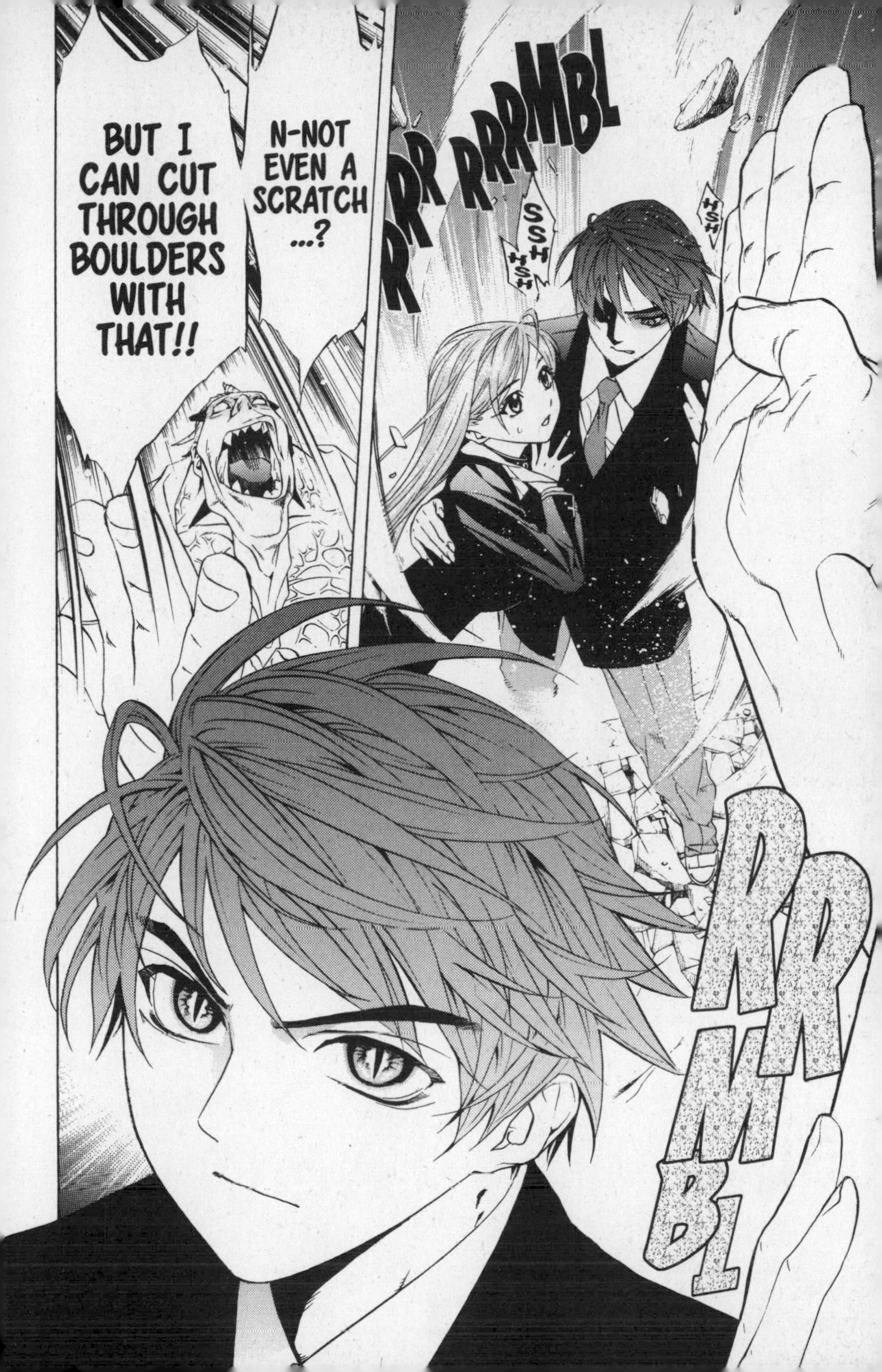
HSH
RRRR RRRRMBL
SSH
HSH
N-NOT EVEN A SCRATCH ...?
BUT I CAN CUT THROUGH BOULDERS WITH THAT!!
RRRMBL

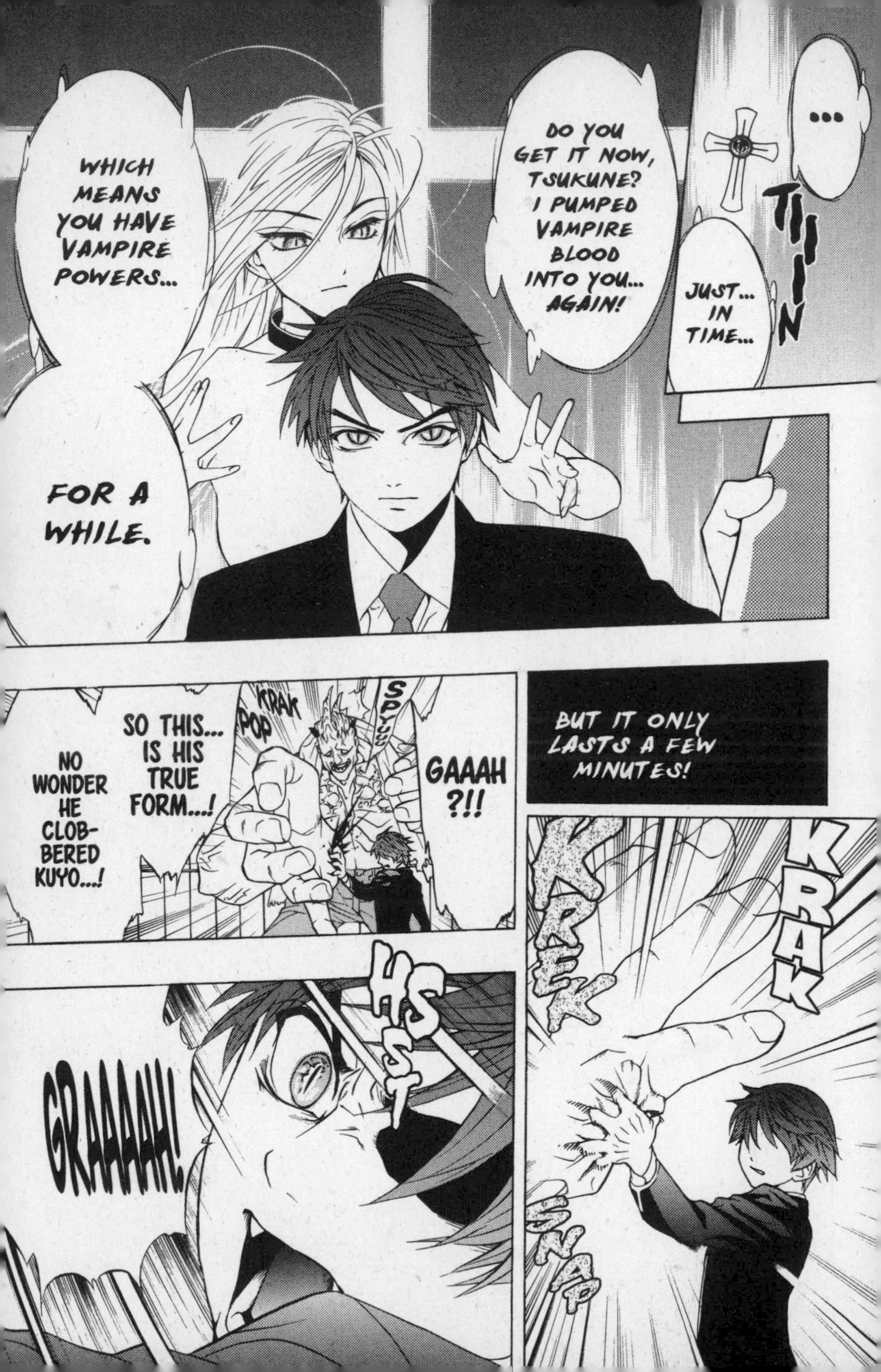
...
TIIIN
JUST... IN TIME...
DO YOU GET IT NOW, TSUKUNE? I PUMPED VAMPIRE BLOOD INTO YOU... AGAIN!
WHICH MEANS YOU HAVE VAMPIRE POWERS...
FOR A WHILE.
BUT IT ONLY LASTS A FEW MINUTES!
GAAAH ?!!
SPYUUU
KRAK
POP
SO THIS... IS HIS TRUE FORM...!
NO WONDER HE CLOB-BERED KUYO...!
KRAK
KREK
SNAP
HSST
GRAAAAH!

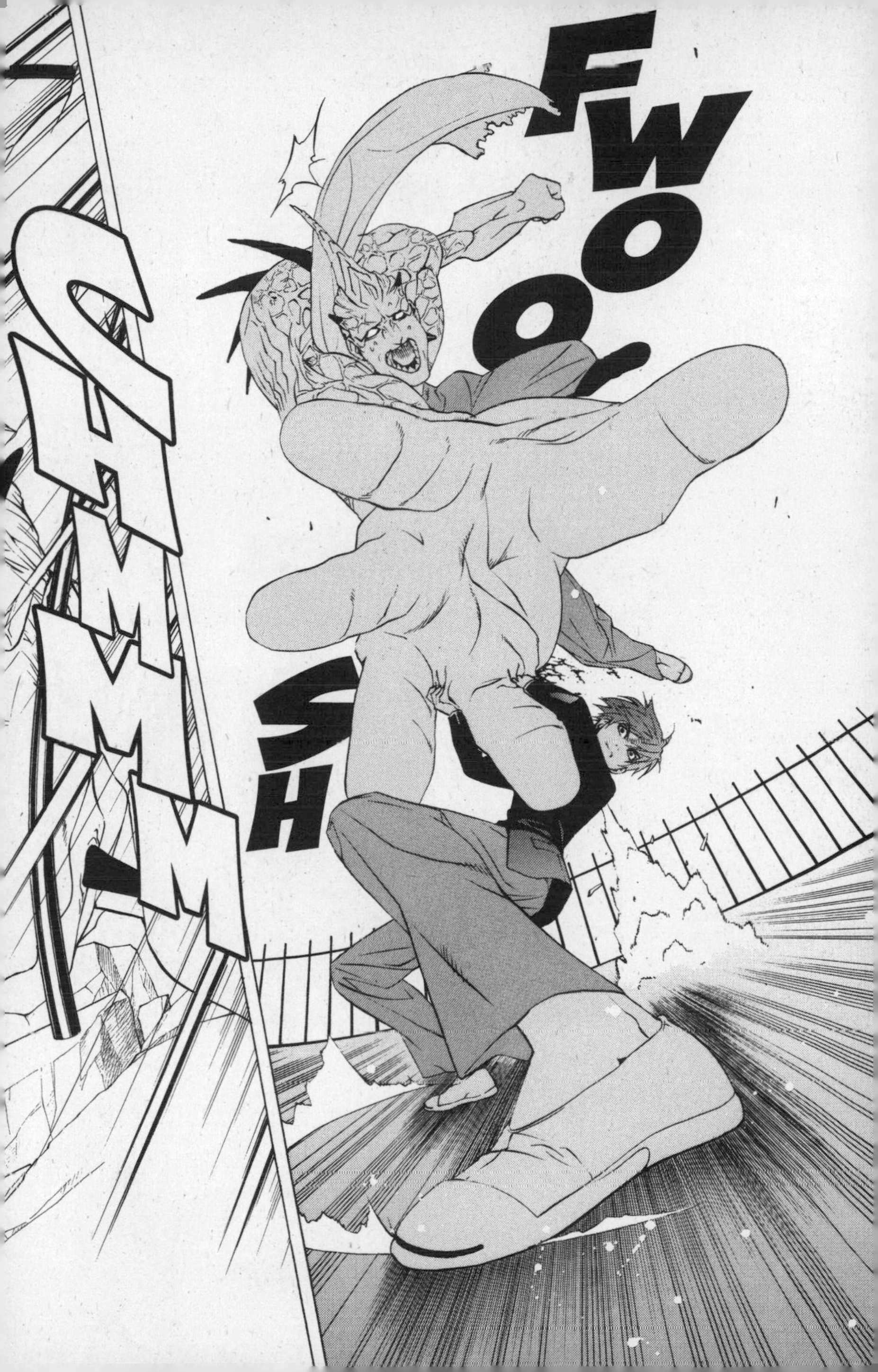
FWOO!
SH

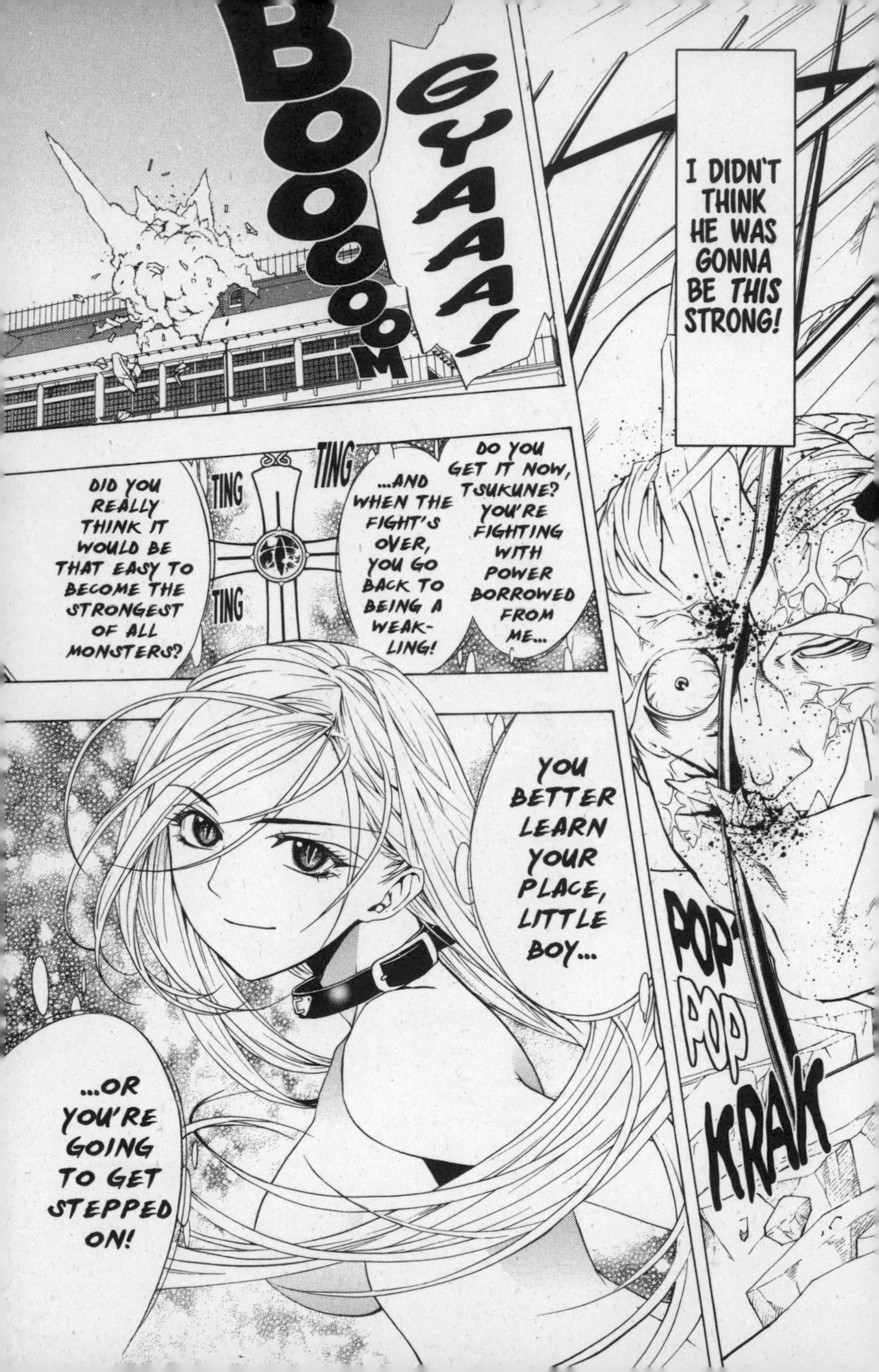
I DIDN'T THINK HE WAS GONNA BE THIS STRONG!
POP POP
KRAK
BOOOOOOM
GYAAA!
DO YOU GET IT NOW, TSUKUNE? YOU'RE FIGHTING WITH POWER BORROWED FROM ME...
...AND WHEN THE FIGHT'S OVER, YOU GO BACK TO BEING A WEAK-LING!
TING
TING
TING
DID YOU REALLY THINK IT WOULD BE THAT EASY TO BECOME THE STRONGEST OF ALL MONSTERS?
YOU BETTER LEARN YOUR PLACE, LITTLE BOY...
...OR YOU'RE GOING TO GET STEPPED ON!

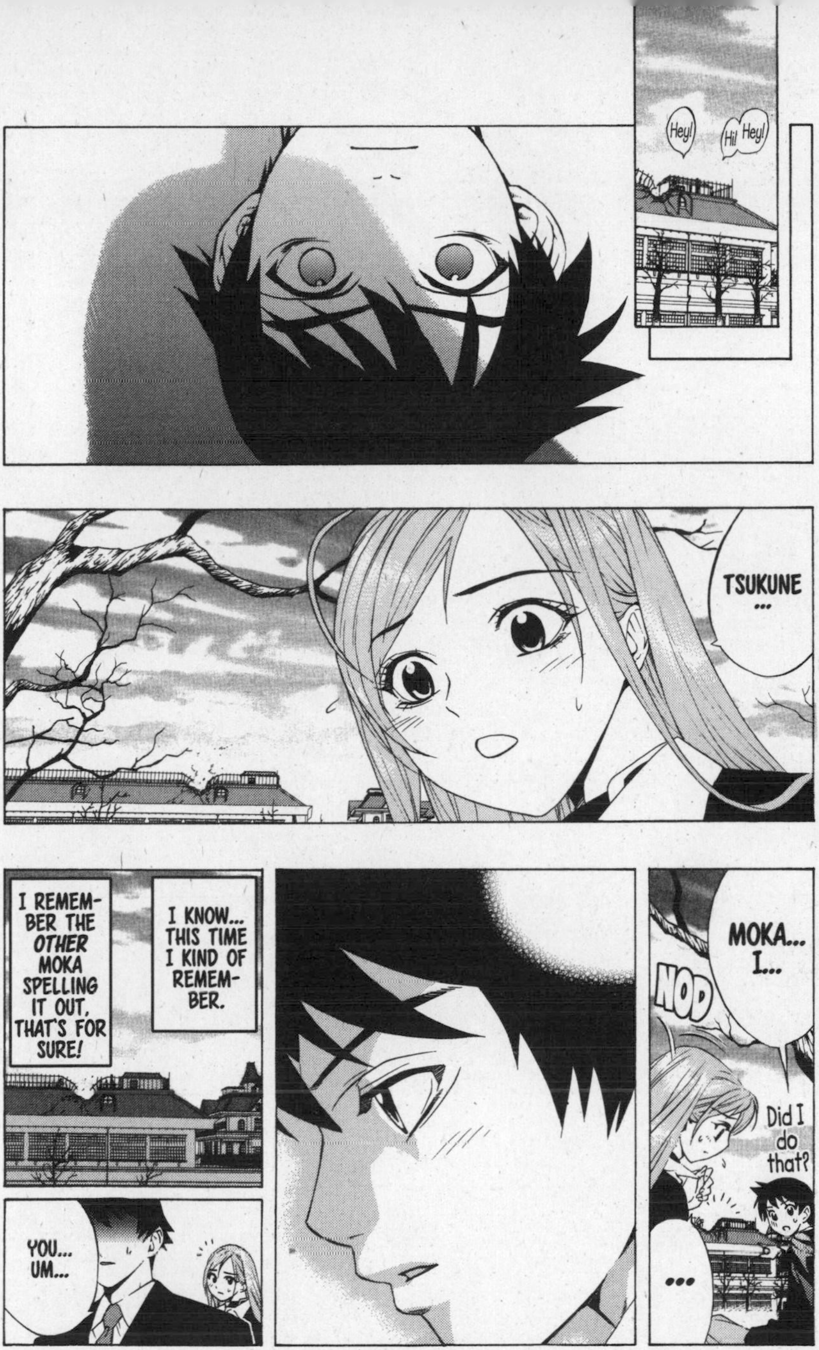
Hey!
Hi!
Hey!
TSUKUNE...
MOKA... I...
NOD
Did I do that?
...
I KNOW... THIS TIME I KIND OF REMEMBER.
I REMEMBER THE *OTHER* MOKA SPELLING IT OUT, THAT'S FOR SURE!
YOU... UM...

READ THIS WAY

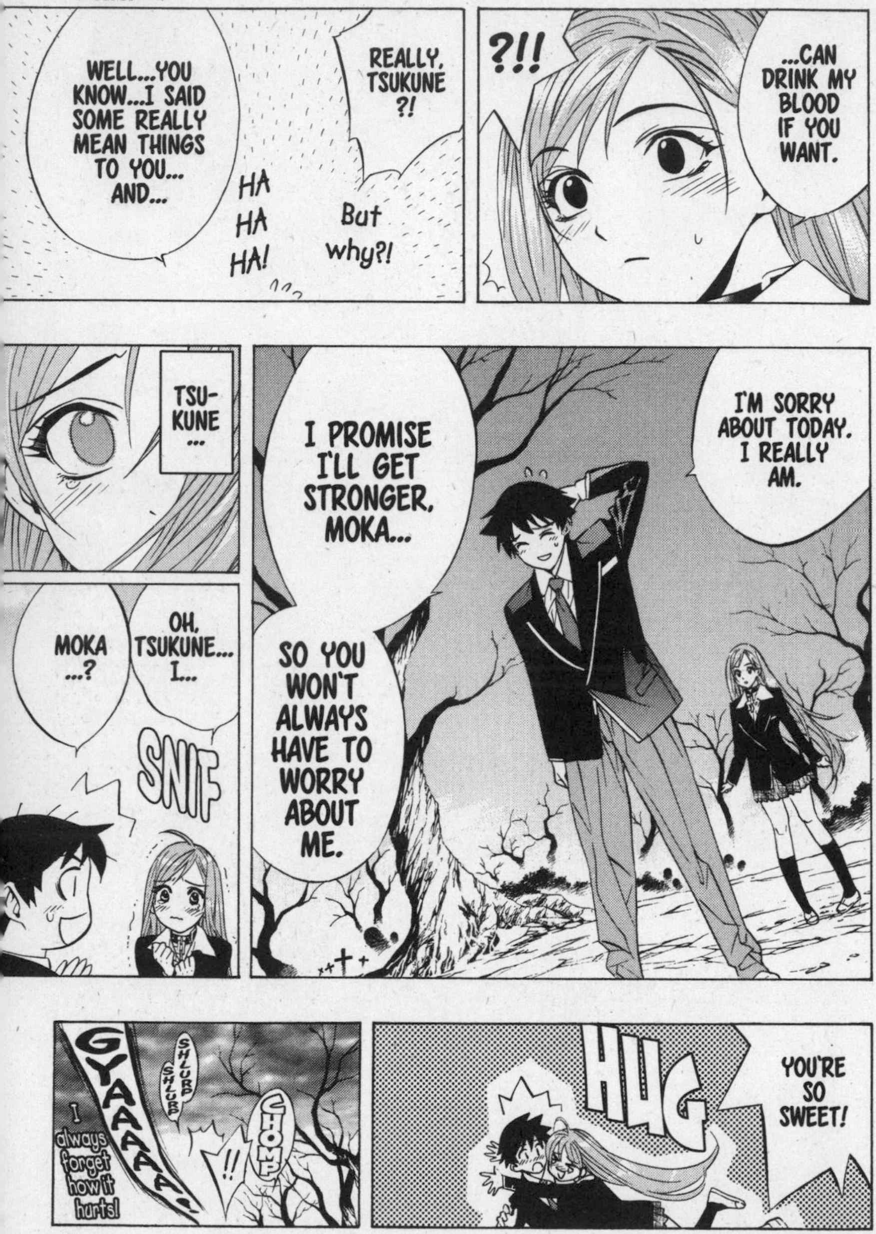

?!!
...CAN DRINK MY BLOOD IF YOU WANT.
REALLY, TSUKUNE ?!
WELL...YOU KNOW...I SAID SOME REALLY MEAN THINGS TO YOU... AND...
But why?!
HA HA HA!
I'M SORRY ABOUT TODAY. I REALLY AM.
I PROMISE I'LL GET STRONGER, MOKA...
SO YOU WON'T ALWAYS HAVE TO WORRY ABOUT ME.
TSU-KUNE ...
OH, TSUKUNE... I...
MOKA ...?
SNIF
YOU'RE SO SWEET!
HUG
CHOMP
SHLURP SHLURP
!!
GYAAAAAA!
I always forget how it hurts!

ROSARIO+VAMPIRE

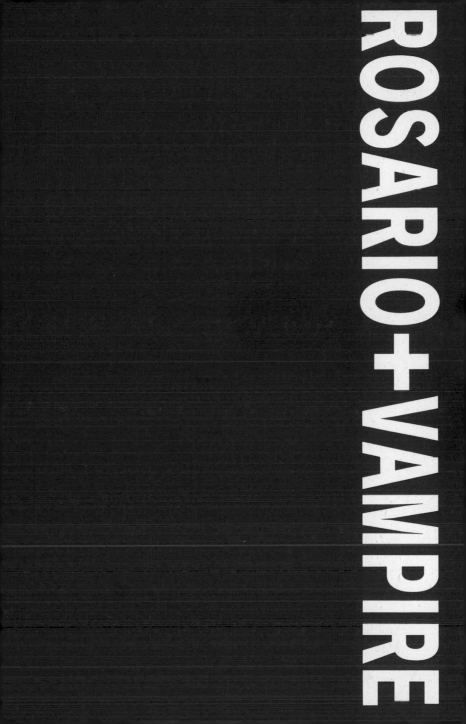

12 : Teach Me!

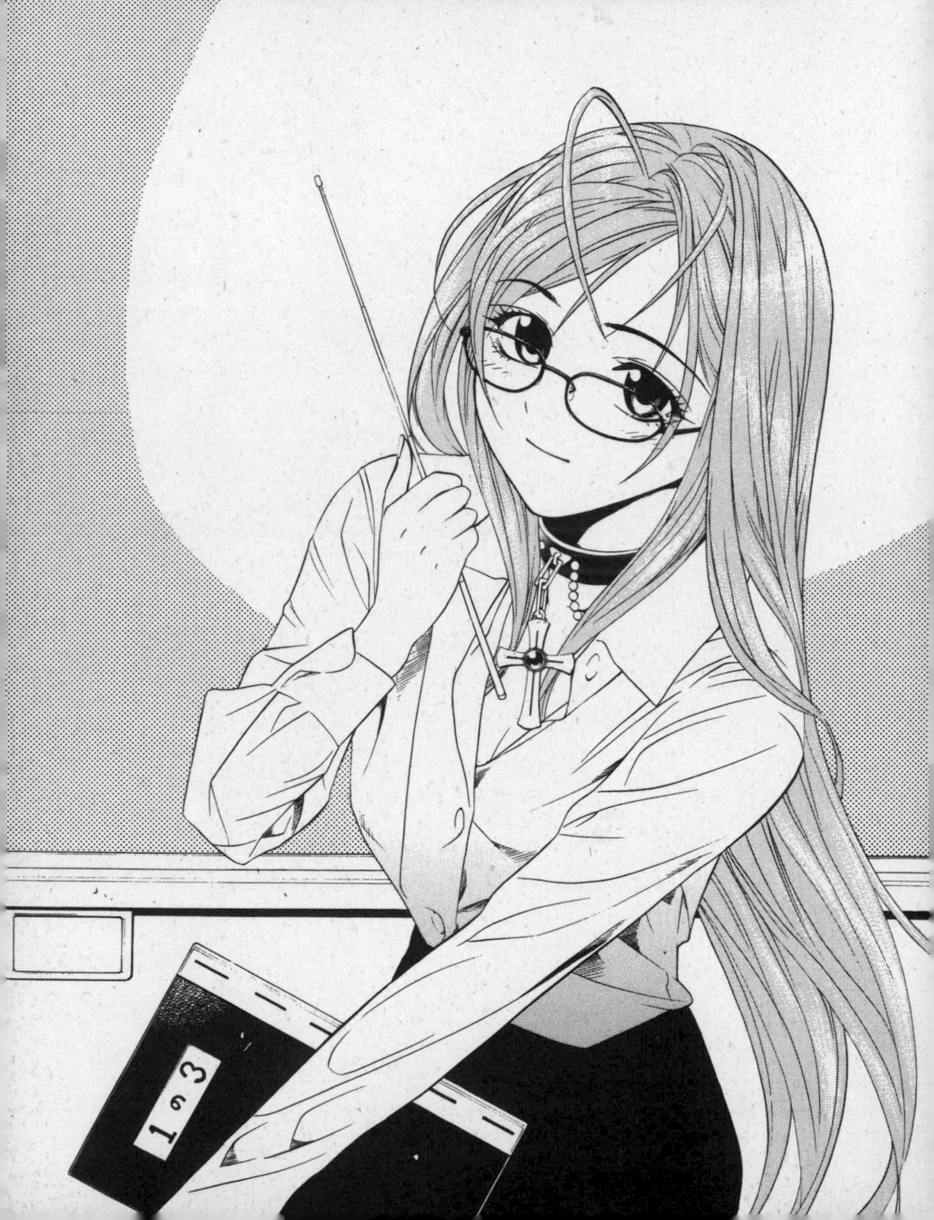
1の3

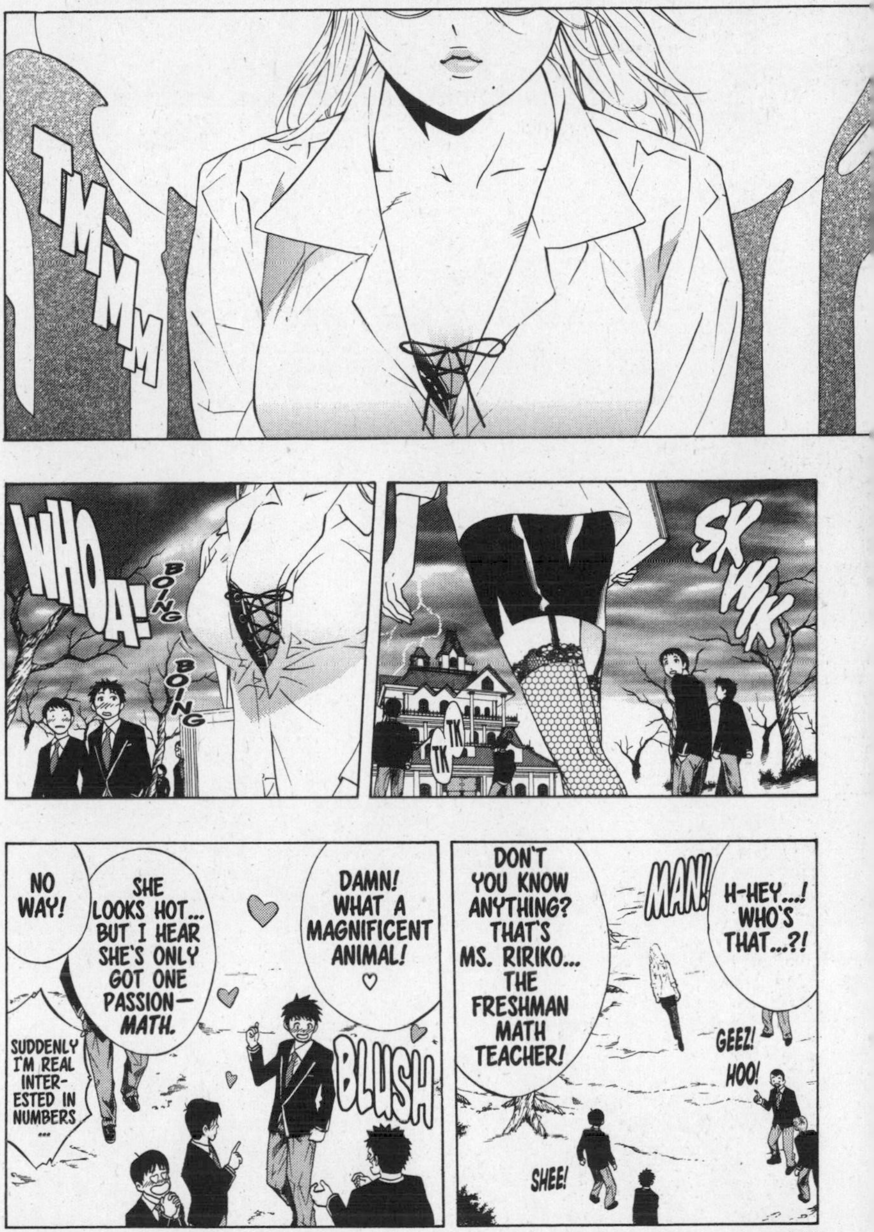
TMMMM
SKWIK
TK
TK
WHOA!
BOING
BOING
H-HEY...! WHO'S THAT...?!
MAN!
DON'T YOU KNOW ANYTHING? THAT'S MS. RIRIKO... THE FRESHMAN MATH TEACHER!
GEEZ!
HOO!
SHEE!
DAMN! WHAT A MAGNIFICENT ANIMAL!
BLUSH
SHE LOOKS HOT... BUT I HEAR SHE'S ONLY GOT ONE PASSION—MATH.
NO WAY!
SUDDENLY I'M REAL INTER-ESTED IN NUMBERS...

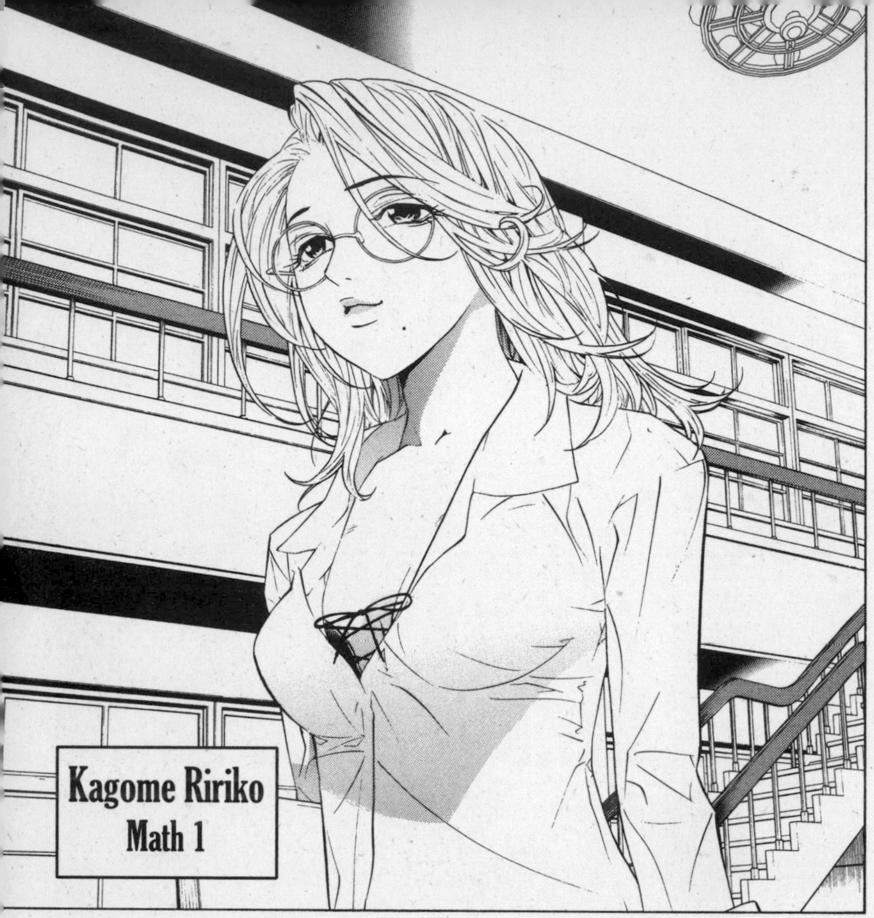
Kagome Ririko
Math 1

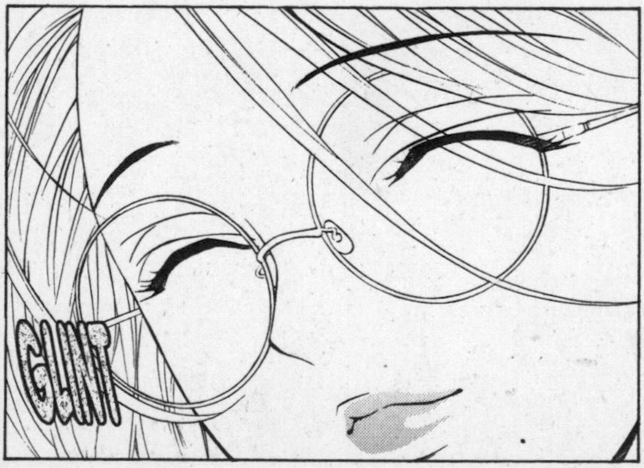
GLINT

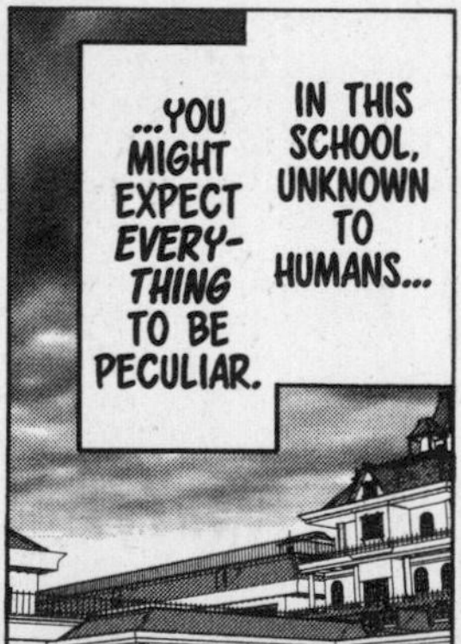
IN THIS SCHOOL, UNKNOWN TO HUMANS...
...YOU MIGHT EXPECT *EVERYTHING* TO BE PECULIAR.

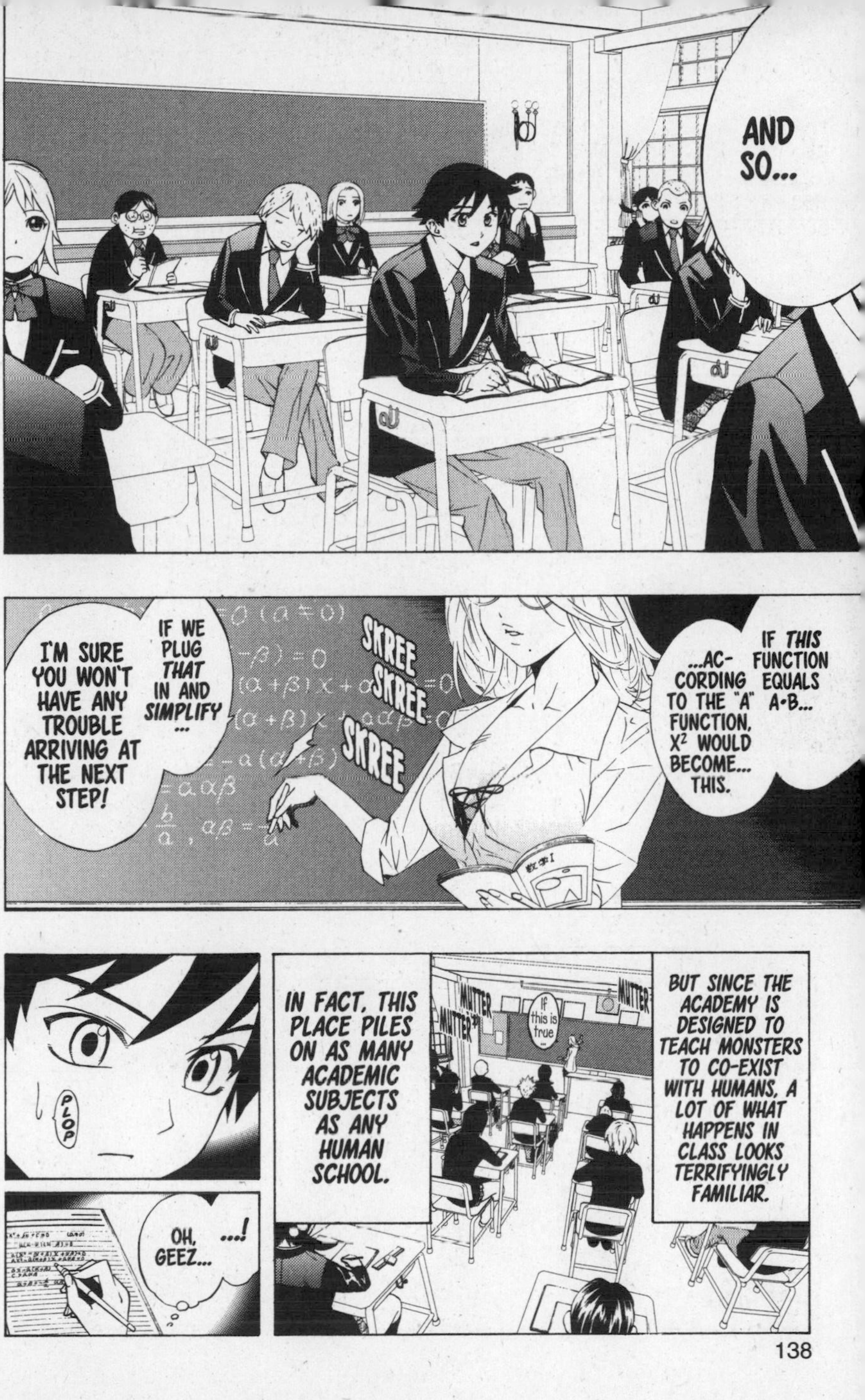
AND SO...
IF THIS FUNCTION EQUALS A-B...
...ACCORDING TO THE "A" FUNCTION, X^2 WOULD BECOME... THIS.
SKREE SKREE SKREE
数学I
IF WE PLUG THAT IN AND SIMPLIFY...
I'M SURE YOU WON'T HAVE ANY TROUBLE ARRIVING AT THE NEXT STEP!
BUT SINCE THE ACADEMY IS DESIGNED TO TEACH MONSTERS TO CO-EXIST WITH HUMANS, A LOT OF WHAT HAPPENS IN CLASS LOOKS TERRIFYINGLY FAMILIAR.
MUTTER
MUTTER MUTTER
If this is true...
IN FACT, THIS PLACE PILES ON AS MANY ACADEMIC SUBJECTS AS ANY HUMAN SCHOOL.
PLOP
...!
OH, GEEZ...

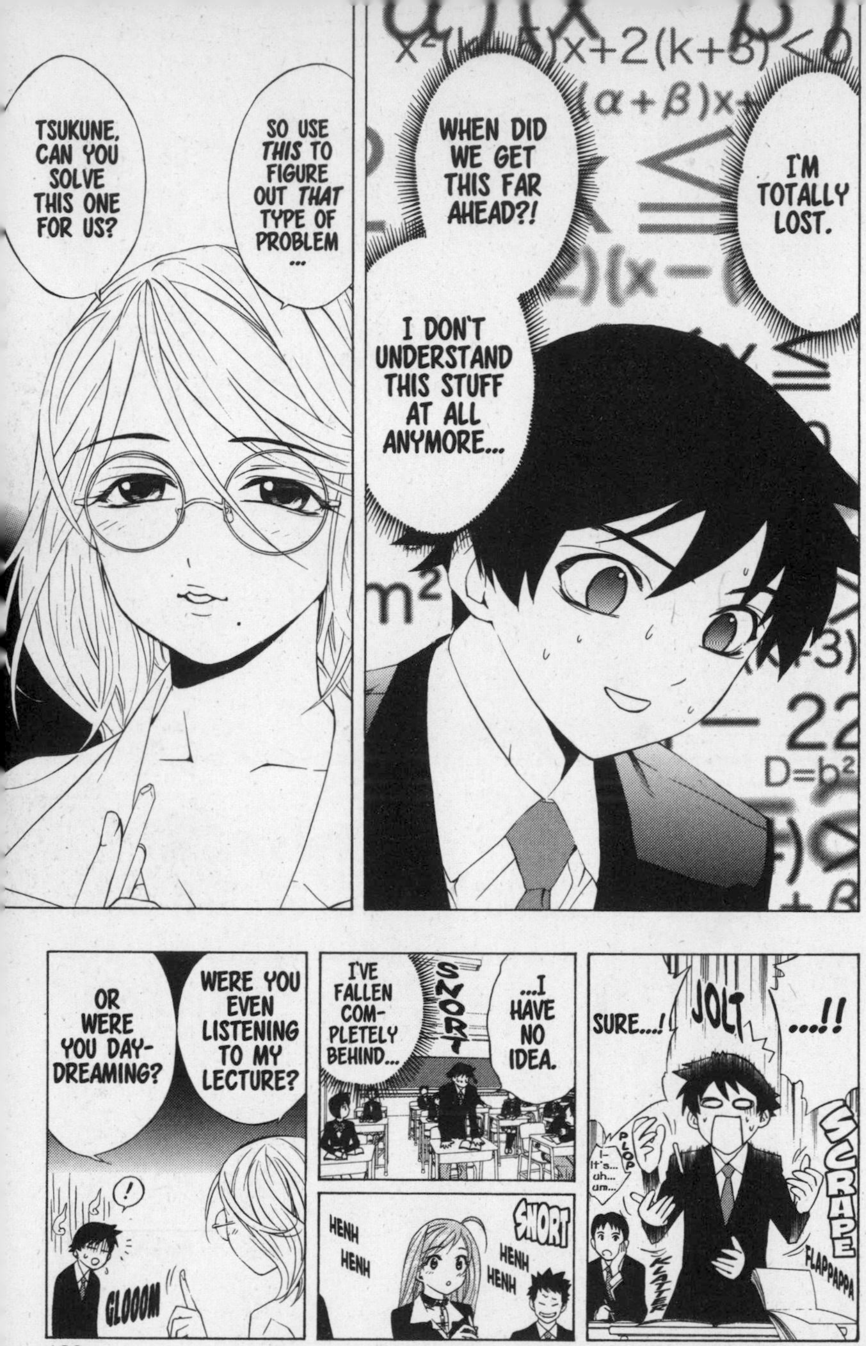
I'M TOTALLY LOST.
WHEN DID WE GET THIS FAR AHEAD?!
I DON'T UNDERSTAND THIS STUFF AT ALL ANYMORE...
SO USE *THIS* TO FIGURE OUT *THAT* TYPE OF PROBLEM ...
TSUKUNE, CAN YOU SOLVE THIS ONE FOR US?
...!!
JOLT
SURE...!
SCRAPE
PLOP
I-It's... uh... um...
KLATTER
FLAPPAPPA
...I HAVE NO IDEA.
SNORT
I'VE FALLEN COM-PLETELY BEHIND...
SNORT
HENH HENH
HENH HENH
WERE YOU EVEN LISTENING TO MY LECTURE?
OR WERE YOU DAY-DREAMING?
!
GLOOOM

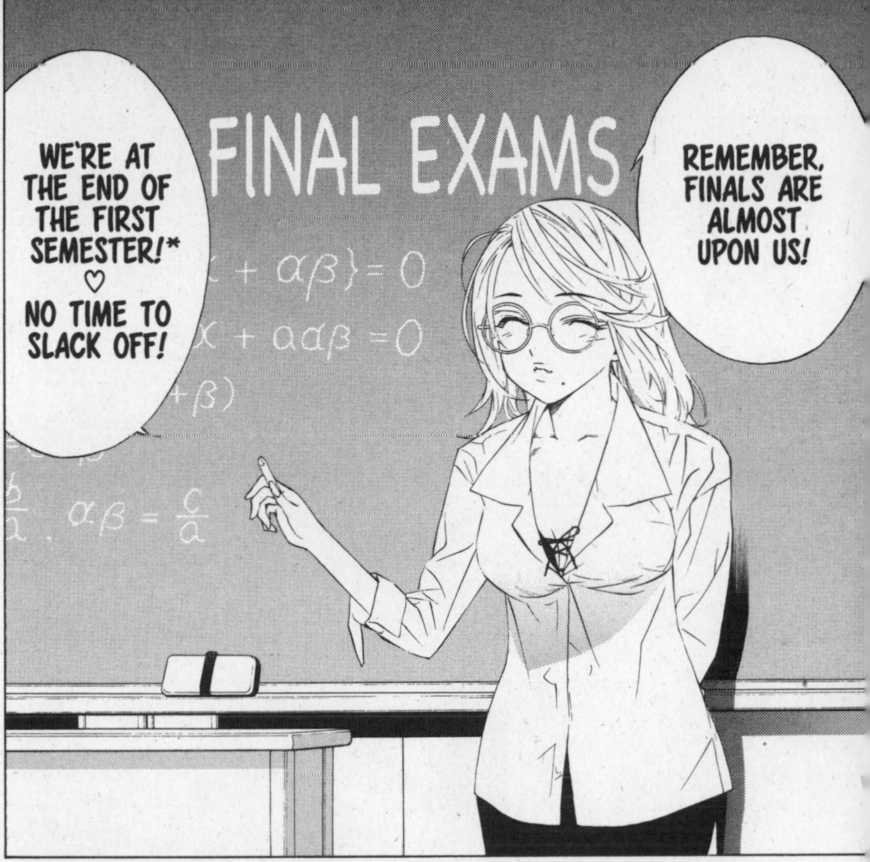
REMEMBER, FINALS ARE ALMOST UPON US!
FINAL EXAMS
WE'RE AT THE END OF THE FIRST SEMESTER!* ♡ NO TIME TO SLACK OFF!

*LIKE THE JAPANESE SCHOOL YEAR, THE MONSTER SCHOOL YEAR STARTS IN APRIL.

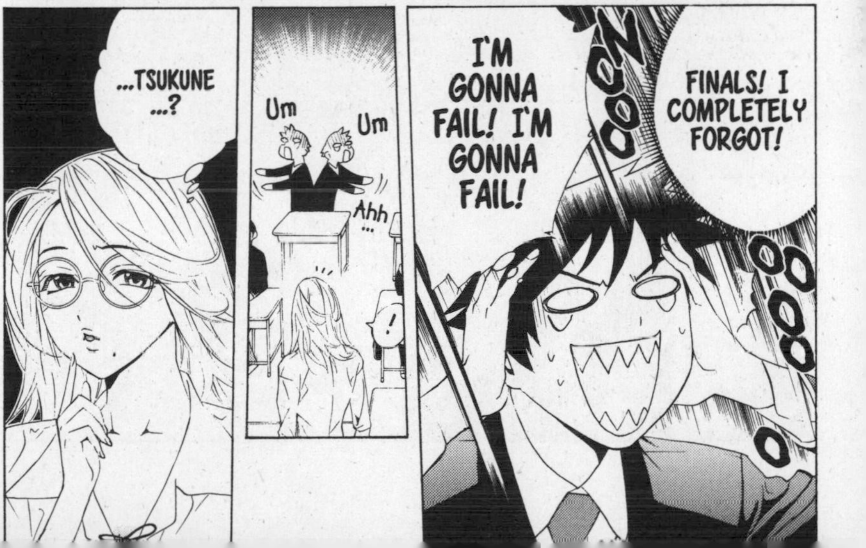
FINALS! I COMPLETELY FORGOT!
I'M GONNA FAIL! I'M GONNA FAIL!
Um
Um
Ahh...
!
...TSUKUNE ...?

READ THIS WAY

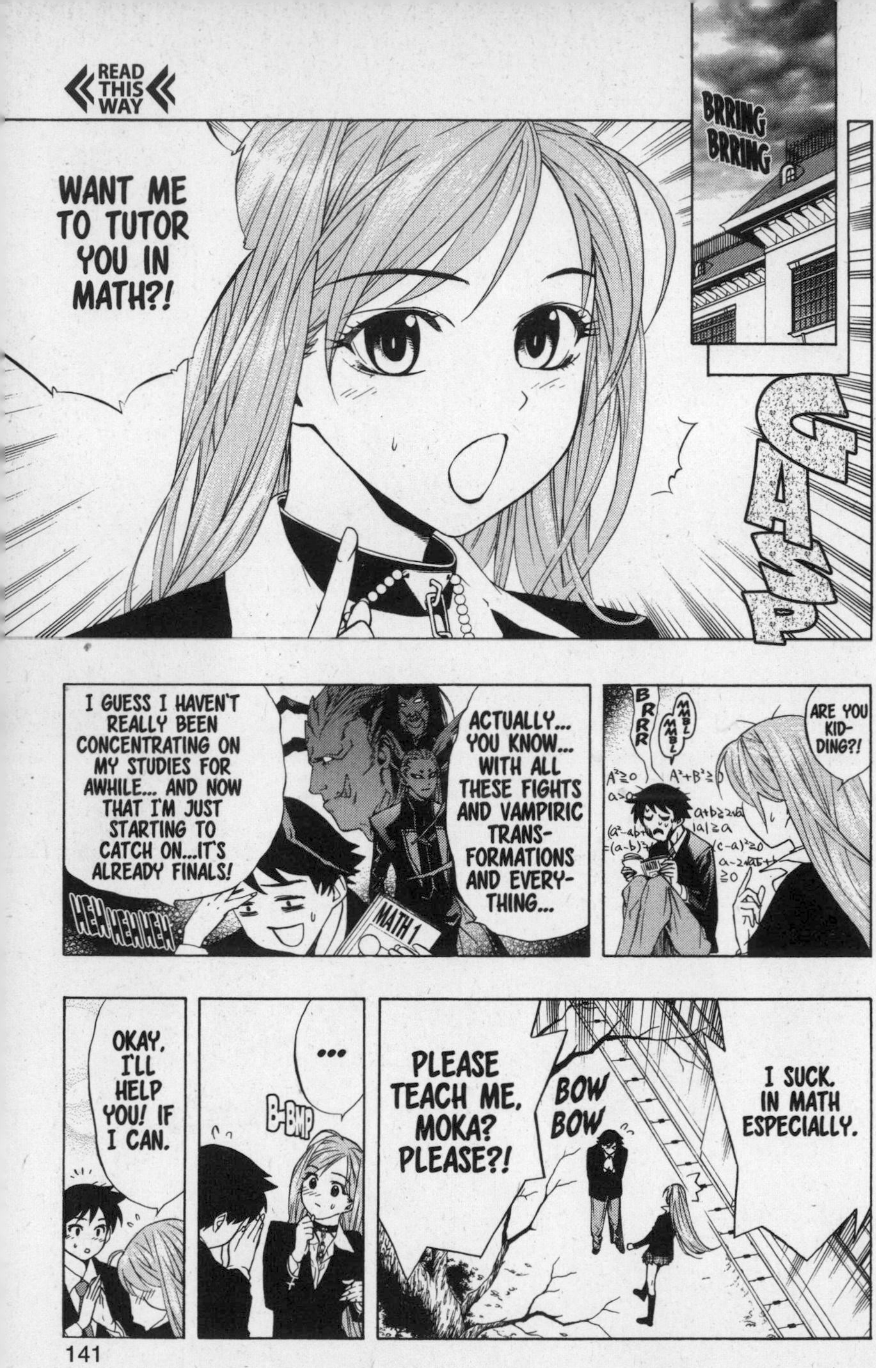
BRRING BRRING
GASP
WANT ME TO TUTOR YOU IN MATH?!
ARE YOU KID-DING?!
BRRR
MMBL MMBL
ACTUALLY... YOU KNOW... WITH ALL THESE FIGHTS AND VAMPIRIC TRANS-FORMATIONS AND EVERY-THING...
I GUESS I HAVEN'T REALLY BEEN CONCENTRATING ON MY STUDIES FOR AWHILE... AND NOW THAT I'M JUST STARTING TO CATCH ON...IT'S ALREADY FINALS!
HEH HEH HEH
MATH 1
I SUCK. IN MATH ESPECIALLY.
BOW BOW
PLEASE TEACH ME, MOKA? PLEASE?!
...
B-BMP
OKAY, I'LL HELP YOU! IF I CAN.

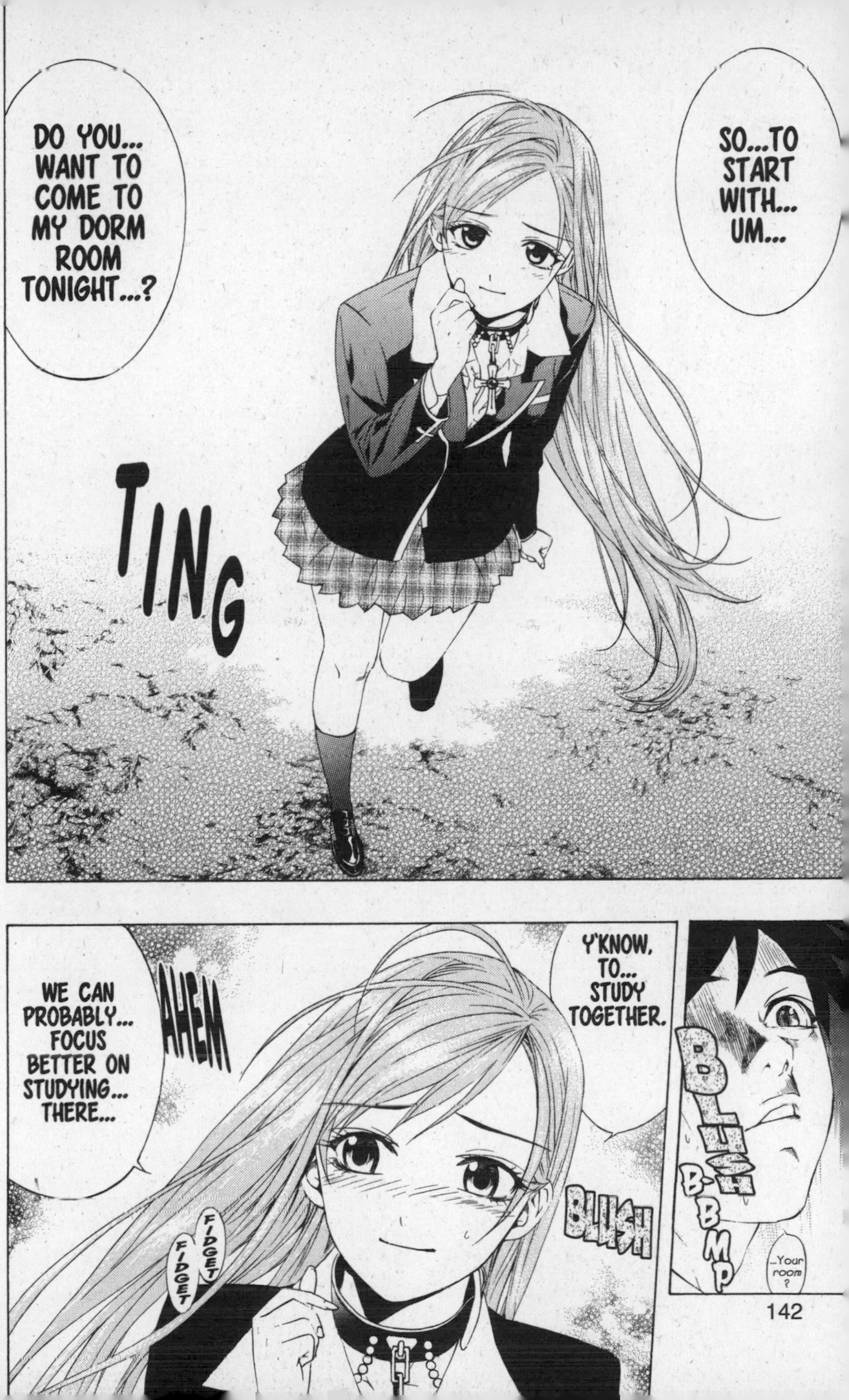
SO...TO START WITH... UM...
TING
DO YOU... WANT TO COME TO MY DORM ROOM TONIGHT...?
BLUSH
B-BUMP
...Your room?
Y'KNOW, TO... STUDY TOGETHER.
AHEM
WE CAN PROBABLY... FOCUS BETTER ON STUDYING... THERE...
BLUSH
FIDGET FIDGET

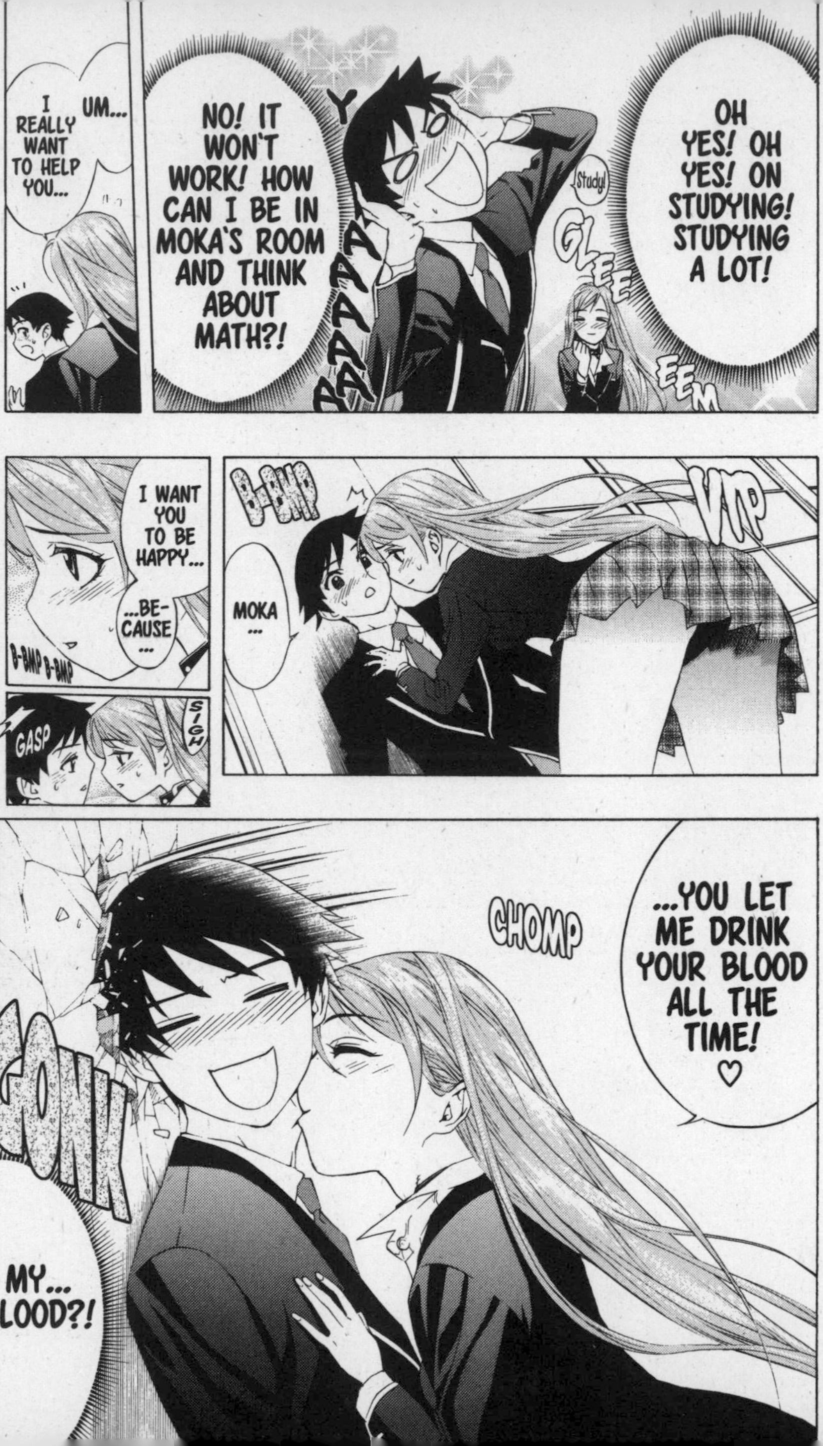
OH YES! OH YES! ON STUDYING! STUDYING A LOT!
Study!
GLEEEEM
NO! IT WON'T WORK! HOW CAN I BE IN MOKA'S ROOM AND THINK ABOUT MATH?!
YAAAAAA
UM...
I REALLY WANT TO HELP YOU...
VIP
B-BMP
MOKA ...
I WANT YOU TO BE HAPPY...
...BE-CAUSE ...
B-BMP B-BMP
SIGH
GASP
...YOU LET ME DRINK YOUR BLOOD ALL THE TIME! ♥
CHOMP
GONK
MY... BLOOD?!

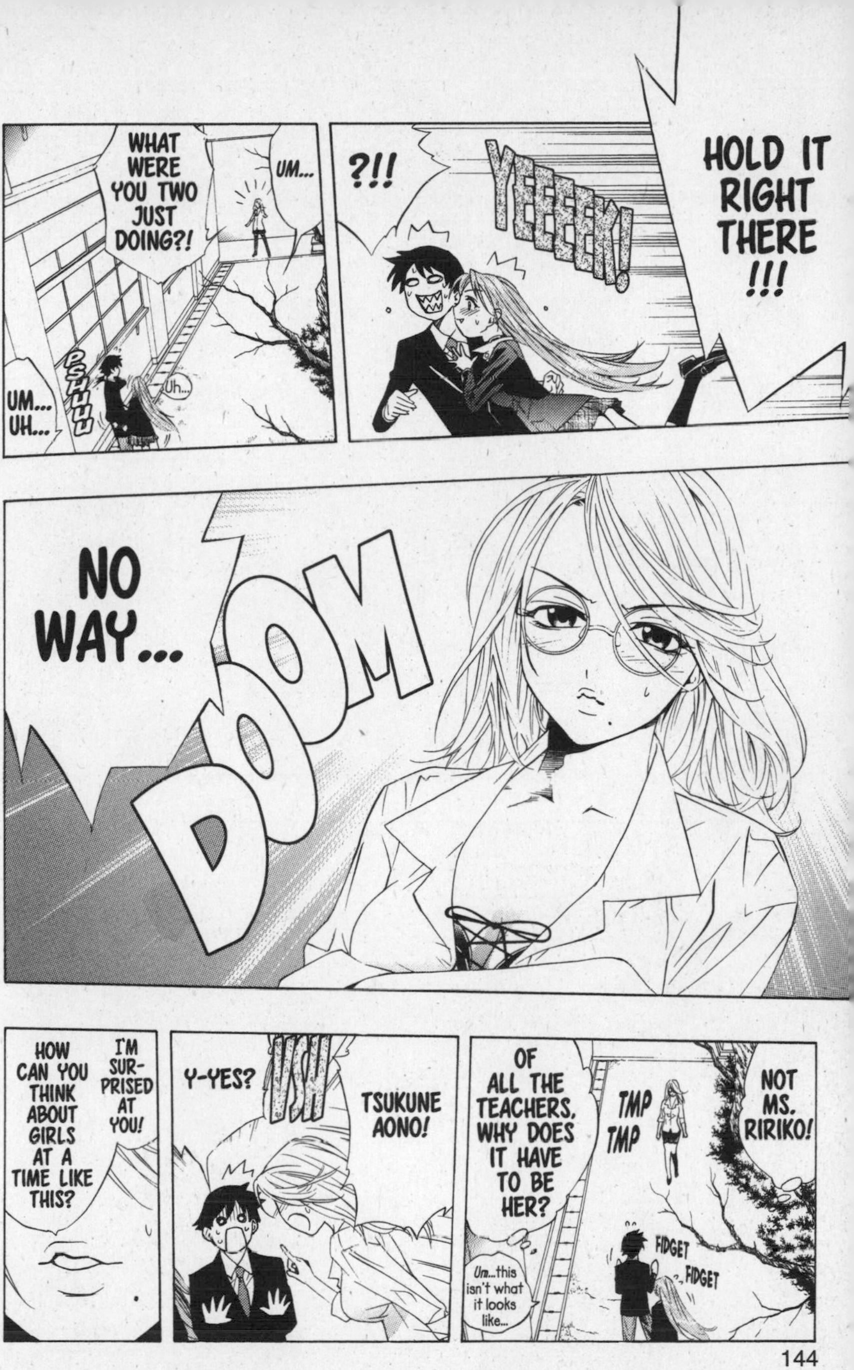
HOLD IT RIGHT THERE!!!
YEEEEK!
?!!
UM...
WHAT WERE YOU TWO JUST DOING?!
Uh...
PSHUUU
UM... UH...
DOOM
NO WAY...
NOT MS. RIRIKO!
TMP TMP
OF ALL THE TEACHERS, WHY DOES IT HAVE TO BE HER?
FIDGET FIDGET
Um...this isn't what it looks like...
VSH
TSUKUNE AONO!
Y-YES?
I'M SUR-PRISED AT YOU!
HOW CAN YOU THINK ABOUT GIRLS AT A TIME LIKE THIS?

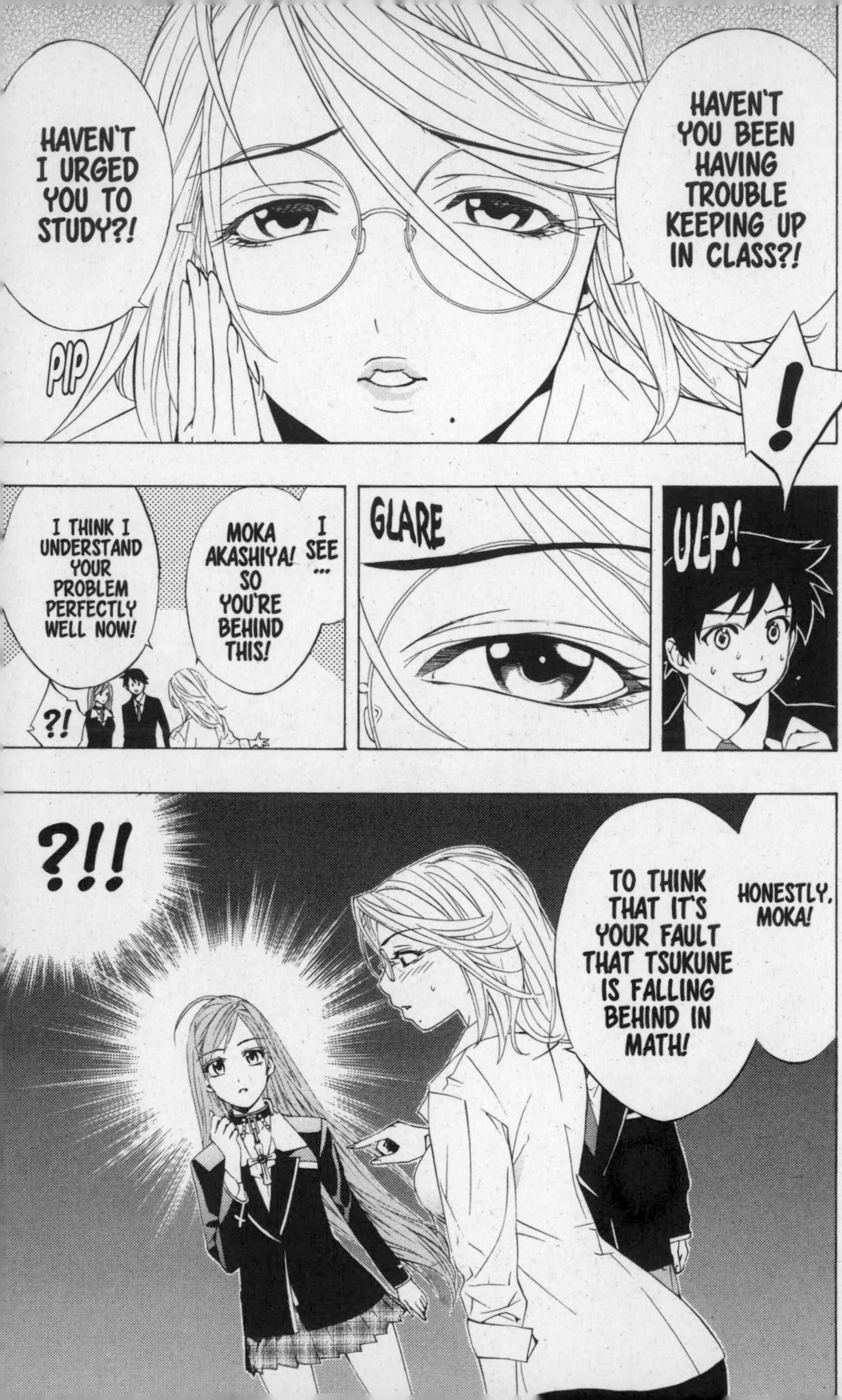
HAVEN'T YOU BEEN HAVING TROUBLE KEEPING UP IN CLASS?!
HAVEN'T I URGED YOU TO STUDY?!
PIP
!
ULP!
GLARE
I SEE...
MOKA AKASHIYA! SO YOU'RE BEHIND THIS!
I THINK I UNDERSTAND YOUR PROBLEM PERFECTLY WELL NOW!
?!
HONESTLY, MOKA!
TO THINK THAT IT'S YOUR FAULT THAT TSUKUNE IS FALLING BEHIND IN MATH!
?!!

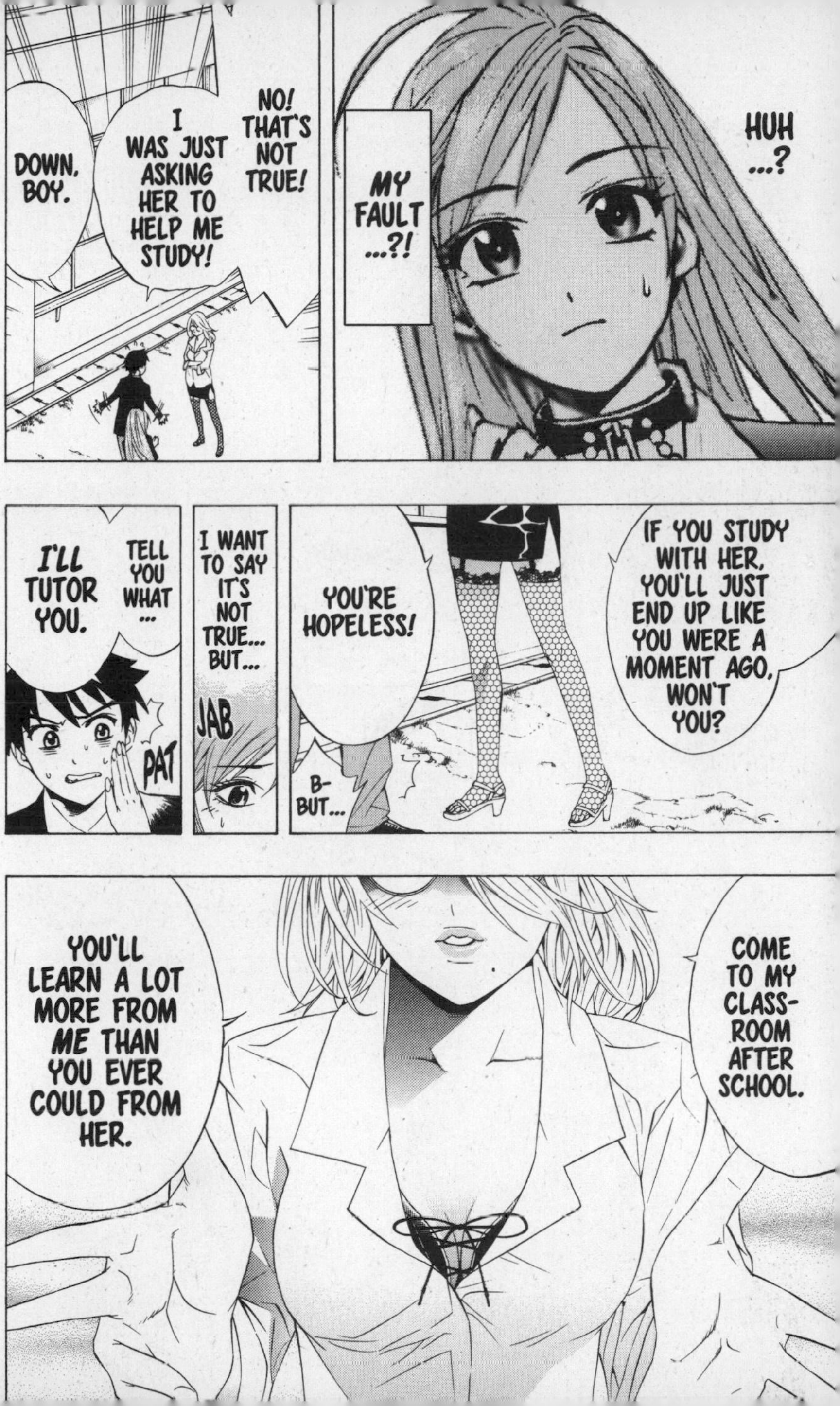
HUH ...?
MY FAULT ...?!
NO! THAT'S NOT TRUE!
I WAS JUST ASKING HER TO HELP ME STUDY!
DOWN, BOY.
IF YOU STUDY WITH HER, YOU'LL JUST END UP LIKE YOU WERE A MOMENT AGO, WON'T YOU?
YOU'RE HOPELESS!
B-BUT...
I WANT TO SAY IT'S NOT TRUE... BUT...
JAB
TELL YOU WHAT...
I'LL TUTOR YOU.
PAT
COME TO MY CLASS-ROOM AFTER SCHOOL.
YOU'LL LEARN A LOT MORE FROM ME THAN YOU EVER COULD FROM HER.

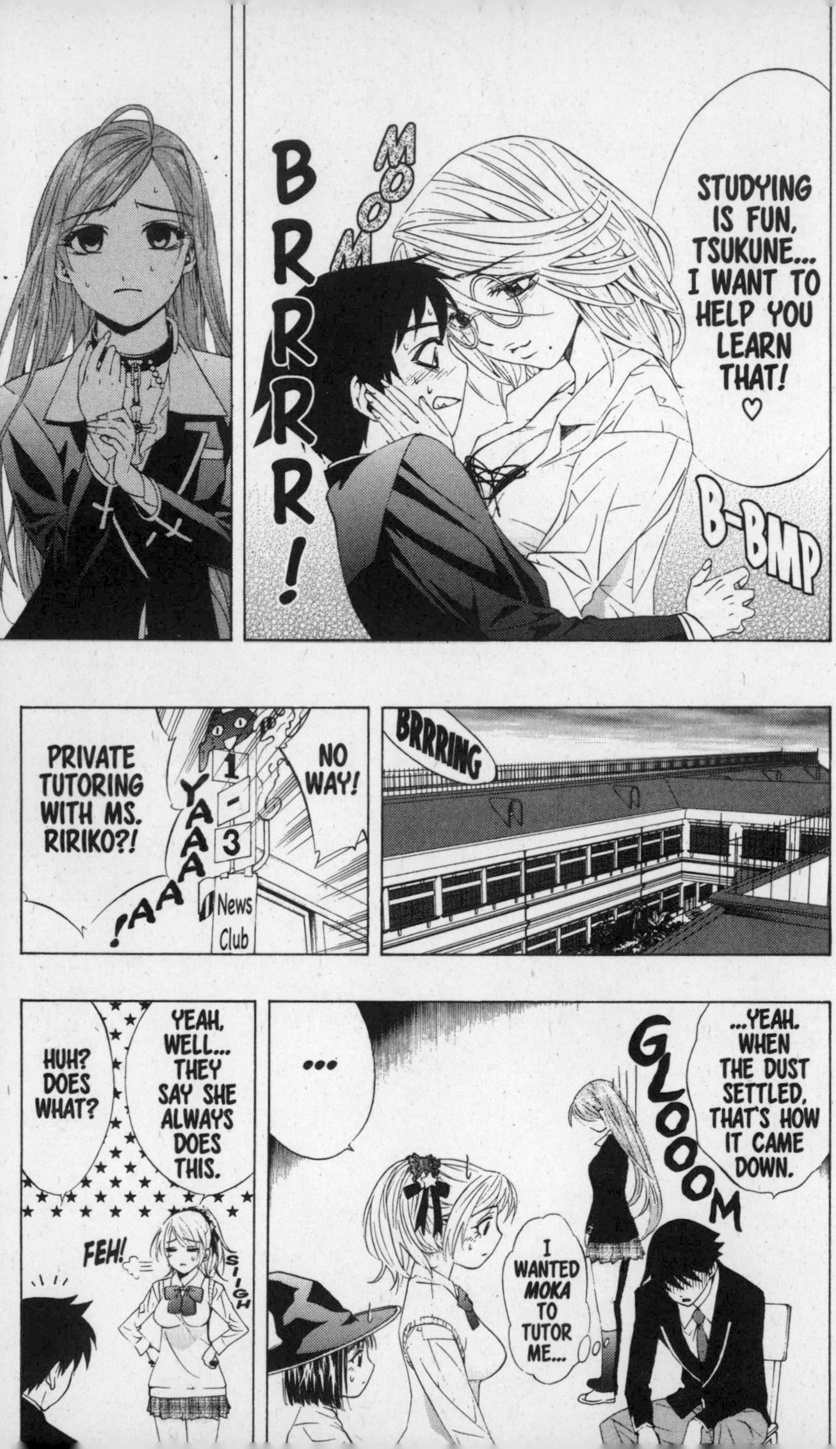

STUDYING IS FUN, TSUKUNE... I WANT TO HELP YOU LEARN THAT! ♡
B-BMP
BRRRRR!
MOOM
BRRRING
NO WAY!
YAAAAA!
PRIVATE TUTORING WITH MS. RIRIKO?!
1-3
News Club
...YEAH. WHEN THE DUST SETTLED, THAT'S HOW IT CAME DOWN.
GLOOOOM
I WANTED MOKA TO TUTOR ME...
...
YEAH, WELL... THEY SAY SHE ALWAYS DOES THIS.
HUH? DOES WHAT?
FEH!
SIGH

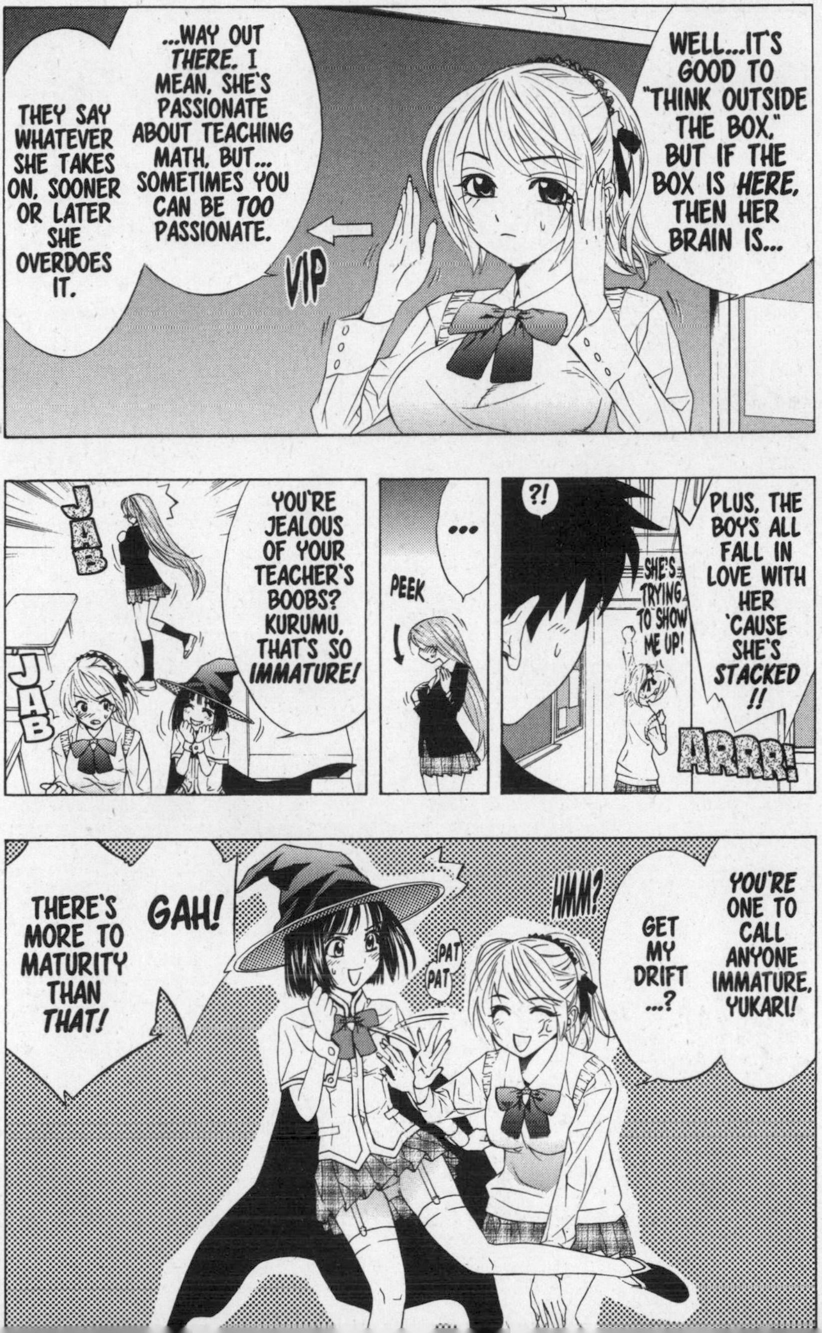
WELL...IT'S GOOD TO "THINK OUTSIDE THE BOX," BUT IF THE BOX IS *HERE*, THEN HER BRAIN IS...
...WAY OUT *THERE*. I MEAN, SHE'S PASSIONATE ABOUT TEACHING MATH, BUT... SOMETIMES YOU CAN BE *TOO* PASSIONATE.
VIP
THEY SAY WHATEVER SHE TAKES ON, SOONER OR LATER SHE OVERDOES IT.
PLUS, THE BOYS ALL FALL IN LOVE WITH HER 'CAUSE SHE'S *STACKED* !!
?!
SHE'S TRYING TO SHOW ME UP!
ARRR!
...
PEEK
YOU'RE JEALOUS OF YOUR TEACHER'S BOOBS? KURUMU, THAT'S SO *IMMATURE!*
JAB
JAB
YOU'RE ONE TO CALL ANYONE IMMATURE, YUKARI!
GET MY DRIFT ...?
HMM?
PAT PAT
GAH!
THERE'S MORE TO MATURITY THAN *THAT!*

READ THIS WAY

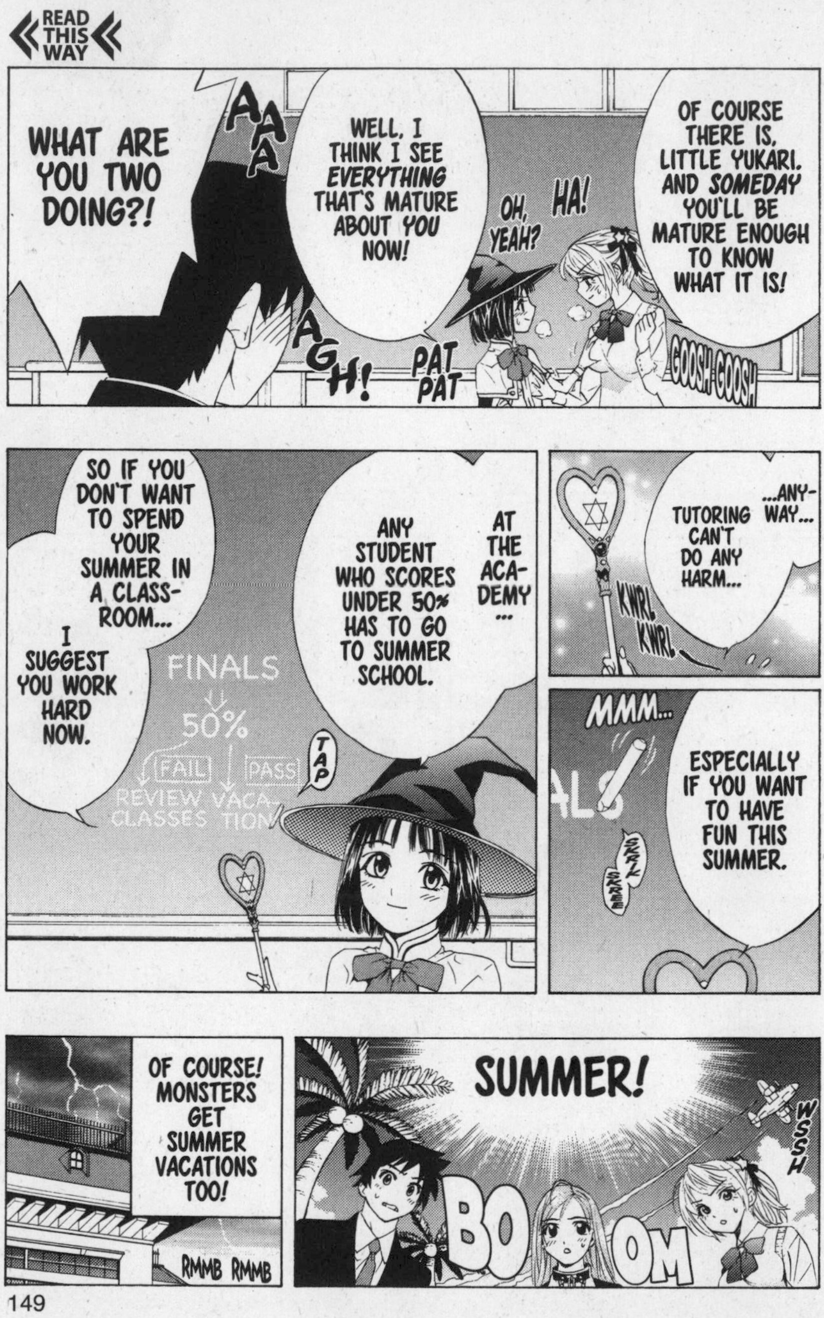

OF COURSE THERE IS, LITTLE YUKARI. AND SOMEDAY YOU'LL BE MATURE ENOUGH TO KNOW WHAT IT IS!
HA!
OH, YEAH?
GOOSH-GOOSH
PAT PAT
WELL, I THINK I SEE EVERYTHING THAT'S MATURE ABOUT YOU NOW!
AAAAGH!
WHAT ARE YOU TWO DOING?!
...ANY-WAY...
TUTORING CAN'T DO ANY HARM...
KWRL KWRL
MMM...
ESPECIALLY IF YOU WANT TO HAVE FUN THIS SUMMER.
SKRIK SKREE
AT THE ACA-DEMY...
ANY STUDENT WHO SCORES UNDER 50% HAS TO GO TO SUMMER SCHOOL.
TAP
SO IF YOU DON'T WANT TO SPEND YOUR SUMMER IN A CLASS-ROOM...
I SUGGEST YOU WORK HARD NOW.
FINALS
50%
FAIL
PASS
REVIEW CLASSES
VACA-TION
SUMMER!
WSSH
BOOOM
OF COURSE! MONSTERS GET SUMMER VACATIONS TOO!
RMMB RMMB

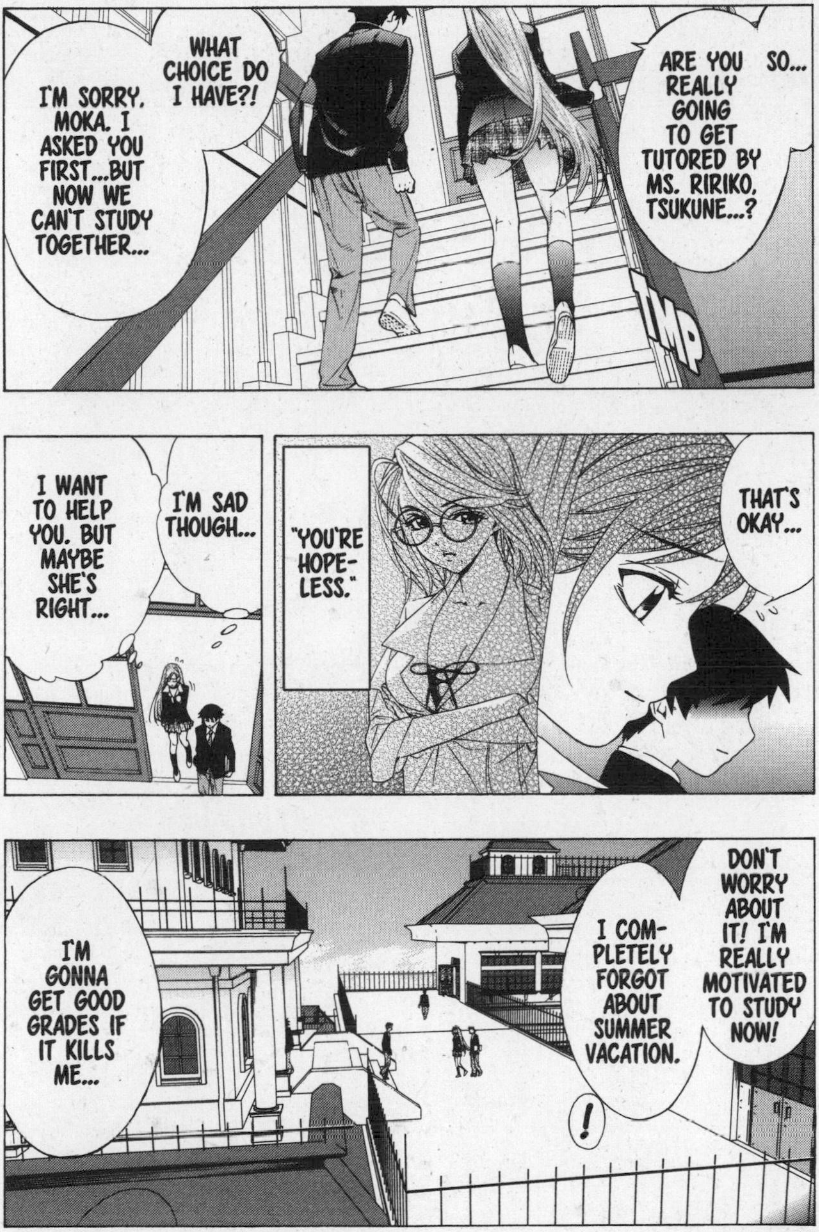
SO... ARE YOU REALLY GOING TO GET TUTORED BY MS. RIRIKO, TSUKUNE...?
WHAT CHOICE DO I HAVE?!
I'M SORRY, MOKA. I ASKED YOU FIRST...BUT NOW WE CAN'T STUDY TOGETHER...
TMP
THAT'S OKAY...
"YOU'RE HOPELESS."
I'M SAD THOUGH...
I WANT TO HELP YOU. BUT MAYBE SHE'S RIGHT...
DON'T WORRY ABOUT IT! I'M REALLY MOTIVATED TO STUDY NOW!
I COMPLETELY FORGOT ABOUT SUMMER VACATION.
!
I'M GONNA GET GOOD GRADES IF IT KILLS ME...

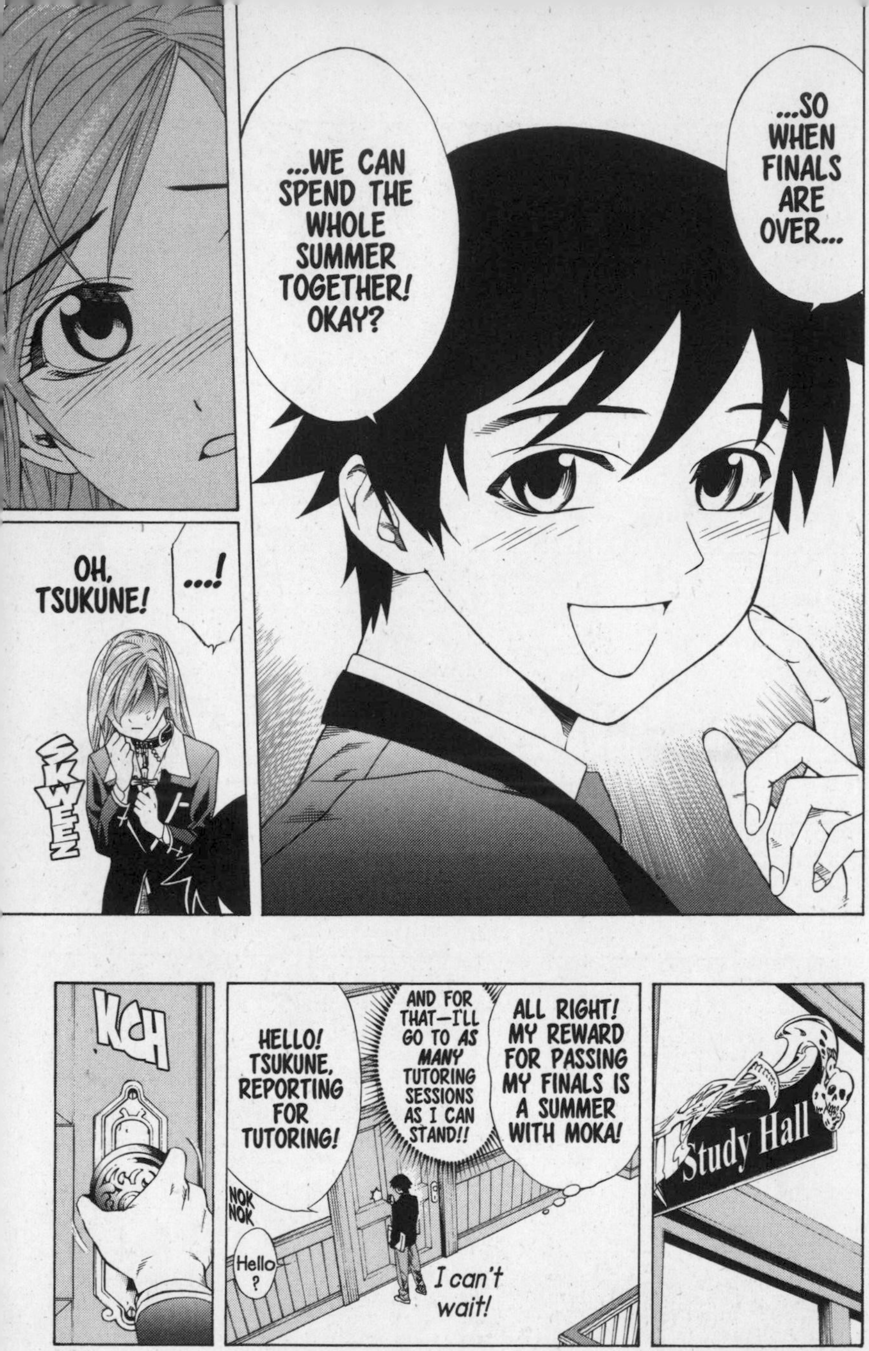
...SO WHEN FINALS ARE OVER...
...WE CAN SPEND THE WHOLE SUMMER TOGETHER! OKAY?
...!
OH, TSUKUNE!
SKWEEZ
Study Hall
ALL RIGHT! MY REWARD FOR PASSING MY FINALS IS A SUMMER WITH MOKA!
AND FOR THAT—I'LL GO TO AS *MANY* TUTORING SESSIONS AS I CAN STAND!!
HELLO! TSUKUNE, REPORTING FOR TUTORING!
NOK NOK
Hello?
I can't wait!
KCH

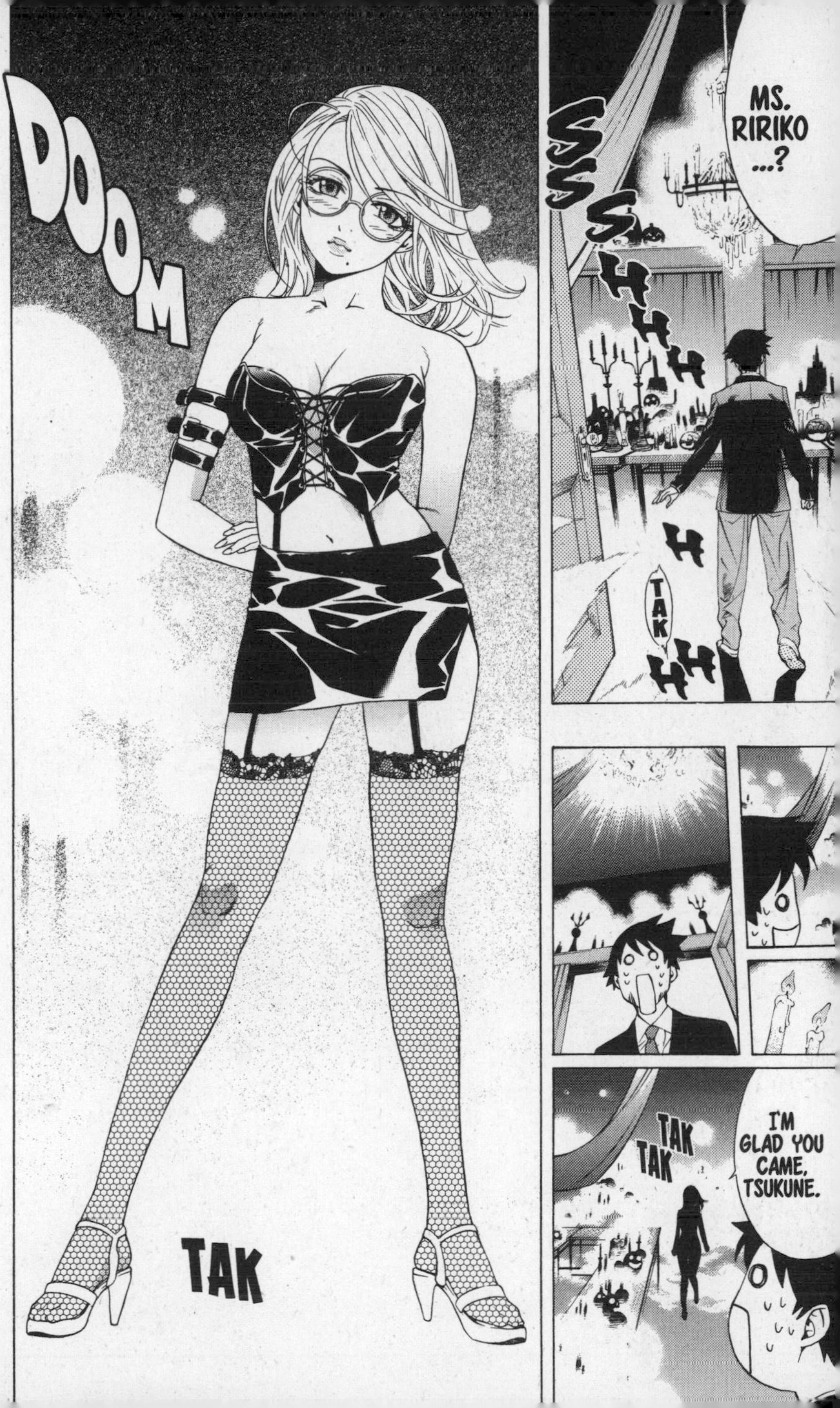
MS. RIRIKO ...?
SSSHHHHH
TAK
HHH
I'M GLAD YOU CAME, TSUKUNE.
TAK TAK
DOOOM
TAK

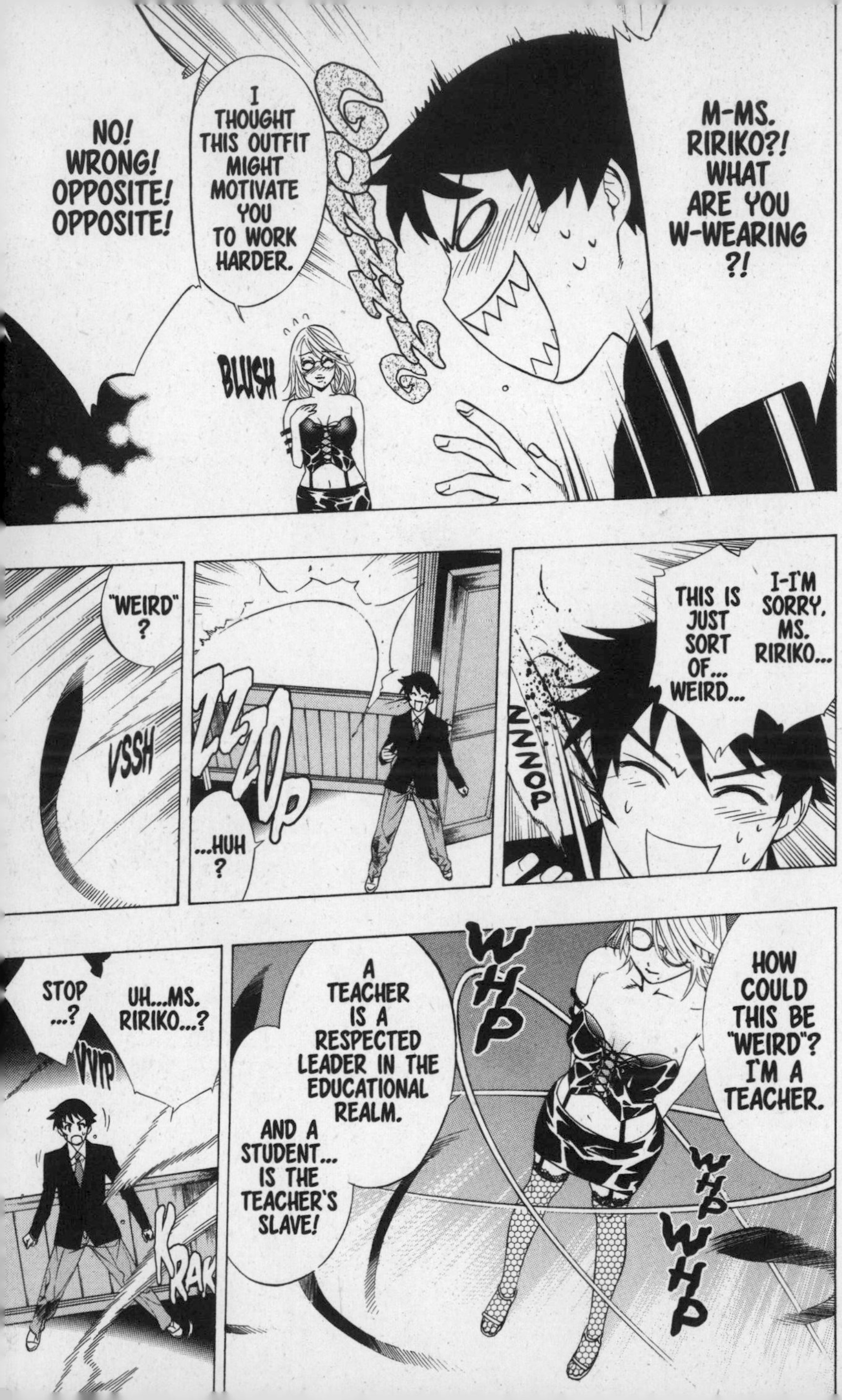
M-MS. RIRIKO?! WHAT ARE YOU W-WEARING?!
I THOUGHT THIS OUTFIT MIGHT MOTIVATE YOU TO WORK HARDER.
NO! WRONG! OPPOSITE! OPPOSITE!
BLUSH
I-I'M SORRY, MS. RIRIKO...
THIS IS JUST SORT OF... WEIRD...
ZZZZOP
ZZZOP
...HUH?
"WEIRD"?
VSSH
HOW COULD THIS BE "WEIRD"? I'M A TEACHER.
WHP
A TEACHER IS A RESPECTED LEADER IN THE EDUCATIONAL REALM.
AND A STUDENT... IS THE TEACHER'S SLAVE!
WHP WHP WHP
UH...MS. RIRIKO...?
STOP...?
VVIP
KRAK

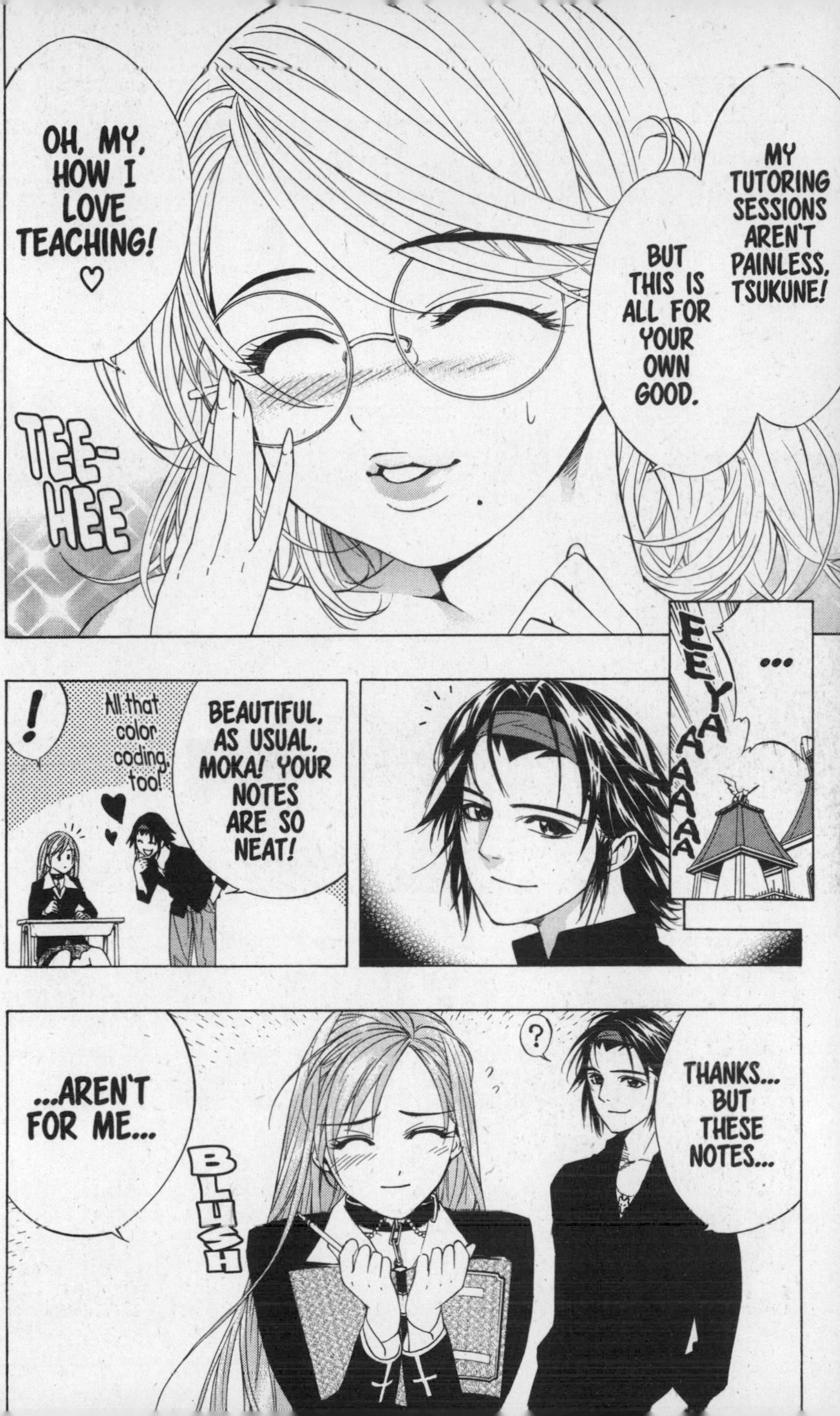
MY TUTORING SESSIONS AREN'T PAINLESS, TSUKUNE!
BUT THIS IS ALL FOR YOUR OWN GOOD.
OH, MY, HOW I LOVE TEACHING! ♡
TEE-HEE
...
EEYAAAAAA
BEAUTIFUL, AS USUAL, MOKA! YOUR NOTES ARE SO NEAT!
All that color coding, too!
!
THANKS... BUT THESE NOTES...
?
...AREN'T FOR ME...
BLUSH

READ THIS WAY

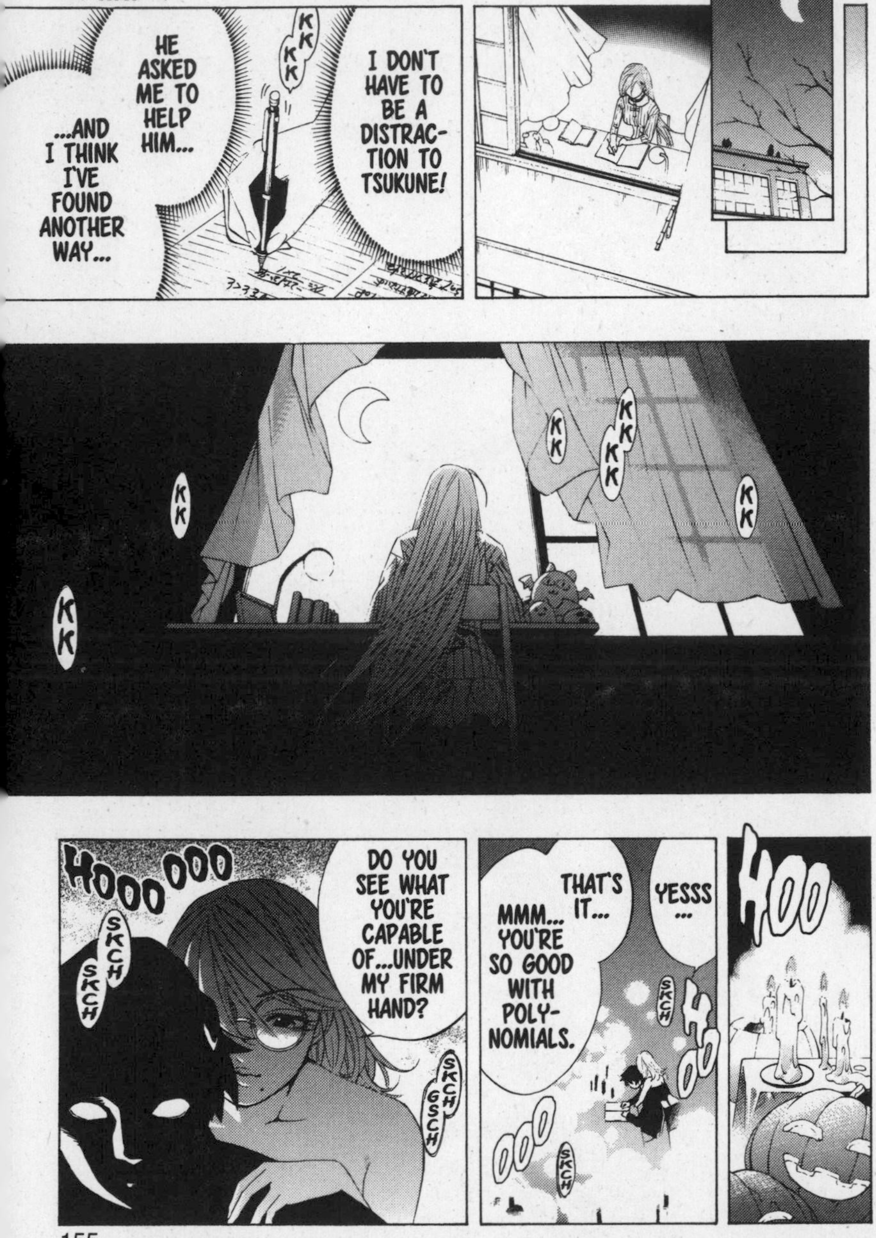

I DON'T HAVE TO BE A DISTRACTION TO TSUKUNE!
KK KK
HE ASKED ME TO HELP HIM...
...AND I THINK I'VE FOUND ANOTHER WAY...
KK
KK KK
KK
KK
KK
HOO
YESSS...
THAT'S IT...
MMM... YOU'RE SO GOOD WITH POLY-NOMIALS.
SKCH
HOO
OOO
SKCH
DO YOU SEE WHAT YOU'RE CAPABLE OF...UNDER MY FIRM HAND?
SKCH GSCH
HOOOOOO
SKCH
SKCH

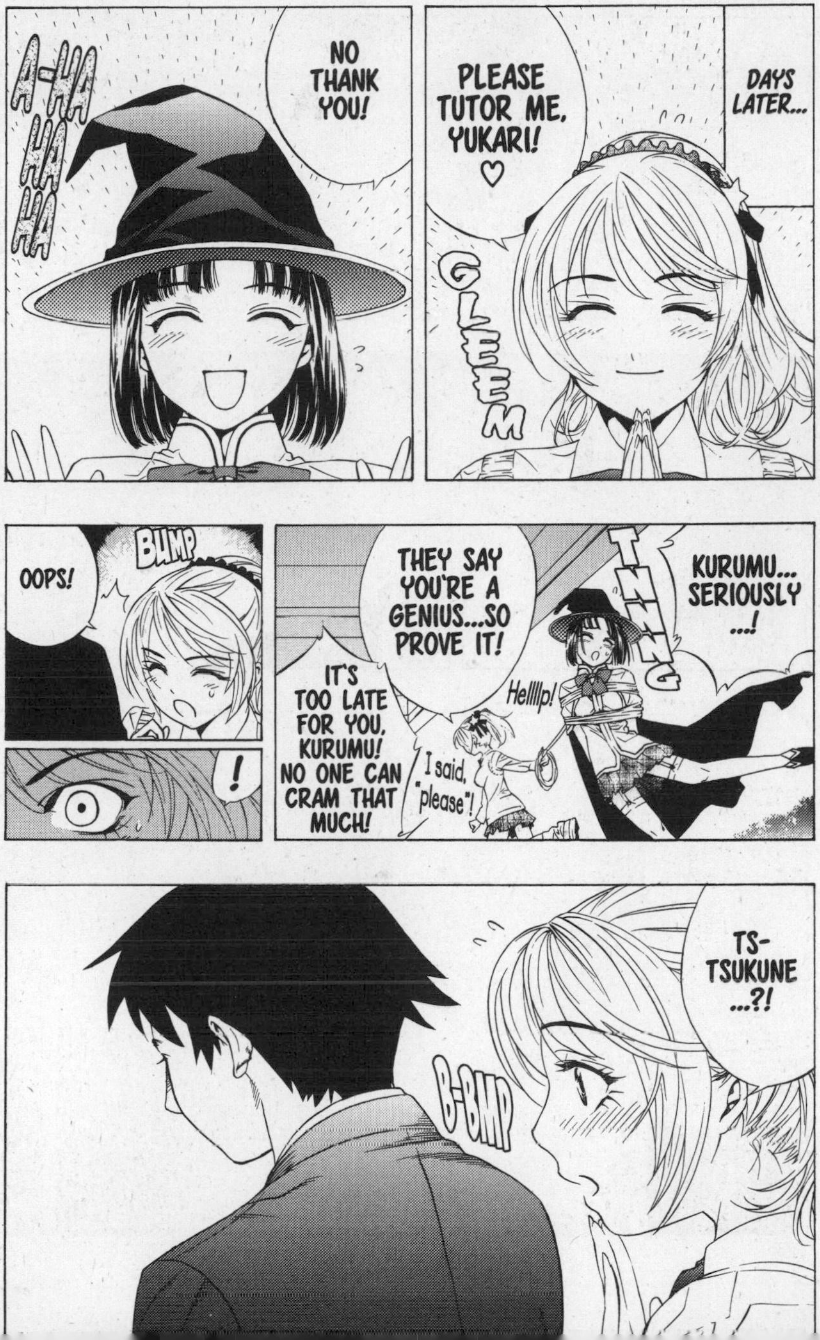
DAYS LATER...
PLEASE TUTOR ME, YUKARI! ♡
GLEEM
NO THANK YOU!
A-HA HA HA HA
KURUMU... SERIOUSLY ...!
TNNG
THEY SAY YOU'RE A GENIUS...SO PROVE IT!
Hellllp!
I said, "please"!
IT'S TOO LATE FOR YOU, KURUMU! NO ONE CAN CRAM THAT MUCH!
BUMP
OOPS!
!
TS-TSUKUNE ...?!
B-BMP

READ THIS WAY

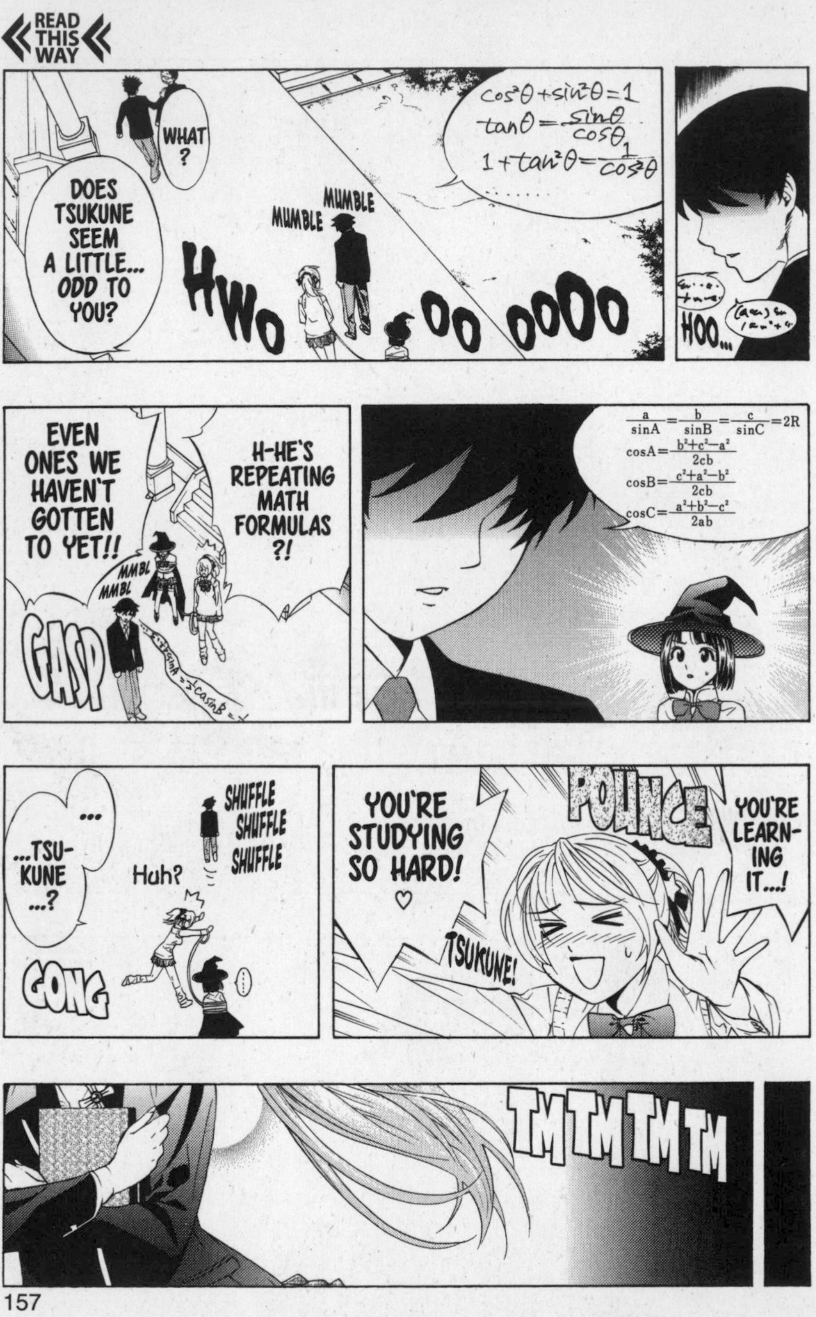
HOO...
$\cos^2\theta+\sin^2\theta=1$
$\tan\theta=\frac{\sin\theta}{\cos\theta}$
$1+\tan^2\theta=\frac{1}{\cos^2\theta}$
......
WHAT?
MUMBLE MUMBLE
DOES TSUKUNE SEEM A LITTLE... ODD TO YOU?
HWO OO OOOO
$\frac{a}{\sin A}=\frac{b}{\sin B}=\frac{c}{\sin C}=2R$
$\cos A=\frac{b^2+c^2-a^2}{2cb}$
$\cos B=\frac{c^2+a^2-b^2}{2cb}$
$\cos C=\frac{a^2+b^2-c^2}{2ab}$
H-HE'S REPEATING MATH FORMULAS?!
EVEN ONES WE HAVEN'T GOTTEN TO YET!!
MMBL MMBL
GASP
POUNCE
YOU'RE LEARNING IT...!
YOU'RE STUDYING SO HARD! ♥
TSUKUNE!
SHUFFLE SHUFFLE SHUFFLE
... ...TSUKUNE...?
Huh?
...
GONG
TM TM TM TM TM

TSUKUNE?
SHUFFLE
HAVE YOU BEEN...
...STUDYING HARD?
MUMBLE
MUMBLE
UM...I WANT TO HELP YOU, AT LEAST A LITTLE.
'CAUSE, YOU KNOW... YOU'VE HELPED ME WITH SO MUCH.
I MEAN... YOU'RE THE REASON SCHOOL IS FUN EVERY DAY!
SO...UM... I MADE THIS NOTEBOOK FOR YOU.
VIP
IT COVERS ALL THE TOPICS ON YOUR TESTS.

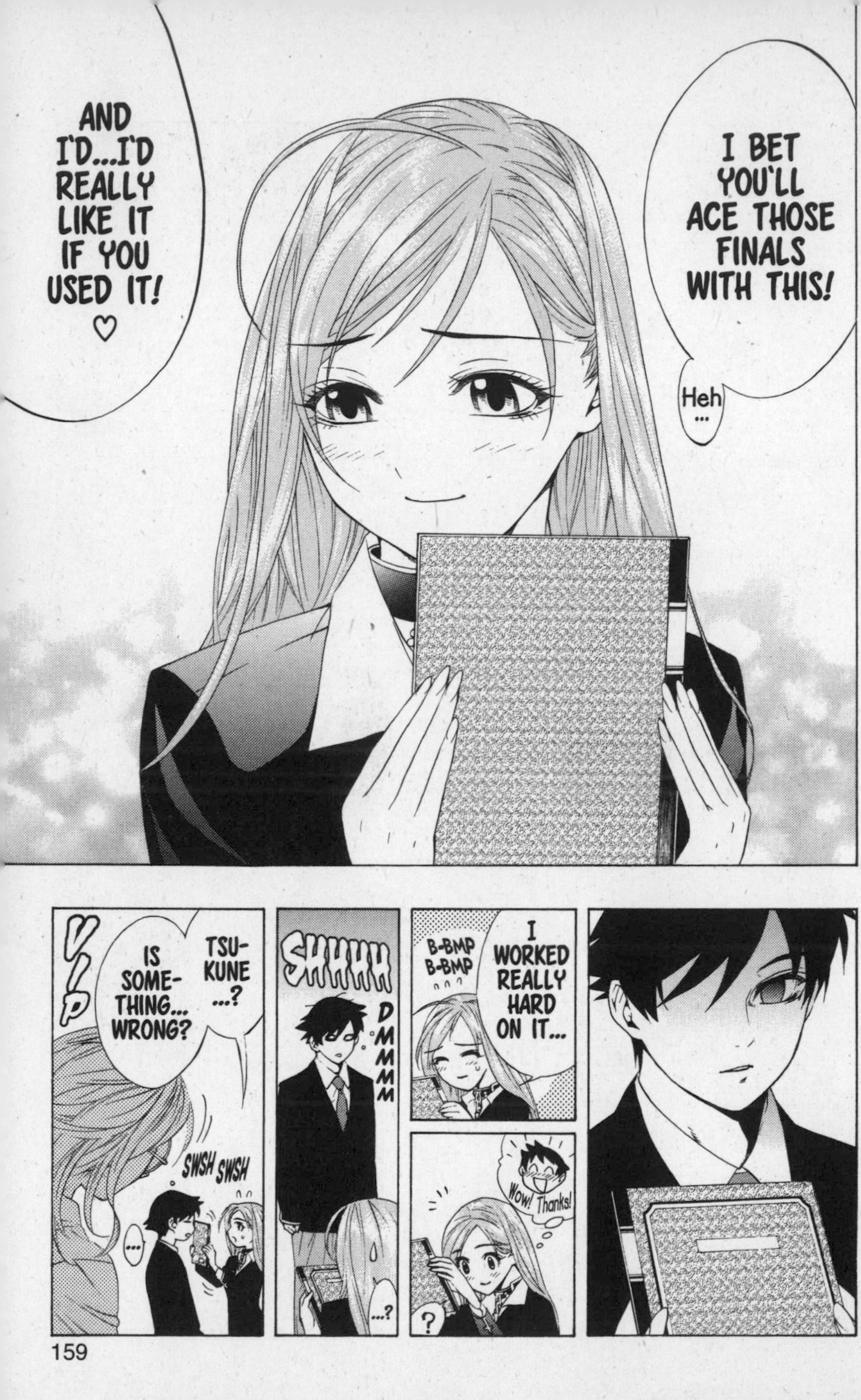
I BET YOU'LL ACE THOSE FINALS WITH THIS!
Heh...
AND I'D...I'D REALLY LIKE IT IF YOU USED IT! ♡
I WORKED REALLY HARD ON IT...
B-BMP B-BMP
Wow! Thanks!
?
SHHHH
DMMMMM
...?
TSU-KUNE...?
IS SOME-THING... WRONG?
VIP
SWSH SWSH
...

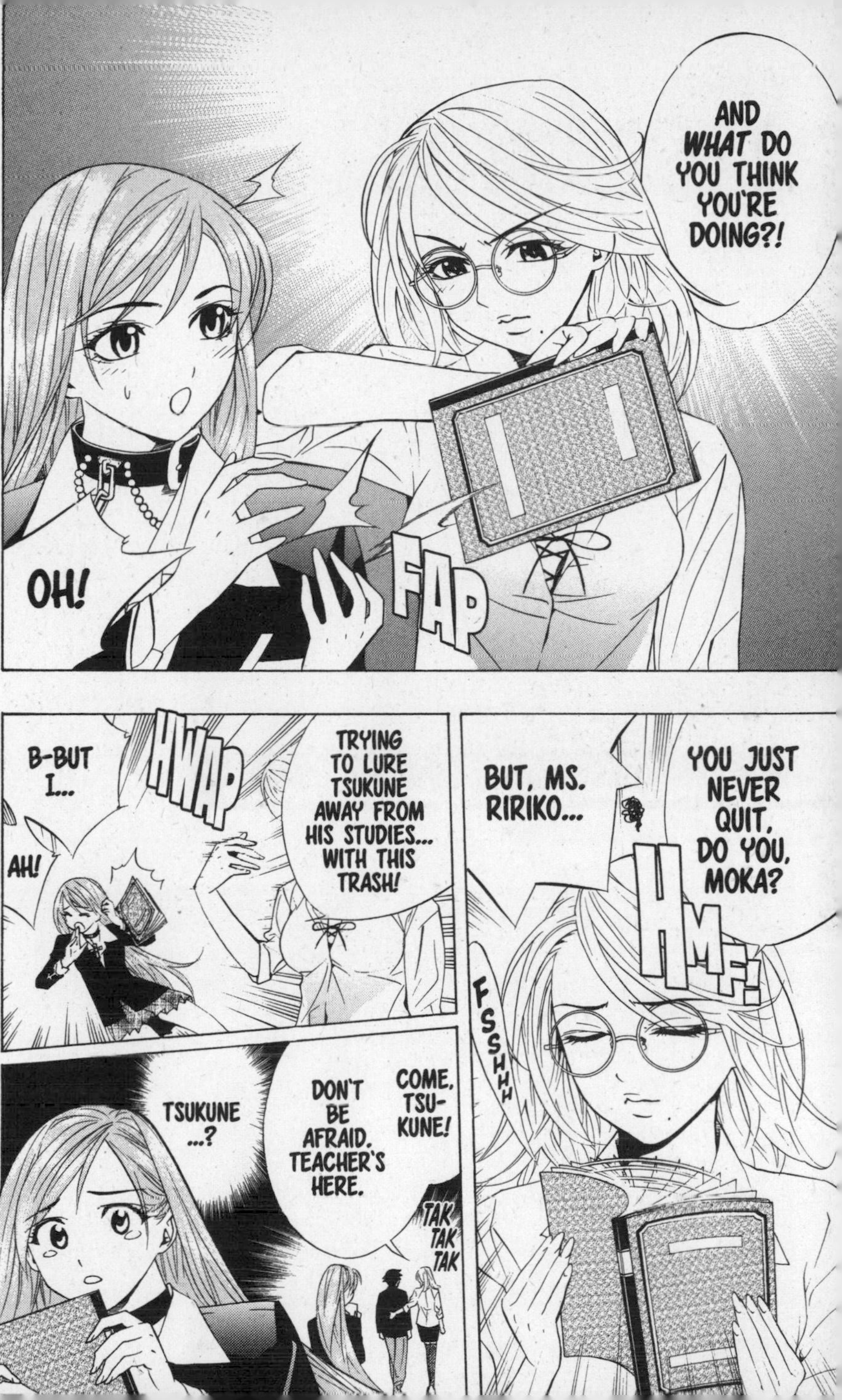
AND *WHAT* DO YOU THINK YOU'RE DOING?!
FAP
OH!
YOU JUST NEVER QUIT, DO YOU, MOKA?
BUT, MS. RIRIKO...
HMF!
FSSHHH
HWAP
TRYING TO LURE TSUKUNE AWAY FROM HIS STUDIES... WITH THIS TRASH!
B-BUT I...
AH!
COME, TSU-KUNE!
DON'T BE AFRAID. TEACHER'S HERE.
TSUKUNE ...?
TAK TAK TAK

READ THIS WAY

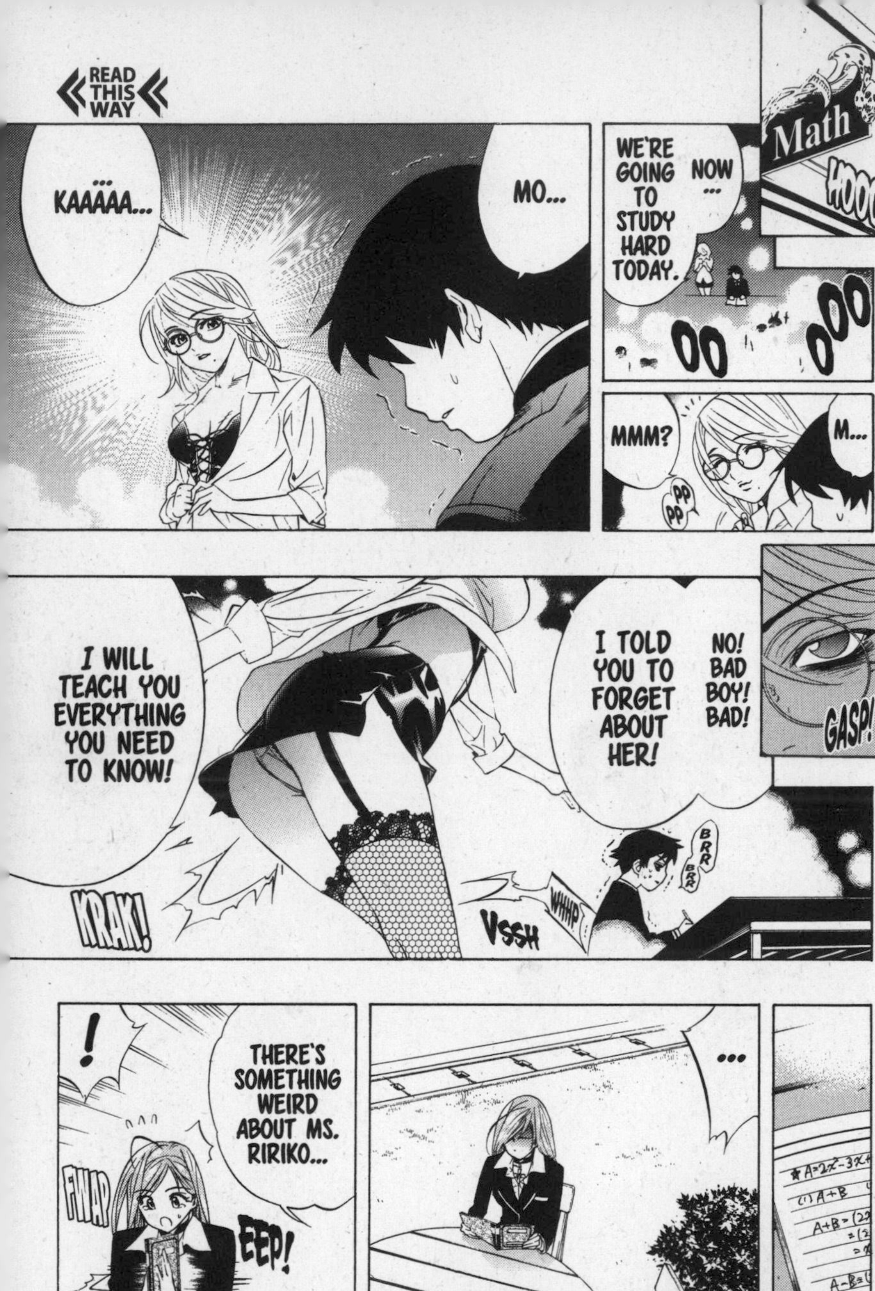
Math
HOOO
NOW...
WE'RE GOING TO STUDY HARD TODAY.
OOO
OO
M...
MMM?
PP PP
MO...
...KAAÄÄA...
GASP!
NO! BAD BOY! BAD!
I TOLD YOU TO FORGET ABOUT HER!
BRR BRR
WHHP
VSSH
I WILL TEACH YOU EVERYTHING YOU NEED TO KNOW!
KRAK!
...
THERE'S SOMETHING WEIRD ABOUT MS. RIRIKO...
!
EEP!
FWAP

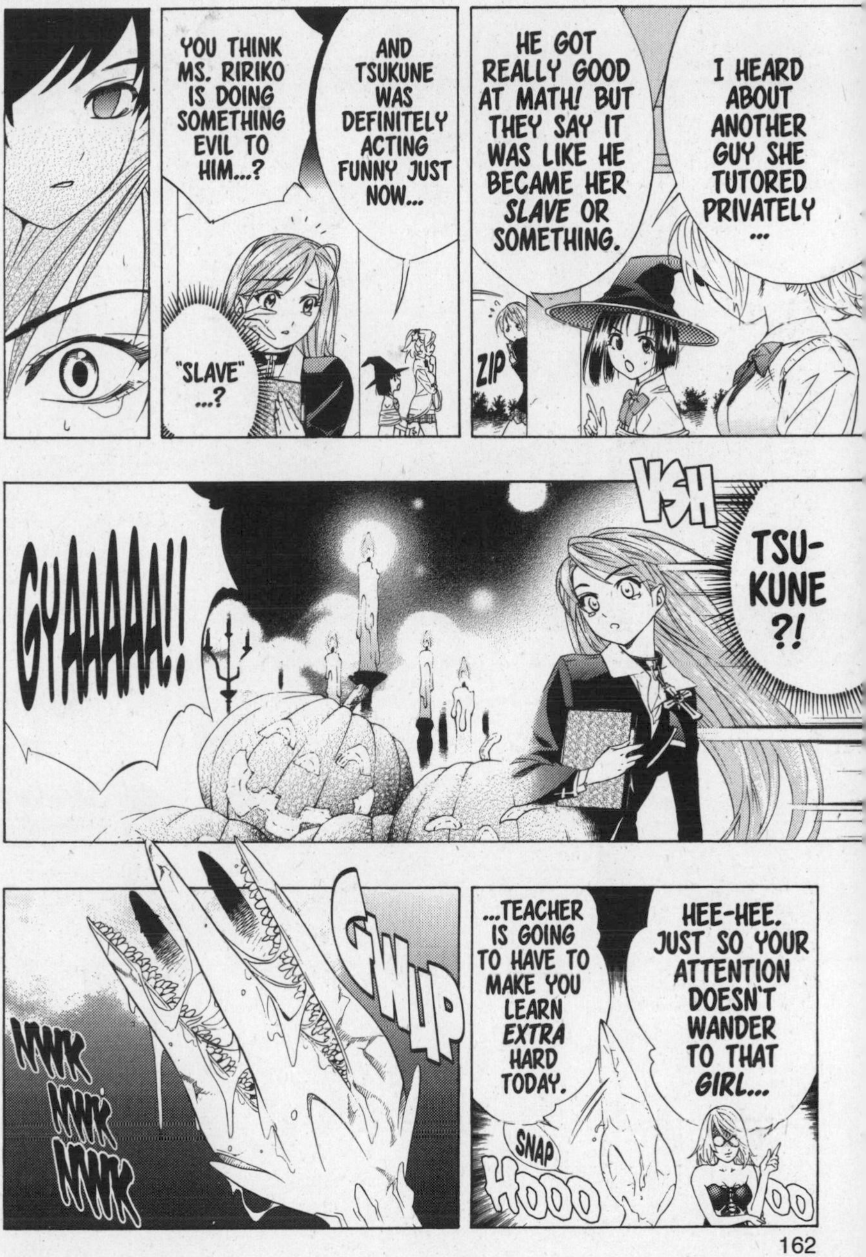
I HEARD ABOUT ANOTHER GUY SHE TUTORED PRIVATELY ...
HE GOT REALLY GOOD AT MATH! BUT THEY SAY IT WAS LIKE HE BECAME HER SLAVE OR SOMETHING.
ZIP
AND TSUKUNE WAS DEFINITELY ACTING FUNNY JUST NOW...
YOU THINK MS. RIRIKO IS DOING SOMETHING EVIL TO HIM...?
"SLAVE" ...?
VSH
TSU-KUNE?!
GYAAAAA!!
HEE-HEE. JUST SO YOUR ATTENTION DOESN'T WANDER TO THAT GIRL...
...TEACHER IS GOING TO HAVE TO MAKE YOU LEARN EXTRA HARD TODAY.
SNAP
HOOO
OO
GNUP
NNK NNK NNK

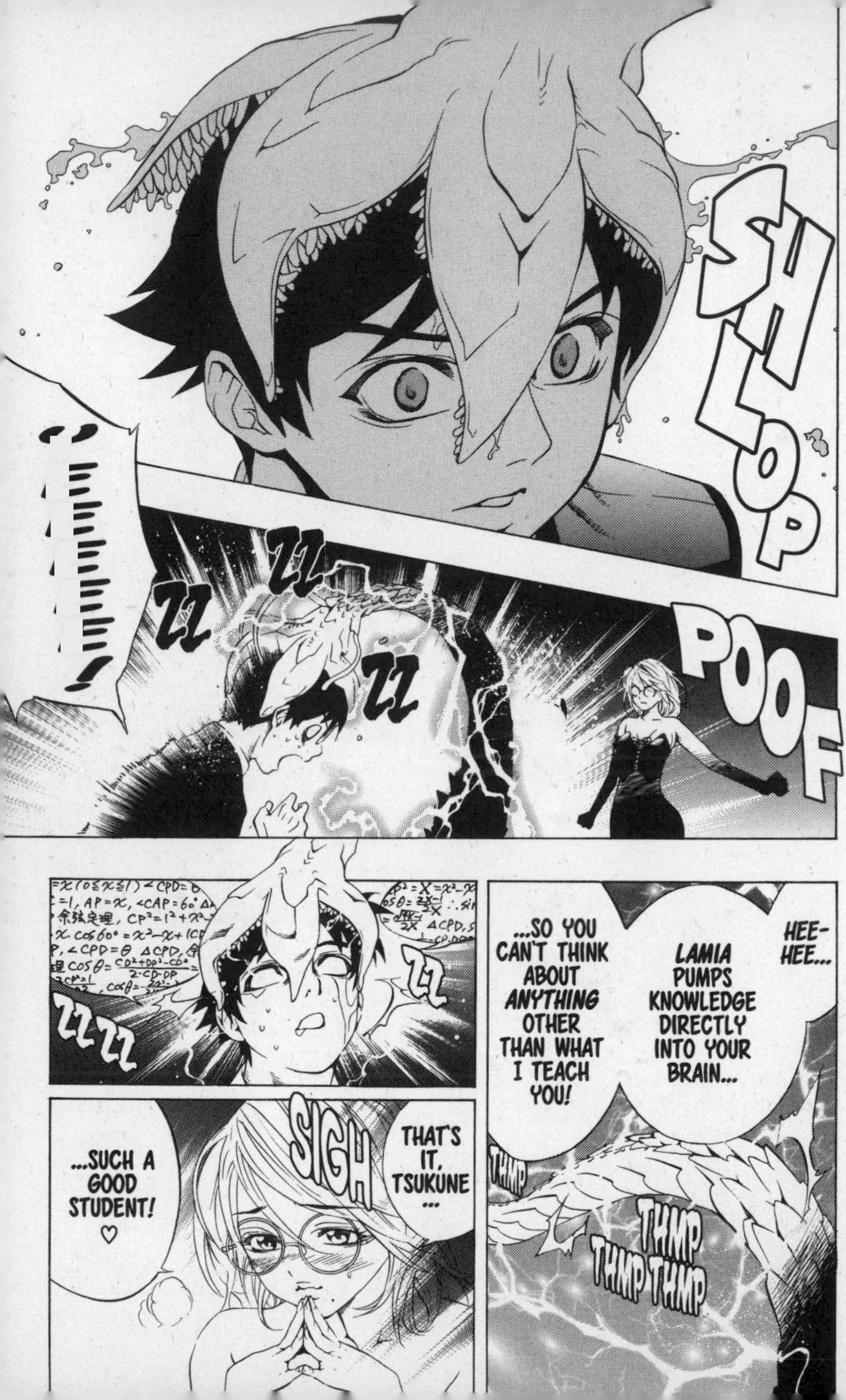
SHLOP
POOF
ZZ
ZZ
ZZ
HEE-HEE...
LAMIA PUMPS KNOWLEDGE DIRECTLY INTO YOUR BRAIN...
...SO YOU CAN'T THINK ABOUT ANYTHING OTHER THAN WHAT I TEACH YOU!
THMP
THMP THMP THMP
ZZ
ZZ ZZ
THAT'S IT, TSUKUNE...
SIGH
...SUCH A GOOD STUDENT! ♡

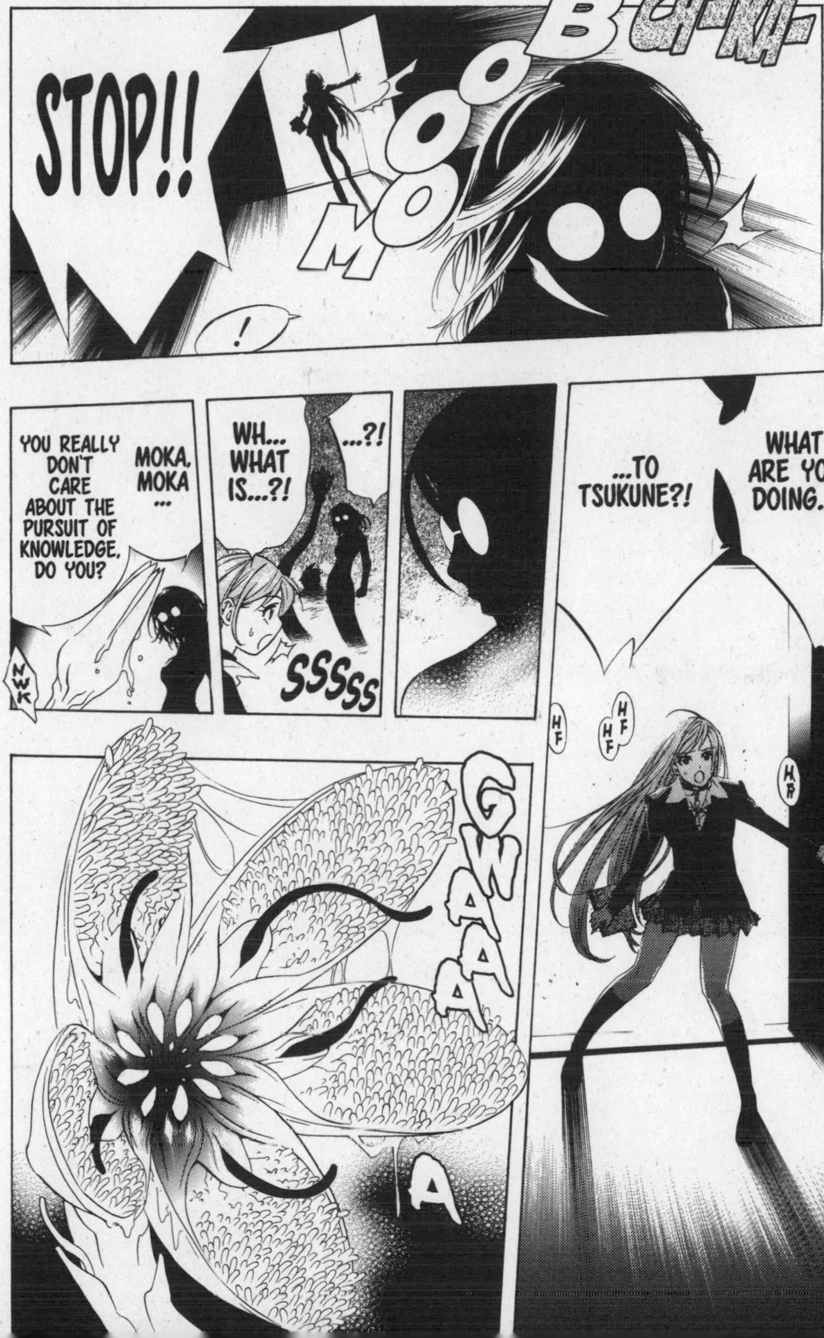
CH-KA-
BOOOOM
STOP!!
!
WHAT ARE YOU DOING...
...TO TSUKUNE?!
HF
HF
HF
HF
HF
...?!
WH... WHAT IS...?!
SSSSS
MOKA, MOKA ...
YOU REALLY DON'T CARE ABOUT THE PURSUIT OF KNOWLEDGE, DO YOU?
NWK
GWAAAA
A

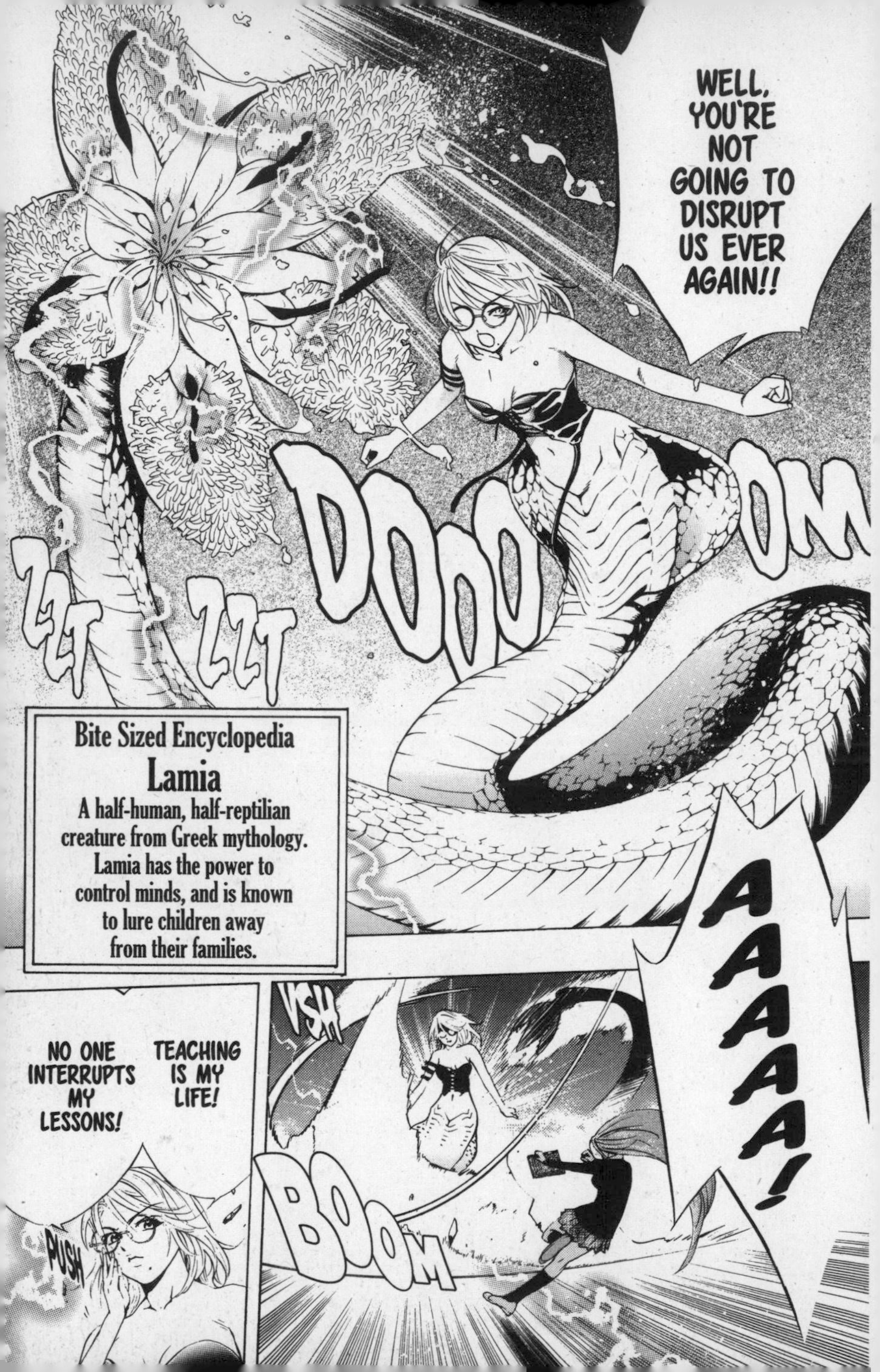
WELL, YOU'RE NOT GOING TO DISRUPT US EVER AGAIN!!
DOOOOOM
ZZT
ZZT
Bite Sized Encyclopedia
Lamia
A half-human, half-reptilian creature from Greek mythology. Lamia has the power to control minds, and is known to lure children away from their families.
AAAAA!
VSH
BOOOM
TEACHING IS MY LIFE!
NO ONE INTERRUPTS MY LESSONS!
PUSH

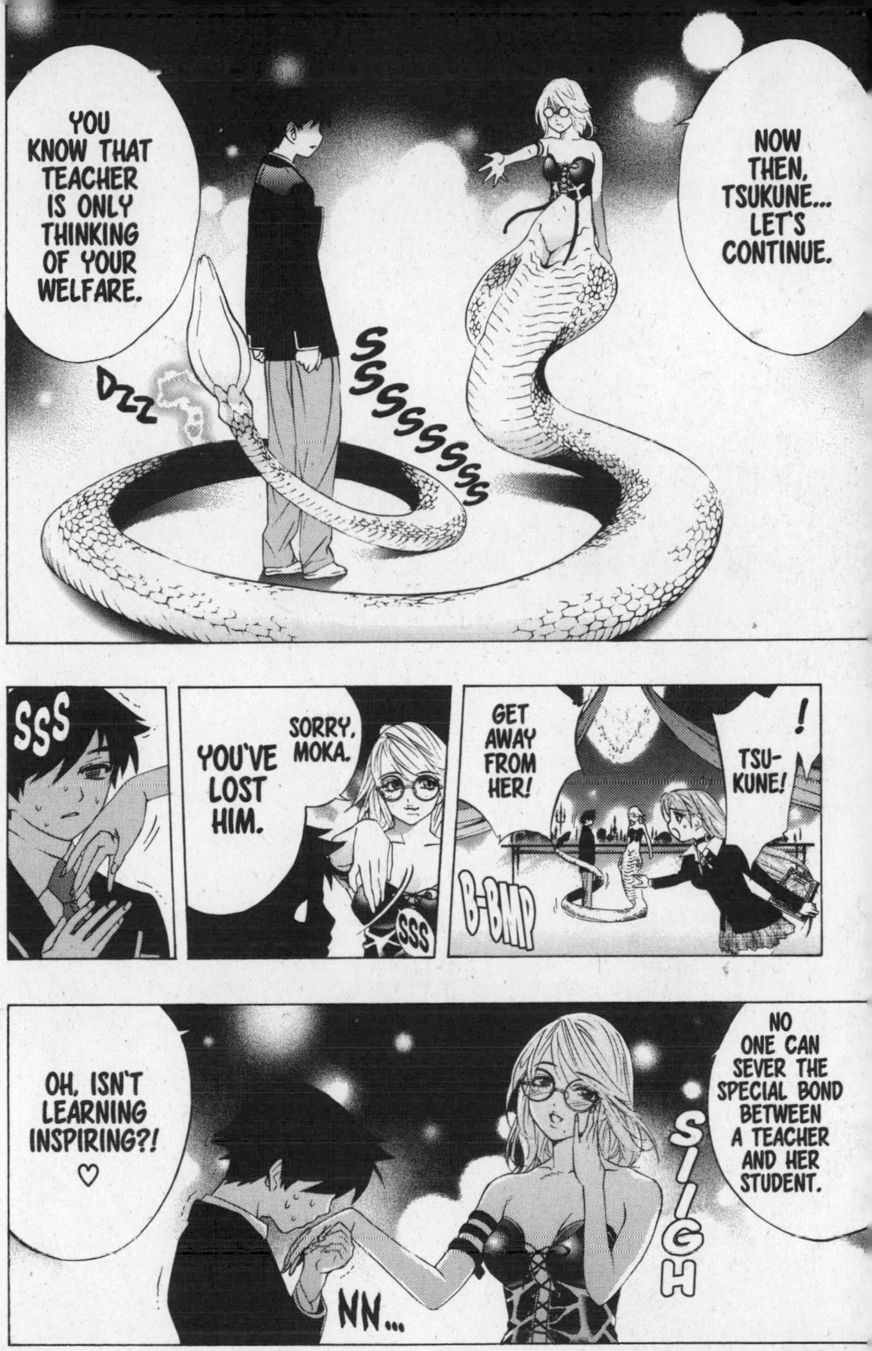
NOW THEN, TSUKUNE... LET'S CONTINUE.
YOU KNOW THAT TEACHER IS ONLY THINKING OF YOUR WELFARE.
SSSSSSSSS
DZZ
!
TSU-KUNE!
GET AWAY FROM HER!
B-BMP
SORRY, MOKA.
YOU'VE LOST HIM.
SSS
SSS
NO ONE CAN SEVER THE SPECIAL BOND BETWEEN A TEACHER AND HER STUDENT.
SIGH
OH, ISN'T LEARNING INSPIRING?! ♡
NN...

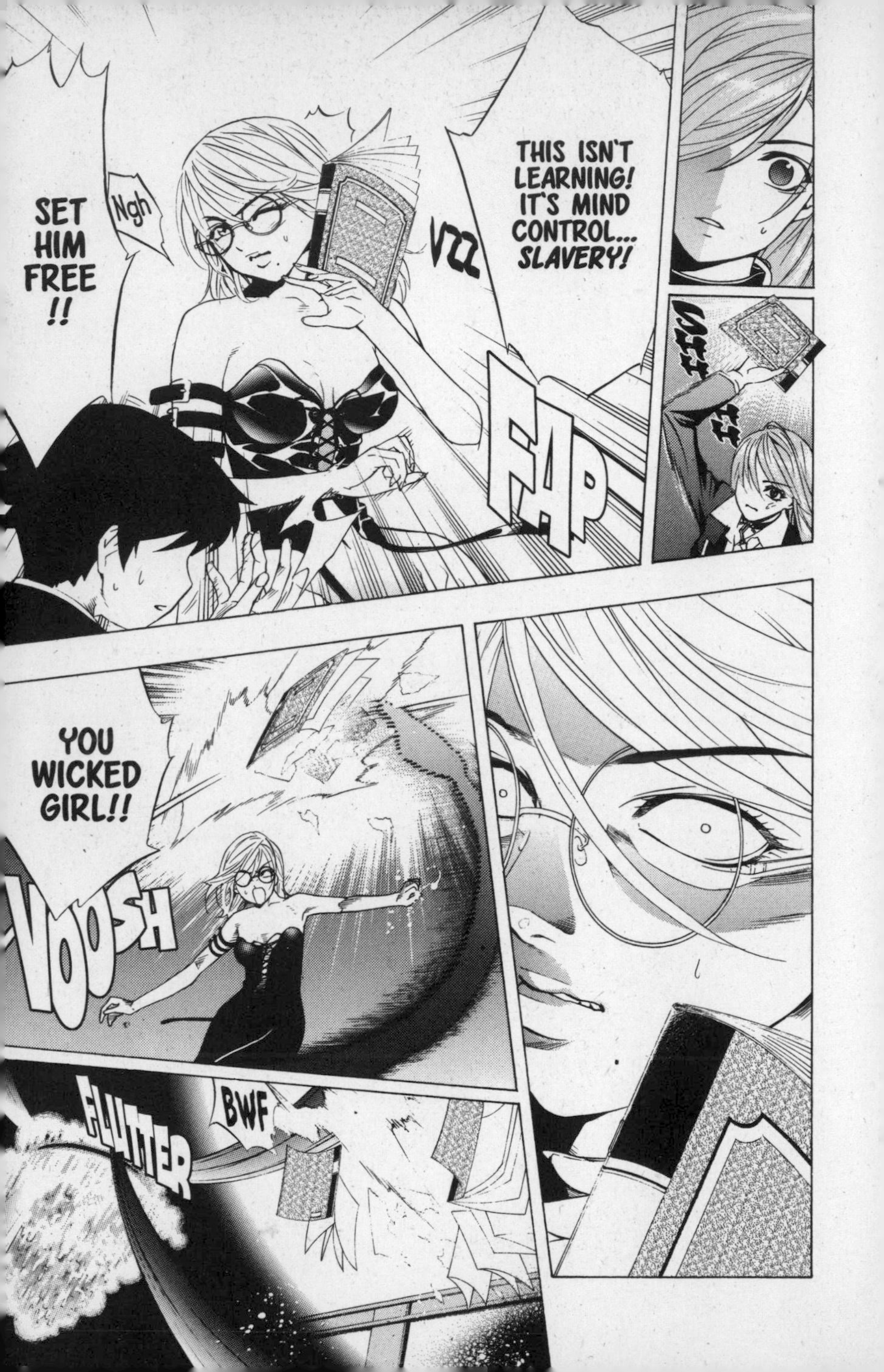
THIS ISN'T LEARNING! IT'S MIND CONTROL... SLAVERY!
VZZ
FAP
Ngh
SET HIM FREE!!
YOU WICKED GIRL!!
VOOSH
BWF
FLUTTER

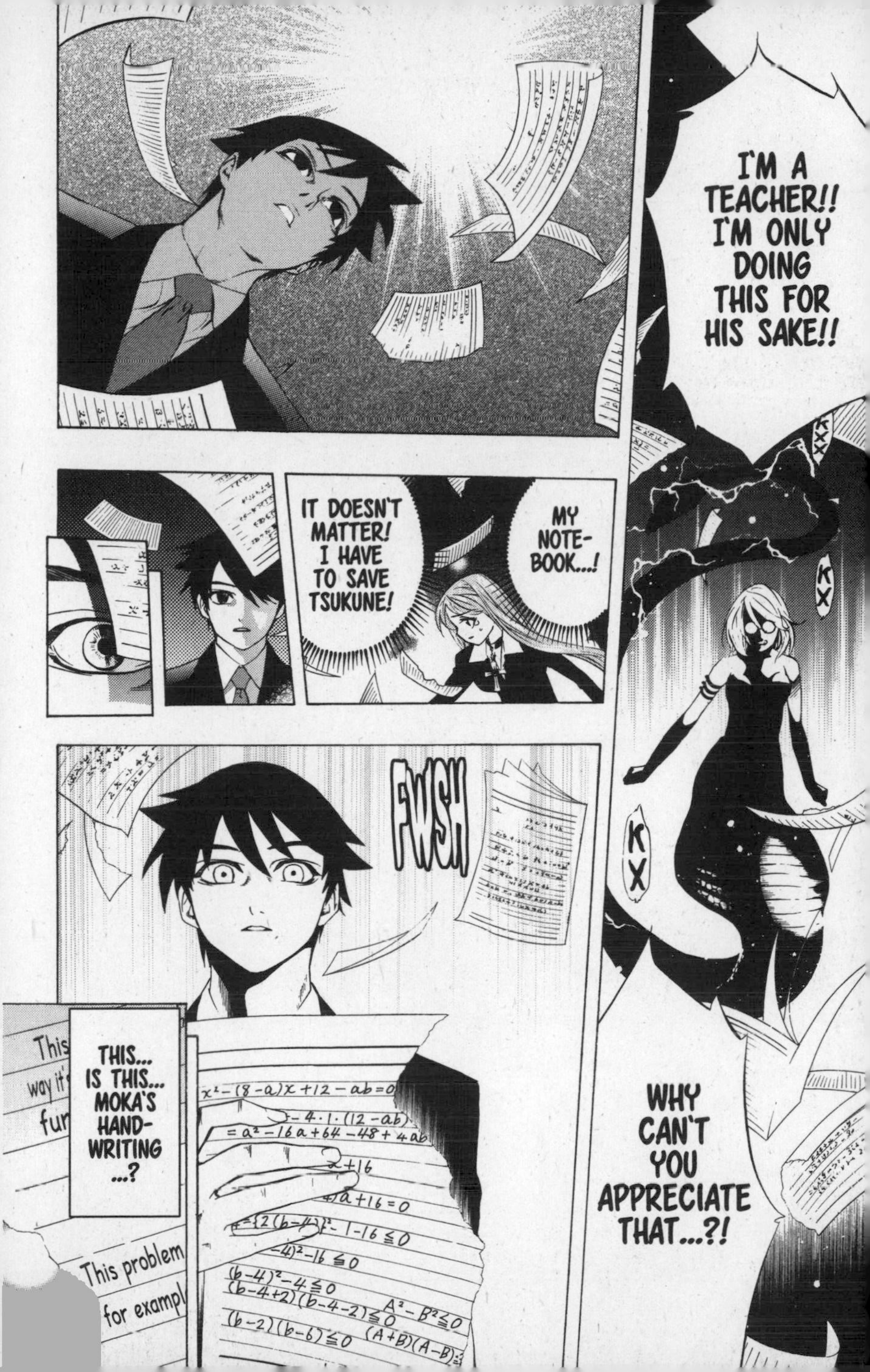

I'M A TEACHER!! I'M ONLY DOING THIS FOR HIS SAKE!!
KXX
KX
KX
WHY CAN'T YOU APPRECIATE THAT...?!
MY NOTE-BOOK...!
IT DOESN'T MATTER! I HAVE TO SAVE TSUKUNE!
FWSH
THIS... IS THIS... MOKA'S HAND-WRITING ...?

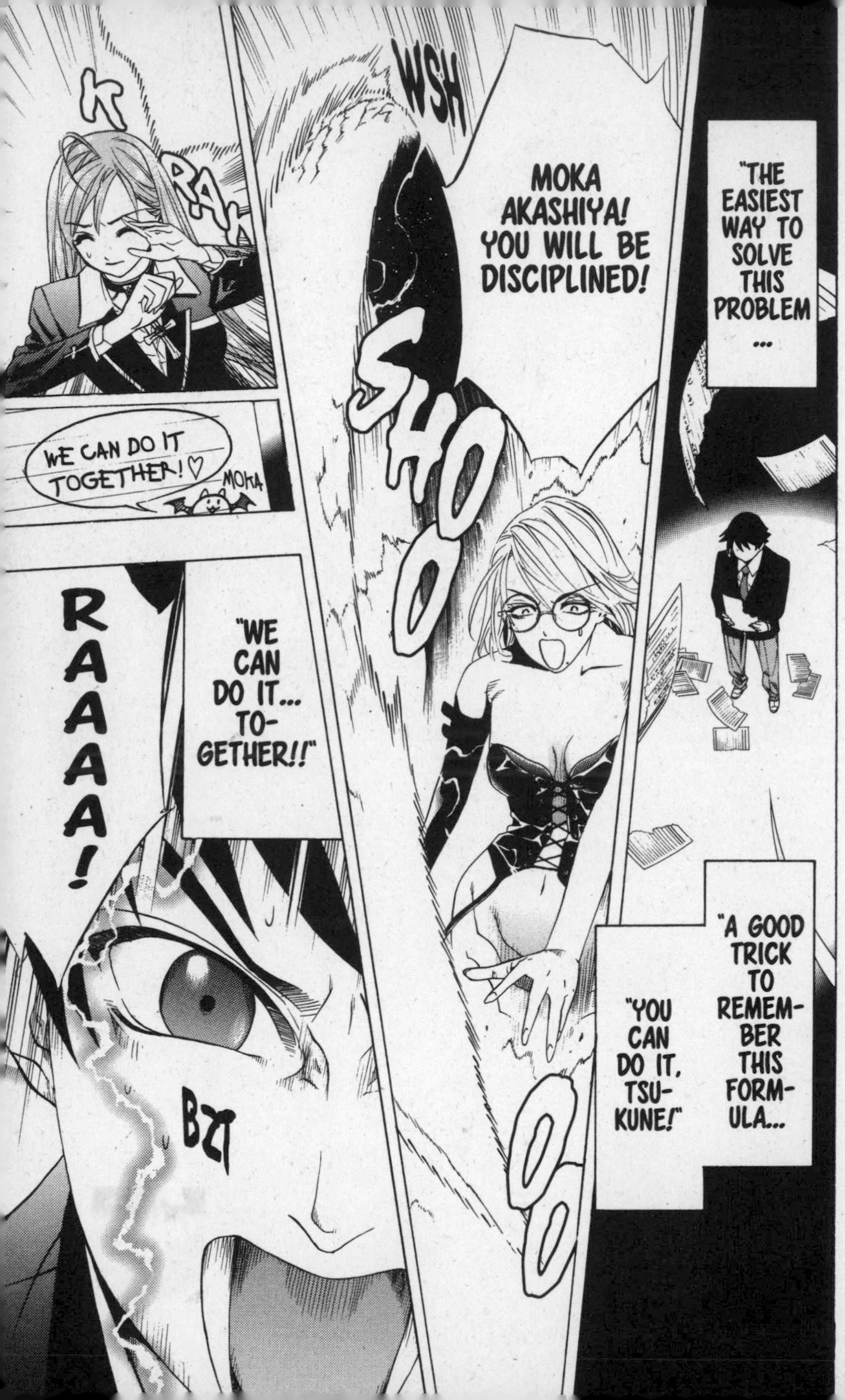
"THE EASIEST WAY TO SOLVE THIS PROBLEM ...
"A GOOD TRICK TO REMEMBER THIS FORMULA...
"YOU CAN DO IT, TSUKUNE!"
WSH
MOKA AKASHIYA! YOU WILL BE DISCIPLINED!
SHOOO
OOO
K
RA
WE CAN DO IT TOGETHER! ♡
MOKA
"WE CAN DO IT... TOGETHER!!"
RAAAAA!
BZT

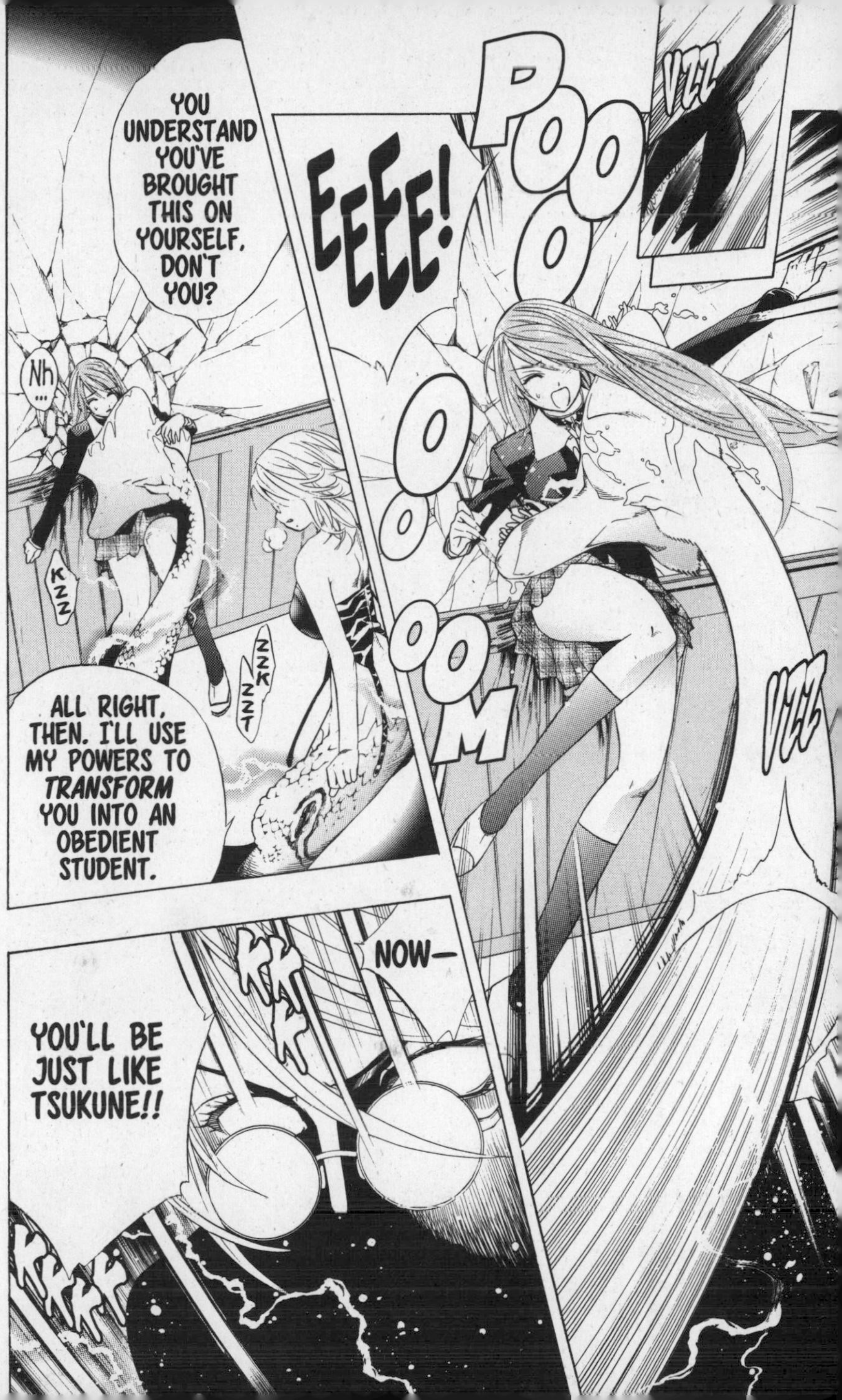
VZZ
POOOOOOOOM
EEEE!
VZZ
YOU UNDERSTAND YOU'VE BROUGHT THIS ON YOURSELF, DON'T YOU?
Nh...
KZZ
ZZK ZZT
ALL RIGHT, THEN. I'LL USE MY POWERS TO *TRANSFORM* YOU INTO AN OBEDIENT STUDENT.
NOW—
KK
YOU'LL BE JUST LIKE TSUKUNE!!
KKKK

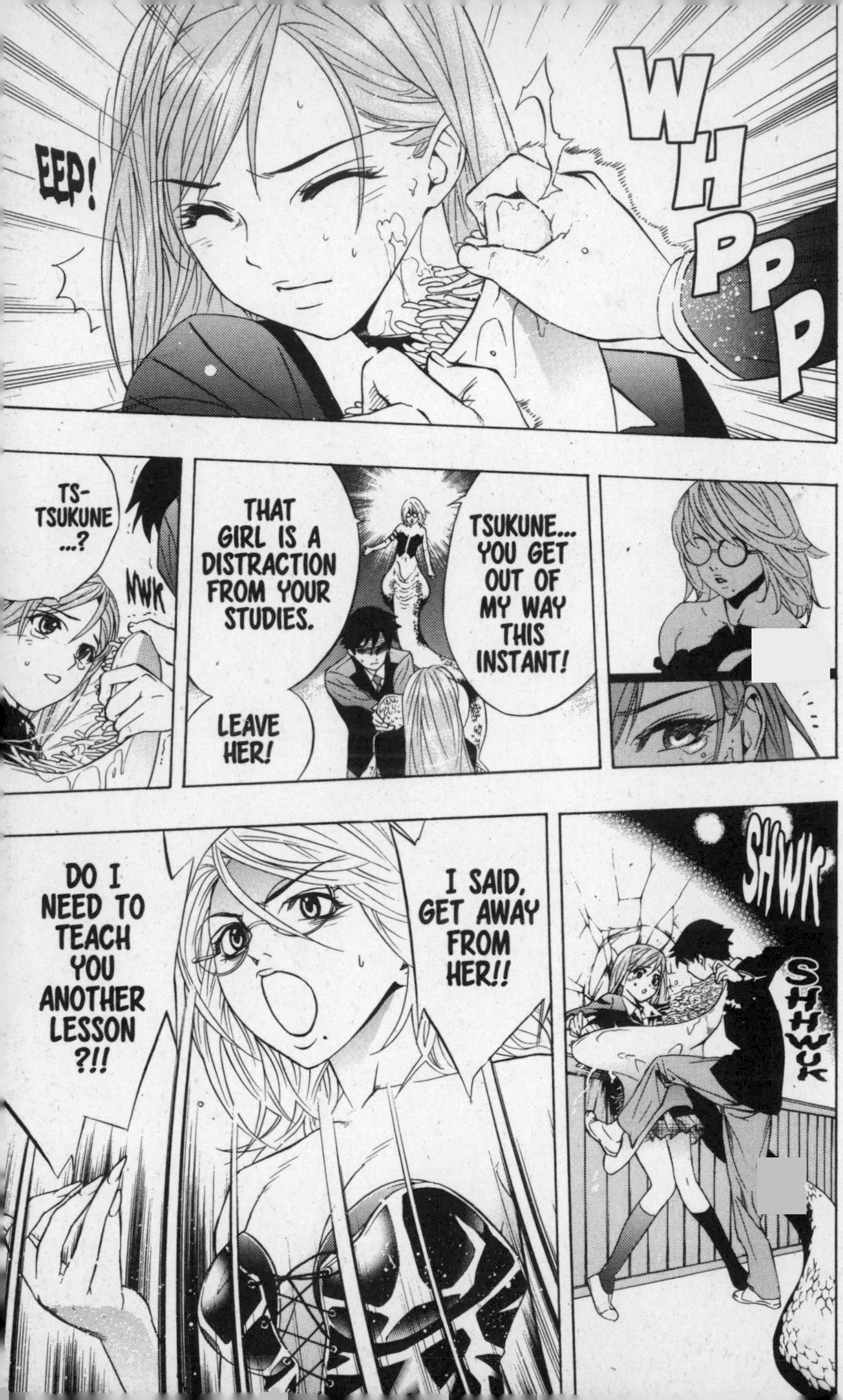
WHPPP
EEP!
TSUKUNE... YOU GET OUT OF MY WAY THIS INSTANT!
THAT GIRL IS A DISTRACTION FROM YOUR STUDIES.
LEAVE HER!
TS-TSUKUNE ...?
NWK
SHWK
SHHWUK
I SAID, GET AWAY FROM HER!!
DO I NEED TO TEACH YOU ANOTHER LESSON ?!!

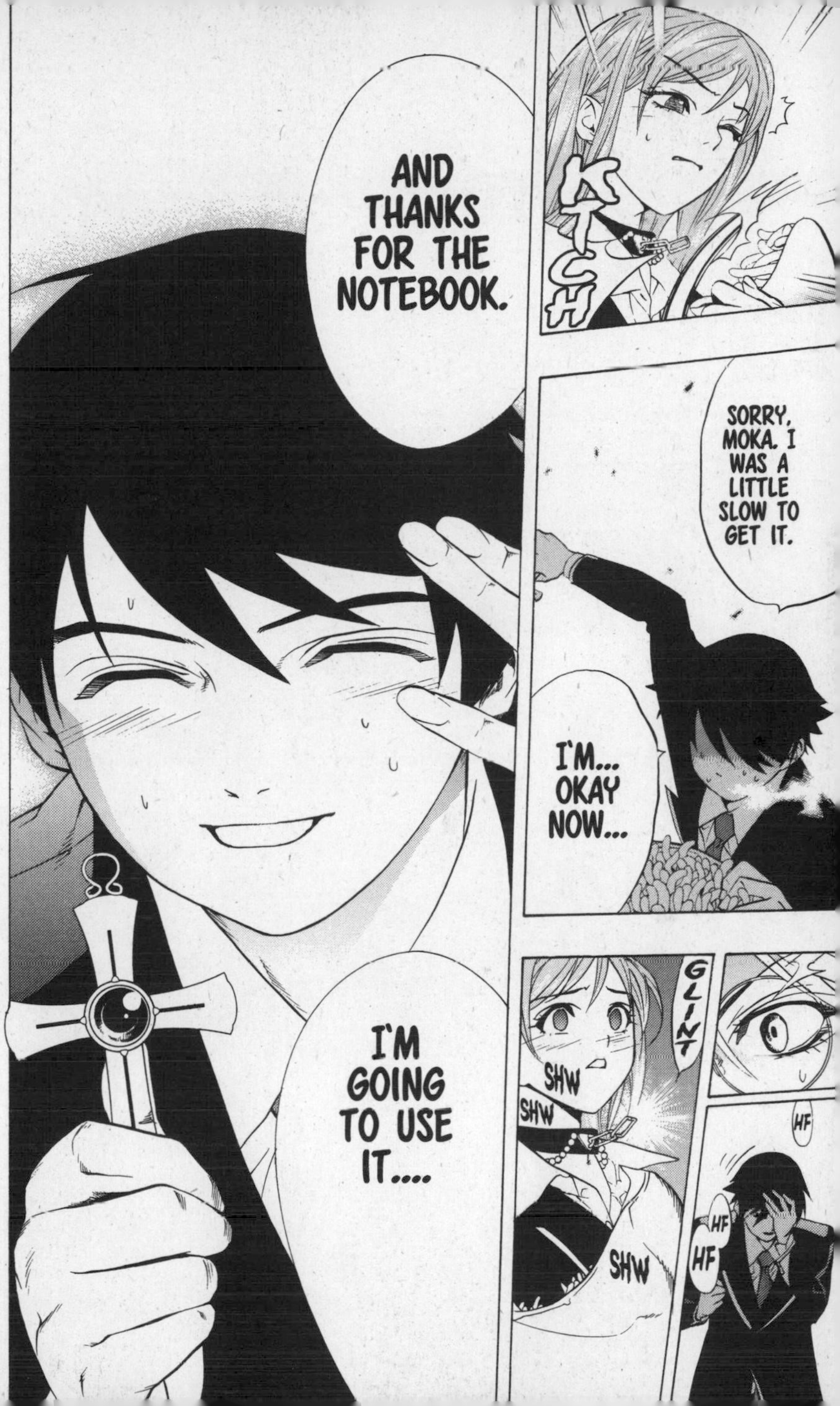
KTCH
SORRY, MOKA. I WAS A LITTLE SLOW TO GET IT.
I'M... OKAY NOW...
HF
HF
HF
GLINT
SHW
SHW
SHW
AND THANKS FOR THE NOTEBOOK.
I'M GOING TO USE IT....

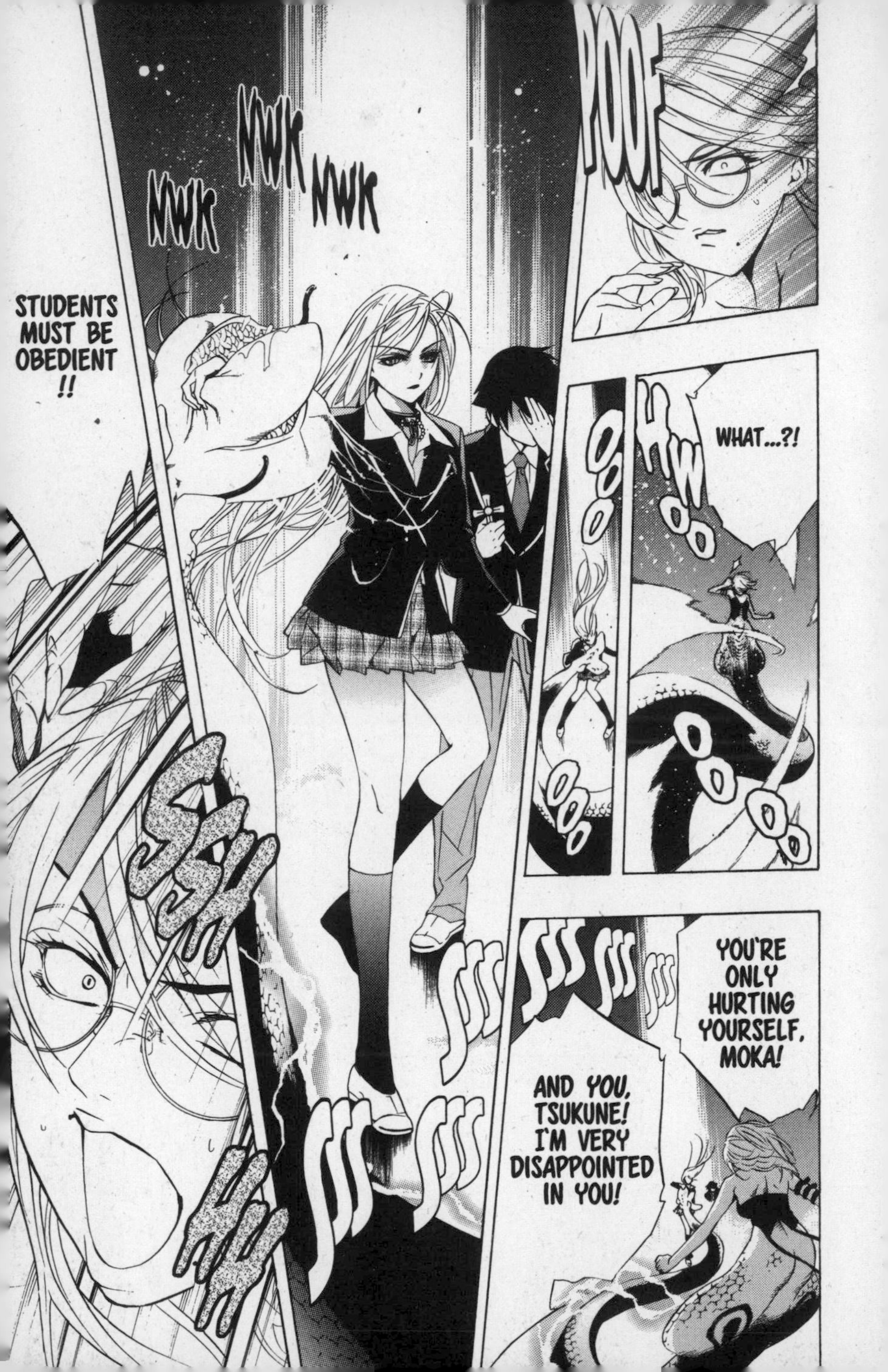
POOF
HWOOO
WHAT...?!
OOOOOO
SSS SSS SSS SSS
YOU'RE ONLY HURTING YOURSELF, MOKA!
AND YOU, TSUKUNE! I'M VERY DISAPPOINTED IN YOU!
NWK NWK NWK
SSS SSS
STUDENTS MUST BE OBEDIENT!!
SSH

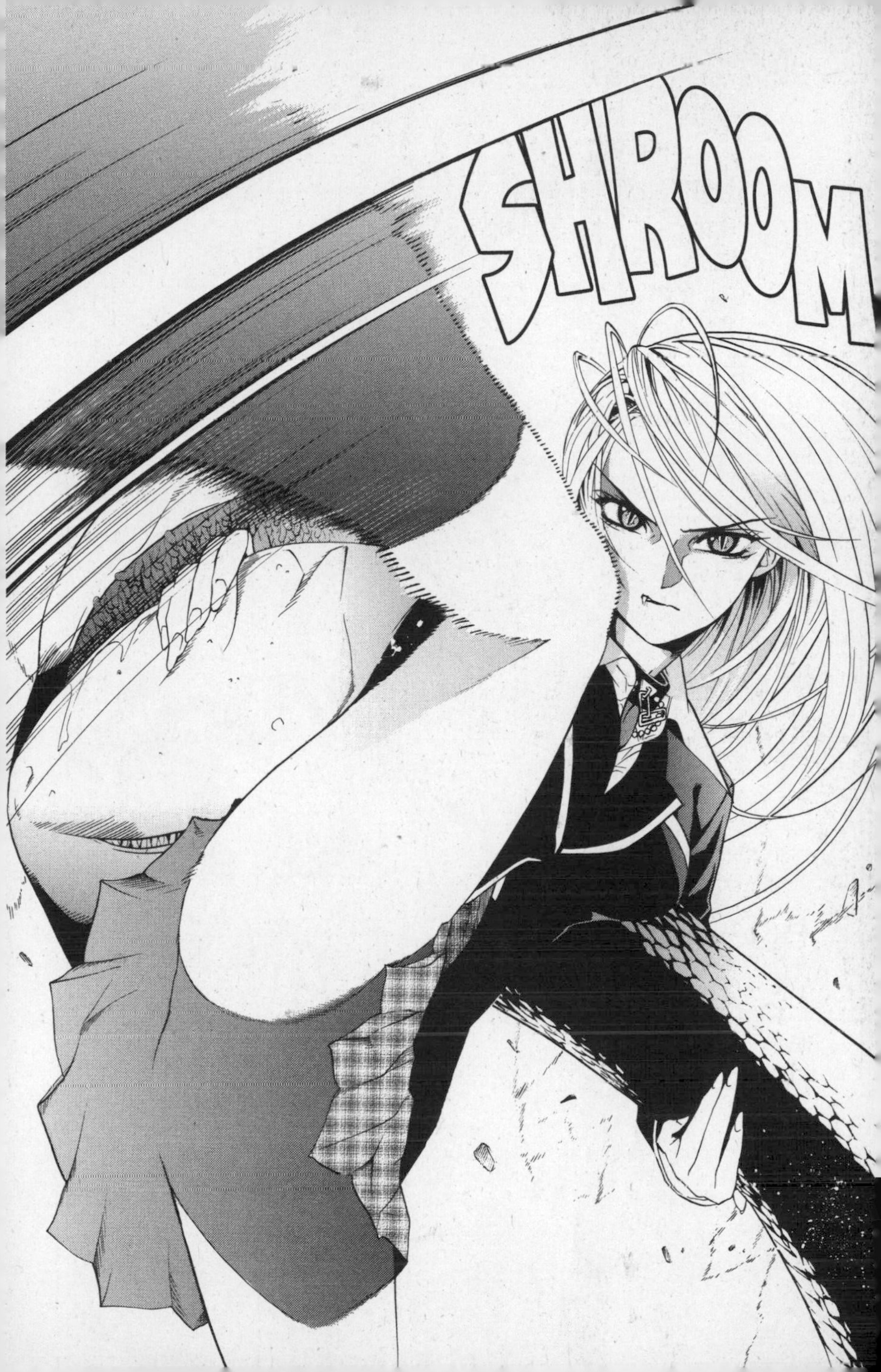
SHROOM

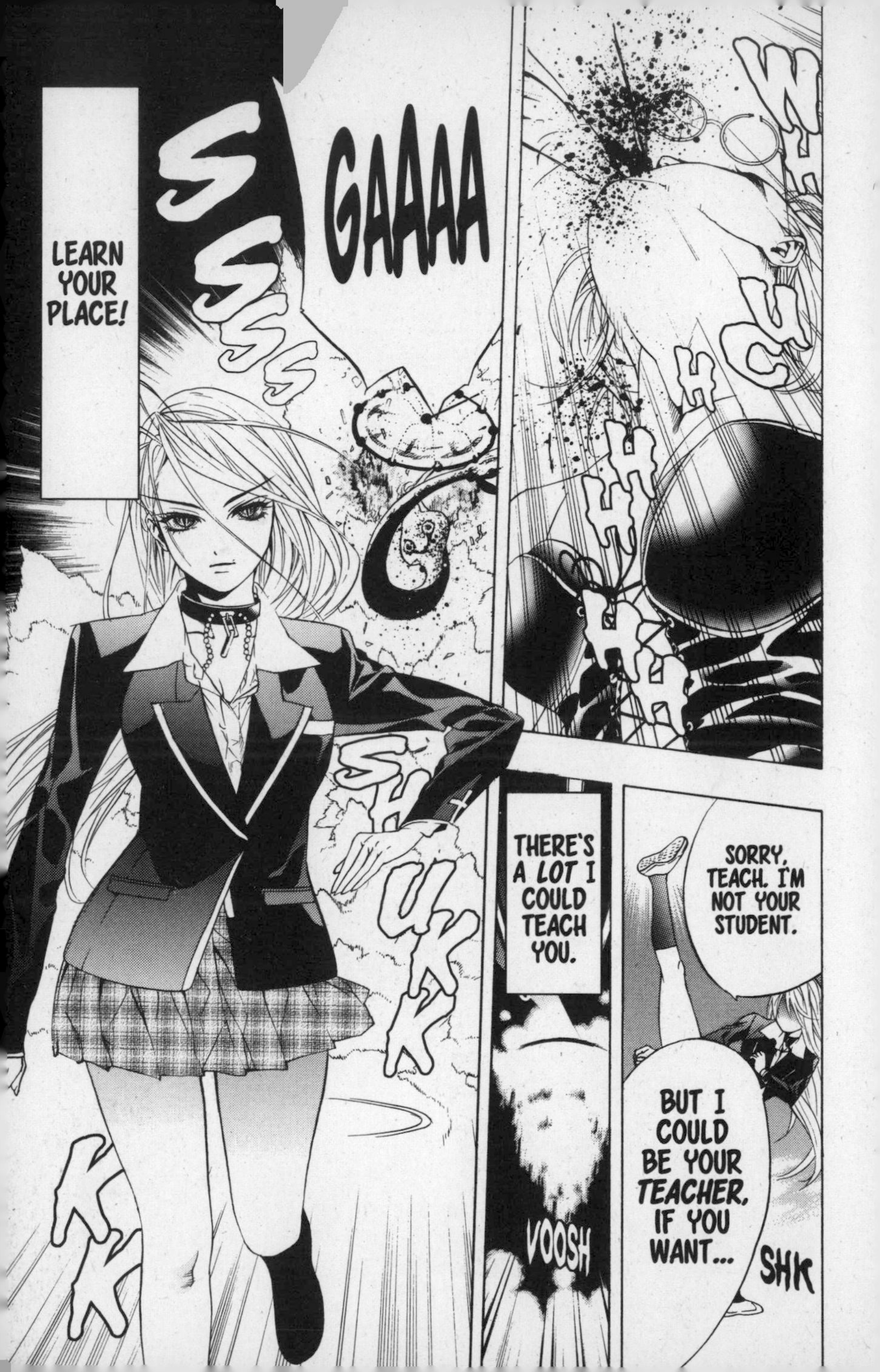
SORRY, TEACH. I'M NOT YOUR STUDENT.
BUT I COULD BE YOUR *TEACHER,* IF YOU WANT...
SHK
THERE'S A *LOT* I COULD TEACH YOU.
VOOSH
LEARN YOUR PLACE!
GAAAA
SHUK

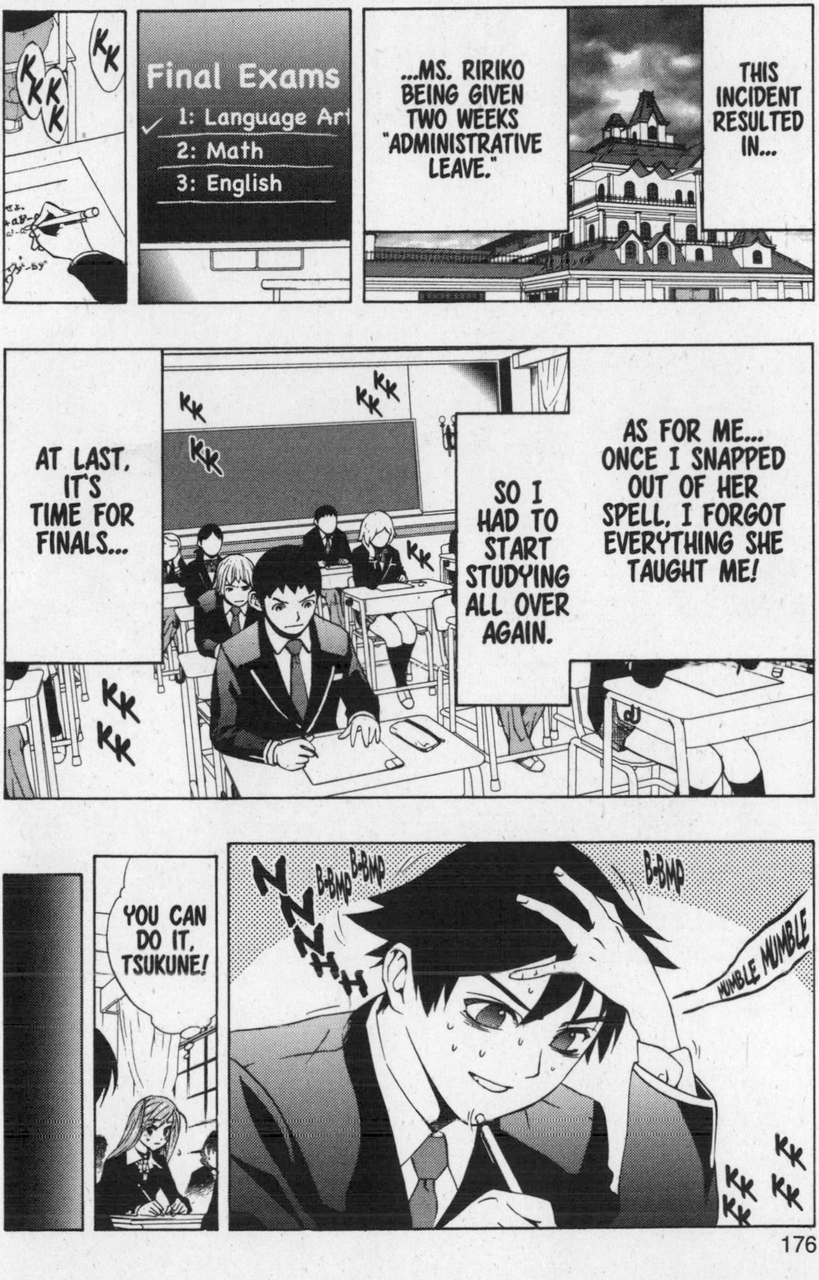
THIS INCIDENT RESULTED IN...
...MS. RIRIKO BEING GIVEN TWO WEEKS "ADMINISTRATIVE LEAVE."
Final Exams
1: Language Art
2: Math
3: English
KK
KKKK
AS FOR ME... ONCE I SNAPPED OUT OF HER SPELL, I FORGOT EVERYTHING SHE TAUGHT ME!
SO I HAD TO START STUDYING ALL OVER AGAIN.
KK
KKKK
KK
KK
AT LAST, IT'S TIME FOR FINALS...
KK
KK
B-BMP
MUMBLE MUMBLE
B-BMP B-BMP
NNNHH
KK KK KK KK
YOU CAN DO IT, TSUKUNE!

READ THIS WAY

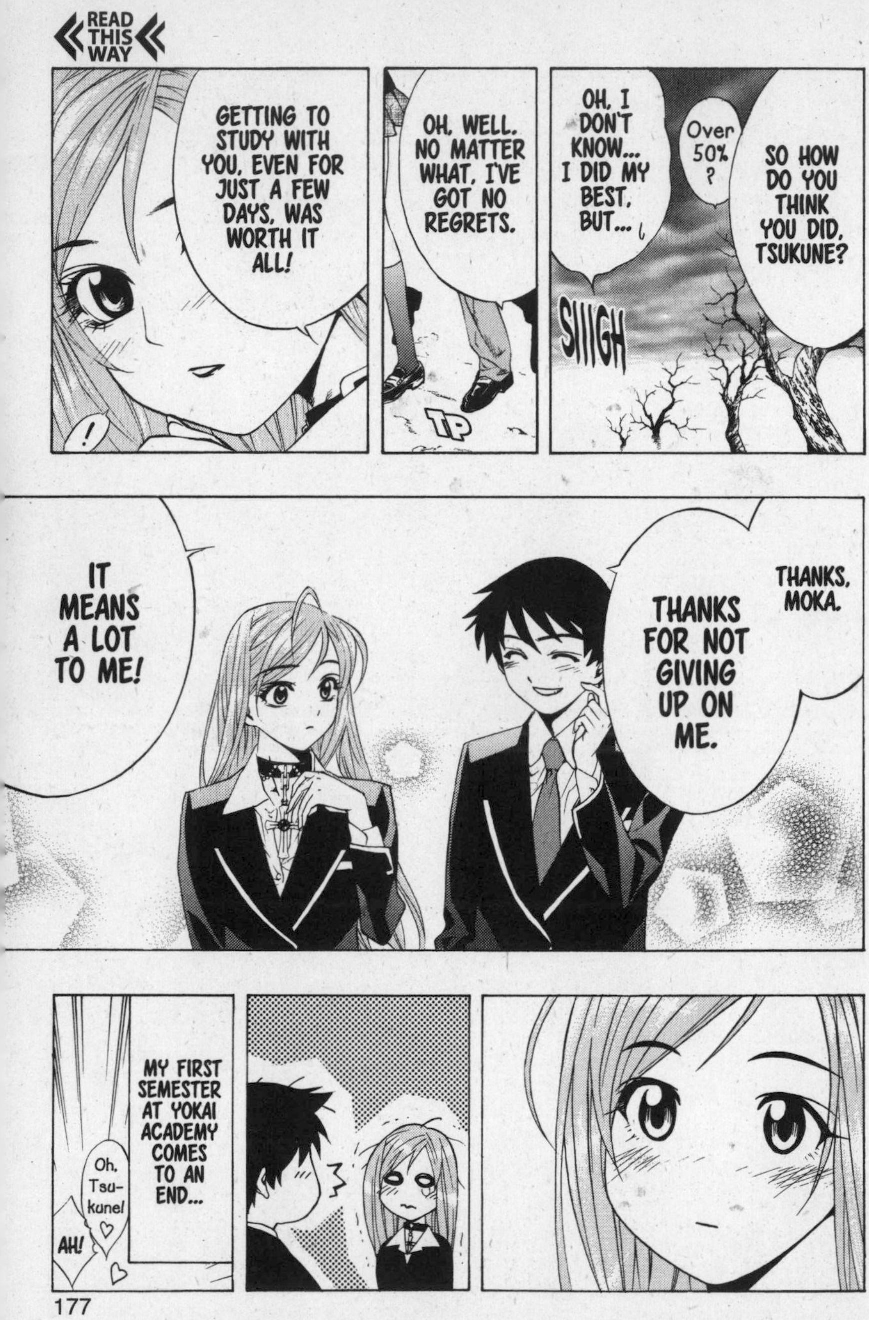
SO HOW DO YOU THINK YOU DID, TSUKUNE?
Over 50%?
OH, I DON'T KNOW... I DID MY BEST, BUT...
SIIIGH
OH, WELL. NO MATTER WHAT, I'VE GOT NO REGRETS.
TP
GETTING TO STUDY WITH YOU, EVEN FOR JUST A FEW DAYS, WAS WORTH IT ALL!
!
THANKS, MOKA.
THANKS FOR NOT GIVING UP ON ME.
IT MEANS A LOT TO ME!
MY FIRST SEMESTER AT YOKAI ACADEMY COMES TO AN END...
Oh, Tsukune! ♡
AH!

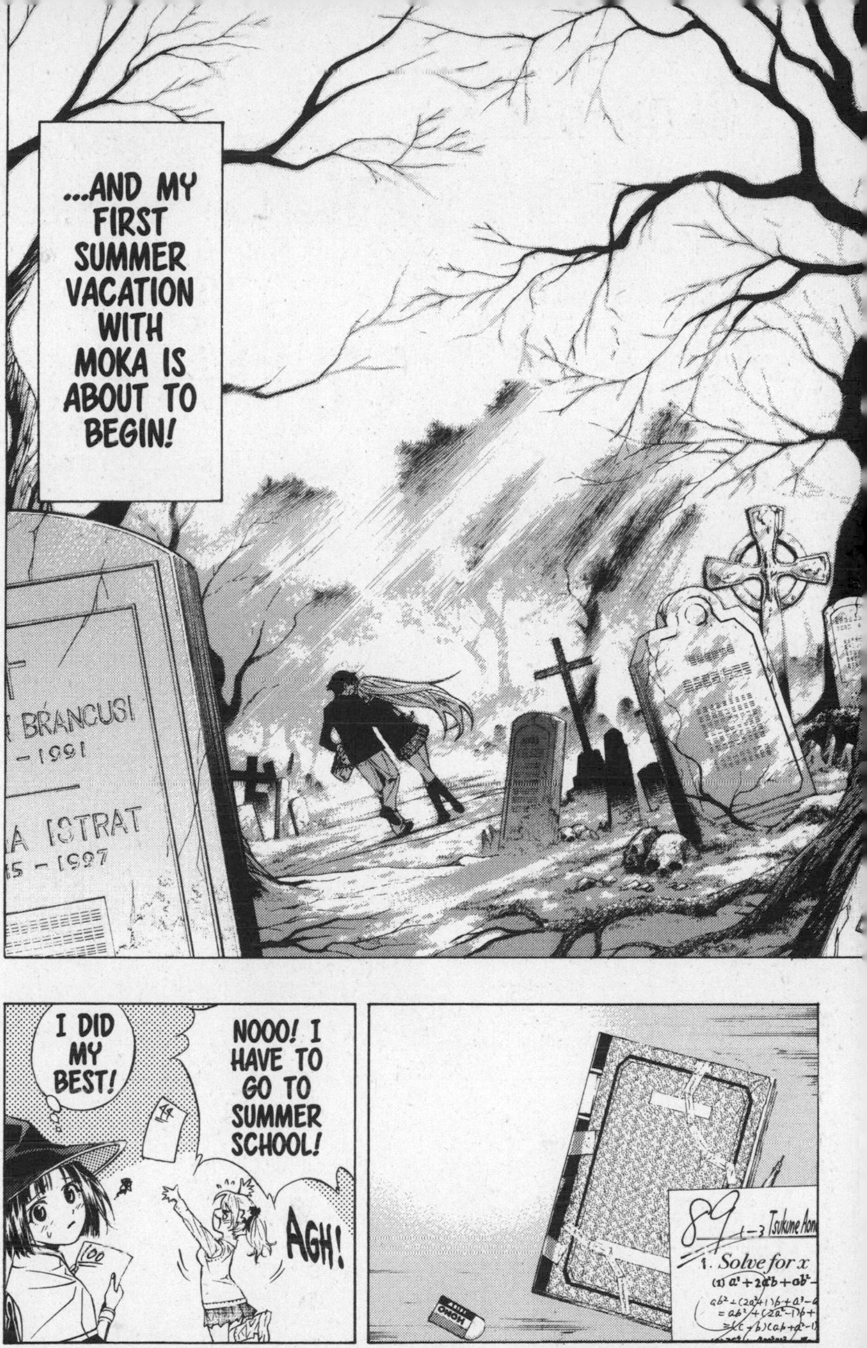
...AND MY FIRST SUMMER VACATION WITH MOKA IS ABOUT TO BEGIN!
BRANCUSI
-1991
A ISTRAT
-1997
89
1-3
1. Solve for x
NOOO! I HAVE TO GO TO SUMMER SCHOOL!
AGH!
I DID MY BEST!
100

ROSARIO + VAMPIRE

End-of-Volume Theater

Q+A Section

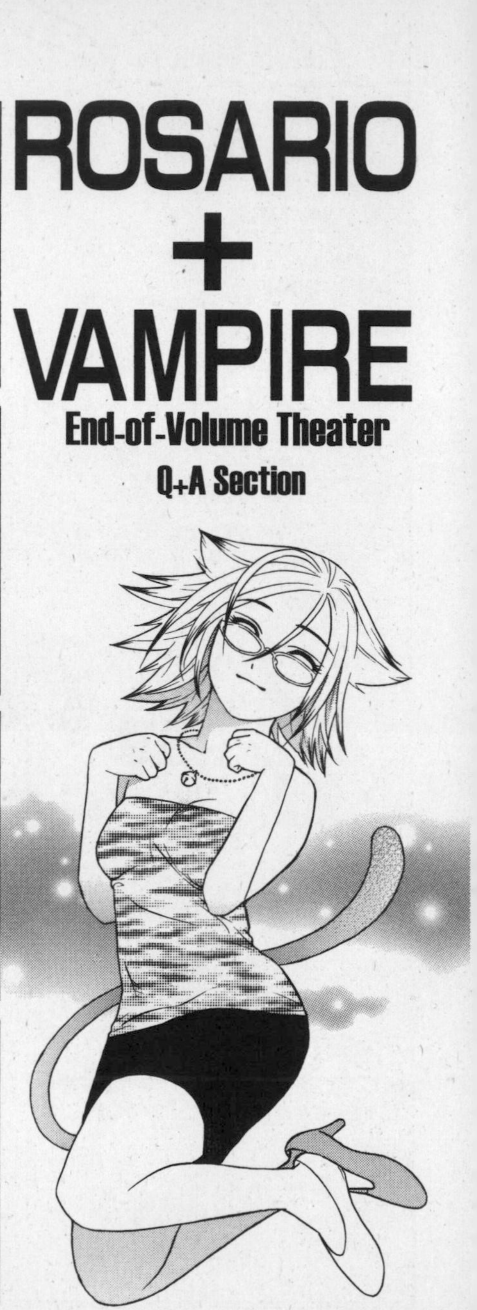

• Ms. Nekonome... •

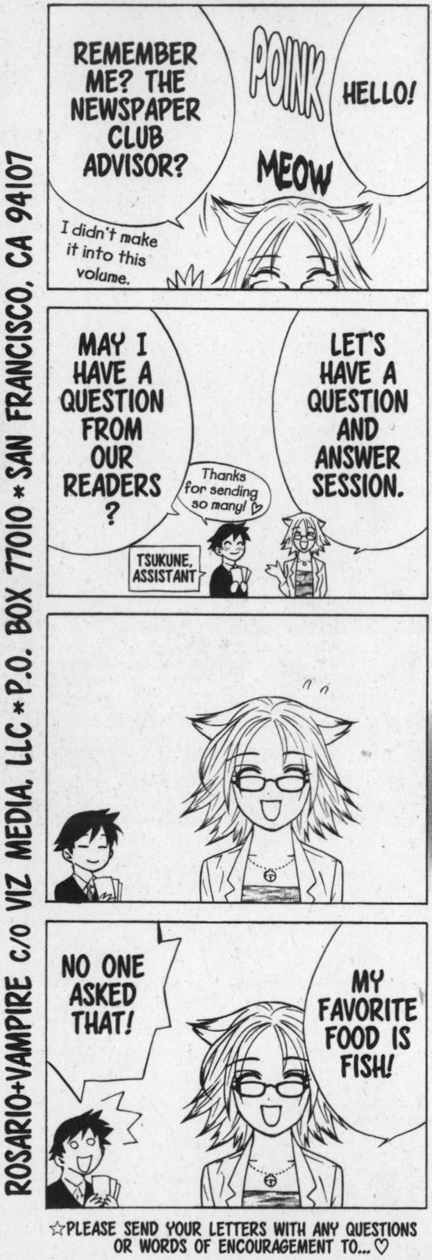

HELLO!
POINK
MEOW
REMEMBER ME? THE NEWSPAPER CLUB ADVISOR?
I didn't make it into this volume.
LET'S HAVE A QUESTION AND ANSWER SESSION.
Thanks for sending so many! ♡
MAY I HAVE A QUESTION FROM OUR READERS?
TSUKUNE, ASSISTANT
MY FAVORITE FOOD IS FISH!
NO ONE ASKED THAT!

☆PLEASE SEND YOUR LETTERS WITH ANY QUESTIONS OR WORDS OF ENCOURAGEMENT TO... ♡

ROSARIO+VAMPIRE c/o VIZ MEDIA, LLC * P.O. BOX 77010 * SAN FRANCISCO, CA 94107

• I Love Warm Places •

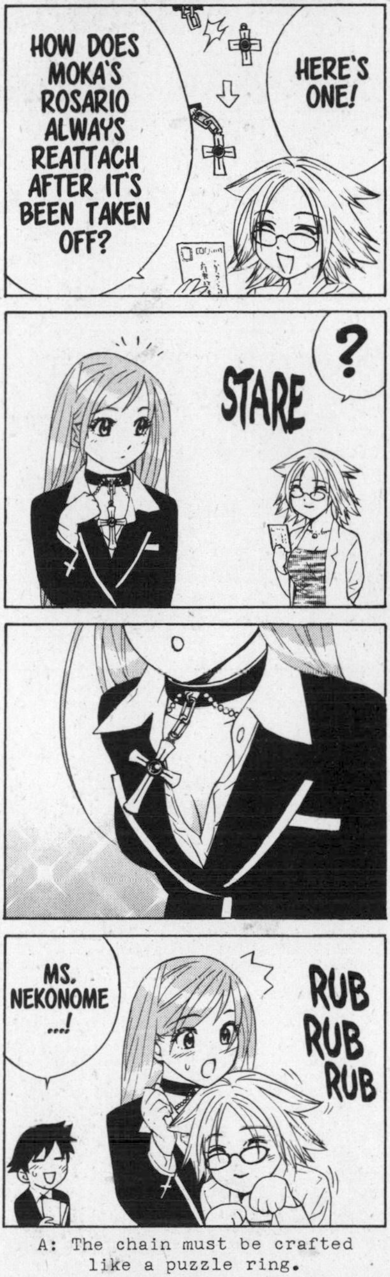
HERE'S ONE!
HOW DOES MOKA'S ROSARIO ALWAYS REATTACH AFTER IT'S BEEN TAKEN OFF?
?
STARE
RUB RUB RUB
MS. NEKONOME ...!

A: The chain must be crafted like a puzzle ring.

• Full of Curiosity •

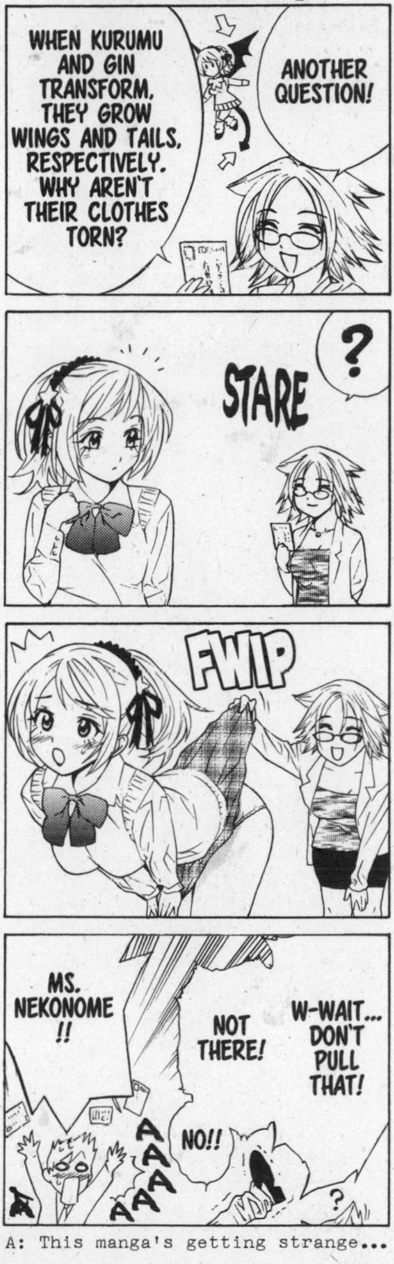
ANOTHER QUESTION!
WHEN KURUMU AND GIN TRANSFORM, THEY GROW WINGS AND TAILS, RESPECTIVELY. WHY AREN'T THEIR CLOTHES TORN?
?
STARE
FWIP
W-WAIT... DON'T PULL THAT!
NOT THERE!
MS. NEKONOME !!
NO!!
?
AAAAA

A: This manga's getting strange...

Rosario + Vampire

Akihisa Ikeda

•Staff•

Makoto Saito   Takafumi Okubo   Mio Isshiki

•3D Modeling•

Takaharu Yoshizawa   Akihisa Ikeda & Crew

•Editing•

Satoshi Adachi

•Comic•

Mika Asada

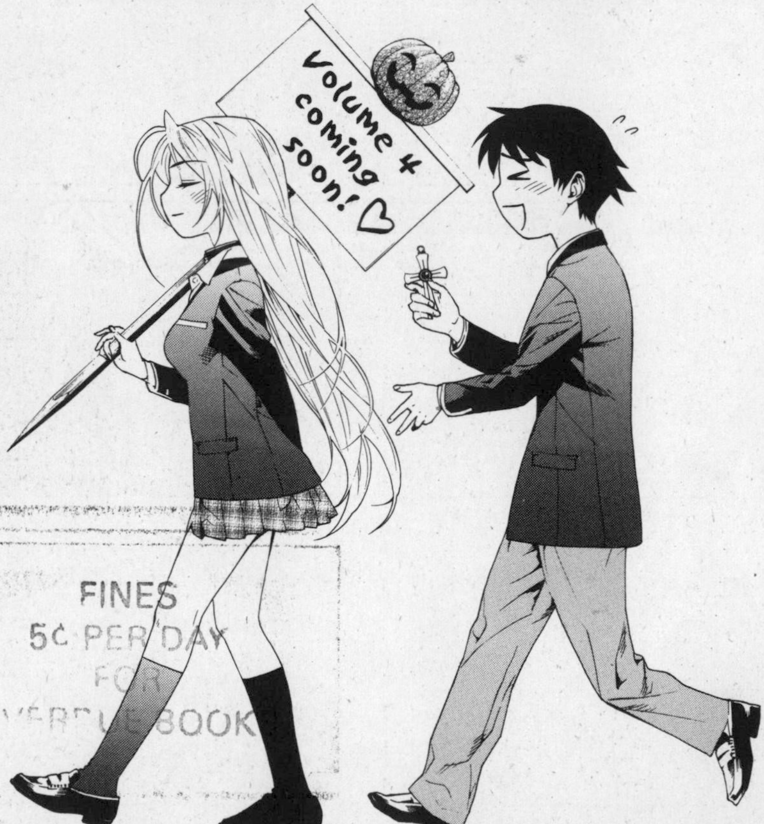
Volume 4 coming soon! ♥

Next volume...summer vacation at Yokai Academy!

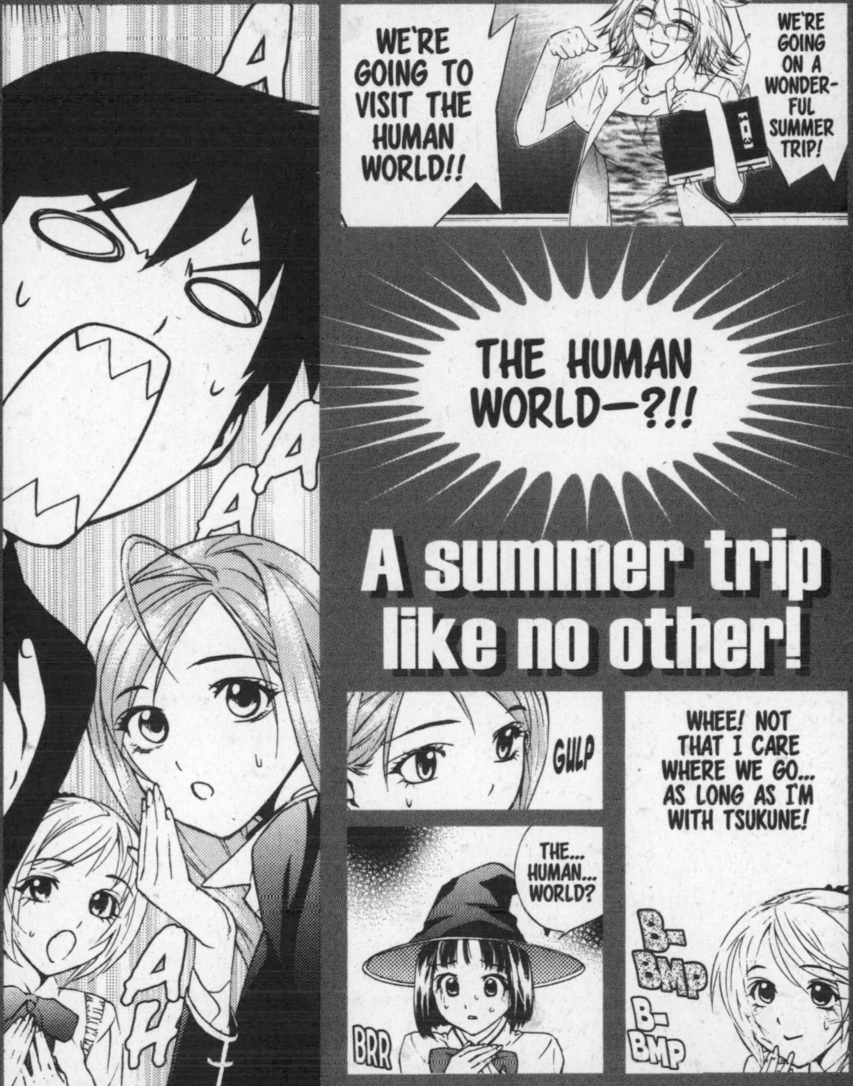
WE'RE GOING ON A WONDER-FUL SUMMER TRIP!
WE'RE GOING TO VISIT THE HUMAN WORLD!!
THE HUMAN WORLD—?!!
WHEE! NOT THAT I CARE WHERE WE GO... AS LONG AS I'M WITH TSUKUNE!
B-BMP
B-BMP
GULP
THE... HUMAN... WORLD?
BRR
AAAAA

A summer trip like no other!

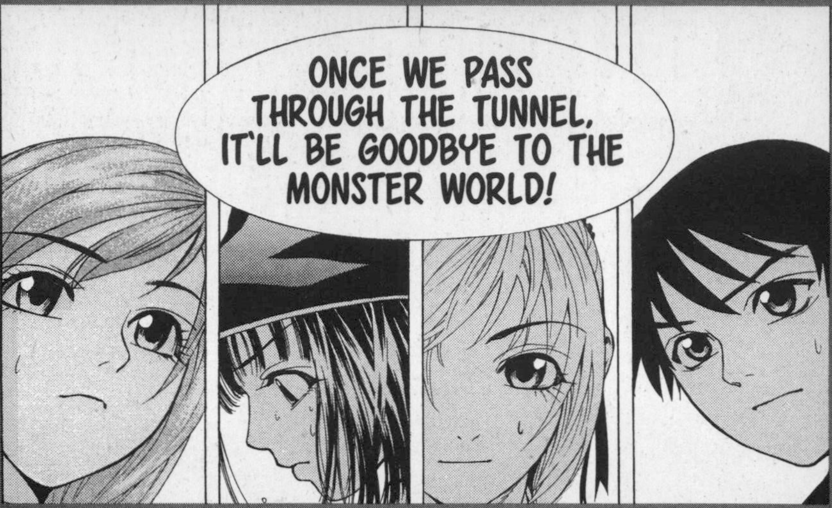
ONCE WE PASS THROUGH THE TUNNEL, IT'LL BE GOODBYE TO THE MONSTER WORLD!

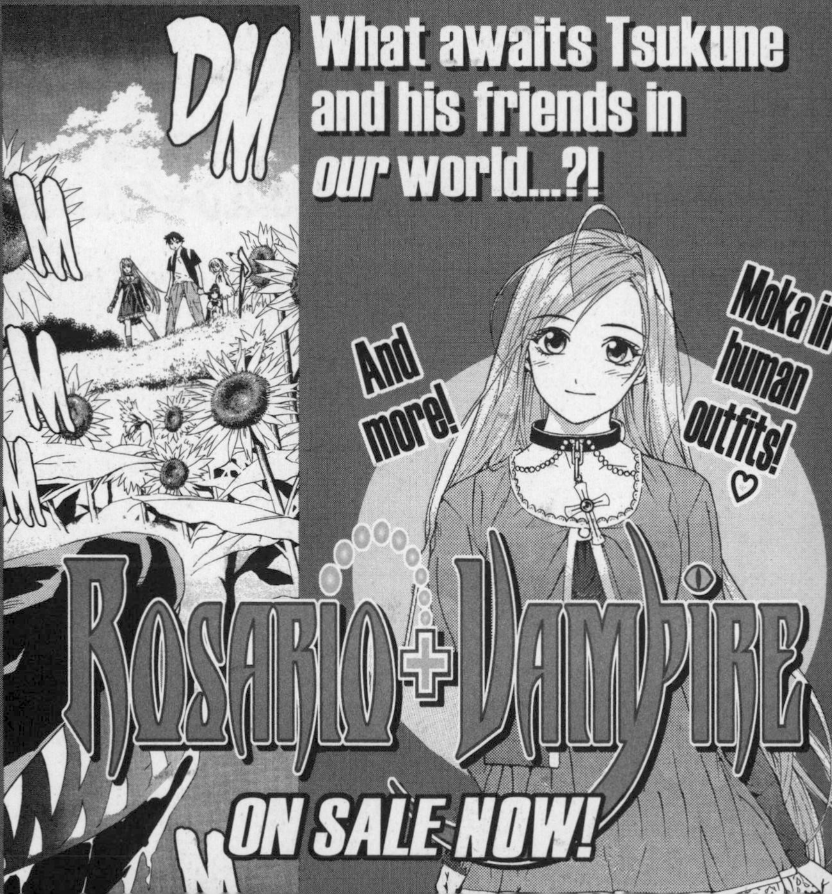
What awaits Tsukune and his friends in *our* world...?!
DMMMMM
Moka in human outfits! ♡
And more!
ROSARIO+VAMPIRE
ON SALE NOW!

Crypt Sheet for Volume 4: Carnivorous Plants!

QUIZ 4

WHEN TAKING A FIELD TRIP TO THE HUMAN WORLD AND OBSERVING HUMAN SPAWN BEING PREYED UPON BY CARNIVOROUS PLANTS...

a. let them eat the kids—after all, it's not like they're inhuman

b. save them and form an alliance to save the environment

c. harvest yourself a lively salad

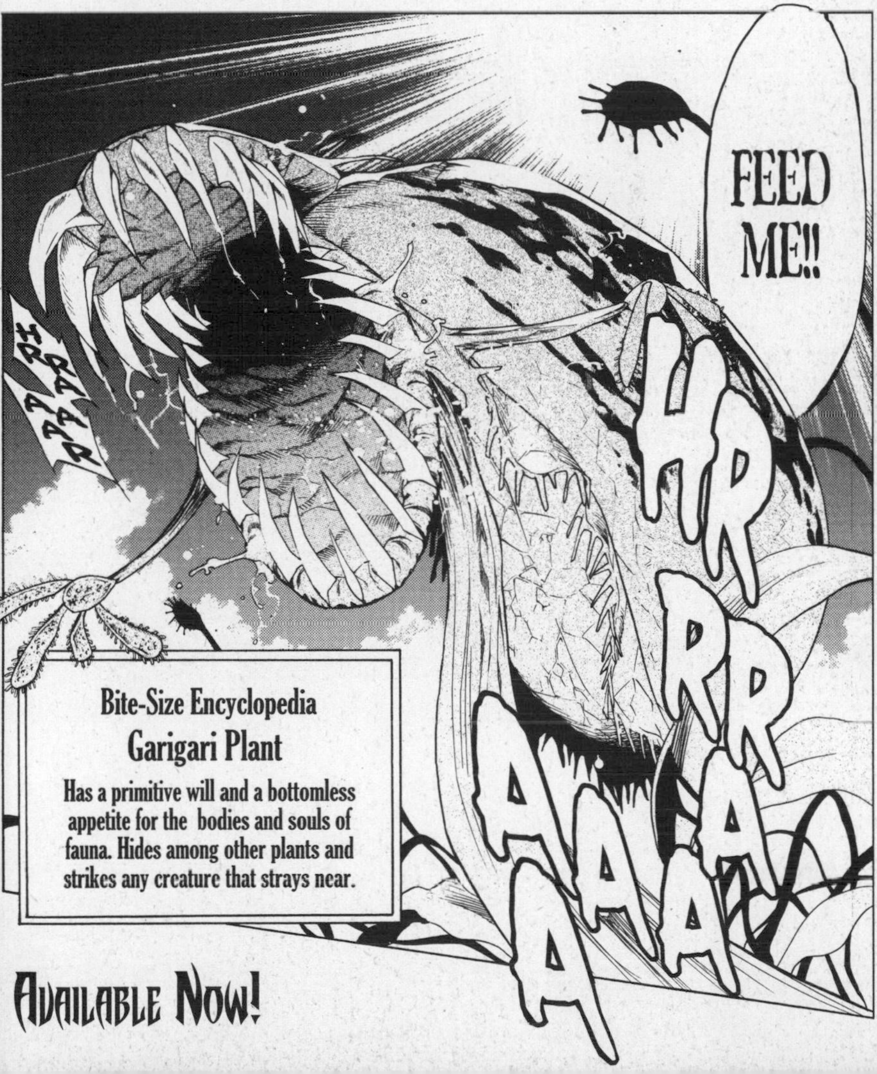
FEED ME!!
Bite-Size Encyclopedia
Garigari Plant
Has a primitive will and a bottomless appetite for the bodies and souls of fauna. Hides among other plants and strikes any creature that strays near.

Available Now!

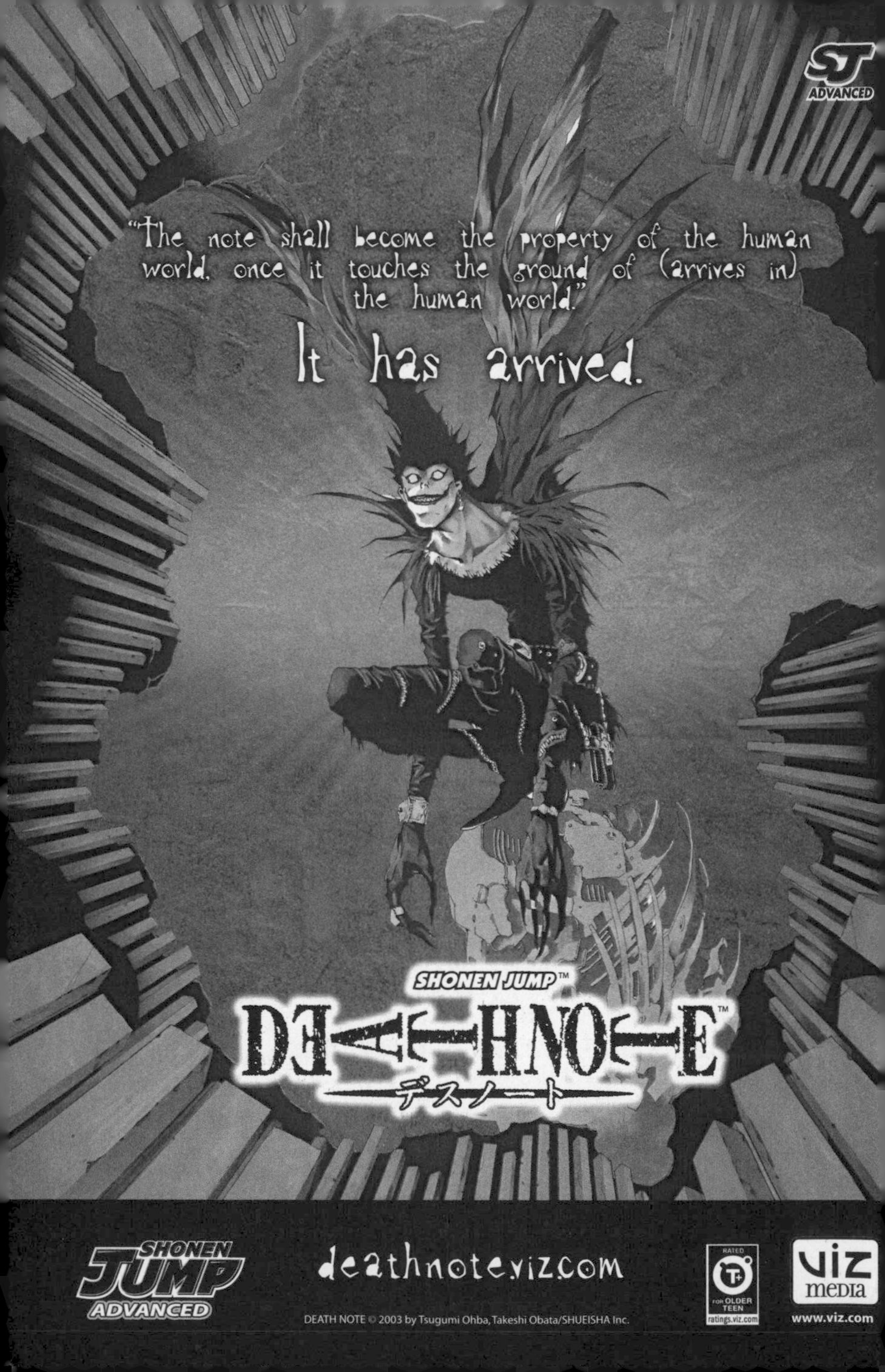
SJ ADVANCED
"The note shall become the property of the human world, once it touches the ground of (arrives in) the human world."
It has arrived.
SHONEN JUMP™
DEATH NOTE™
デスノート
SHONEN JUMP ADVANCED
deathnote.viz.com
RATED T+ FOR OLDER TEEN ratings.viz.com
viz media
www.viz.com
DEATH NOTE © 2003 by Tsugumi Ohba, Takeshi Obata/SHUEISHA Inc.

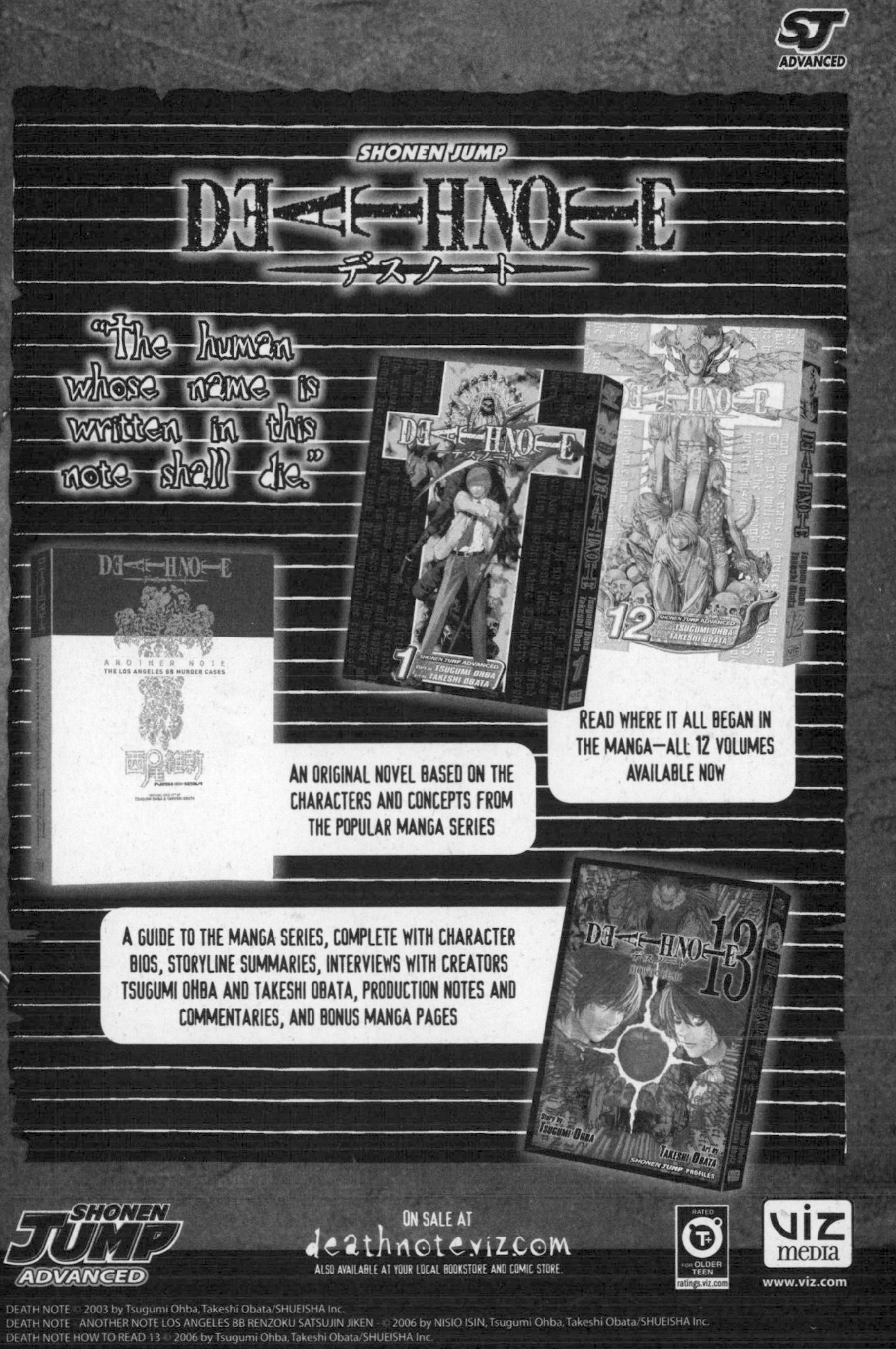
SJ ADVANCED
SHONEN JUMP
DEATH NOTE
デスノート
"The human whose name is written in this note shall die."
AN ORIGINAL NOVEL BASED ON THE CHARACTERS AND CONCEPTS FROM THE POPULAR MANGA SERIES
READ WHERE IT ALL BEGAN IN THE MANGA—ALL 12 VOLUMES AVAILABLE NOW
A GUIDE TO THE MANGA SERIES, COMPLETE WITH CHARACTER BIOS, STORYLINE SUMMARIES, INTERVIEWS WITH CREATORS TSUGUMI OHBA AND TAKESHI OBATA, PRODUCTION NOTES AND COMMENTARIES, AND BONUS MANGA PAGES
SHONEN JUMP ADVANCED
ON SALE AT
deathnote.viz.com
ALSO AVAILABLE AT YOUR LOCAL BOOKSTORE AND COMIC STORE.
RATED T+ FOR OLDER TEEN
ratings.viz.com
VIZ media
www.viz.com
DEATH NOTE © 2003 by Tsugumi Ohba, Takeshi Obata/SHUEISHA Inc.
DEATH NOTE - ANOTHER NOTE LOS ANGELES BB RENZOKU SATSUJIN JIKEN - © 2006 by NISIO ISIN, Tsugumi Ohba, Takeshi Obata/SHUEISHA Inc.
DEATH NOTE HOW TO READ 13 © 2006 by Tsugumi Ohba, Takeshi Obata/SHUEISHA Inc.

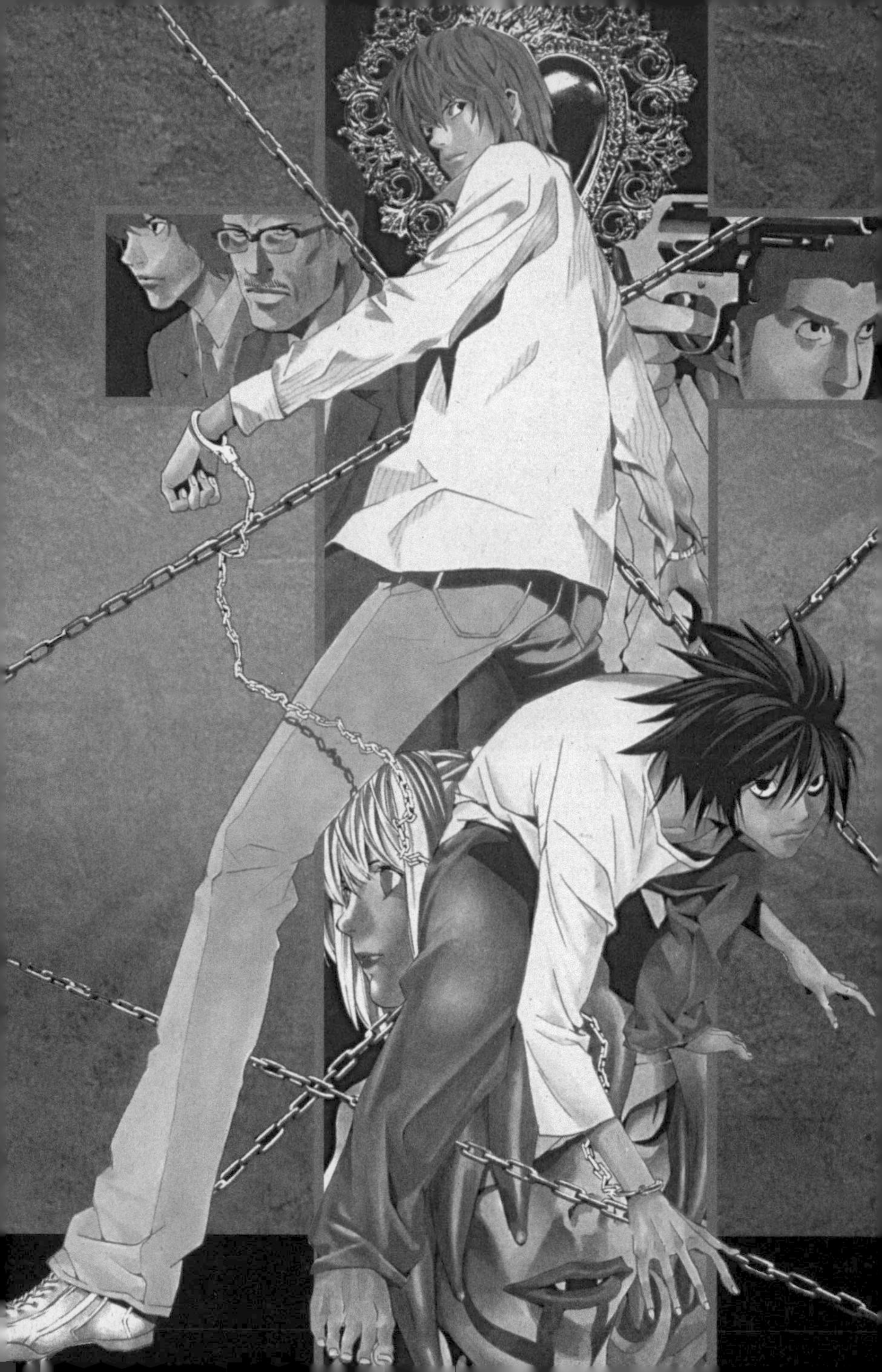

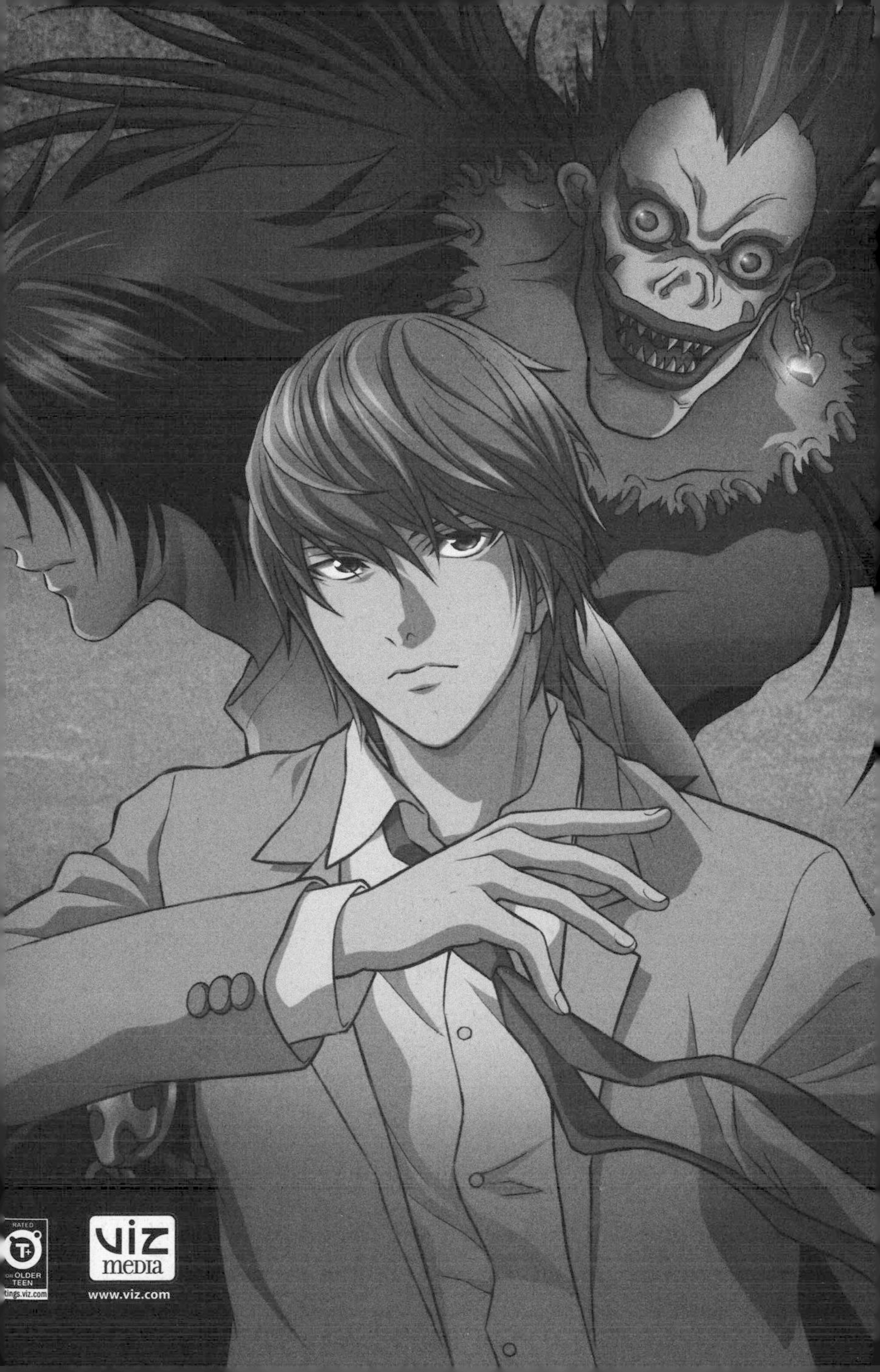

RATED
T+
OLDER
TEEN
tings.viz.com
viz
media
www.viz.com

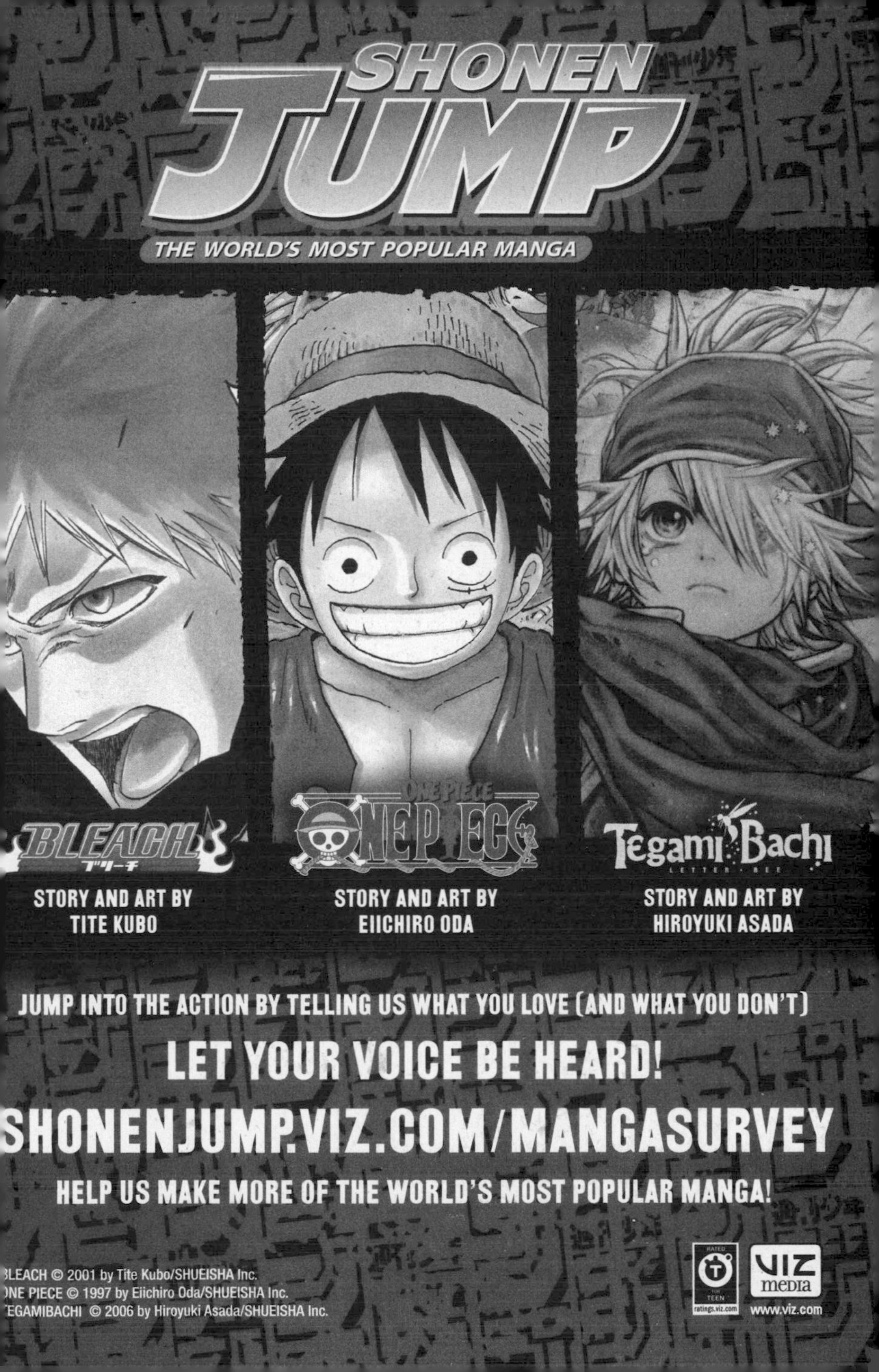
SHONEN JUMP
THE WORLD'S MOST POPULAR MANGA
BLEACH
ブリーチ
STORY AND ART BY
TITE KUBO
ONE PIECE
STORY AND ART BY
EIICHIRO ODA
Tegami Bachi
LETTER BEE
STORY AND ART BY
HIROYUKI ASADA
JUMP INTO THE ACTION BY TELLING US WHAT YOU LOVE (AND WHAT YOU DON'T)
LET YOUR VOICE BE HEARD!
SHONENJUMP.VIZ.COM/MANGASURVEY
HELP US MAKE MORE OF THE WORLD'S MOST POPULAR MANGA!
BLEACH © 2001 by Tite Kubo/SHUEISHA Inc.
ONE PIECE © 1997 by Eiichiro Oda/SHUEISHA Inc.
TEGAMIBACHI © 2006 by Hiroyuki Asada/SHUEISHA Inc.
RATED T FOR TEEN
ratings.viz.com
VIZ media
www.viz.com

The World's Greatest Manga
Now available on your iPad

Full of FREE previews and tons of new manga for you to explore

From legendary manga like *Dragon Ball* to *Bakuman*₀, the newest series from the creators of *Death Note*, the best manga in the world is now available on the iPad through the official VIZ Manga app.

- ## Free App
- ## New content weekly
- ## Free chapter 1 previews

ROSARIO+VAMPIRE 3
SHONEN JUMP ADVANCED Manga Edition

STORY & ART BY AKIHISA IKEDA

Translation/Kaori Inoue
English Adaptation/Gerard Jones
Touch-up Art & Lettering/Stephen Dutro
Cover Design/Hidemi Dunn
Interior Design/Julie Behn
Editor/Annette Roman

Published by VIZ Media, LLC
P.O. Box 77010
San Francisco, CA 94107

10 9 8 7 6 5
First printing, October 2008
Fifth printing, September 2011

www.viz.com

www.shonenjump.com

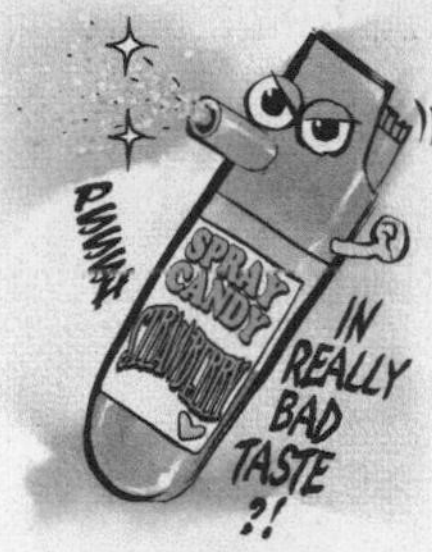
SPRAY CANDY
IN REALLY BAD TASTE ?!

池田晃久
AKIHISA IKEDA

I like things to be simple. A UCC black coffee beside me while I work. Chicken ramen for dinner. No grainy stuff on my strawberry Pocky. For games, Nintendo of course. Simple! The standards! But maybe deep down I like weird things...Today I bought some unknown cheap candy and got yelled at by my staff. ← Yahoo!

Akihisa Ikeda was born in 1977 in Miyazaki. He debuted as a mangaka with the four-volume magical warrior fantasy series *Kiruto* in 1999, which was serialized in *Monthly Shonen Jump*. *Rosario+Vampire* debuted in *Monthly Shonen Jump* in March of 2002, and is continuing in the new magazine *Jump Square* (Jump SQ). In Japan, *Rosario+Vampire* is also available as a drama CD. In 2008, the story was released as an anime.

Ikeda has been a huge fan of vampires and monsters since he was a little kid.

He says one of the perks of being a manga artist is being able to go for walks during the day when everybody else is stuck in the office.